An Introduction with Readings

Marxism and Asia

Hélène Carrère d'Encausse and Stuart R. Schram

Allen Lane The Penguin Press

Le Marxisme et l' Asie 1853-1964
first published in France by Armand Colin, 1965
This translation, with additions,
first published in 1969
Copyright © Hélène Carrère d'Encausse
and Stuart R. Schram, 1969
Allen Lane The Penguin Press
Vigo Street, London W1

Penguin Books Inc.
7110 Ambassador Road
Baltimore, Maryland 21207

SBN 7139 0056 3
Library of Congress Catalogue Number 74-94354

Printed in the United States of America by
Universal Lithographers, Inc.
Set in Monotype Baskerville

CONTENTS

PREFACE TO THE ENGLISH EDITION

The theme of this book is both narrower and broader than could be indicated in a brief title. It is narrower, for the Marxism in question is primarily that of Lenin and his disciples. (We nevertheless preferred the present title to 'Communism and Asia', which would have misled the reader by suggesting that the subject was the role of a movement rather than the metamorphoses of a system of ideas.) It is broader, for we are concerned not merely with Asia, but with the relations between revolution in Europe and revolution elsewhere, considered as an aspect of relations between the advanced industrial societies of Europe and North America and the countries of Asia, Africa and Latin America.

Our aim has been to make a contribution towards the understanding of recent developments by placing them in an historical perspective. This approach called forth objections on the part of certain historians when the French edition was published four years ago. The past, they maintained, should be contemplated in its entirety; facts should be selected with an even hand, and evaluated in terms of their significance at the time and not of their subsequent impact. We are not altogether convinced by these arguments. History is always selective, and the selection can only be made from the standpoint of the historian, which is never unrelated to the moment at which he is writing. In any case, this book is not a work of history. It might perhaps best be described as an essay accompanied by illustrative materials. As such, it does not claim to demonstrate anything according to rigorously scientific methods. We regard it rather as a contribution to an ongoing debate to which no conclusion is yet in sight.

The central problem on which we have endeavoured to throw light is that of the widening abyss between the disciples of Marx in Europe and in Asia. The most obvious outward manifestation and symbol of this phenomenon is, of course, the Sino-Soviet dispute. Although this conflict reached the stage of open rupture and mutual excommunication precisely at the time when this book was first written, in the winter of 1963–4, our concern has never been with the dispute as such, but rather with the factors which had made the participants grow apart. In two respects, however, the events of the past few years have rendered even more complex and problematical the links between the current situation, and the facts and theories of the past to which a large part of this anthology is devoted.

First of all, for Lenin and the Comintern 'Marxism and Asia' meant essentially the application of Marxist modes of reasoning *to* Asia, in order to develop methods for the conquest of power adapted to the peculiar conditions prevailing in Asian societies. This is the aspect of the question to which the Soviets have continued to give primary emphasis, and in a sense it constitutes the unifying strand around which much of our discussion is woven. For the Chinese, on the other hand, 'Marxism and Asia' means above all Marxism *in* Asia – the adaptation of Marxism to Asian conditions by the Asians themselves, not only in order to find new techniques for seizing power, but with the aim of breaking new paths in the revolutionary transformation of society. This aspect of Chinese Marxism was dealt with to a considerable extent in the first edition of this book, but it appears increasingly as *the* central issue – more important than the discussions regarding collaboration with the 'national bourgeoisie' and other classes or groups in the non-European countries to which the Soviets devote so much attention. And yet, the long history of the debates within the world communist movement (when there still was such a thing) regarding the proper way to go about making revolution in Asia constitutes the indispensable background to the more recent quarrels about 'paths to socialism'. In other words, the logical discontinuity which is evident in the latter part of this book is implicit in reality itself – though perhaps if we had succeeded in achieving a deeper understanding we might have done more to show the inherent unity of the two aspects of the problem.

A second and even more important change in the way this problem presents itself to our attention lies in the fact that ideological influence between Europe and Asia is no longer a one-way street. In the past, Mao Tse-tung limited himself to insisting on the right of the Chinese to develop their own form of Marxism, adapted to Chinese traditions; in recent years, 'Mao Tse-tung's Thought' has been proclaimed the only correct and authentically revolutionary doctrine, applicable not only in Asia but throughout the world. And whereas half a century ago China was shaken out of her torpor by the mass demonstrations of students, some of whom had been reading Marx, the little red book is brandished today by student activists in London, Berkeley and Paris.

This does not prove, of course, that Chinese ideological influence is a decisive factor in the European political situation today. There are profound differences of opinion, among both those friendly and those hostile to the Chinese and/or to the students, as to whether there is really anything in common between the Chinese cultural revolution and the aims of the students in the West. Moreover, despite all the books about the events of May

1968 in Paris, it remains to be seen whether the student movement in Europe and North America can be regarded as even potentially revolutionary, in the sense of opening the way to profound changes in the political and economic system. Nevertheless, it no longer seems quite so obvious as it did to us in 1964 that the only significant revolutionary phenomena in the latter part of the twentieth century will necessarily take place in Asia, Africa and Latin America. But if there are (or may perhaps be) significant Marxist currents outside Asia, it is clear that the interaction between Marxism and Asia will continue to be of decisive importance, both because it affects the destinies of the greater part of the world's population, and by virtue of its impact on political and ideological developments in Europe.

The changes in the content of the present edition, as compared to the French original, consist primarily of additions designed to bring the book up to date, but we have also made some revisions in the Introduction in the light of subsequent events. Section XII of the documents has been split into two parts, and a number of new items from the years 1964–8 added to the resulting Section XIII. A similar sub-division has been made in the Introduction, and a long passage added regarding the cultural revolution in China and its relevance to the problems of revolution in other countries. A few additional documents have also been incorporated into Section X, and a corresponding passage into the Introduction, in order to put more stress on the evolution in China towards a new and original revolutionary model in the years 1955–8. A new Conclusion sums up our present ideas regarding the theme of the book as a whole.

Hitherto in this Preface, although we have been talking about Marxism and Asia, we have referred only to the Chinese interpretation. This does not mean that we regard the Chinese revolution as the prototype of revolutions everywhere. In a passage of the Introduction to the French edition, omitted here because it seemed to be belabouring the obvious, we wrote:

> It is clear that henceforth for everyone, Soviets, Chinese, European or non-European countries, the problems of the revolution will be seen through various prisms in which subjective judgements growing out of a background of unique cultural traditions will play a considerable role, and that the multiplicity of revolutionary perspectives cannot fail to develop.

But we found it more fruitful to examine in detail the forms of 'Asian Marxism' elaborated by the Chinese and (for the earlier period) by the Muslim Bolsheviks of the Soviet Union, and to contrast these with the orthodox line of the Soviet Union and the Comintern, rather than to present a broad and superficial image of the whole problem of revolution in Asia.

This volume is, in the fullest sense of the word, the fruit of a joint effort by the two authors. While certain passages deal with problems which fall within the competence of only one of us, the whole of the book was planned in common and drafts were exchanged and revised until they incorporated the ideas of both. The English translation represents a collective undertaking on an even broader scale. The texts of which the original is in Russian were translated directly into English by Anthony Bishop. Those of which the original is in Chinese were translated from French into English by Carol Marciano, with the exception of some recent items which have been published in English in Peking. The English versions were then checked against the Chinese text by Hu Chi-hsi. The items from French originals were also translated by Mrs Marciano. Stuart Schram translated the Introduction and the materials from the German; he also prepared the composite translation of the debates of the Second Comintern Congress. The whole manuscript was then scrutinized by the two authors, who assume joint responsibility for the result.

Hélène Carrère d'Encausse
Stuart R. Schram

PART 1. Introduction

Marxism, as everyone knows, although it originally took form as a response to the problems of the most advanced capitalist countries of Europe and North America, has hitherto triumphed above all in relatively underdeveloped countries. Moreover, despite the recent eruption of protest movements in Europe and the United States, the most powerful ideological centres claiming allegiance to Marxism, both in terms of revolutionary fervour and in terms of influence on the world scene, are to be found today in Asia and in Latin America.

The progressive shift in the centre of gravity of revolution towards the non-European countries constitutes, in fact, one of the most striking and least-disputed traits in the history of the world over the past half century. Moreover, this shift itself is only one aspect of a still broader current of change inspired by the determination of the peoples of Asia and Africa to become the masters of their own destiny, and not merely the objects of a history made by the European nations. This claim to dignity and independence, which had been latent in a variety of intellectual and political movements in the East at the end of the nineteenth century, was given a new impetus by the defeat of Russia at the hands of Japan in 1905. Japan's victory appeared to offer tangible proof that Western superiority was not a permanent and unchangeable fact of history; it thus first aroused hopes which were to be realized only half a century later, when the liberation of a large number of Asian and African countries brought about a radical change in the former world equilibrium.

Long before this concrete result was attained, there was wide awareness in Asia and Africa that an irreversible change was under way. In the West, on the other hand, even the most revolutionary long stubbornly refused to understand and accept the profound transformation of the world in which they were living, and continued to think exclusively in terms of Europe. Thus the awakening of Asia and Africa, and the growing importance which this new world came to assume in the revolutionary movement as a whole, inspired frustration and bitterness among European communists, while the communists of the formerly dependent countries greeted this evolution with enthusiasm. To communists everywhere, these developments posed difficult theoretical problems.

The aim of this book is to trace the historical development of this process. We shall also endeavour to interpret in this perspective the present situation of the world communist movement. More broadly, we shall try to present the conflicts within what used to be called the 'socialist camp' as merely one manifestation of the great upheaval which has changed the face of the world in the twentieth century.

Marxism is an intrinsically European current of thought, which unites several of the most characteristic traits of European civilization as a whole: the sense of history inherent in the Judeo-Christian tradition, and the Promethean urge to transform nature that has manifested itself since the Renaissance, and especially since the industrial revolution. Transplanted to Asia, to societies most of which did not have this sense of history, and none of which traditionally had such a vision of man '*maître et possesseur de la nature*' (in Descartes's well-known phrase), it caused a profound shock. Nor did Marxism itself escape unchanged from the encounter.

This encounter between Marxism and the non-European world required a mediation, which was carried out by Lenin. To be sure, the work of Marx himself contains the elements of an adaptation to the conditions of the East to a far greater extent than the 'orthodox' interpretation of Marxism would lead one to believe. But they are only elements, which were never systematically developed by Marx. Moreover, if Marx was more inclined than many of his disciples to attribute to Asia an important role in the world revolution, there was no place in his scheme of things for an original contribution by Asian culture. On the contrary, he declared that the only salvation for the peoples of the East lay in 'Europeanization'. It was Lenin, citizen of an empire belonging both to Europe and to Asia, who first opened wide the door to the implantation of Marxism in Asia. But if he opened the door, he could not foresee the use which would be made of his variant of Marxism by revolutionaries in Asia, Africa, and Latin America. His vision was limited not only by the fact that he died at the very beginning of the new era he had helped to open, but also because, despite a feeling for the problems of Asia remarkable among Social Democrats of his generation, he was himself very European in his mentality and experience. How could this man, whose ideas had taken shape during years of exile spent in Paris and Zürich, have imagined the fate of those ideas when they had been transmuted by minds formed in the traditional societies of Asia or in the jungles of Africa?

The evolution just summarily evoked provides the framework for this volume. We shall first sketch the development, from Marx to Lenin, of theories concerning the revolution in non-European countries put forward by various schools of Marxism. Secondly, we will endeavour to convey an idea of the wide spectrum of nationalist heresies and deviations which manifested themselves after the October Revolution among the non-European peoples of Russia, as well as in China. At the same time, we shall show that nationalist deviations are by no means the monopoly of non-European revolutionaries, and that the European communists have often been inclined to treat their Asian and African comrades in an authoritarian and even contemptuous manner. Finally, in the third part of our Introduction, we will analyse the evolution of the communist world since the establishment of the Chinese People's Republic in 1949 resulted in the creation of a second political and ideological centre, and since the collapse of the former colonial empires brought about the massive entry on the world scene of Asian and African countries haunted by the memory of their humiliation at the hands of the West. Thus we shall attempt to show that the roots of the dramatic conflict between European and Asian communism and their respective champions in Moscow and Peking are to be found in the dis-Europeanization of the world which has been under way for a long time.

In the course of our discussion of the three main phases in the history of communism – prior to the October Revolution, from 1917 to 1949, since 1949 – we shall endeavour to keep constantly in view three aspects of the problem, which are related but nevertheless distinct: the tactical aspect, the strategic aspect, and the cultural aspect. By tactical aspect, we mean to designate the controversies among Marxists regarding the way in which the revolutionary struggle should be carried on within the non-European countries. By strategic aspect, we mean strategy on a global scale, and in particular the problem of the relative weight which should be attributed to the proletarian revolution in the advanced capitalist countries, and to the national revolution in the dependent countries, in the overall struggle for the overthrow of the capitalist system. By cultural aspect, we mean to evoke the dilemma which confronts each of the non-European countries: that of modernizing while remaining themselves.

The order in which we have just enumerated these factors is a logical order, from the more concrete to the more abstract. But it is also an historical order. The problem of tactics was worked out in general terms during Lenin's lifetime, at least on the theoretical level – even if the choice of one of the tactical arms stored up in 'the arsenal of Marxism-Leninism' is still frequently the subject of sharp controversy. On the other hand, the strategic problem, despite its constantly growing importance, has still not been satisfactorily resolved, and lies at the heart of the current Sino-Soviet polemics. And yet, even this problem is perhaps less difficult to solve than the problem of culture. For on the strategic level, we are dealing with men's actions, whereas on the cultural level we are concerned with much deeper levels of existence. When there is a conflict between two different strategic conceptions rooted in differing situations and differing interests, a compromise can be sought through a rational analysis of the divergencies. It is much more doubtful whether intellectual analysis can contribute to the solution of problems involving a cultural dimension. For behind the obvious conflict between the national pride of the Asian communists and the attitude of superiority of their European comrades, there lies a more fundamental issue: the determination of the newly independent peoples to escape from their present condition of economic and technical backwardness, and at the same time to preserve their national identity. To the extent that the remedy for underdevelopment – modernity – implies Westernization, it calls into question the very specificity which has been the most cherished aim for which the non-European peoples have struggled.

Today, within the communist world, so recently considered as monolithic, psychological problems have arisen not unlike those which complicate the relations between former colonies and 'mother countries' within the capitalist world. Like those who brought 'civilization' to the colonies, those who brought 'revolution' to Asia are unwilling to admit that their former pupils are capable of creating a new society which is not simply a copy of their own. The future will tell whether such an achievement on the part of the non-Europeans, and its acceptance by the Europeans, will be reached earlier within the world of those who call themselves Marxist-Leninists, or outside it.

1. MARXIST VIEWS OF THE NON-EUROPEAN WORLD PRIOR TO THE OCTOBER REVOLUTION

The Legacy of Marx

Few people would deny today that Marx left to his disciples an ambiguous heritage. This ambiguity is, on the one hand, a consequence of the very richness and complexity of his personality and his writings. It also results from the fact that his life work remained unfinished, and in large part was not even published during his own lifetime. No doubt the contrast between the 'young Marx' and the Marx of *Das Kapital* is not so total as it has sometimes been made out to be. The fact that he came progressively to devote himself less to philosophy and more to economics and sociology does not mean that he had repudiated all the ideas of his youth. Nevertheless, on a certain number of problems his position did vary, so that it is possible to justify more than one 'Marxist' viewpoint by references to Marx.

In the domain which interests us in this volume, that of the analysis of the economic and political development of the non-European countries, the difficulties in the way of distinguishing *the* Marxist position are further aggravated by the fact that in his writings Marx devoted only relatively brief and fragmentary passages to extra-European societies, so that in this case, even more than as regards the evolution of the capitalist countries of Europe, his disciples have been obliged to elaborate their theories out of disparate and sometimes contradictory elements.

The major contradiction in Marx's thought regarding the non-European countries is that between his rather narrow europocentrism on the cultural level, and his world-wide vision on the strategic level. In his celebrated articles on the consequences of British rule in India, Marx develops a conception of Indian civilization, and of Asian civilization in general, as not only different from that of Europe, but clearly inferior. He saw in it a society where individual initiative played virtually no role, and where every aspect of economic and political activity was stifled by 'oriental despotism' (see Text I 1).

There is no doubt that, beginning in 1853, Marx held the view that a certain number of non-European countries were characterized by an economic and social system qualitatively different from those which had prevailed during all the phases which had marked the development of European societies – even if, in one celebrated text, he inserted the 'Asiatic mode of production' in a succession of historical epochs which also included classical antiquity and the feudal and capitalist modes of production.[1] Marx regarded the Asiatic mode of production as the socio-economic formation closest to primitive tribal society. True to his europocentric vision of the world, he was persuaded that in Greco-Roman times European societies had skipped this stage in his ideal typology and moved directly to ancient slave-holding society, which was a more advanced system because it involved an element of private property.

At one point, Marx characterized the absence of private property in land as 'the true key, even to the Oriental heaven' and one of the foundations of oriental despotism.[2] But this was not, in his opinion, an absolutely indispensable trait of the Asiatic mode of production, for even at a time when he had learned of the existence of private property in land in China, he continued to regard this country, like India, as an example of the 'Asiatic' system.[3] The two really basic traits of the Asiatic mode of production were, in Marx's view, an economy resting on the foundation of a multitude of tiny village communities isolated from one another, engaging in small-scale agriculture and handicrafts; and, at the top of the pyramid, a despotic state which appropriated part of the surplus produced by the village communities, and which took charge of the public works, especially for irrigation, indispensable to the functioning of such an economy.[4]

The implications of these ideas on the cultural level are obvious. The Asiatic mode of production was regarded by Marx as a very early stage in the development of humanity, growing directly out of primitive communism. To declare that the Asian countries are still at a phase corresponding to the dawn of civilization, and that

[1] See the preface to the *Critique of Political Economy*.

[2] See his letter to Engels of 2 June 1853, *Briefwechsel*, vol. I, p. 413.

[3] *Das Kapital* (Berlin, Dietz Verlag, 1956), vol. III, pp. 365–6. On the question of whether China is or is not an example of the Asiatic mode of production, see the controversy between Wittfogel and Meisner in *China Quarterly*, nos. 11, 12 and 16. Although on the whole it seems to us that Wittfogel goes much too far in systematizing Marx's views on Asiatic society so as to make of them a uniform model (the application of which to contemporary problems is even more debatable), we agree with him that Marx classified China among the Asiatic societies, even if it was not a typical example.

[4] This conception is sketched out in Text I 1; it was subsequently developed by Marx in a series of fragmentary but suggestive texts of which the most important is a long passage from the rough draft of *Capital*, *Grundrisse der Kritik der Politischen Ökonomie*. This has been translated into English under the title Karl Marx, *Pre-Capitalist Economic Formations* (London, Lawrence and Wishart, 1964), with an introduction by E. J. Hobsbawm. See also the excellent article of George Lichtheim, 'Marx and the Asiatic Mode of Production', *St Antony's Papers*, no. 14 (London, Chatto and Windus, 1963), pp. 86–112. A number of communist intellectuals in both Eastern and Western Europe have also taken an interest in this theory in recent years; we will have the occasion to refer to their writings later in this Introduction.

they would never have emerged from their stagnation without Western intervention, is to condemn in advance any attempt by the peoples of these countries to modernize while retaining their own personalities.

At the same time, one must emphasize that Marx did not in the least believe that Asia was condemned to live perpetually in such a condition of stagnation. On the contrary, he was persuaded that the Indians, whose human qualities he praises highly, were entirely capable of playing a role in the world and of developing in their turn a dynamic civilization – but only on condition that they become 'Europeanized'. For Marx, who was a humanist marked both by the Greek tradition and by the experience of the industrial revolution, the essence of Europeanization consisted in assimilating the individualism and the Promethean spirit in which he rightly saw one of the essential traits distinguishing European civilization from all the great civilizations of Asia. This credo found expression in one of the most eloquent passages of his articles on India, where he writes that Indian civilization 'transformed a self-developing social state into never changing natural destiny, and thus brought about a brutalizing worship of nature, exhibiting its degradation in the fact that man, the sovereign of nature, fell down on his knees in adoration of Hanuman, the monkey, and Sabbala, the cow' (see Text I 1).

Such were Marx's views regarding Asian society. But he was not only an economist or a sociologist analysing society; he was also a revolutionary who was resolved to change it. To be sure, he was above all interested in changing the European society in which he lived, but he none the less envisaged Europe in a world-wide context, and in this context he believed that Asia could play a certain role, even in connexion with the European revolution. As early as 1853, in his article on revolution in China and in Europe (see Text I 2), he sketched out the two essential ideas which were to constitute the core of the diverse theories of imperialism developed by various Marxist thinkers half a century later. First of all, he held that capitalist development in Europe, and the expansion of European capitalism throughout the world, were in the process of creating a single world economic system.[1] Secondly, he believed that the convulsions in the non-European part of this system could react back on Europe itself, and even provoke revolution there. '... The next uprising of the people of Europe ...', he wrote, 'may depend more probably on what is now passing in the Celestial Empire ... than on any other political cause that now exists.'

'What is now happening in the Celestial Empire' was the Taiping rebellion – in other words a development which at first sight did not seem to have anything to do with the socialist revolution or even with the bourgeois revolution. Hence the strategic concep-

[1] This idea had already been put forward in the *Manifesto*.

tions of Lenin and his successors, who proposed to channel the nationalist forces in Asia in the service of the world revolution, are not altogether without precedent in Marx's own writings. Engels even went so far as to speak, in 1857, of a war '*pro aris et focis*' in China (see Text I 6). But it must be recognized that the views of Marx and Engels on the evolution of Asian society under the impact of the West are even more fragmentary than their ideas on the origins and nature of that society. The articles of 1853 on British rule in India, which had laid heavy emphasis on the progressive character of the destruction of the small village communities and the introduction of private property and the germs of individualism, gave the impression that India, and no doubt the other countries of Asia as well, would have to pass through a capitalist stage of development. Later, Marx and Engels were to set forth different ideas – this time with reference to a rather peculiar example of 'oriental despotism', namely Russia.

The views of Marx and Engels on Russia are of obvious theoretical and practical importance. At the time of the revolution of 1848 and its sequels in Eastern Europe, their attitude reduced itself essentially to a bitter hatred for tsarist Russia as the principal bastion of reaction in Europe, and the principal obstacle to revolution. In some instances, they even went beyond this political judgement to attitudes which can only be called racist.

Thus, in 1849, when the 'Southern Slavs' of the Austrian Empire supported the imperial power against the insurrection of the German and Hungarian revolutionaries, Engels wrote:

> Among all the peoples . . . of Austria, there are only three who have been carriers of progress, who have played an active role in history, and who still retain their vitality: the Germans, the Poles, and the Magyars. For this reason, they are now revolutionary.
>
> The chief vocation of all the other races and peoples, great and small, is to perish in the revolutionary holocaust. . . .[1]

Although at this time Marx and Engels scarcely had any more sympathy for the Russians than for the Southern Slavs, whom they so light-heartedly consigned to oblivion, Russia was too massive a phenomenon to be thus casually dismissed. They considered it, as we have already said, to be an Asian or semi-Asian country. But on the one hand, with the passage of time Marx and Engels showed a tendency to trace the boundary less rigidly between Asian societies and those of Europe, and to explain the peculiarities of Asia more in terms of the stage of economic and social development which prevailed there. Apart from this, they came to take a somewhat less negative view of the traditional society of Asia, at least in comparison with the ravages caused by the incursion of European capitalism.[2] This change in their outlook led them to judge Russia,

[1] Article of January 1849, entitled 'Hungary', *Nachlass*, vol. III, p. 236.

[2] On these developments see Lichtheim, op. cit., pp. 97–8.

too, in a somewhat less hostile light, and to develop, regarding Russia's future path, the idea that this country could even benefit in some respects from its backwardness as compared to Western Europe. This train of thought is extremely important, not only because of its implications for Russia, but because the same logic was extended by certain of Marx's disciples, and in particular by Lenin, to other 'Asian' societies, and served as a starting-point for theories of a 'non-capitalist path of development' in the backward countries.

This conception was first sketched by Engels in an article of 1875, which began with a highly unflattering picture of Russian society at the time:

> Such complete isolation of the various villages from one another is . . . the natural basis of *oriental despotism*, and from India to Russia, wherever it has existed, this social form has always produced despotism. . . . The despotism of the Tsar . . . is a necessary and logical product of Russian social conditions.[1]

Despite this beginning, in the same article Engels envisaged the possibility of transforming the Russian village community into a higher form of socialist property, without passing through the intermediate stage of individual land ownership – but only on the condition that a victorious socialist revolution took place in the West before the complete disintegration of communal property in Russia. For his part, Marx wrote in 1877 that if Russia continued the evolution towards capitalism on which she had embarked in 1861, she would lose 'the finest occasion that history had ever offered to a people', and would afterwards be obliged to 'undergo all the meanders of the capitalist system'.[2]

In their preface to the Russian edition of the *Communist Manifesto* published in 1882, Marx and Engels were still more affirmative:

> Can the Russian *obshchina* [village commune] . . . be transformed directly into the higher form of communist property in land, or must it go through the same process of decomposition displayed in the historical development of the West?
>
> Today, only one reply to this question is possible. If the Russian revolution gives the signal for a proletarian revolution in the West, so that the two complete one another, the form of communal property in the land which now exists in Russia can constitute the starting-point for a communist development.[3]

Finally, in a text written in 1894, shortly before his death,

[1] F. Engels, 'Soziales aus Russland', in K. Marx and F. Engels, *Werke* (Berlin, Dietz Verlag, 1962), vol. 18, pp. 563–4.

[2] Letter of Marx to the Russian periodical *Otechestvennye Zapiski*, in K. Marx and F. Engels, op. cit., vol. 19, p. 108.

[3] ibid., p. 296.

Engels confirmed this position in principle, and even extended its application beyond the case of Russia. He declared that in general 'the countries which have just succumbed to capitalist production', and which have conserved at least some rudiments of communal forms of property, can find in the latter 'a powerful means of shortening appreciably the process of their development towards socialist society, and for avoiding the greatest part of the suffering and struggles through which we have had to pass in Western Europe'. He no longer seemed to attribute to Russian society, or even to Indian society, a distinctive 'Asiatic' character; on the contrary, he mentioned the traits common to all 'savage or barbaric social formations, characterized by communal property of the means of production', whether it be among the Slavs, in India, or among the ancient Celts or Germans.

But if Engels thus extended the application of the ideas formulated in the preface of 1882 to the Russian edition of the *Manifesto*, he emphasized even more strongly than before the indispensable precondition, namely the support of the proletariat of the advanced countries. 'The initiative for such an eventual transformation of the Russian commune,' he wrote, 'cannot come from this commune itself, but solely from the industrial proletariat in the West. The victory of the Western European proletariat over the bourgeoisie, and the replacement of capitalist production by socially-organized production which will accompany this victory – this is the necessary precondition to the raising of the Russian commune to this level.' Not only would the 'backward countries' require the support of the Western proletariat, but Europe would also have to show them 'how it is done', before they would be able to embark on such a shortened development towards socialism.[1] Here the europocentric world view which characterized the founders of Marxism manifests itself in particularly striking fashion.

If Marx and Engels thus developed the idea that the backward countries could avoid the capitalist stage, provided they were supported by the proletarian revolutionaries of the more advanced countries, they said little about the way in which this transformation would take place, even in the case of the particular backward country they were discussing – Russia. Engels's article of 1875, cited above, is a good example. The coming revolution in Russia, he wrote, would be started by 'the upper classes in the capital – perhaps by the government itself', but afterwards the peasants would have to carry it further.[2]

One is struck by the absence of any reference to the proletariat. Can we conclude from this that Engels foresaw a purely peasant revolution in Russia, and by extension throughout Asia? This

[1] F. Engels, 'Nachwort zu Soziales aus Russland', in K. Marx and F. Engels, op. cit., vol. 22, pp. 421–35.

[2] K. Marx and F. Engels, op. cit., vol. 18, p. 567.

would be extrapolating his ideas to far too great an extent. In fact, Marx and Engels wrote so little on the form which the revolution would take in Asia – or in Russia, considered as an oriental despotism – that their successors and disciples were obliged to construct their theories in this domain by relying to a great extent on analogies with what the founders of 'scientific socialism' had written in very different contexts. This is particularly the case as regards the two fundamental problems of the role of the peasantry, and the national factor.

Marx did not at first view the peasantry in any very favourable light. In a well-known passage from the *Communist Manifesto*, he declared that the bourgeoisie, by increasing the population of the cities, had thus rescued 'a great part of the population from the idiocy of rural life'. He also described the middle classes, both urban and rural, as conservative by nature.[1] But apart from the fact that the aim of the *Manifesto* was not to present a carefully-balanced analysis, but to call the proletariat to battle, Marx and Engels were basing themselves in large part, in 1848, on the example of England. And as Marx himself wrote a few years later, England, because of her highly developed industrialization, was the country in which the role of such intermediate classes as the peasantry had the least importance.[2] Afterwards, when Marx had occasion to examine the problems posed by the role of the peasantry in France, he came to less negative conclusions.

To be sure, in the first installment of his study of the events of 1848 in France, he produced a celebrated and highly unflattering characterization of the peasantry:

> The 10th December 1848 was the day of the peasant insurrection. . . . The symbol which expressed their entry into the revolutionary movement – clumsy and shrewd, rascally and naïve, loutish and sublime, calculated superstition, pathetic burlesque, brilliant and foolish anachronism, prank of world history, hieroglyphic undecipherable for the reason of civilized man – this symbol was marked unmistakably with the physiognomy of the class which represents barbarism in the midst of civilization.[3]

But in the following installment of the same work, he wrote that the peasants, made wiser by experience, were coming to understand that their interests were linked not to those of the bourgeoisie, but to those of the workers. (It is in this context that he made the well-known statement: 'Revolutions are the locomotives

[1] *The Communist Manifesto.*

[2] K. Marx, 'Letter to the Labour Parliament', *The People's Paper*, 18 March 1854, in *Karl Marx and Frederick Engels on Britain* (Moscow, Foreign Languages Publishing House, 1953), p. 402.

[3] K. Marx, *Die Klassenkämpfe in Frankreich* (Berlin, Dietz Verlag, 1951), pp. 70–71.

of history'.)[1] Two years later, in *The 18th Brumaire of Louis Bonaparte*, Marx developed at some length the viewpoint that the peasant smallholders, who had been in the first instance the instrument of the bourgeoisie in its struggle against feudalism, had now come to oppose the bourgeoisie and to see in the urban proletariat their natural ally and guide. And he continued:

In losing hope in the Napoleonic restoration, the French peasant loses faith in his small holding, overthrows the whole state apparatus built on that small holding, and thus the proletarian revolution obtains the chorus without which, in all peasant countries, its solo becomes a swan song. (See Text I 5.)

To be sure, Marx eliminated this resounding phrase from the second edition of his book, but in more sober form, the idea that the peasantry would be more and more inclined to ally itself with the urban workers remained, and would afterwards serve to justify the most divergent theoretical conceptions.

But would not the behaviour of the peasantry – and of all the other classes of society – be affected by the political or economic domination of the countries of Asia by Europe? In dealing with this problem, Marxist theoreticians have relied above all on the writings of Marx and Engels about the national problems in Eastern Europe.

In this connexion, one must first of all emphasize that Marx and Engels did not, as was to be the case of Lenin and other twentieth-century Marxists, bestow universal approval on all national independence movements. At the time of the 1848 revolution, when they wrote most of their articles regarding the national problem in Eastern Europe, the fundamental criterion by which they judged national movements was hatred of Russia. As a corollary of their view of tsarism as the principal bastion of reaction in Europe, they came to regard as positive any national uprising that weakened the Russian empire, and to condemn as reactionary any national movement which might possibly prove advantageous to Russia.

In the case of national liberation movements which they regarded as legitimate and progressive, such as that of Poland in particular, Marx and Engels did, however, draw certain interesting conclusions regarding the influence of the national factor on revolutionary tactics. Thus, in discussing the consequences of the partition of Poland among the powers, Engels declared that this foreign servitude had given birth in Poland to the alliance of all the classes of society, with the exception of the upper nobility, which was in league with the powers (see Text I 4). We have here a clear prefiguration of the innumerable theories regarding the alliance of the proletariat and the peasantry with the bourgeoisie

[1] ibid., p. 124.

in the dependent countries, which have been elaborated in the course of the past half century.

If the typical examples of the national problem in the middle of the nineteenth century were to be found in Eastern Europe, the typical example of the colonial problem was Ireland. It is precisely with reference to Ireland that Marx has left a text which, despite its brevity, has very broad implications. Writing to Engels in 1867, he expressed the view that the English working class would never accomplish anything until the British political system was shaken by the loss of Ireland. 'It is in Ireland', he wrote, 'that the lever must be applied' (see Text I 3). By thus giving priority to action in the colony over action in the mother country Marx opened the door to all the 'asiocentric' visions of the world revolution which were to be propagated once Asia had ceased to be a simple object of analysis and become an actor in its own right.

The Second International and Colonial Problems

If the writings of Marx and Engels on the problems of the non-European countries are fragmentary and inconclusive, this is in large part because, in their lifetime, colonial expansion was still only in its early stages. The increasingly rapid progress of European colonization in Asia and Africa would soon oblige Marx's disciples to take a definite stand on these questions.

Even before the establishment of the Second International in 1889, the European socialist parties had begun to take an interest in colonial problems and the question had been placed on the agenda of the Paris Congress in 1900.[1] But it was only in 1904, at the Amsterdam Congress, that contradictory tendencies manifested themselves openly in the international socialist movement. At the Stuttgart Congress of 1907, these tendencies clashed in a lengthy and impassioned debate.

The natural reaction of most European socialists towards colonial expansion in its early stages had been negative, both on humanitarian grounds and because the enterprise appeared to profit only the bourgeoisie. Two factors were now working against such a negative attitude towards colonization. On the one hand, it was more and more widely believed that the whole population of Europe, including the workers, could live better thanks to the profits obtained from the colonies. In 1902, Hobson developed this idea systematically, for the purpose of combatting it, in his celebrated work *Imperialism*, which was to have such great influence on Lenin. And if liberals such as Hobson or revolutionaries such as Lenin were disturbed by this evolution, the possibility of living better thanks to the labour of the Chinese coolies or the Negroes of Africa was not equally distasteful to all socialists. This selfish reac-

[1] For an excellent historical survey see the article of M. Rebérioux and G. Haupt in *Le Mouvement Social,* no. 45, October–December 1963, pp. 7–37.

tion was reinforced by the europocentrism on the cultural level which characterized, as we have already seen, Marx himself. As early as 1882, Engels had expressed, in a letter to Kautsky, his disappointment at the tendency of the English workers to 'joyfully share in the feast of England's monopoly of the world market and in the colonies' (see Text I 7). But at the same time, he continued to adopt a patronizing attitude towards the 'natives' of Asia and Africa in which one can even glimpse an embryo of justification for the policy of the 'tutelage' of the civilized countries over the 'immature peoples' which was to be urged, beginning in 1904, by Van Kol, David and Bernstein. At least Engels opposed armed repression in the colonies by the former mother countries, once the revolution had been carried out.

The tendency at the Congresses of 1904 and 1907 to support a 'positive' colonial policy, and the counter-attack against this position by the 'orthodox' faction, especially by Kautsky, are so clearly formulated in the extracts reproduced in this volume (see Texts I 8 and I 9) that it hardly seems necessary to analyse the debates here. Thanks to the prestige of Kautsky, the Congress failed to heed Van Kol's warning that the Europeans must accomplish their civilizing mission fully armed, if they did not want to be eaten by the cannibals, and rejected the motion calling for 'a socialist colonial policy' in favour of the traditional condemnation of the colonial atrocities of the bourgeoisie. But the tendency illustrated by the debates of 1907 remained strong in all the socialist parties of Europe, as Lenin, who was present at the Stuttgart Congress, took pains to emphasize.

Lenin and his Contemporaries before the Founding of the Third International

If the debate at Stuttgart revealed a certain lack of understanding of the colonial problem on the part of the social democrats, the problem had none the less been raised, and would henceforth constitute a subject of reflection for socialists of various tendencies in the years which preceded the First World War. But before analysing Lenin's ideas on this subject, it is necessary to sketch briefly the essential traits of his thought as a whole, which distinguish it from all other schools of Marxism.

At the beginning of this Introduction, we suggested that Lenin was in a certain sense the mediator between Marxism and the non-European world. If he was able to carry out this role, it was partly because the presence in the tsarist empire of a large percentage of non-Russians had given him direct experience of the colonial problem. But a more important reason was that Russia itself was a country half-way between Europe and Asia from the standpoint of economic and social development. We have seen that Marx considered it to be an oriental despotism. To be sure, at the turn of the century substantial changes were taking place. In particular, the beginnings of industrialization were giving rise to a numerically limited, but concentrated and politically conscious, industrial proletariat. Nevertheless, even if Russia was no longer characterized by Asiatic stagnation, it was still far from corresponding to the idea commonly held by Marxists of a highly developed capitalist country, ripe for revolution.

Without in any sense regarding as negligible the conscious action of human beings, Marx himself, and even more the 'orthodox' Marxists such as Kautsky, tended to emphasize economic and social determinism. In their view, the development of the productive forces brought about changes in the position of the various classes of society; and when the gap between the legal position and the real importance of a rising class reached a certain point, the class struggle was exacerbated to such an extent that a revolution broke out. For the orthodox Marxists, any attempt by a given class to seize power before it had been put in a dominant position by the development of the economy would be premature and condemned to failure.

Such was also the position of the Russian Mensheviks, who held that one must first let the bourgeoisie carry out its own revolution, and then wait until the ensuing development of capitalism had put the proletarian revolution on the order of the day. Lenin, like the leaders of the communist parties of the underdeveloped countries today, did not have that much patience. He was thus led to shift the accent from the determinist to the voluntarist strand in Marx's thought. This does not mean, of course, that he believed there were no limits to the action of the revolutionaries; he always stressed the fact that one must adapt oneself to concrete revolutionary situations. But he nevertheless believed in the possibility of, as it were, pushing forward the wheel of history, in situations where orthodox Marxists thought revolutionary action impossible for the time being.

Because of this voluntarist tendency, the cast of Lenin's thought is particularly well adapted to the requirements of revolutionary action in underdeveloped countries. Moreover, in addition to a turn of mind, he brought to the solution of the problems of the revolution in the East a series of organizational and tactical principles developed on the basis of Russian experience. This is above all the case as regards the relations between class and party, and as regards the alliance between the proletariat and the peasantry.

Lenin, who was resolved to carry out the revolution in a country where the working class was not yet very large, was obliged to compensate for this numerical weakness by organization and discipline. And in pursuing this aim of an effective revolutionary organization, he made extremely important changes in the Marxist conceptions regarding the relation between the Communist party and the proletariat. His views on this point were first systematically developed in *What Is To Be Done?*, written in 1902. Here, at one stroke, Lenin set forth the ideas which were henceforth to guide the action of the Bolsheviks, both before and after the October Revolution. Building on an idea formulated by Kautsky, according to which socialist consciousness is 'an element imported from outside into the class struggle of the proletariat', he explains at length that the workers, left to themselves, cannot rise above 'trade union consciousness' – i.e., the idea of struggling for immediate material advantages. A real political struggle, according to Lenin, presupposes, on the contrary, knowledge regarding society as a whole which cannot come to the workers from their own experience but is brought to them from outside by intellectuals of bourgeois origin. The task of the revolutionaries is thus not simply to go to the workers and assimilate their aspirations; such an attitude could only lead to 'the crushing of consciousness by spontaneity', and hence to failure. What is wanted is on the contrary to make of the social democratic party an organization of professional revolutionaries. Some of the latter may be workers who have acquired the necessary knowledge; the majority will not be, but this will not prevent the party from incarnating the real will of the proletariat.

In *What Is To Be Done?* Lenin justifies the small and disciplined character which he proposes to give to the social democratic party by the conditions under which political work was carried out in tsarist Russia, where clandestinity was indispensable to avoid police repression. This factor certainly played a role, but there is no doubt that the idea of a party which leads the proletariat and is not simply the emanation and the spokesman of the real working class corresponds to Lenin's élitist turn of mind. This élitist tendency is, moreover, closely linked to Lenin's voluntarism. It is evident that the further economic conditions are from being ripe for revolution, the greater is the gap between the overall vision of the transformations to be carried out and the immediate experience of the workers, and hence the greater the need to inculcate this vision from outside.

Although in *What Is To Be Done?* Lenin set forth his ideas regarding the role of the proletariat in the revolution in terms of the situation of the Russian Social-Democratic Workers' Party, which was struggling for the leadership of a backward working class, his conceptions in fact had much wider implications. They were, moreover, based not only on Russian experience, but on the reformist tendencies of Western social democracy. In his pamphlet, Lenin denounced the attempt of Bernstein and Millerand to orient social democracy towards bourgeois reformism. Kautsky had written about class consciousness imported from outside not with reference to Russia but in discussing the programme of the

Austrian Social Democratic Party. For his part, Lenin, while he referred to Russian conditions, was even more concerned to combat the reformist tendencies which had begun to manifest themselves early in the twentieth century, and which were to lead in 1914 to an open crisis in the social democratic movement.

Lenin also drew another conclusion from the strength of the reformist tendencies in the advanced capitalist countries: that the backward and predominantly agrarian countries appeared to offer the best chance of revolution, because of the weakness of the capitalist sector. Although the idea that the capitalist chain should be broken at its 'weakest link' is implicit rather than explicit in Lenin's writings of this early period, it nevertheless exists in embryonic form in his strategy of the revolutionary vanguard, and in his attempt to make a place for the peasantry in theory and strategy.

In order to understand the spirit in which Lenin would later deal with the problems of the revolution in the non-European countries, one must consider not only the way in which he dissociated the 'proletarian' party from the real proletariat, but also the dissociation between the class nature of a given historical phase and the actual role of the various classes during this phase. Marx considered as a matter of course that the capitalist stage in the development of society would be characterized by the domination of the bourgeoisie, just as the feudal stage had been marked by the domination of the nobility. The bourgeois-democratic revolution which constituted the transition from feudalism to capitalism would likewise be carried out by the bourgeoisie. As for the proletariat, it would support the bourgeoisie in the democratic revolution, until the time came to put an end to the capitalist system by the socialist revolution, in which the workers in their turn would play the leading part. Trotsky was the first to break radically with this conception, by postulating in his theory of the 'permanent revolution', put forward in 1905, that the bourgeois-democratic revolution could take place under the hegemony of the proletariat – which would moreover transform the democratic revolution without a pause into the socialist revolution.

Lenin was more prudent. At the time of the 1905 revolution, he referred to the 'revolutionary-democratic dictatorship of the workers and peasants'. But he interpreted this formula, as early as September 1905, in a sense which clearly suggested that hegemony in this joint dictatorship would belong to the proletariat – or to the 'party of the proletariat'. At the same time, he referred to an 'uninterrupted revolution' which appeared to bear a strong family resemblance to Trotsky's 'permanent revolution'.[1]

[1] This celebrated passage of Lenin regarding the 'uninterrupted revolution' is to be found in 'The Attitude of Social Democracy towards the Peasant Movement'; translation in *The Alliance of the Working Class and the Peasantry*

As pointed out earlier, Marx, too, believed that the peasantry could furnish an ally or 'chorus' for the proletarian revolution. But he formulated these ideas with reference to the France of 1852, which was one of the most advanced countries at the time, where the urban proletariat had long played a significant political role, and was, in Marx's opinion, rapidly growing in economic importance as well. To state, on the other hand, that a worker and peasant dictatorship, led in fact by the proletariat, was possible in the Russia of 1905, was to attribute political power to a class which did not yet occupy a dominant position in the economy, and did not appear capable of doing so. This naturally led to the idea that politics dominates economics, and in fact Lenin set forth most explicitly this very principle. 'Politics,' he wrote, 'is the concentrated expression of economics. . . . Politics cannot fail to take priority over economics. Not to understand this is to forget the ABC of Marxism.'[1]

To be sure, Lenin wrote this in a particular context, that of the discussion regarding the respective roles of the party and of the trade unions in Russia in 1920. But there is no doubt that these words express a basic trait of his whole system of thought. This trait is particularly evident precisely in Lenin's ideas regarding the evolution of the non-European countries. In Russia, the working class, although a minority, was relatively strong and concentrated. One could therefore find a certain justification for attributing the leading role to this class, or to the party which was supposed to represent it. The situation in Asia was quite different. Economically and numerically, the working class was infinitely weaker there than in Russia. Under such conditions, to postulate a revolution led by a Marxist party signified, even more than in Russia, giving politics priority over economics.

Such are the principal traits of Lenin's thought, and such is the spirit in which he undertook to analyse the problems of the revolution in the non-European countries. We have spoken of voluntarism, and of the priority attributed to politics. One could also refer to an empirical attitude – or an opportunistic attitude, depending on whether one wishes to praise him or blame him. There is no doubt that Lenin constantly kept his eyes fixed on his basic aim, which was the conquest of power in Russia, and more broadly the triumph of the world revolution. His attitude towards the national liberation struggles of the colonial and dependent peoples was all the more utilitarian because he did not attach any value to

(Moscow, Foreign Languages Publishing House, 1962), pp. 236–7. For a brief comparison of the attitudes of Lenin and Trotsky regarding the dissociation between the class character of a stage and the role of the actual classes during that stage, see S. Schram, *La 'révolution permanente' en Chine* (Paris, Mouton, 1963), pp. xxi–iv.

[1] Lenin, *Polnoye Sobraniye Sochinenii*, vol. 42, p. 278.

the nation as such. 'The slogan of national culture,' he wrote, 'is a bourgeois fraud. . . . Our slogan is the international culture of democracy and of the world working-class movement.'[1] Consequently, if he vigorously combatted the position of Rosa Luxemburg, who rejected the right of self-determination as reactionary, it was only because he was convinced that in many cases it would be possible to promote social revolution by supporting national movements.

The source of Lenin's understanding of the explosive and revolutionary character of national factors is obvious enough. Though he had been formed in the Western Marxist tradition, he was a native of a multi-national state where aspirations to social reform were often inseparable from aspirations to national independence, and where the latter offered solid support to the former in the struggle against the established order. It is significant, moreover, that the analysis of the national problem was carried out above all by Austrian and Russian Marxists that is to say, by men who had lived in multi-national empires where the demands of the national minorities constantly claimed their attention.[2]

The 1905 revolution, in particular, had shown what great force could be generated by the combination of the opposition on social and national grounds. Another lesson of that revolution was precisely that the development of the revolutionary movement led to a prodigious development of national aspirations, which manifested itself from 1907 to 1908 in the flourishing of a variety of national democratic movements of the Muslims around the colonial periphery of the Russian empire, and in the Turkish and Persian revolutions.

It is in a pamphlet of 1914 entitled *On the Right of Nations to Self-Determination*, devoted to the refutation of Rosa Luxemburg's ideas, that Lenin defined his position regarding the progressive role which could be played by national demands. On the one hand, he emphasized that historically the framework of the independent nation-state had always been the one which best permitted the free development of a capitalist economy in the place of feudalism, thus opening the way to further changes. On the other hand, knowing the strength of national sentiments, he was convinced that the best way to prepare the ground for closer ties in the future, especially among the peoples of the tsarist empire, was to recognize the right of the subject peoples to secede, in the hope that they would rapidly come to understand the advantages of a wider

[1] Lenin, 'Critical remarks on the national question', *Collected Works*, vol. 20 (Moscow, Progress Publishers, 1964), p. 23.

[2] For the history of the debates within the social democratic movement on the national question, see E. H. Carr, *The Bolshevik Revolution 1917–1923* (London, Macmillan, 1950), vol. I, pp. 259–75, and also D. Boersner, *The Bolsheviks and the National and Colonial Question (1917–28)* (Geneva, Droz, 1957), chapter II.

market. Finally, the recognition of the right to self-determination was in his eyes indispensable in the interest of the dominant people itself, for a people which oppresses another cannot itself be free: 'The century-long history of the repression of the movements of the oppressed nations, and the systematic propaganda in favour of such repression by the upper classes, have created in the Great-Russian people prejudices, etc. which are enormous obstacles to the cause of its own liberty.'[1]

It is obvious that all these arguments, and especially that which refers to the importance of nation-states as a framework for the development of capitalism, apply in particular to Asia, as Lenin emphasized very strongly in the text of 1914 just cited.[2] But in the case of the East, another factor came into play: the pernicious influence which Lenin very early came to attribute to the colonial possessions as a means for corrupting the working class of the mother countries.

As early as 1907, in his comments on the Stuttgart Congress, Lenin sketched out the idea that as a result of colonization the European workers were in danger of falling into a situation similar to that of the proletarians of antiquity, who lived at the expense of society instead of supporting society by their labour. And 'the class of non-working have-nots is incapable of overthrowing the exploiters' (see Text II 1).

That colonization would make it possible to improve the fate of the European workers and thus to delay social revolution in Europe was a belief shared, at the beginning of the twentieth century, by all those who had thought about the problem, whether they were socialists like Kautsky,[3] Hilferding,[4] or Rosa Luxemburg,[5] liberals like Hobson, or partisans of imperialism like Cecil Rhodes, who saw in the colonies a means for avoiding civil war.[6] The problem for the revolutionaries was how to put an end to this system. Rosa Luxemburg was persuaded that the domination of the imperialist powers over the non-European world was such as to render any initiative on the part of the oppressed nations completely illusory. Salvation could only come from the European proletariat. We have seen that virtually the totality of the leading figures of the Second International, despite their disagreements regarding the policy to be followed in the colonies, also believed, at the beginning of the twentieth century, that the victims of colonization were utterly impotent. Lenin was not so pessimistic regarding the possibility of revolutionary action in Asia, but he

[1] Lenin, *Selected Works* (Moscow, Progress Publishers, 1967), vol. 1, p. 616. See also Text II 5.

[2] ibid., p. 605.

[3] K. Kautsky, *Sozialismus und Kolonialpolitik* (Berlin, 1907).

[4] R. Hilferding, *Das Finanzkapital* (Berlin, 1910).

[5] R. Luxemburg, *Die Akkumulation des Kapitals* (Berlin, 1912).

[6] See his remarks cited by Lenin in Text II 6.

took a long time to elaborate his position regarding the tactics which should be followed.

How uncertain and tentative were his first reflections on this theme is attested by his article of 1908, 'Inflammable Materials in World Politics' (Text II 2). On the one hand, he here salutes the appearance in Asia of 'tens of millions of proletarians'. But at the same time, he predicts that the latter will carry on 'a victorious struggle – like that of the Japanese – against their oppressors'. We have already emphasized the decisive role of the defeat of Russia by Japan in the awakening of Asia, but the part played in this achievement by the proletariat was, to say the least, problematical.

Already, in 1912, in his article on Sun Yat-sen (Text II 3), Lenin was evolving towards a more realistic conception of the social forces at work in Asia, for he attributed the principal role to the peasants. At the same time he showed that he belonged to the intellectual universe of Marx by declaring that 'the East has definitely embarked on the path of the West', and that Sun Yat-sen was 'a worthy successor' to the men of the Enlightenment. The following year, in another celebrated article, 'Backward Europe and Advanced Asia', he set forth similar ideas. Whereas in Europe 'the proletariat *alone* is *the* advanced class', since the European bourgeoisie is altogether corrupt, in Asia the bourgeoisie '*still* sides with the people against reaction' (Text II 4). Despite the title, which appears to give priority to Asia, Lenin nevertheless continued to assume, in this text of 1914, that the European proletariat would play the essential role in the world revolution. It was, he wrote, the victory of the European workers which would 'free both the peoples of Europe and the peoples of Asia'.

The war of 1914 was to mark a new phase in Lenin's intellectual itinerary. He could not but meditate on the dramatic split in the ranks of European social democracy caused by the attitudes adopted towards the war. This cleavage corresponded to a great extent with that which had been visible since Stuttgart between the socialist parties of the great colonial powers and the parties of the nations without colonies. The parties of the first group, which were in general solidly established, adopted a very moderate attitude towards the colonial problem. Those of the second group, which in general led a precarious and semi-clandestine existence, had always taken a more radical line on colonial questions. Lenin, as he reflected on the collapse of social democracy in the advanced countries possessing colonies, and as he considered likewise the force of socialism in Russia and the vitality of the movements of resistance in the colonies, endeavoured to fit these various facts into a coherent system. It is in the phenomenon of imperialism that he found the explanation of the crisis which gripped the European socialist movement, and the means to integrate the movements in the backward countries into a global strategy which could resolve this crisis.

In his celebrated work, *Imperialism, the Highest Stage of Capitalism*, of which we give only a brief extract here (Text II 6), Lenin set forth a theory about the evolution of the world as a whole since the beginning of the twentieth century. He developed systematically the idea he had sketched as early as 1907, according to which it was colonial exploitation that lay at the root of the corruption of the proletariat, for the profits from the colonies had made it possible for the bourgeoisie to encourage 'opportunist' (i.e. moderate and reformist) tendencies in the working class. But imperialism, which eats away at the dynamism of the proletariat of the advanced countries, has, in the dependent countries, exactly the contrary effect, since it there serves to develop nationalist tendencies. Given this link between the national problem and imperialism, Lenin considered that no revolutionary could henceforth deny the importance of national movements. For his part, he regarded the national struggle against imperialism as an integral part of the overall struggle of the proletariat for its liberation, since the national struggle could not achieve its objectives without the destruction of the colonial system. Furthermore, seen in the context of imperialism, the national problem is the factor which connects the non-European world to the problem of the world revolution, and constitutes a link between the developed West and the backward East.

With this analysis Lenin went a step further, as compared with his previous attitude, towards a position according a full measure of attention to the revolutionary potential of the Orient. And in the face of the totally europocentric position adopted by Rosa Luxemburg in her pamphlet *The Crisis of Social Democracy* (published in 1916 under the pseudonym of 'Junius'; see Text II 7) Lenin reaffirmed once more his belief in the possibility and the utility of movements of liberation in the colonies (Text II 8). But he was still very far, in 1916, from a vision of the world revolution attaching equal weight to Asia – still less a greater weight than to Europe. This is attested by his remark, in a discussion of the Irish uprising, that a blow struck there against British imperialism is infinitely more important than 'an uprising of much greater magnitude in a distant colony' (Text II 9).

As for Stalin, who occupied the post of Commissar for Nationalities in the years immediately after the revolution, it is true that he urged his comrades, at a time when all eyes were fixed on Germany, not to forget the East (Text II 10). But he nevertheless declared, in this very article written in December 1918, that 'the chains of imperialism' would 'be broken in the first place' in the West. His vision of the revolution thus remained also, in the last analysis, a europocentric one.

Prior to the establishment of the Soviet power, Lenin had developed his ideas on the national question primarily in a dialogue with Russian and European revolutionaries. In 1920, at the Second Congress of the Communist International, he was to find himself confronted for the first time with Asian interlocutors, in the double context of the international situation of Soviet Russia and of the national problem within the country.

2. PROBLEMS OF THE REVOLUTION IN THE EAST IN THE DAYS OF THE COMINTERN

The Second Congress of the Communist International

When, beginning in November 1917, problems of all kinds presented themselves to the Bolsheviks, no longer in an exclusively theoretical form, but in concrete terms, the attention of Lenin and his colleagues was first absorbed by the task of establishing their power in the face of the double threat of intervention and civil war. To the extent that they had the leisure to focus their attention on the outside world, it was rather by Europe that they were preoccupied, both because the danger of intervention came from there, and because they still considered the European revolution, and especially the German revolution, as the key to the world revolution and a necessary condition of their own survival. Thus the First Congress of the new Communist International, which met in 1919, accorded little attention to the problems of the Asian revolution.

In the summer of 1920, on the other hand, despite the wave of enthusiasm inspired by the Red Army's victorious offensive in Poland at the very moment when the Second Congress was in session, revolution in Europe no longer appeared to be a foregone conclusion, at least in the immediate future. There was also an important change in the origins of the participants. In 1919 Soviet Russia had been largely isolated from the outside world by the Allied blockade, so that it had often been necessary to appoint individuals who happened to be on hand as 'delegates' of their respective countries to the First Congress. In 1920, the situation had changed sufficiently so that a certain number of revolutionaries not only from Europe, but from Asia and from other continents, had been able to make their way to Moscow. It is in this context that the first great debate took place within the International regarding the problems of the revolution in the non-European countries.

This debate was of very broad scope. It dealt with both the tactical and strategic aspects of the problem. It was marked by a clash between the most diverse tendencies. The theses which were finally adopted were considered throughout the whole existence of the Comintern as defining the orthodox Leninist view in this domain, and are often cited by communist theoreticians even today. For all these reasons, the debate at the Second Congress merits special attention.

It is particularly difficult to give a summary analysis of the proceedings of the Congress because the leading protagonists in the debate did not divide along the same lines in dealing with the various issues. To give only one example, the Italian Serrati, who represented the most extreme europocentrism, and the Indian M. N. Roy, who defended a resolutely asiocentric position, were in agreement over tactics in according very little credit to the bourgeois revolutionaries in the Eastern countries, and in advocating exclusive reliance on the proletariat.

Most accounts of the Second Congress begin by analysing the debate on the tactical level. It seems to us that it is more instructive to begin with the problem of strategy on a world scale. On this level, three tendencies were represented at the Congress: the europocentrism of Serrati, the asiocentrism of Roy, and an intermediate position defended by Lenin and by certain other Russian and European delegates.

Serrati's attitude was expressed not only in his intervention at the end of the debate, of which the essential passages are included in our extract (Text III 4), but in repeated attempts to put an end to the discussion, which he obviously regarded as a waste of time. Little need be said about this extreme europocentric tendency, except that it was almost unanimously rejected by the Congress. In view of the failure of the European revolution (even though this failure was supposed to be only temporary), all eyes were turned on the East to find new forces capable of assuring victory on a world scale, and a position which regarded Asia as of no account could hardly expect to attract much sympathy from the delegates.

The real debate was between Lenin and Roy, and it took place above all in the commission. The extracts from the summary of this clash, which are translated here at some length (Text III 2), show in striking fashion how deep was the gulf between a European revolutionary – even a revolutionary with as broad a vision as Lenin – and an Asian profoundly convinced of the pre-eminent role which Asia was destined to play in world history.[1] Roy declared flatly that the fate of the European revolution depended entirely on the revolution in Asia; unless the latter triumphed, the communist movement in Europe would simply count for nothing at all. In the face of such extreme statements even Lenin, who had been the first to grasp and to emphasize the importance of the revolution in the colonies, could not do otherwise than tell Roy that he was going too far.

Given the composition of the Second Congress of the Com-

[1] Although he did not include a translation of the debates in the commission, Allan Whiting summarized the essence of this clash between Lenin and Roy in his *Soviet Policies in China 1917–1924* (New York, Columbia University Press, 1954), pp. 54–5.

munist International, given too the inherent logic of Marxism, which may be regarded as an attempt to europeanize the world, this controversy necessarily had to be decided in favour of Lenin. Roy was thus obliged to accept modifications in his theses which transformed his categorical profession of faith in the Asian revolution as the key to everything into the much less sweeping claim that revolution in Asia was important and could play a role in the worldwide victory over imperialism (see Roy's speech, Text III 4). The position originally defended by Roy nevertheless remains in the history of the world communist movement the clearest prefiguration of the current asiocentrism of the Chinese.

On a tactical level, the central problem was that of the collaboration with the bourgeoisie in the non-European countries. Here again the chief protagonists were Lenin and Roy. As *rapporteur* on the national and colonial question, Lenin had prepared theses emphasizing that it was necessary in the colonial and dependent countries to support the 'bourgeois-democratic' liberation movement. To be sure he also indicated very clearly that it was the duty of the communists to keep their own organization intact, and not to merge it with that of the bourgeois democrats. Nevertheless, the idea that temporarily the communists should allow the bourgeoisie to retain the hegemony over the revolutionary movement was implicit in Lenin's theses (see Text III 3).

Such an attitude was natural in the case of Lenin, whose principal concern, as head of the Soviet government, was to find allies capable of weakening the rear of the colonial powers which were adopting a hostile and threatening attitude towards his régime in Europe. It could not satisfy an Asian revolutionary, who had no intention of accepting indefinitely the domination of the bourgeoisie of his own country. Here, too, the debate between Lenin and Roy constitutes a prefiguration of the conflict between the diplomatic interests of the Soviet Union and the natural ambitions of the revolutionaries of Asia and Africa which runs through the whole history of Soviet foreign policy, from the Turkey of Kemal to Nasser's Egypt.

On the tactical level, Lenin made a few concessions to Roy. In particular, he agreed to replace in his theses the term 'bourgeois-democratic' by the vaguer word 'revolutionary'. As he explained himself in his report to the plenary session (see Text IV 2), this modification did not have the effect of excluding all collaboration with the bourgeoisie – for he held that any national-revolutionary movement in the backward countries must necessarily be bourgeois-democratic. The point of the stipulation that communists must collaborate only with 'revolutionaries' among the bourgeoisie was simply to separate the sheep from the goats among such movements. In Lenin's view, a 'good' bourgeois movement, which the communists should support, was a movement which did not oppose the efforts of the communists to organize the peasantry and the broad masses of the exploited. Having thus made explicit certain aspects of his own thinking, Lenin obtained in exchange from Roy the insertion, in the latter's 'complementary theses', of a brief sentence regarding the utility of cooperating with bourgeois nationalists. The emphasis in Roy's theses none the less remained different from that in Lenin's theses. In particular, Roy maintained that, from the very beginning of the revolution, the communist vanguard must seize the leadership and not allow it to remain in the hands of the bourgeoisie. Moreover, this position, which was at once more asiocentric and more sectarian, was to some extent recognized, since the two sets of theses were both officially adopted. But in fact it was above all Lenin's theses which served henceforth to define the orthodox position, though there were occasional references to those of Roy. The lack of serious attention to the latter is symbolized by the fact, which has often been pointed out, that it is Roy's original text, and not that adopted by the Congress after the important changes made in the commission, which was included in both the German and Russian editions of the proceedings of the Second Congress, and that this error was not even detected until 1934.[1]

If Lenin and Roy disagreed as to the tactics by which the communists in the Eastern countries could finally succeed in seizing power, they were both equally persuaded that, once the Soviet power was established, these countries could avoid the capitalist stage of development and move directly to socialism. Once more, however, there was a minor divergence between their positions. For Roy, the soviets which would be established would necessarily be, if not purely proletarian, at least *workers'* and peasants' soviets. This attitude was a natural consequence of his overall view according to which there already existed in the Asian countries a proletariat which was, to be sure, numerically limited, but which had attained a high level of class consciousness and was capable of playing a decisive political role. Lenin, on the other hand, spoke at considerable length of soviets which would *not* be workers' soviets, but peasant soviets, or 'soviets of toilers' or 'soviets of the exploited'. In this context he declared: 'The idea of a soviet organization is a simple one; it can be applied not only in the framework of proletarian relations, but also in the framework of peasant relations, of a feudal or semi-feudal nature.'

Lenin's ideas regarding peasant soviets have played a considerable part in the controversies regarding the originality of the Chinese pattern of a communist revolution supported primarily by the peasantry. Lenin's two speeches on this question at the Second Congress (see Texts III 1 and III 4) appear to distinguish between

[1] On this point see Whiting, op. cit., p. 56, and E. H. Carr, *The Bolshevik Revolution 1917–1923* (Macmillan, 1953), vol. III, p. 252.

the communist parties which must be founded in the backward countries on the one hand, and the peasant soviets which these parties are advised to establish on the other. The implications of his remarks regarding the class composition of the communist parties themselves are much less clear. New light is thrown on this aspect of Lenin's thinking by a text recently published in the fifth edition of his works, in which he declares that one must '*adapt* not only the soviet institutions, but the communist party (its composition, its special tasks) to the level of the *peasant* countries of the colonial East'.[1] To be sure, the fact that Lenin said one must adapt both the soviets and the party did not necessarily mean that one must adapt them to the same degree. If 'peasant soviets' would necessarily, as the name implies, be composed primarily of peasants, Lenin no doubt envisaged that the communist parties would include a certain percentage of proletarian elements. And it would naturally be the task of the parties, supported by the International, to organize the soviets as an instrument for mobilizing the masses. Hence one cannot conclude from the text by Lenin just cited that already in 1920 he envisaged the possibility of a communist party composed almost exclusively of peasants. But there is no doubt that Lenin had already taken the first steps in a direction which was ultimately to lead to Mao Tse-tung's peasant communism as its logical conclusion.

In Lenin's view, a non-capitalist path of development could be followed only if 'the victorious proletariat of the Soviet republics' gave its support to the revolutionary movement in the backward countries. Roy was more explicit, referring to 'the Soviet republics of the advanced capitalist countries'. Did Lenin mean the same thing? Or was he thinking of the various 'soviet republics' scattered over the territory of the former Russian empire, which were soon to unite to establish the Soviet Union? It seems likely that, if he had not yet, in July 1920, abandoned all hope of a revolution in Germany or in other European countries, he was already moving towards a vision in which, for a relatively long time, Soviet Russia alone would extend a hand to the peoples of Asia and give them the support which would allow them to avoid the capitalist stage. Thus the schema of Marx and Engels, according to which Russia could avoid the capitalist stage if the victorious proletariat of the advanced countries of Western Europe supported the Russian revolution, was transposed towards the East. From a backward country, living under the rule of oriental despotism, Russia was to become, first in theory and then in fact, an advanced country, which in turn would offer its aid to even more backward countries of Asia and Africa.

If the principal spokesman of the asiocentric view at the Second Congress was the Indian Roy, while Lenin adopted a more

[1] Lenin, *Polnoye Sobraniye Sochinenii*, vol. 41, p. 457.

balanced position, the other speakers who participated in the debate were not all divided along geographic lines. Thus it was a Persian in the service of the Soviet government, Sultan-Zadé, who rejected most brutally the 'error' of Roy in attributing too much weight to the revolution in Asia. In the opposite sense, the Dutchman Maring (whose real name was Henricus Sneevliet), who already had considerable revolutionary accomplishments to his credit in Indonesia, and who was later to play an important role in the Chinese revolution, emphasized most strongly the importance of the Asian revolution, though he did not go quite so far as Roy.

Finally, it is worth pointing out that the cultural dimension of the revolution in the colonies is even more completely absent from the discussions of the Second Congress than it was from the debates of the Second International. At Amsterdam and Stuttgart, the Englishman Hyndman had praised the civilization of India, 'which is perhaps superior to ours'. At Moscow in 1920, the Indian Roy was primarily concerned to demonstrate that the way which would be followed by Asia was identical to that of Europe (see his reply to Serrati, towards the end of the debate). For his part, Lenin no longer employed at this Congress the concept of the Asiatic mode of production, but neither did he expound a unilinear theory regarding the development of all societies of the East and the West.

In reality, his true concern lay elsewhere, and therefore the absence of cultural problems from the debates of the Second Congress was quite logical. The exclusive concentration on problems of strategy and tactics which characterizes this Congress is, in fact, a concrete illustration of the mutation which Lenin brought about in Marxism. From the rich and complex thought of Marx, Lenin extracted above all certain recipes for the conquest of power. This was his strength, and also his weakness, as history has shown.

The Congress of Baku and the Colonial Problem in Russia itself

Formerly you were accustomed to cross the desert to visit the holy places; now you cross deserts, mountains and rivers to meet together and discuss how you can free yourself from your chains and join in a fraternal union to live an equal, free and fraternal existence.[1]

This commentary on the invitation addressed by the Comintern to the representatives of the 'enslaved popular masses' of the East, summoning them to come and discuss their fate at Baku the following month, prefigures in striking fashion both the tone of this debate, and the problems posed in the course of it. The Baku Congress was characterized like the Second Comintern Congress by the encounter between two conceptions of the colonial revolution.

[1] *Kommunisticheskiy Internatsional*, no. 12, 20 July 1920, column 2264.

But for the first time, these two conceptions were rooted in a concrete situation: the experience then going on around the periphery of the Soviet state. The spokesmen for the East[1] at Baku were primarily Muslims from Central Asia, which had been a veritable colony of the Russian empire, and their interventions constituted the first attempt at a theoretical analysis of the problems of revolution in Asia by men who had actually lived through such a revolution. One must remember that these Muslims had come to communism, or to the support of the Soviet power, from the reformist national movements which had developed in Russia after the 1905 revolution.[2] During the summer of 1917, the incapacity of the Provisional Government to satisfy their hopes had pushed them towards the Bolsheviks, whose slogans regarding the self-determination of nations attracted them. In the policies of the Bolsheviks they thought they glimpsed at last the possibility of realizing in common their dream of political and social regeneration. It was in Turkestan, where there existed a colonial situation and a mass of Russian colonists and functionaries, that the disillusion was most rapid. This disillusion was to mark the first steps of the indigenous communists in the party organizations. At the first Conference of Muslim Communists of Central Asia (24–30 May 1919) a delegate was to declare regarding the revolutions in Central Asia:

> We were still obliged to endure a contemptuous attitude on the part of the former privileged classes towards the indigenous masses. This attitude is that of the communists, who retain a mentality of oppressors and regard the Muslims as their subjects.[3]

The truth of this allegation is attested by G. Safarov, who was Lenin's emissary in Central Asia. His judgement is extremely interesting, for it is unquestionably applicable to other colonial situations:

> It was inevitable that the Russian revolution in Turkestan should have a colonialist character. The Turkestani working class, numerically small, had neither leader, programme, party nor revolutionary tradition. It could therefore not protest against colonialist exploitation. Under tsarist colonialism, it was the privilege of the Russians to belong to the industrial proletariat. For this reason, the dictatorship of the proletariat took on a typically colonialist aspect.[4]

Like Safarov, the Muslims of Russia grasped very early that a

[1] Of the 1891 delegates to the Congress, there were 235 Turks, 192 Persians, 8 Chinese, 8 Kurds, and 3 Arabs. The others came primarily from the non-Russian areas of Soviet Russia, especially from Central Asia and the Caucasus.

[2] For these events see H. Carrère d'Encausse, *Réforme et Révolution chez les Musulmans de l'Empire Russe. Bukhara 1867–1924* (Paris, Armand Colin, 1966).

[3] G. Safarov, *Kolonial'naya Revolyutsiya. Opyt Turkestana* (Moscow, 1921), p. 97.

[4] G. Safarov, *Revolyutsiya i Kul'tura* (Tashkent, 1934), vol. I, p. 10.

difference quite naturally arose between the actual conditions of the proletarians of the former colonial power, and the indigenous workers. This being the case, they found it logical to endow the latter with their own organizations, where the concept of class (which was as yet but feebly developed) would be linked or even subordinated to a reality which had not disappointed them: solidarity among the peoples of Turkish origin. This is why, at the Third Congress of Muslim Communist Organizations in January 1920, they demanded that the organization of the Russian Communist Party in Turkestan should be transformed into a Turkish Communist Party, which would be the rallying-point for all Communists of Turkish origin in Russia. They were doubly attached to this idea because they had become persuaded that the revolution in the East was of fundamental importance for the future of the world revolution. They had expressed this conviction at the Second Congress of the Communist Organizations of the Peoples of the East (November 1919) in terms much more vigorous than those used by Lenin in his report (Texts IV, 1, A and B), thus drawing upon themselves a rebuke from the organ of the Commissariat for Nationalities.[1]

Thus, on the eve of the Congress of Baku, the Muslim Communists of Russia had developed, in the light of their revolutionary experience, a conception of the problems posed by the colonial revolution which combined several ideas. In their opinion, the revolution did not solve the problem of the relations between the labouring masses of the dominant industrial societies and those of the agrarian societies they dominated. In the latter, solidarity among the various social strata was indispensable to escape from domination. Finally, the revolutionary potential of the East was indispensable to the world revolution. It must be emphasized that these ideas were as yet largely implicit, and were expressed in fragmentary and scattered fashion. They by no means constituted as yet a clear theory of the colonial revolution. Moreover – and this is an important point – these ideas were as yet largely unknown to the Russian Bolsheviks, for Lenin's emissaries had come to Turkestan only in the summer of 1920 and of them only Safarov, who participated in the second mission, had a real grasp of the problems.[2]

Whereas the Muslims came to Baku in September 1920 embittered by their experiences and intuitively persuaded of the specificity of the colonial revolution, the leaders of the Comintern came there impressed by the debates at the Second Congress, and

[1] *Zhizn' Natsional'nostey*, no. 45 (53), 30 November 1919, calls attention to the idea, put forward at this Congress, of the crucial importance of the revolution in the East, and points out the danger of such statements.

[2] The first commission of inquiry, sent to Tashkent at the end of 1919, had seen in the demands of the Muslims simply an attempt to seize power.

also struck by the collapse of the hopes for an immediate revolution in the West following the defeat which had meanwhile taken place before Warsaw. This probably explains the tone of the opening speech by Zinoviev, the president of the Congress, who invoked the revolutionary potentialities of the East, and strongly emphasized the originality of the revolution in the Orient. Zinoviev's conclusion, calling on his audience to participate in a holy war against imperialism, unleashed extraordinary enthusiasm. The delegates brandished their sabres and revolvers, amid cries of '*Jihad*', 'Long live the resurrection of the East!' and 'Long live the Third International!' (see the description in the proceedings of the Congress, Text IV 2). But it was only later, when the Muslims explained their problems and their conception of the revolution, that the Congress really found itself for the first time face to face with the concrete problems of the colonial revolution.[1] The non-Russian delegates showed how fragile was the concept of class solidarity in a colonial situation. They emphasized the necessity of an adaptation of communist ideology to the specificity of the East, and insisted on the fundamental character of *national* revolutions, which were the only guarantee of the genuine emancipation of the Orient. A natural consequence was to attribute an important role to the national bourgeoisie. Here the theories elaborated at the Second Congress collided with a demonstrable reality: the difficulty of establishing a bridge between the proletariat of the advanced countries and the peasantry of the colonies.

The Muslims' demand that, in the light of the stabilization in the West, priority should be given to the revolution in the East, due account being taken of the specificity of the East, was in fact rejected by the leaders of the Comintern. Indeed, the position of the International was even more reserved on this point than it had been at the Second Congress. It is quite clear from the speeches of Radek, Bela Kun and Pavlovich, and from the theses they presented, that the liberation movements of the peoples of the East were, in their view, destined to remain a secondary force supporting the world revolution, and did not constitute a distinct revolutionary possibility. This being the case, they naturally laid it down that the revolution in the East should conform to the general pattern of the revolution as a whole. Thus national revolution was expected to be accompanied by social revolution, so that the alliance with the bourgeoisie could only be temporary and condi-

[1] E. H. Carr (*The Bolshevik Revolution*, vol. III, p. 262, note 1) says that, according to information from Georgian Mensheviks the stenographic report of the Baku congress was considerably abridged, as regards the speeches of certain Muslims particularly hostile to the Bolsheviks. This appears quite likely, for some of the speeches are given only in abridged translations, and others (particularly that of Ryskulov) give in several points the impression of having been cut.

tional, and not of long duration, as the Muslims demanded. And as there was no proletariat, the class that should lead the movement was the poor peasantry of the Eastern countries. By refusing to support national movements led by the bourgeoisie, the leaders of the Comintern appeared to deviate from the line laid down by Lenin at the Second Congress. At the same time, they did not fail to proclaim the necessity of extending the revolution to the East, and the Congress came to an end in an atmosphere of great enthusiasm. In view of the grave conflicts which had emerged in the course of the debates, this shows the complexity of the problems and the incapacity of the participants to decide clearly what they actually wanted.

One of the important aspects of this Congress is that it brought into play the three dimensions we have singled out. It raised the problem of a re-examination of strategy on a world scale, sought to elaborate tactics appropriate to local conditions, and above all attacked the question at the fundamental level of the specificity of the colonial world. For the Muslims of Russia, the revolution was above all a means for recapturing their national identity, a continuation of the dream of the reformists. This aspiration, as yet not clearly expressed in 1920, was later to be a fundamental preoccupation of other communist parties in the non-European world.

Following the Baku Congress, the resolutions adopted there were put into practice around the periphery of Russia, where steps were taken to curb the national communist governments, and cadres belonging to the minority nationalities were purged. The highpoint of the crisis was reached in 1923, with the denunciation of nationalist deviations and the elimination of virtually all natives from local positions and their replacement by 'proletarian elements'.

The best known of the victims of this repression was a Tatar communist, Sultan Galiev.[1] Galiev, who had been, immediately after the October Revolution, Assistant Commissar for Nationalities under Stalin, has unfortunately left very few writings. The one from which we have selected extracts for this volume (Text IV 3) dates from 1919, a period when he had not yet despaired of collaboration with the Russian revolutionaries.

Beginning in 1923, on the other hand, after he had been attacked and expelled from the Communist Party, he developed much more radical ideas, which are known only from the passages cited by his adversaries. Declaring that there was a fundamental difference between the proletariats of the West and of the East, and that the

[1] See A. Bennigsen and C. Quelquejay, *Le Sultangalievisme au Tatarstan* (Paris, 1960), pp. 176–82, where Sultan Galiev's ideas are set forth; and also Arsharuni and Gabidullin, *Ocherki Panislamizma i Panturkizma v Rossii* (Moscow, 1931), pp. 76–91.

two were irreconcilable, he characterized as follows the nature of the Muslim East:

The Muslim peoples are proletarian nations. There is a great difference between the economic situation of the English and French proletariat, and the proletariat (?) of Morocco or Afghanistan. It may be stated that the national movement in the Muslim countries has the character of a socialist revolution.[1]

The fundamental distinction for Sultan Galiev was therefore between the Western proletariat, which was a social *class*, and Eastern *nations* which were entirely proletarian because of the economic conditions imposed upon them. In his view, the replacement of the Western bourgeoisie by the Western proletariat as the dominant class could not lead to any change whatever in the relations of the latter class with the oppressed countries of the East, for the Western proletariat mechanically inherited the attitude of the class to which it had succeeded as far as national questions were concerned. The only solution for the East was to substitute for the dictatorship exercised by the Western mother countries the dictatorship of the proletarian nations of the East over the former colonial powers of the West.[2] In order to bring about such a reversal of the historic situation, Sultan Galiev envisaged the creation of a colonial communist international, which would have been independent of the Third International and which would have defended against the advanced countries the interests of the proletarian nations. The first step in the regrouping of these nations was to have been a great Turkish national state, Turan. Both Turan and the colonial international were to have been led by a Muslim 'socialist and workers' ' party, representing the broad masses of the Muslims: peasantry, proletariat, and petty bourgeoisie.

In these theoretical conceptions one finds many of the demands of the Muslims after 1917, and many of the conclusions which they had reached. The state of Turan recalled the Republic of Turkestan which had been proposed in 1919, and the socialist and workers' party was the descendant of the 'Muslim Communist Party' suppressed in 1918, and of the 'Turkish Communist Party' which never came into being.

Sultan Galiev also emphasized repeatedly the problem of incorporating into communism the Muslim cultural heritage, and of according a certain tolerance to Islam, at least in the beginning.

On this point, of the utmost importance as far as the cultural

[1] Quoted by Arsharuni and Gabidullin, op. cit., p. 78.

[2] This is stated in the programme written by Sultan Galiev in 1928; this programme has disappeared, and one can merely reconstruct the essential outlines on the basis of the analysis of it given by Arsharuni and Gabidullin, op. cit., p. 79.

aspect of things is concerned, it is appropriate to recall the ideas of another Muslim nationalist converted to communism, Hanafi Muzzafar. According to Arsharuni and Gabidullin, Muzzafar was 'the ideologist of Sultangalievism', and attempted to justify theoretically the conciliation of communism and Islam, that is to say the formation of an Islamized communism.[1] For Hanafi Muzzafar the problem of the Muslims was that of 'the existence of our nation, of the entire Islamic world, and of all the subject nationalities and states'.[2] The enemy of these nations, who was responsible for their misfortunes, was imperialism, and communism was struggling against imperialism. Consequently an alliance with communism was indispensable, but this alliance should be concluded without abandoning an iota of the truths professed by the Muslim peoples, i.e. Islam. It was possible to combine the two for, wrote Muzzafar, 'religion, and especially our religion, Islam, is not a class religion, it is a religion which transcends classes, it is universal. It is possible that each class understands the religious domain in its own way, and considers it from its own point of view, but that constitutes precisely a class approach and not an Islamic approach.'[3] The desire to harmonize the transformations of modern times with the values inherent in Islam lay at the heart of Hanafi Muzzafar's thinking. Here again we find an echo of the position of Ryskulov who demanded at the Baku Congress that the religious and cultural heritage of the colonial peoples be integrated into Marxism. The dominant concern of Hanafi Muzzafar, as had been the case with Sultan Galiev and the Turkestanis in 1919, was to preserve the *unity* of the Islamic world, by making of it the centre of a socialist development of the community.

The period from 1920 to 1923 was marked not only by the development of a theory of the colonial revolution by the Muslims, but also by changes in the ideas and above all of the actions of the Bolsheviks regarding the national question. Down to 1920, the need to gain the spontaneous support of the non-Russian peoples in order to struggle against the forces hostile to the revolution had led the Bolsheviks to declare their fidelity to the principle of the self-determination of nations. But progressively the Bolsheviks discovered, as Stalin was to emphasize afterwards in his writings, that the vigour and complexity of the national movements, and the consequences of their unhindered development, went far beyond what they had imagined in their theoretical reflections, and offered more drawbacks than advantages.[4] The internal disintegration of Russia was accelerating. Lenin's attention was

[1] His work on religious and national questions, *Din Ve Millet Masalari*, has remained unpublished, but Arsharuni and Gabidullin quote extensively from it.

[2] Arsharuni and Gabidullin, op. cit., p. 80.

[3] loc. cit.

[4] Stalin, *Sochineniya*, vol. III, pp. 30–1.

constantly drawn to this problem, during the years 1919–20, by Safarov, who saw the movement gathering momentum in the peripheral areas of Turkestan. On the basis of this example, Safarov developed his own conception of a colonial revolution, emphasizing both the necessity and the limits of such a revolution (Text IV 4). When the failure of the European revolution grew more obvious, beginning in 1921, it became clear to the Russian leaders that the salvation of the revolution required the rapid reunification of the former empire. From that point onwards, the Bolsheviks embarked upon the repression and liquidation of all the centrifugal national movements, and also upon the creation of a centralized state. On the one hand, the national movements were progressively decapitated, and then eliminated. Muslim leaders such as Sultan Galiev were liquidated, and all the communist parties of the minority nationalities were purged, their membership having often undergone a turnover of from sixty to ninety per cent between 1921 and 1924. On the other hand, the constituent republics (Ukraine, Bielorussia, etc.) were progressively brought into the Soviet federation, on the basis of a clearly manifest centralism. To be sure, this unification took place in principle on the basis of the will of the proletariat, and on the basis of a strict equality among all the peoples belonging to the federation. The texts by Stalin of which extracts are included here denounce Great-Russian chauvinism as well as local chauvinisms (Texts IV 5 and IV 6). Stalin also emphasized the importance of the colonial revolution (Text IV 7) and the need to make a place in the Soviet organs for elements from the minority nationalities (Text IV 6). Nevertheless, the reassuring declarations made at the time when the Bolsheviks were engaged in their effort at national reconstruction could not hide the reality of their actions, still less the psychological background of those actions: the profound lack of confidence of the Bolsheviks in the backward peoples, and their certainty that, despite the failure in Europe, the centre of gravity of the revolution remained the industrial proletariat. At the Twelfth Congress of the Communist Party in 1923, Stalin declared: 'The political basis of the dictatorship of the proletariat comprises first of all and most fundamentally the industrial regions in the centre and not at all the outlying regions which are agrarian lands.'[1] And if at this same Congress Great-Russian chauvinism was denounced, Kalinin none the less declared that the policy of the Soviets should henceforth have as its aim 'to teach the peoples of the Kirghiz steppe, the Uzbeks and the Turkmens, to accept the ideals of the worker of Leningrad'.[2]

[1] ibid., vol. V, p. 265.
[2] M. Kalinin, *Za Eti Gody* (Moscow, 1929), vol. III, pp. 385–6.

The Communist International and the Revolution in the East from the Third to the Fifth Congress

We have seen that the interaction between national realities and social revolution within the former Russian empire engendered, during the years immediately following the revolution, a growing tension which the leaders in Moscow finally attempted to eliminate by a policy of centralization and repression. But in the eyes of Lenin and his colleagues this conflict was not inevitable. Despite the susceptibilities of the national minorities, friendly collaboration between Russian and non-Russian revolutionaries was regarded as not only desirable but possible.

The situation was quite different with respect to the tactics of collaboration between communists and nationalists in other countries laid down at the Second Congress of the International. Here there was a fundamental contradiction at the very start. In as much as the ultimate objective of a proletarian dictatorship had by no means been abandoned, collaboration with bourgeois revolutionaries was only a stage. Thus those who tomorrow would be treated as enemies were asked to participate in an enterprise of which they were destined to be afterwards the victims. For their part, the nationalists were perfectly well aware of these mental reservations in the Comintern's policy of alliance, and when they none the less agreed to collaborate, it was with the firm intention of using the communists rather than allowing themselves to be outmanoeuvred by them.

The contradiction just mentioned was openly recognized at the time by the theoreticians of the International, who repeatedly emphasized that to collaborate with the bourgeois nationalists did not mean either that the communists abandoned the class struggle, or that they would allow their hands to be tied in the future. Already in itself this contradiction would have sufficed to ensure that the history of collaboration between communists and nationalists would be an agitated one. But the situation was further complicated by another contradiction of which the Soviets contested (and continue to contest) the very existence: that between the interest of the world revolution and the interest of the Soviet state.

This problem could arise only when the perspective of an immediate revolution in Europe had receded sufficiently so that, on both sides, people began to envisage the existence of the Soviet state side by side with bourgeois states during a relatively long period. In this respect, March 1921 marks a truly decisive turning point. On the one hand, the attempt at armed insurrection known as the 'March Action', launched by the German Communist Party on 17 March 1921, and completely crushed by the *Reichswehr* in less than two weeks, showed conclusively that Germany was not ripe for a communist revolution. On the other hand, the signature on 16 March of a commercial agreement with the United Kingdom, and on 18 March of a peace treaty with Poland, appeared to open prospects for the stabilization of the relations between the Soviet state and the Entente powers.

In this new context, the problem of the exploitation of nationalist currents to revolutionary ends would henceforth be inextricably mixed up with that of the exploitation of conflicts between capitalist countries to prevent a coalition against Russia. This dual motive can be clearly seen in the fact that at this time Soviet policy endeavoured to exploit nationalism not only in the non-European countries, but in Germany. To be sure, for a brief period during the summer of 1923, following the French occupation of the Ruhr, an attempt was made to obtain from the nationalists and even from the fascists a contribution to the proletarian revolution.[1] And in his last article, published in March 1923, Lenin sketched a schema regarding the corruption of the proletariat in the countries of the Entente thanks to the profits from the exploitation of Germany closely modelled on his theory of the corrosive effects of colonial profits (see Text V 4). Nevertheless, the innumerable declarations of sympathy for Germany, considered as an 'oppressed people', were manifestly inspired by the interests of the Soviet state rather than by revolutionary aims, as the Rapallo policy and the collaboration between the *Reichswehr* and the Red Army abundantly show.

The situation as regarded the exploitation of the national movements in the East was more complex, but there too, it seemed clear, even before Lenin's disappearance from the political scene, that priority was frequently given to the interests of the Soviet state. The most important and instructive example is that of Turkey. In the spring of 1920, following the establishment at Ankara of a nationalist government presided over by Kemal, the latter exchanged with Moscow messages referring to their common struggle against imperialism. Subsequently, the Soviet government repeatedly proclaimed its solidarity with Kemal in his efforts to maintain himself in power despite the hostility of the Entente.

In the beginning, there was at least the appearance of a justification for this policy in revolutionary terms, for Kemal, who needed Soviet support, went so far as to speak in his messages of an alliance between the workers of the West and the peoples of Asia and Africa to put an end to the domination of the bourgeoisie.[2]

[1] On this episode, known as the 'Schlageter Line', from the name of a nationalist executed for sabotage by the French authorities, of whom the communists later made a symbol in their propaganda, see E. H. Carr, *The Interregnum* (London, Macmillan, 1954), pp. 174–89.

[2] For extracts from Kemal's telegram of 29 November 1920, and more generally for an analysis of Soviet-Turkish relations beginning in 1920, see

But as he gradually consolidated his power, the Turkish leader moved towards a more conservative position, repressing the revolutionary movements within the country and carrying out a *rapprochement* with England and France. Nevertheless, even at the end of 1922, despite the fact that in January 1921 Kemal had executed seventeen leaders of the Turkish Communist Party, Moscow continued to see revolutionary potentialities in his movement (see Text V 2, the debates at the Fourth Congress of the International, especially Radek's speech). It is only in 1923, after Kemal had openly disdained Soviet diplomatic support at the Conference of Lausanne in order to seek a compromise with the Entente, that the Soviet leaders began to reconsider their policy towards him.

The priority accorded by the Soviet government to diplomatic considerations was strikingly illustrated by the debates at the Third Congress of the International, which met in June 1921. The commercial agreement signed three months earlier with London had stipulated that the two countries undertook to curb all mutally hostile propaganda, and more particularly that Soviet Russia would abstain from all propaganda which might incite the peoples of Asia to act contrary to British interests. The leaders in Moscow had no desire to endanger the hope of a provisional *modus vivendi* with the Western powers, at a time when the economic situation of Russia was particularly difficult, by openly violating this promise.

In his long report in the name of the Executive Committee of the International, Zinoviev, after analysing at great length the situation in the West, devoted only a few sentences to the problems of the East: 'The Propaganda Council created by the Baku Congress is working actively in the Middle East. From the standpoint of organization much remains to be done. The same is true regarding the Far East.'[1]

This passing reference to the East indicated clearly the place which the Third Congress was prepared to assign to the national and colonial question. That place was a minimal one. In fact, the 'Western' tendency in the Comintern dominated the debates of 1921. Commenting on Trotsky's report 'The World Crisis and the New Aims of the Comintern', Roy emphasized the revolutionary potential of the East, but his arguments had only a very limited impact on Trotsky, who continued to hold that 'of the three beds in which the revolutionary tide flowed, the third was the colonial world'.[2]

An incident which took place at the Congress is symbolic of the

---

E. H. Carr, *The Bolshevik Revolution*, vol. III, pp. 244–9, 263–6, 294–304, 473–8, 484–9.

[1] *Protokolle des III. Kongresses der Kommunistischen Internationale*, p. 211.

[2] ibid., p. 137.

lack of attention accorded to the Eastern question. In the course of the debate on the colonies, the delegates from the colonial countries showed a tendency to speak at some length, and the presidium decided to limit each orator to five minutes. This provoked an outburst of indignation from M. N. Roy (Text V 1). Charles-André Julien of the French delegation shared Roy's bitterness. To their interventions, Kolarov replied, in the spirit of the Stuttgart Congress, that the principal aim of the debate was to show the solidarity of the communists in the West with the peoples of the East.

Between the Third and Fourth Congresses new events led the Comintern to take a greater interest in the colonial question. In Europe, the year 1922 saw the rise of fascism in Italy, and the International moved towards united front tactics in order to oppose these reactionary tendencies. These tactics of the united front applied in the West could also serve as a model for a united front of a different kind with the national movements in the East. At the same time, the Turkish problem led to a conflict between Moscow and the United Kingdom, which had opposed Soviet presence at the Lausanne Conference, then about to begin. Hence when the Fourth Congress met in November and December 1922, the Soviet leaders no longer had the same reasons as in 1921 to limit the propaganda against British imperialism.

The whole course of this Congress shows how much more 'Asian' it was than the previous one. The delegates from the East were able to speak at length during the two sessions devoted to their problems, and this time Zinoviev's report devoted a great deal of attention to the revolutionary situation in the East. Among the representatives of the Asian countries, this Congress revealed the existence of two very different tendencies. One of them, which can be called moderate, was represented by the Indonesian, Tan Malaka, who raised a question regarding the support to be accorded to national movements which was all the more important because his position was contrary to that defended by Lenin at the Second Congress. How far, he asked, should one go in supporting national movements? Lenin had condemned pan-Islamism and limited collaboration with national movements to those which were regarded as not reactionary. Such a distinction, said Tan Malaka, was wrong, and particularly harmful in the case of pan-Islamism. Islam had a great hold on the popular mind in the East, and to struggle against it meant to alienate popular sentiment. Moreover, it played a central role in the national struggle, and was therefore progressive and anti-imperialist.

In opposition to Tan Malaka, who demanded support for all national movements, M. N. Roy defended a much more leftist position, based on an analysis of the new economic tactics of capitalism. In Roy's view, since the war, capitalism, far from wishing to hinder industrial development in the colonies, was bent on speeding it up, in order to create new markets in the overseas countries. This being the case, the national bourgeoisie of the colonies was naturally inclined to seek an understanding with the imperialist powers, whose policy was favourable to its interests, and thus found itself radically opposed both to the urban proletariat and to the peasantry. It was only in the most backward countries that the privileged strata, even the feudal aristocracy, could momentarily play an objectively revolutionary role. According to Roy, it was therefore above all necessary to prepare the communist parties for taking over the leadership of the national liberation movements in the relatively near future.

Apart from the differences regarding the tactics to be applied in the non-European countries, this congress provided an occasion for the expression of divergent views on both the strategic and cultural levels. Radek especially displayed a scepticism regarding the real force of the revolutionary movements of the East which was entirely contrary to the position of all the Asian delegates. He also showed a contempt for the 'Confucian' mentality of the Chinese communists which contrasted brutally with Tan Malaka's plea for recognition of the specificity of the East.

The resolutions and theses adopted by the Congress made a place for all the positions which had been expressed during the debates. The principle of collaboration with the revolutionary bourgeoisie in the East was clearly recognized. In certain cases, one could even go so far as to support pan-Islamism. But such collaboration must be of limited duration, and the proletariat must struggle to establish its hegemony over the national liberation movement. Finally, the Comintern insisted on the necessity, for the Western communist parties, to give unfailing support to the revolutionary effort in the East. This recommendation was underscored by the denunciation of the behaviour of the French Communist Party (see Text V 2 A, the speech of Safarov).

The Fourth Congress was the last one attended by Lenin, who suffered his second stroke shortly afterwards. Between this second stroke, which took place on 16 December 1922, and the third one, in March 1923, which finally put an end to his political and literary activity, he dictated a certain number of notes, including one on the national question in Russia which illustrates once more his understanding for the human problems created by colonization.[1] But if he had a remarkable sympathy for the susceptibilities of the non-European peoples towards their former masters, he had not achieved, even at the end of his life, any comprehension of the

[1] This document was first published by Richard Pipes, who found it in the Trotsky Archives (see his study *The Formation of the Soviet Union*, Cambridge [Mass.], Harvard University Press, 1954). It is now part of the official corpus of Lenin's works. See *Polnoye Sobraniye Sochinenii*, vol. 45, pp. 356–62.

explicitly cultural dimension of the Asian revolution. This is flagrantly apparent in reading his last article (Text V 4), which attributes to Asia decisive weight in global revolutionary strategy, but which poses the problem of 'civilization' exclusively in terms of the level of economic and technical development.

When the Fifth Congress met on 17 June 1924, Lenin was dead and Stalin already had considerable influence. The orientation and decisions of the Congress, and even its tone, were already characteristic of the Stalinist era. Superficially, the Fifth Congress marked a decisive turning point towards a more 'colonial' orientation of the Comintern. The importance of the debate on this theme, and the sharp criticisms directed at certain Western communist parties (especially the French and British parties) seemed to indicate that henceforth the Comintern took the revolution in the East very seriously. But these verbal protestations did not suffice to convince Nguyen Ai Quoc (Ho Chi Minh) that the International had really abandoned its europocentric errors, and he proclaimed with the utmost emphasis that Europe was no longer the centre of the revolution.[1]

In the course of the debates M. N. Roy once more defended the most extreme viewpoint. But this time, he clashed head on with the spokesman of the presidium, and his position was finally condemned. The fundamental divergence between Roy and the leaders of the Comintern pertained as usual to relations with the bourgeoisie. In the view of Manuilsky and the other defenders of the official line, the alliance with the bourgeoisie corresponded to the tactics which were suitable during the whole of the bourgeois democratic stage in the backward countries, and this alliance should be maintained as long as imperialism had not been defeated and social conflicts had not arisen. Roy held, on the contrary, that as soon as the bourgeoisie had taken power it attempted to get rid of its allies, thus setting back the revolutionary movement in general. This is why he was prepared to accept an alliance only in certain cases where, precisely, the bourgeoisie was as yet in no position to seize power.

The resolutions adopted by the Fifth Congress rejected Roy's view and proclaimed the tactics of collaboration with the bourgeoisie as the basic line valid for the whole of the East. They also insisted on the importance of the revolutionary movements in the colonies, and on the need to avoid concentrating the whole effort of the Comintern in the West. Did these declarations correspond to a fundamental shift in the orientation of the Comintern? The policies applied by Stalin in the peripheral areas of the U.S.S.R.

[1] His declarations were reduced to a few colourless lines in the 'Compte rendu analytique' published by the Librairie de l'Humanité in 1924, in which the criticisms of the French Communist Party by Manuilsky were also greatly attenuated.

inhabited by Muslim peoples, and the foreign policy of the Soviet Union at the same period, hardly bear out this hypothesis. By preaching virtually unconditional support to national liberation movements, the leadership of the Comintern hampered in reality the development of the communist parties in the Eastern countries, and placed the latter at the mercy of the national leaders when they seized power. The Turkish example clearly demonstrates this. On the other hand, by denying the possibility of a class struggle in the East, except as an altogether secondary phenomenon, at least in the immediate future, the leaders of the Comintern obviously cast doubt on the revolutionary capabilities of the masses in the colonies. As between suspicion regarding the revolutionary capacities of the bourgeoisie and suspicion regarding the revolutionary capacities of the worker and peasant masses, the Comintern chose the second, and this choice is already characteristic of Stalin's policy. The refusal to see in the East any revolutionary possibilities except that of a national revolution clearly implied that only the West could carry out a social revolution. To be sure, for a time the emphasis was placed on revolution in the East, but in the final analysis this policy might well hide a considerable dose of precisely that 'Western spirit' which the Fifth Congress denounced. This was to be demonstrated once more by the Chinese example.

Chinese Communism, from the Origins down to 1927

It is clear today that Chinese communism is neither a simple transposition to a slightly different cultural environment of a kind of Platonic idea of communism which is everywhere the same, nor a 'new dynasty' succeeding to a host of others without breaking the continuity of Chinese history, but a complex, dynamic and perhaps explosive mixture of Leninist and Chinese elements. Like virtually all other Asian nations, China was an overpopulated peasant country. At the same time, it differed radically from all the countries of South and South-east Asia by the nature of its political and intellectual tradition, which was still a massive and coherent phenomenon at the beginning of the twentieth century, despite its decadence. It is not an easy task to define in brief compass – or even in an entire volume – the essential characteristics of Chinese civilization. And yet virtually nothing in the evolution of Chinese communism can be adequately understood apart from this context.

If China continues to be marked so indelibly with the imprint of its past, even today, this is not merely because the Chinese tradition was an extremely rich one. It is also because that civilization possessed two attributes which no doubt prepared it better than any other great non-European civilization to adapt to the modern world. These are in the first place a sense of history, and in the second place a philosophical tradition oriented above all towards political and ethical problems rather than towards metaphysical speculation.

To be sure, the Chinese idea of history was not that of history as a continual forward movement in the direction of progress, as we know it today in the West. But it must be remembered that the idea of progress is a relatively recent invention, even in the European cultural tradition. The Chinese conception of history, which is that of alternating periods of centralization and disintegration of the empire, is not too far from that of classical antiquity. In any case, the Chinese were better prepared to accept the idea that they were part of a world-wide universal history than peoples, such as those of India, which traditionally had not even had a written history.

As for Chinese philosophy, it is well known that Confucian orthodoxy almost completely neglected religious and ontological problems and concentrated on the one hand on the moral self-cultivation of the individual, and on the other hand on problems of family, social and political relationships. To be sure, nearly all the solutions to these problems proposed by Confucianism were so many obstacles to the assimilation of revolutionary or even of liberal ideas. In the intellectual domain, Confucius preached respect for the prevailing orthodoxy, and in the domain of social relationships, he preached respect for the hierarchical superior, whether it be the emperor, the father or the husband. Westernization, even in the most moderate form, thus clashed head on with the Chinese tradition, and led to a sudden break in traditional patterns of life and forms of thought, followed by a period of disarray. Nevertheless, the Confucian tradition aided in the comprehension of Western political ideas to the extent that it was oriented towards the problems of this world, and to the extent that it attached the highest value to political and social order. In particular, it inculcated the idea of the national community as the central reality in the life of the individual, even if that community was conceived as a universal empire covering the whole of the civilized world rather than as one state among others. In this respect also, there is a striking contrast with the mystical civilizations of South and South-east Asia, for which political realities completely dropped out of sight as a result of the exclusive concentration on relations between the individual and the absolute.

If we leave the plane of tradition for that of history, two facts give to the encounter with the West a dimension in China which it does not have elsewhere. On the one hand, this process began very early, with the Opium War of 1840, so that it extended over more than a century. On the other hand, although China underwent a humiliation analogous to that of colonial domination, as a result of the imposition of concessions and spheres of influence, the control of the customs by foreign powers, extra-territoriality, and so forth, it nevertheless conserved something of its independence and sovereignty. As a result, the Chinese political and intellectual *élites* were able to discuss the best way of resisting the West with much greater freedom than was granted to other Asian nations under direct colonial domination.

Elsewhere, one of the authors of this volume has tentatively put forward a three-part schema to describe the process of modernization in China, and perhaps in other non-European countries.[1] In a first phase, which might be called that of 'tradition-oriented nationalism', Chinese intellectuals and statesmen on the whole reaffirmed the absolute superiority of Chinese moral and political principles over those of the barbarians – even if they made a slight concession in recognizing the value of certain Western technical discoveries for purely military purposes. In a second phase, a certain number of Chinese, convinced of the tragic incapacity of traditional society to apply Western techniques effectively, or to resist Western military and economic pressure, were led to propose the complete abandonment of Chinese ideas and customs and their replacement by those of the West. Finally, this phase of radical Westernization was succeeded by a third phase, that of revolutionary nationalism. In this case, the aim is once more to assimilate certain essential elements of Western civilization, in particular its Promethean will to master nature, but in the political context of a radical transformation of the existing society in order to resist Western domination.

Naturally, like all historical schemas, this one represents an oversimplification of reality. On the one hand, the three phases just defined did not succeed one another at definite dates, but overlapped. Moreover, attitudes belonging to two or even three of these archetypes often coexisted in a single individual. Nevertheless, this schema appears to us to be a useful guide to the direction in which China was evolving at the end of the nineteenth century and the beginning of the twentieth.

Since it is manifestly impossible in this brief volume to examine in detail all the intellectual influences which played a role in the birth of the Chinese Communist Party, we shall take as examples the intellectual itineraries of the two founding fathers of the party, Li Ta-chao and Ch'en Tu-hsiu. In a sense, these two men are characteristic representatives of the two currents of which revolutionary nationalism, in its Leninist guise, was to constitute the synthesis.

Ch'en was above all a Westernizer, who turned to Communism as the most efficient method for modernizing Chinese society. Li, on the other hand, was a nationalist, who found in the Leninist

[1] S. Schram, *The Political Thought of Mao Tse-tung* (Harmondsworth, Penguin Books, 1969), pp. 18–19.

theory of imperialism a justification for his chauvinistic views. These very different turns of mind, which characterized the two men even when they had both adopted the same ideology, had led them to clash long before they were converted to Leninism. In their celebrated polemics of 1914–15, of which we have translated here the essential passages (see Texts VI 1 and VI 2), the one appears as the perfect incarnation of nationalism, and the other as a spokesman for radical Westernization.

In Ch'en Tu-hsiu's article, which was the first to appear, Chinese political customs are rejected as absolutely inferior to those of the West. In Europe and America, what is called a state is 'an organization for pursuing in common the happiness of the citizens', whereas in China it is merely a system employed by the despot and his family for plundering the inhabitants. The proper goal for China and the key to the future is to acquire 'knowledge', i.e. Western scientific knowledge. (A few years later, Ch'en would develop these ideas in the form of a cult of 'Mr Democracy' and 'Mr Science'.) Finally, the independence or even the existence of the Chinese state does not appear to him to be anything very important, still less a reason for pride.

It would be hard to imagine a more brutal contrast with Li Ta-chao's position, expressed in a letter to the editor protesting against the publication of Ch'en's article. To be sure, writing in 1915, during the First World War which had inaugurated a period of rapid transformation in China, Li does not express himself in the terms which would have been used by a defender of the Chinese tradition a quarter of a century earlier. Not only does he invoke the authority of European writers, but the very concept of a state, around which his whole argument is organized, is foreign to traditional Chinese thought. The moderate conservatives of the second half of the nineteenth century who wanted to borrow certain techniques from the West without modifying the Chinese essence were attached not to the Chinese state, but to the Chinese 'way', which they regarded as the only way worthy of human beings. To employ the accepted terminology, they were 'culturalists' rather than 'nationalists'.[1] There is nevertheless a strong family resemblance between these men and the pre-Marxist Li Ta-chao of 1915. Like them, he was above all preoccupied by the salvation of the entity 'China'; and though he defined this entity as a state rather than a culture, he did not envisage any significant changes in the social structure of China in order to strengthen it. In this sense, the Li Ta-chao of this period remains not only a nationalist, but a conservative nationalist.

Moreover, if the state was not a central value in Chinese thought

[1] The classic study of the transition from 'culturalism' to nationalism is that of Joseph Levenson, *Confucian China and its Modern Fate* (London, Routledge and Kegan Paul, 1958), vol. I.

prior to the impact of the West, the idea of preserving the nation was not without antecedents. At the beginning of the seventeenth century, when the Chinese dynasty of the Ming was overthrown by the Manchu invaders, the great scholar Wang Fu-chih wrote:

> Now man partakes of *yin* and *yang*, food and breath, equally with other things, and yet he cannot but be distinguished absolutely from other things; the Chinese in their bone structure, sense organs, gregariousness and exclusiveness, are no different from the barbarians, and yet they must be distinguished absolutely from the barbarians. Why is this so? Because if man does not mark himself off from things, then the principle of Heaven is violated. If the Chinese do not mark themselves off from the barbarians, then the principle of earth is violated. . . .
>
> Even the ants have leaders who rule their ant-hills, and if other insects come to attack their nests, the leader gathers the ants together and leads them against their enemies to destroy them and prevent further intrusion. Thus he who would lead the ants must know the way to protect his group. . . .[1]

To be sure, Wang Fu-chih was an isolated figure in his own time, but at the beginning of the twentieth century he had a great reputation and considerable influence. (Mao Tse-tung, while he was a student in Changsha, participated in the meetings of a society for the study of Wang's writings.) It was thus from indigenous roots, as well as from imported elements, that modern nationalism developed and took shape in China half a century ago.

If it is proper to consider Li Ta-chao as an example of nationalism, and Ch'en Tu-hsiu as an example of Westernization, it must be recognized that beginning in 1915 the evolution of the two men, like that of the Chinese intellectuals as a whole, was to be extremely rapid and rather chaotic. Three factors played an important part in this acceleration of the political and cultural transformation of China: the anti-Japanese sentiments aroused by the twenty-one demands in 1915 and by Japanese policy towards China in general; the disappointment regarding the intentions of the victors of the First World War inspired by the decision of the Peace Conference to hand over to Japan the former German concessions in China rather than to return them to the Chinese; and the October Revolution in Russia.

Among the future leaders of the Chinese Communist Party, Li Ta-chao was the first to discover the Russian revolution. As early as July 1918 he compared it to the French revolution, and found it to be superior because it was inspired by humanism and internationalism, whereas the French revolution was based on patriotism and nationalism. His enthusiasm for the 'social revolution' in Russia by no means implied that he had already been

[1] Wang Fu-chih, preface to *Huang Shu*, as translated in W. Th. de Bary (ed.), *Sources of the Chinese Tradition* (New York, Columbia University Press, 1960), pp. 599–602.

converted to Marxism, still less to Leninism; on the contrary, in this same article he wrote that history was nothing but the annals of the human spirit. Nor did his preference, in this article of 1918, for the internationalist humanism of the Russian revolution imply that he was no longer concerned with the reality of the nation. On the contrary, he saw in each nation the incarnation of a particular civilization, and he emphasized that these national civilizations followed a pattern of flourishing and decline. In his opinion, the countries of Western Europe had already reached the limit of a phase of expansion. Russia, on the other hand, thanks to the fact that its civilization had been brought back to a primitive stage by the Mongol yoke, still had reserves of energy for its future development. Moreover, the people of Russia, which was a country spread across Europe and Asia, combined the religious talents of Asia and the political talents of Europe, and this gave them a unique capacity for creating a new world civilization constituting a synthesis between the East and the West. And in the new synthesis of which Russia was to be the instrument, Li Ta-chao believed that China's contribution would be considerable.[1]

In this period, while Li Ta-chao's internationalist enthusiasm was leading him so far as to take as his aim 'the destruction of the frontiers between races and states' (see Text VI 3), Ch'en Tu-hsiu underwent an evolution in the opposite direction, towards a more nationalist position. As late as October 1918, in his celebrated article on the monument to von Ketteler, the German Minister killed by the Boxers (see Text VI 4), he had expressed in vigorous terms the idea that all of China's misfortunes were the result, not of the hostile interventions of the foreigners, but of her own backwardness, and proclaimed that salvation could be found only in Western science. A year and a half later, at a time when he already regarded himself as a Marxist, he published, in the Hunanese capital of Changsha, a 'Salute to the Spirit of the Hunanese' (Text VI 5) which had as its sole theme the contribution of the 'spirit of struggle' of the Hunanese to the preservation of the Chinese nation. The list of those whom he regarded as exemplars of that spirit is an exceedingly mixed one. Alongside of Wang Fu-chih, the anti-Manchu scholar whom we have already mentioned, one encounters revolutionary heroes such as Huang Hsing, Sun Yat-sen's lieutenant in the 1911 revolution, and Ts'ai Ao, who led the combat against Yüan Shih-k'ai when the latter

[1] Li Ta-chao, 'Fa-O ko-ming chih pi-chiao-kuan', *Yen chih*, no. 3, 1918, reprinted in *Li Ta-chao Hsüan-chi*, pp. 101–4. Huang Sung-k'ang, *Li Ta-chao and the Impact of Marxism on Modern Chinese Thinking* (Paris and The Hague, Mouton, 1964), pp. 29–31, gives a translation of this text. The materials translated by Miss Huang are useful, but her analysis is merely a summary of the official view. For a discussion of this article of Li's on quite a different level, see Maurice Meisner, *Li Ta-chao and the Origins of Chinese Marxism* (Cambridge [Mass.], Harvard University Press, 1967), pp. 61–6.

attempted to make himself emperor in 1915 and 1916. Wang, Huang, and Ts'ai are all considered in China today as patriots who played a progressive role in their own time. But Ch'en Tu-hsiu does not distinguish between them and figures such as Tseng Kuo-fan and Lo Tse-nan, the artisans of the repression of the Taipings, who are denounced today in Peking as reactionaries who sold themselves to the imperialists. Obviously, if Ch'en puts all five of these men in the same category, it is because he feels that all of them contributed to the strengthening and the survival of China.

At the very period when he wrote his 'Salute to the Hunanese', Ch'en Tu-hsiu was in the process of developing an interpretation of Marxism in which classes were everything, and nations nothing.[1] Thus, like Li Ta-chao, he manifested simultaneously more or less contradictory nationalist and internationalist tendencies which coexisted in his mind without being fused together in a coherent viewpoint. In this respect, the two men were altogether typical of Chinese intellectuals at the time. It was Lenin's ideas regarding the revolution in the Eastern countries, as they had been formulated and adopted at the Second Congress of the International, which would help them to resolve these contradictions.

Despite the presence in China as early as 1920 of an emissary of the Communist International, the decisions of the Second Congress regarding collaboration with bourgeois revolutionaries appear to have had no influence whatever in China at the time. On the contrary, the First Congress of the Chinese Communist Party, in July 1921, adopted a resolution declaring that the new party should 'stand up on behalf of the proletariat, and should allow no relationship with the other parties or groups'.[2]

The psychological roots of this black-and-white vision were the same as those to which we alluded in connexion with the debate between Roy and Lenin at the Second Congress of the International, namely the impatience of Asian revolutionaries who did not want to wait indefinitely until the economic and social development of their countries sapped the foundations of bourgeois rule and made conditions ripe for the proletarian revolution. Mao Tse-tung expressed this sentiment very well when he wrote in 1920 that if one waited a century until communism came by peaceful methods, this would mean that for a whole century two thirds of humanity would be cruelly exploited by the capitalists. 'How can we bear this?' he observed.[3]

[1] On the intellectual development of Ch'en Tu-hsiu, see Benjamin Schwartz, *Chinese Communism and the Rise of Mao* (Cambridge [Mass.], Harvard University Press, 1958), pp. 8–30 passim. Meisner, op. cit., offers an excellent brief characterization of the differences between Li Ta-chao and Ch'en Tu-hsiu.

[2] *The Communist Movement in China.* An essay written in 1924 by Ch'en Kung-po. Edited, with an introduction, by C. Martin Wilbur (New York, East Asian Institute of Columbia University, 1960), p. 109.

[3] See *The Political Thought of Mao Tse-tung*, p. 40 and Text VI A 1, pp. 296–8.

Mao expressed these ideas in correspondence with his friend Ts'ai Ho-sen, then studying in France. In Europe Ts'ai absorbed a certain number of revolutionary ideas current at the time, but he interpreted them in his own way. The letter which he wrote to Ch'en Tu-hsiu in February 1921 (Text VI 6) illustrates very well the mixture of ideological radicalism and asiocentrism which characterized the thinking of many communist intellectuals in China at the time. Although he limits his analysis to two classes, the bourgeoisie and the proletariat, he concludes that precisely because of its backwardness Asia can make a sort of 'great leap forward' and forge ahead of Europe in the race towards social revolution. Furthermore, by reducing the Chinese bourgeoisie to a mere handful of people who are actually nothing but an appendix of the bourgeoisie of the capitalist countries, he succeeds in expressing, in the vocabulary of social classes, a vision essentially nationalist or regionalist of the world revolution.

It was the Congress of the Toilers of the Far East, held in Moscow in January 1922, which was to set the Chinese communists on the road to solving this contradiction between a pre-Leninist Marxist vocabulary and a content strongly marked by revolutionary nationalism.[1] At this Congress, which was attended not only by a certain number of Chinese communists but by a delegate of the Kuomintang, Zinoviev conjured his Chinese comrades not to look down on these 'publicans and sinners', the non-communist revolutionaries (see Text VI 7). The preface to the record of the Congress states that the Chinese Communist Party grasped this lesson in the course of the debates. It is true that, at their own Second Congress six months later, the Chinese communists adopted resolutions very different from those of their First Congress, showing a good understanding of Leninist tactics.[2]

In August 1922, the Comintern imposed on the Chinese Communist Party a policy without precedent in the history of the world communist movement, according to which the members of the Communist Party were to join the Kuomintang as individuals, while retaining their own organization. After discussions with Sun Yat-sen and his friends, this policy was effectively put into practice on a large scale beginning with the first Congress of the Kuomintang in January 1924.[3] We have already seen that the 'united front' with the nationalists corresponded to the line of the Comintern at the time, but this organic fusion constituted a further step in the same direction.

[1] For a detailed analysis of the proceedings of this Congress, see Whiting, op. cit., chapter V.

[2] See in particular the decision on the national united front, Ch'en Kung-po, op. cit., pp. 126–8.

[3] On this period see Conrad Brandt's study, *Stalin's Failure in China* (Cambridge [Mass.], Harvard University Press, 1959).

For Stalin, this policy of close collaboration with the Kuomintang, and of the subordination of the Chinese Communist Party's own aims to the maintenance of good relations with Sun Yat-sen (and later with his successor Chiang Kai-shek) was nothing more than a tactical manoeuvre in the framework of his foreign policy. Like Lenin, he attached no value whatever to the nation as such – unless it be to the Russian nation. But now a fundamental problem arose. The Chinese nation was not a matter of indifference even to Ch'en Tu-hsiu, still less to Li Ta-chao. By pushing the Chinese communists in this direction, Stalin thus contributed to opening a Pandora's box which his successors have still not succeeded in closing.

Already Leninist theory conferred a certain legitimacy on the exploitation of nationalist sentiments. Called as they were to apply it in the framework of the alliance with the Kuomintang, the Chinese Communists interpreted it in such a way as to give priority more and more to the national factor over the class factor. Thus Li Ta-chao, in an article of November 1922, placed heavy emphasis on the role of the oppressed peoples, side by side with the oppressed classes, in the world revolution, and drew the conclusion that the whole of the Chinese people should sympathize with the Russian revolution (see Text VI 8). For his part, Mao's friend Ts'ai Ho-sen wrote in one of the first issues of the new organ of the Chinese Communist Party, *Hsiang-tao* (*The Guide Weekly*), an article on the victory of the Kemalist revolution in Turkey dominated by two themes: the importance of the national factor in general, and the importance of China in particular. Turkey and China, wrote Ts'ai, are the two key countries in the revolution in the colonies, who show the way to all the others (see Text VI 9).

It is appropriate to recall that, as pointed out above, the line of the Comintern at this time exalted the significance of the nation not only in the dependent countries of Asia and Africa, but even in the European countries which had been the 'victims' of the Versailles treaty, and especially in Germany. The article which the weekly of the Chinese Communist Party devoted to the German problem in January 1923, during the occupation of the Ruhr, shows the curious results to which the 'Schlageter Line' could lead when it was interpreted in the Chinese context. Particularly noteworthy is the statement regarding the solidarity between the two 'oppressed peoples' of China and Germany (see Text VI 10).

Clearly the phase during which Li Ta-chao himself had spoken of the abolition of all barriers and of universal brotherhood was merely an interlude which belonged henceforth to the past. A striking proof of this was the article on the Boxers published by Ch'en Tu-hsiu in September 1924 (see Text VI 12). The man who, six years earlier, had seen in the Boxers 'detestable' people and a disgrace to China now glorified them as the vanguard of the national revolution.

But the Westernizer Ch'en Tu-hsiu, even after his conversion to Leninism, could not compete with the former conservative nationalist Li Ta-chao. On 13 May 1924, before the political club of the students at Peking University, Li made a speech on the 'racial question' which is one of the most extraordinary documents in the ideological history of the Chinese Communist Party.[1] In it, Li Ta-chao carries the priority of nation over class to such a point that he presents the class struggle on a world scale as a racial war (Text VI 11).

In May 1926, Li Ta-chao published in one of the organs of the Chinese Communist Party a complete translation of Marx's article on revolution in China and in Europe which we discussed earlier in this Introduction (Text I 2). In his accompanying commentary (Text VI 13), Li found in Marx's article further confirmation of the fact that China's role in the world revolution would be a pre-eminent one. He showed much less concern to define precisely the class character of the Chinese revolution.

In Moscow, on the other hand, the casuistry regarding the class nature of the political forces in China was just then reaching a high point, as a crisis approached both in the relations between the Chinese Communist Party and the Kuomintang, and in the struggle between Stalin and the opposition. In June 1926 Chiang Kai-shek had begun his 'Northern Expedition', with the aim of overthrowing the government of the warlords in Peking and of unifying the country. Already in March 1926 a preliminary trial of strength had taken place between Chiang and the communists. In the autumn of 1926, in the face of the mounting wave of revolutionary agitation in the countryside unleashed by the Northern Expedition, it was clear that cooperation between the Communist Party and the Kuomintang would be more and more difficult. In this context the Trotskyite opposition began to attack Stalin's China policy, claiming that it consisted in tying the hands of the communists in order to avoid offending Chiang Kai-shek. In order to defend himself, Stalin caused to be adopted at the Seventh Plenum of the Executive Committee of the International, in November and December 1926, a somewhat less negative line. In particular, it was laid down that the proletariat should assume hegemony in the revolution, and the Chinese communists were advised to encourage the struggles of the peasantry (see Text VI 14 B). But at the same time, Stalin continued to insist on the participation of the Communists in the Kuomintang, which in

[1] The text published at the time was not written down by Li himself, but is based on notes taken by one of his listeners. Nevertheless, it was included in a bibliography of his writings published in Peking in 1957, and the content may be regarded as authentic. See Meisner, op. cit., pp. 188–93, and note 36, p. 291.

fact made impossible any truly effective independent policy.[1]

It is well known that the peasant movement, which had been powerfully stimulated by the Northern Expedition, ultimately proved to be the key to the victory of the Chinese revolution. Mao Tse-tung, in his celebrated 'Report on an Investigation of the Peasant Movement in Hunan', showed himself to be mightily impressed by this 'hurricane', which he described as irresistible, and went so far as to speak of the 'leadership of the poor peasantry' over the whole revolution.[2]

This report, which was attributed to 'one of our agitators', even though Mao was already an alternate member of the Central Committee, was well received in Moscow,[3] but this did not at all imply that Stalin and his comrades had grasped the fundamental importance of the peasant revolution in China. On the contrary, the Chinese communists were ordered to employ all the influence at their command to keep the peasant movement within limits acceptable to the Kuomintang – thus depriving of any real effect the decision of December 1926 in favour of the development of the struggle in the countryside. And Stalin continued to discourse solemnly on the class character of the Kuomintang.

In May 1927, a few weeks after Chiang Kai-shek had sealed the break with the communists by a massacre of the Shanghai workers from which the labour movement was not to recover prior to 1949, Stalin explained his China policy to the students at the Sun Yat-sen University in Moscow. Not only did he still attempt to justify the 'four-class bloc' – workers, peasants, urban petty bourgeoisie and national bourgeoisie – which he had advocated since 1925 (see Text VI 14 A), but he endeavoured to demonstrate, with incomparably ponderous casuistry, that the Comintern had foreseen everything two years earlier (Text VI 14 C). He did even better. In August 1927, when the leaders of the 'Left Kuomintang' in Wuhan had followed Chiang Kai-shek in breaking with the communists, Stalin was still trying to promote collaboration with the remnants of the 'revolutionary Kuomintang', and advised the Chinese communists against any independent action under their own flag. Naturally he presented once more the history of the Chinese revolution as a ballet perfectly planned in advance by the Comintern (Text VI 14 D).

Trotsky had no difficulty in ridiculing Stalin's theories regarding the 'four-class bloc' (Text VI 15). But he himself, as we shall see in detail below, had little understanding of the specific problems

[1] On this period see Brandt, op. cit., and also Schwartz, op. cit., pp. 46–73.

[2] See *The Political Thought of Mao Tse-tung*, pp. 53–5 and 250–59.

[3] See Bukharin's speech at the Eighth Plenum of the Executive Committee of the Communist International in May 1927, in *Die Chinesische Frage auf dem 8. Plenum der Executive der Kommunistischen Internationale* (Hamburg-Berlin, 1928), pp. 12–13.

of the Chinese revolution, and in particular of the importance of the national factor. Moreover, it is worth pointing out that as late as the Eighth Plenum of the Executive Committee of the International, in May 1927 – i.e., after the break with Chiang Kai-shek – Trotsky protested against the charge that he was advocating the withdrawal of the communists from the 'Left Kuomintang' in Wuhan. All he was asking, he said, was that certain conditions should be attached to further participation in the Kuomintang.[1]

In reality, Trotsky was no more capable than Stalin of leading the Chinese communists to victory. Stalin sacrificed the Chinese revolution to the security of Russia's frontiers. Trotsky would have brought about an equally great disaster by attributing to the Chinese proletariat a force which it did not possess and by imagining that the great coastal cities could play a role which they were incapable of filling in an economically and politically divided China. The true solution was to be found by certain of the Chinese communists who were the most profoundly rooted in the life of their own country. Forty years later, even as they defended Stalin against Khrushchev's attacks, they recalled that they had led the Chinese revolution to victory despite the 'errors' of the Soviet leader.[2]

The International and the Problems of the Revolution in the East from 1928 to 1934

The Sixth Comintern Congress, which met in 1928, had the difficult task of drawing the appropriate conclusions from the Chinese catastrophe, and also – even if this was of secondary importance compared to the Chinese problem – of taking account of a decline in the revolutionary prospects throughout the Islamic East (especially in Syria and in North Africa). The policy of collaboration with bourgeois nationalist movements advocated by the Comintern was subjected to extremely violent criticism by Trotsky (see Text VII 2),[3] whose voice was not heard at the Congress. Naturally his position was totally rejected.

As at the previous Congress, the representatives of the colonial and dependent countries came to the Sixth Congress to reproach the Comintern with its attitude towards these regions. They detected in the very terms of the programme europocentric tendencies and a perpetual incomprehension of the real situation in the non-European countries. Many of them found that the tactics now proposed were no more correct than those which had led to defeat in China. It is, however, characteristic of the Sixth Congress that there was no real controversy between the spokesmen for the

[1] ibid., p. 42.

[2] 'On the Question of Stalin', *Hung-ch'i*, no. 18, 1963, p. 5.

[3] See also his criticism of Stalin and Bukharin in *La révolution permanente* (Paris, Rieder, 1930).

position of the leadership of the Comintern and the representatives of Asia as there had been at the earlier Congresses. It is true that the Indian delegate continued the debate opened by Roy at the Fourth Congress regarding the changed nature of colonial policy during the period of its decline (i.e., the encouragement of industrialization in the colonies), but this position was entirely eliminated from the theses adopted by the Congress, and was not even seriously discussed as it had been at the previous Congresses.

In his report regarding the activity of the Comintern, Bukharin was principally concerned to find arguments for denying the responsibility of the International in China, and for putting all the blame on the leaders of the Chinese Communist Party. The latter were accused of having first gone too far in the direction of an alliance with the bourgeoisie (over-estimating the force of the latter), and then having underestimated the force of the bourgeoisie and indulged in revolutionary adventurism pure and simple. This failure, said Bukharin, implied for China a period not of real retreat, but merely of organization and work among the masses in order to prepare the ensuing phase. For the Chinese revolution, far from having been liquidated, as Trotsky claimed, would soon move into a new upsurge.

Despite this highly optimistic view of the defeat in China, Bukharin carefully abstained from presenting the case of China as a universally valid example, and insisted on the necessity of studying each concrete problem. The programme and the theses adopted by the Sixth Congress contained a certain number of new definitions, pertaining both to the international communist movement and to the revolutionary tactics in the colonial and dependent countries.

The first innovation, pertaining to the Comintern as a whole, was to be found in the special place assigned to the U.S.S.R. Henceforth, the Soviet Union was regarded as the first and most important element, coming even ahead of the revolutionary proletariat, in an alliance which would allow the colonial and dependent countries to avoid the capitalist phase. Here the Russian domination of the world communist movement, which had begun to emerge at the Fifth Congress, became even more evident. The very formula employed in the theses, 'the alliance with the U.S.S.R. and with the revolutionary proletariat of the imperialist countries', already suggests the idea of 'socialism in one country'.

A related idea, particularly interesting in the light of recent developments, was the description of the colonies as the 'world's countryside', in contrast to the industrial countries which constitute the 'cities of the world'. This metaphor was applied not merely (as in recent Chinese imagery) to the conquest of power, but to the continuing economic and social transformation which would take place after the victory of the world revolution. In the view of the Comintern, it was indispensable that the 'international proletariat' establish its hegemony over the 'popular masses' of the non-European countries throughout this whole process (Text VII I B).

Several representatives of Asia and Africa, including not only the Indian Tagore but the spokesman of the white South African workers, Bunting, took exception to the slight implied in this language. (See their speeches in Text VII I A.) But, believing implicitly as they did in the logic of Marxism, according to which (as Lenin put it in the passage quoted by Trotsky at the end of Text VII 2) 'the city inevitably leads the village, the village inevitably follows the city', their only argument could be that the colonial countries were not (or need not necessarily remain) simply a vast rural area looking towards the world's industrial heartland for leadership. It was left to Mao Tse-tung to make a virtue out of necessity, and to proclaim that Asia, Africa and Latin America stood in the forefront of the world revolution precisely because they *were* the world's countryside.

As for the revolutionary tactics to be adopted in Asia, the theses of the Sixth Congress were based on the idea that capitalism had reached a new phase, a phase in which it adopted a particularly uncompromising and hostile attitude towards the Soviet state. This being the case, the greatest vigilance was indispensable, and the communists could not allow themselves to make any concessions to elements which were only too ready to come to terms with capitalism. The tactics of alliance with the national bourgeoisie were henceforth rejected, and the Sixth Congress went very far in this direction, for not only did it rule out collaboration with the reformist national bourgeoisie, but it showed itself to be extremely suspicious even towards the petty bourgeoisie, which was regarded as being also for the most part inclined to abandon the revolutionary struggle when its democratic aspirations had been satisfied. If temporary alliances could be concluded in certain cases, provided the communists retained the hegemony, they were to be of limited duration and subject to many conditions. The tasks assigned to the communists were difficult ones. They were to build communist parties, infiltrate the trade unions, organize the peasantry (the tactics of worker and peasant parties were rejected), and prepare the way for the Soviet power, if necessary by armed uprisings. The communist parties in the West were to support the efforts to build a revolutionary movement in the colonies. The essential thing during this period was seen as the establishment of 'the unity of the industrial proletariat with the toiling masses in the colonies'. The duty of communist parties throughout the world to apply these tactics was imperative. The struggle of 'class against class' was to be carried out everywhere.

We have already mentioned Trotsky's criticism of the tactics adopted by the Sixth Congress, in which he saw a door far too freely opened to collaboration with the bourgeoisie, despite all the precautions taken in the formulation of the theses (Text VII 2). But in reality, when one looks at this period in an historical perspective, one is struck rather by the resemblance between Trotsky's position and that of the Comintern, as it was reaffirmed almost without change from 1928 to 1934. The extracts from the decisions and directives of the Comintern regarding the Chinese revolution which appear in this volume (Text VII 3) show a tendency almost as marked as that of Trotsky to the doctrinaire application of concepts and slogans shaped by European conditions and a European mentality to a very different reality. All the established stereotypes are to be found there: priority of the cities over the countryside, insistence on the hegemony of the 'workers' over the peasants, belief in a mass uprising modelled on the Russian revolution. But in reality, these were only vain words, for the man who ultimately was to gather into his hands real control over the policies of the Chinese Communist Party – even though he did not assume the leadership of the party until 1935, during the Long March – was resolved to go about things in quite a different way.[1]

The Problems of the Revolution in Non-European Countries at the Time of the Popular Front and the Second World War

The tactics of 'class against class' laid down by the Sixth Congress in 1928 represented an *a posteriori* attempt to repair the errors previously committed in China. This new line, which came too late to save the situation at the time, did not have happier consequences for the future. By promoting sharp conflict between the workers and the capitalists, and above all between communists and social democrats, it prevented effective union to block the triumph of National Socialism. When the Seventh Congress finally met in 1935, Hitler was already solidly installed in power, and it was very late indeed to discover that the tactics of 'class against class' were a hindrance to the organization of a united front of the democratic countries against Nazi Germany. Nevertheless, as in 1928 the Comintern undertook to draw the appropriate lessons from events, and decided that the decisive problem at the moment was the defence of democratic freedoms against the authoritarian régimes. The struggle of 'class against class' was replaced by the struggle of 'nation against nation', in which the democratic nations were expected to unite in a common front. These tactics were extended, as usual, to the colonial countries, where they implied the abandonment of such aims as might

[1] On the genesis of this strategy, see S. Schram, *Mao Tse-tung* (Penguin Books, 1966, chapters 6 and 7), and also the introduction to Mao Tse-tung, *Basic Tactics* (London, Pall Mall, 1967).

weaken the people's democratic front. On the one hand, the anti-imperialist national struggle had to be sacrificed for the moment, in order to avoid destroying unity on an international level. On the other hand, social revolution could not be pushed within each country, in order to avoid destroying national unity. Every possible alliance was sought if it could somehow contribute to weakening Fascism.

Among the events of this period, the colonial policy of the French Communist Party, especially in Algeria, is particularly interesting, for it faithfully reflects the line laid down by the Comintern. Following the attacks directed against it at the Fourth and Fifth Congresses, the French Communist Party, which had known its day of glory at the time of the war against Abd el Krim, began towards 1930 (date of the Seventh Congress of the French Communist Party) to concern itself, at least intellectually, with the colonial problem.

As soon as the decision was taken to create an anti-fascist front, the French Communist Party adopted a position on colonial problems entirely in conformity with the decisions of the Comintern. In October 1935, Maurice Thorez proclaimed his attachment to the 'defence of the Algerian people',[1] but this defence consisted in establishing the highest possible degree of unity with the bourgeois national-reformists of Algeria. (Among these was Ferhat Abbas, who had been considered a 'counter-revolutionary' during the period of the 'class against class' struggle.) These partisans of assimilation[2] or integration, favourable to the Blum-Violette plan for the reform of the statute of the Muslims of Algeria,[3] were opposed on grounds of national interest by proletarian elements grouped together in the organization called 'l'Etoile nord-africaine'. Although it had fought side by side with the communists and supported the Popular Front, the French Communist Party, when confronted with a choice, preferred Ferhat Abbas. On 26 January 1937, 'l'Etoile nord-africaine' was dissolved by a decree of the Blum government. Two weeks later, the French Communist Party expressed itself on this issue,[4] declaring that although such a measure was 'regrettable', the attitude of 'certain leaders' of the 'Etoile nord-africaine' towards the Popular

[1] M. Thorez, *Oeuvres*, book II, vol. 9, p. 46.

[2] For Ferhat Abbas's statement denying the existence of an Algerian nation, see C. A. Julien, *L'Afrique du Nord en Marche* (Paris, Julliard, 1952), p. 110.

[3] The attitude of the French Communist Party towards the Blum-Violette plan was ambiguous and varied according to the tactical aims of the moment. In 1934, this plan was denounced as an 'attempt at corruption aimed at dividing the *indigènes*' (*L'Humanité*, 7 February 1934). On the other hand, in 1937 the organ of the Algerian Communist Party, *La Lutte Sociale* (30 January 1937) defended the project.

[4] *L'Humanité*, 12 February 1937.

Front, the government, and the Communist Party was suspect.[1]

Later, Maurice Thorez wrote:

> If the decisive issue at the moment is the struggle against fascism, the interest of the colonial peoples lies in their union with the people of France, and not in an attitude which could facilitate the enterprises of fascism and put, for example, Algeria, Tunisia and Morocco under the yoke of Mussolini and Hitler.

The definition of the Algerian 'nation in the process of formation' given by Maurice Thorez at this time is also worthy of mention. On the one hand, this definition implies that the Algerian nation in question is very far from being in a position to aspire to independence. On the other hand, in view of the very small place Thorez attributes to the Arabs, his definition implies union with France rather than independence (see Text VIII 2).

Another important and well-known case is that of India during the Second World War, when the Communist Party was obliged to support the British war effort at a time when the leaders of the Congress were all in prison for demanding independence. The result was to alienate the communists from the Indian masses to a degree that required years to overcome.

It is perfectly clear, when one considers the events of this period, that the process begun at the Fifth Congress, and which tended to confound the cause of the world revolution and that of the U.S.S.R. and to subordinate in certain circumstances the interests of the world revolution to the interests of Soviet foreign policy, continued to develop at an increasing rate. There was, however, one exception, of no small magnitude: China.

To be sure, at the time of the Popular Front, Mao Tse-tung followed the example of the Comintern in elaborating theories which attributed a large place to the bourgeoisie and its political representative, the Kuomintang, in the struggle against Japanese fascism. The united front which he advocated even included the 'patriotic gentry'. But these theoretical developments were the natural outgrowth of a tendency already visible in China prior to the Comintern's about-face at its Seventh Congress, and Mao Tse-tung's position did not follow the fluctuations of Soviet foreign policy so mechanically as that of most other communist parties. Thus, in January 1940, at the high-point of the Germano-Soviet understanding which had led to a new sectarian phase in the tactics of the Comintern in Europe and elsewhere, Mao virtually promised that the national bourgeoisie would enjoy hegemony over the revolution for an indefinite time in the future if it showed itself capable of assuming this role (see Text VIII 3). To be sure, he was probably not very sincere in making this offer, which he

[1] On 26 April 1938 *Moskovskaya Gazeta* raised the question of collusion between the 'Etoile nord-africaine' and fascist Italy.

has eliminated from the current edition of his *Selected Works*, and in other texts written almost at the same time he clearly stated that leadership would belong to the Communist Party.[1] He also followed the Soviet line in denouncing the dangers inherent in the acceptance of American aid. Nevertheless, he knew where the real danger to China lay. Thus, in the original version of 'On New Democracy', he proposed an alliance not simply with the 'national bourgeoisie', but with the big bourgeoisie in general, provided only that the members of this class were prepared to struggle against Japan.

Commenting in 1943 on the dissolution of the Comintern, Mao declared:

Since the Seventh World Congress of the Communist International in 1935, the Communist International has not intervened in the internal affairs of the Chinese Communist Party. And yet, the Chinese Communist Party has done its work very well, throughout the whole Anti-Japanese War of National Liberation.[2]

[1] See S. Schram, *Mao Tse-tung* (Penguin Books, 1966), p. 215.
[2] Schram, *The Political Thought of Mao Tse-tung*, p. 423.

3. TOWARDS ASIOCENTRIC COMMUNISM

From the Seventh Congress of the Chinese Communist Party in 1945 to the Death of Stalin

Throughout this volume, we have had occasion to show how the Soviet leaders have subordinated the interests of the revolution, both in Asia and in Europe, to their foreign policy objectives. But if this has been the case since the time of Lenin himself, the relative weight given to revolutionary aims as compared to diplomatic aims has varied from one period to another. The years immediately following the Second World War were characterized by an almost total priority to foreign policy, which resulted in altogether surprising deformations of the Leninist theory of revolution in the underdeveloped countries.

This priority to foreign-policy objectives did not, of course, rule out vigorous efforts to extend Soviet influence. On the contrary, artificial 'revolutions' supported by the Red Army led, during the first post-war years, to the establishment of direct Soviet control over the whole of Eastern Europe. But the colonies and protectorates of Asia and Africa were quite another matter. On the one hand, they were beyond the scope of direct military intervention by the Soviet Union. Even more important, perhaps, was the fact that Stalin, who had already burned his fingers once in China in 1927, was not particularly desirous of fostering revolutionary movements in these countries, whose inhabitants appeared to him strange and unpredictable. Apart from this, he was primarily concerned with U.S.–Soviet relations, and judged all other factors in terms of their repercussions on this central problem. Thus the French Communist Party, which had been obliged to adopt a moderate line on colonial problems during the years 1945–7, when it participated in the government, in order not to shock its Socialist and Catholic allies and alienate its own supporters (see Text IX 3), continued to oppose Algerian independence after 1947 on the grounds that the departure of the French would only open the door to American influence.[1]

In Asia, the policy advocated by Moscow beginning in 1947 was a policy of armed uprising by the workers and peasants, directed not only against the colonial powers but also against the local bourgeoisie. Such a line, by which the communist parties

[1] L. Feix, 'Quelques vues sur le problème algérien', *Cahiers du Communisme*, September 1947, pp. 851–71.

and the numerically small groups under their influence cut themselves off from the struggles of the Asian peoples for their independence, could only lead to failure. It thus had the great advantage for Stalin of allowing him to be revolutionary and intransigent in words, without running any great risks of fostering a situation in Asia that might disturb his own tranquillity.

As it happened, however, a revolution was even then in course in the most populous nation of Asia which Stalin would not succeed in halting by his counsels of prudence, a revolution which would ultimately transform the world communist movement beyond all recognition. Henceforth there would exist within the communist bloc people belonging to a cultural universe completely different from that of Europe. Not only were these people different, but they were conscious of the differences, and proud of them. They regarded the adaptation of Marxism to the peculiar conditions prevailing in China (which they also referred to as the 'Sinification' or the 'nationalization' of Marxism) as one of the greatest theoretical exploits in the history of the world. Moreover, they proclaimed that Mao Tse-tung's thought, which was the highest example of 'Sinified Marxism', was particularly well adapted to the needs of all the peoples of the East (see Liu Shao-ch'i's speech at the Seventh Congress of the Chinese Communist Party in 1945, Text IX 1).

In this perspective, the leaders of the Chinese Communist Party would henceforth propagate conceptions different from those of Moscow as regarded the tactics of revolutionary struggle in colonial and dependent countries. This behaviour raises two questions: What was the true scope of the divergences between the Chinese and Soviet positions? And to what extent were the Chinese bent on proclaiming their originality?

It is relatively easy to answer the second question. The celebrated passage from Liu Shao-ch'i's speech at a meeting of the World Federation of Trade Unions held in Peking in November 1949, shortly after the establishment of the Chinese People's Republic (see Text IX 6), is only the best known of a mass of similar texts, emphasizing heavily that it is China's vocation to serve as a model for all the countries of Asia.[1]

The first major study of the Sino-Soviet conflict states that, beginning in 1951, the Chinese largely refrained from voicing these pretensions in order to avoid irritating Stalin.[2] It is true that in revising his earlier writings for inclusion in the current canon of his *Selected Works*, which began to appear in Chinese in 1951, Mao Tse-tung considerably attenuated the claims which he

[1] See also Schram, *The Political Thought of Mao Tse-tung*, p. 111.

[2] Donald M. Zagoria, *The Sino-Soviet Conflict, 1956–1961* (Princeton, Princeton University Press, 1962), p. 15.

had put forward regarding the specificity of Chinese experience.[1] But Text IX 8, which is extracted from a pamphlet reprinted in a revised edition in January 1952, shows that at that date the Chinese pretensions had not been abandoned, even if they were expressed less frequently and blatantly.

This text also illustrates another aspect of the problem, namely that one must consider not only explicit affirmations of originality, but also the weight attributed to the Chinese example as compared to Soviet experience and Soviet teachings. A comparison of Texts IX 5 and IX 8 brings this point home very clearly. The first of these, which emanates from an authoritative Soviet academic spokesman, emphasizes above all what the Chinese communists have learned from the Soviet Union, and in particular from Stalin. The author claims that Stalin, who, as we have seen, could not make head or tail of the Chinese revolution, 'predicted its future course with genius'. This Soviet analysis gives the impression that Stalin took the Chinese communists by the hand and showed them the way to victory. To be sure, the author also hails the 'immense influence' of the Chinese revolution throughout South-east Asia – but this theme is altogether secondary in comparison to that of the decisive importance of Soviet support. The Chinese pamphlet, on the other hand, devotes only a single paragraph (translated *in extenso* in our extract) to the Soviet contribution to the liberation of the peoples of the East. In contrast, it is stated that Mao Tse-tung's synthesis of Marxism-Leninism with the practice of the Chinese revolution 'has been uniformly accepted by all the peoples of the East'. But the author goes even further. By identifying Mao's 'New Democracy' with the 'People's Democracy' then being supported by the Soviets in Eastern Europe, and by adding that Mao was the first to advocate such New Democracy, he virtually affirms that all the theoretical innovations introduced in the world communist movement after the Second World War were in fact borrowed from Mao Tse-tung. Finally, he declares that the victory of the Chinese revolution is exercising a 'decisive' influence on the national liberation struggles in all the countries of the East.

There is thus not the slightest doubt that the Chinese did in fact proclaim the originality of their 'way'. But what was the real scope of this claim? It has been suggested that Liu Shao-ch'i, when he declared in November 1949 that the Chinese way should be followed by the peoples of many colonial countries, was in fact acting in agreement with Moscow, which had accepted a variant of the Chinese tactical line.[2] Even at the time, certain facts appeared to

[1] See the variants in *The Political Thought of Mao Tse-tung, passim.*

[2] John Kautsky, *Moscow and the Communist Party of India, A Study in the Postwar Evolution of International Communist Strategy* (London, Chapman and Hall, 1956), p. 96.

contradict this interpretation. For example, the Chinese pamphlet already mentioned (Text IX 8) cites declarations by Asian communists manifesting their determination to follow the Chinese example which were not included in summaries of the discussions at the November 1949 meeting published in organs of the World Federation of Trade Unions.

One could thus suppose that these confirmations of Chinese influence were less acceptable to Moscow than to Peking. Viewing the problem in the perspective of subsequent developments, it seems even more obvious today that the Soviet leaders were never inclined to hand over to the Chinese of their own free will the responsibility for guiding the revolution in Asia, and never accepted with pleasure Peking's pretension of having found an original way for the revolution in non-European countries.

There remains the problem of how the tactics advocated by the Chinese in fact differed from those propagated by Moscow. In 1948, before Mao Tse-tung and his comrades took power, two very clear differences could be observed between the Chinese and Soviet lines. The first pertained to the attitude which should be adopted towards the bourgeoisie. As we have already emphasized, the Soviets were at that time in the midst of the Zhdanovist sectarian period, and supported a classic 'left' strategy based exclusively on the workers, the peasants, and part of the petty bourgeoisie. Mao Tse-tung, on the other hand, continued to follow the basic line laid down by 'On New Democracy' in 1940, and still sought the cooperation of the 'national bourgeoisie'. In July 1949, in his article 'On People's Democratic Dictatorship', he carried the argument even further by including the national bourgeoisie not only among the 'people', but among the 'dictators'.[1] To be sure, he declared at the same time that only the proletariat – that is to say, the Communist Party – could lead the revolution. The bourgeois could thus be only second-class dictators. Mao's position nevertheless appeared as 'rightist' in the eyes of the Soviets.

The other point of divergence concerned the use of violence. Mao Tse-tung was in the process of achieving power thanks to a quarter of a century of virtually uninterrupted fighting. He was thus inevitably led to attribute to guerrilla warfare a central role in his conception of the revolution in Asia. The Soviets, on the other hand, although they authorized a certain number of armed uprisings in 1948 – in particular in Burma, Malaysia and Indonesia – soon came to realize that these tactics, which aroused world-wide hostility among the bourgeoisie which was the victim of these enterprises, did not fit in with the main goal of their global strategy, the struggle against the United States.[2]

[1] See, on this theme, *The Political Thought of Mao Tse-tung*, pp. 76–8.

[2] See Kautsky, op. cit., pp. 33–4, 86–7.

According to John Kautsky, the result of the confrontation between the Soviet and Chinese viewpoints was the elaboration of a compromise, which he calls the 'neo-Maoist' strategy, in which the Soviets abandoned their unconditional hostility towards the bourgeoisie of the non-European countries, while the Chinese recognized that war was not an indispensable element of their 'way'.[1] There is unquestionably some truth in this interpretation, but it is not the whole truth. The texts translated in this volume (see Texts IX 2, IX 4, IX 5, IX 6, IX 7, and IX 8) show on the one hand that the Soviets moved only very slowly towards a less hostile attitude towards the bourgeoisie. (This is illustrated in particular by Text IX 4, of September 1949, which denounces the collusion of the Eastern bourgeoisies with imperialism.) Even with reference to China, at a time when Mao had already admitted the national bourgeoisie among the 'dictators' (provided, of course, that it accepted the hegemony of the Communist Party), the ideologists in Moscow declared that this same national bourgeoisie was incapable of playing the role of a basic participant in the national liberation movement (Text IX 5). These positions are in sharp contrast with the positive attitudes towards the national bourgeoisie which are expressed in all the Chinese texts of Section IX.

As for the role of violence, it is even clearer that the Soviet and Chinese positions were not identical. In his speech of November 1949, Liu Shao-ch'i made of armed struggle an indispensable element of the national liberation struggles of the peoples of Asia. It was impossible, he said, to seek an easier way (Text IX 6). And the 1952 pamphlet (Text IX 8) emphasizes heavily the role of armed struggle, going out of its way to discover, in India and elsewhere, strict parallels with the revolutionary peasant war waged in China. 'The principal form of revolutionary struggle of the peoples of the East,' it is stated in this pamphlet, 'is armed struggle.' In contrast, the Soviet spokesman Zhukov stated in 1951 that among the characteristics of the Chinese revolution, it was precisely the role of the revolutionary army which was unlikely to recur in other countries (Text IX 7).

From Stalin's Death to the Great Leap Forward

We have seen that, even at the time of the establishment of the Chinese People's Republic, there were divergences between the positions of Moscow and Peking both on the tactical level (role of the national bourgeoisie, importance of armed struggle) and on the cultural level (originality and value of Mao Tse-tung's 'Sinified Marxism'). The period which opened with Stalin's death (although some of the new tendencies which characterized it were

[1] ibid., chapter IV.

already visible in his lifetime) was to see the whole problem of relations between the two great communist powers posed in completely different terms. The development of China on the one hand, and the Soviet Union on the other, would bring them first closer together, and then further and further apart. But although there was growing tension between the two countries as early as 1956, until 1959 or 1960 the effects of this conflict on the policies of Moscow and Peking appear to have been very limited as compared to the inherent logic of the development of each country.

On the Soviet side, the years from 1953 to 1956 were marked by the efforts of Stalin's successors to find new methods of leadership, more flexible and better adapted to complex and changing realities. This was true not only of internal affairs, but also of the methods employed in dealing with other members of the communist bloc. China in particular was treated with infinitely more consideration than in the past. In China, once the régime had been established and the after effects of the Korean war had been overcome, the first systematic attempt at economic development began with the five-year plan of 1953–7, closely modelled on the Soviet example. In this context, it is not surprising that the viewpoints of the two countries on a number of important problems should have moved closer together.

Among these was the problem of relations with the national bourgeoisie in the Asian and African countries, and of the attitude that should be adopted towards newly-independent countries under bourgeois leadership. In April 1954, Chou En-lai signed a treaty of friendship with Nehru (whom Mao Tse-tung had denounced in 1949 as a collaborator of imperialism)[1] containing the famous 'five principles of peaceful coexistence'. At the end of 1954 the Soviets also put forward a more positive opinion regarding the role of the neutralist countries, such as India, in world politics, thus abandoning their Zhdanovist dualism.[2]

Such an evolution appeared very natural in the case of China, which was an Asian power desirous of increasing her diplomatic influence in Asia. This tendency found its culmination in Chou En-lai's role at the Bandung Conference. The reasons for the change of the Soviet attitude are more complex, and require some discussion. Even before Stalin's death there had been signs of a re-examination of the established doctrine regarding the national and colonial question. It was becoming clear that the circumstances required a radical revision of the theoretical foundations of the foreign policy of the Soviet Union and of the socialist camp. In Asia and the Middle East national governments had come to power. The zeal with which they repressed the communist parties

[1] See *The Political Thought of Mao Tse-tung*, Text VIII F.

[2] See the article of A. Leontiev in *Kommunist*, no. 13, 1954, pp. 43–58.

and other left-wing groups was greatly increased by the fact that these groups, faithfully applying Zhdanov's views to the effect that *real* independence was impossible under bourgeois leadership, opposed the new leaders and denied that they constituted genuinely independent governments. The universal hostility of the socialist camp towards such governments drove them, quite regardless of their own wishes, towards the capitalist camp, thus reinforcing the latter. Nearly everywhere in the non-European countries communism remained isolated, without influence on the masses, commonly regarded as a foreign ideology.

A new policy was thus indispensable. It was also possible. Immediately after the Second World War the Soviet government had found itself confronted, in the peripheral republics, with sentiments of national frustration – which had been encouraged and developed by the appeal to the national pride of the peoples of the Soviet Union launched by Stalin in 1941 in order to foster resistance against the German invader. The national aspirations of the non-Russian peoples of the Soviet Union, which had never been totally dormant since the revolution, had been one of the great problems facing the U.S.S.R. between 1946 and 1952. In these circumstances, it was difficult indeed to pursue a policy based on the encouragement of national movements in the Islamic countries of Asia and the Middle East without aggravating the demands of the minority peoples of the Soviet Union, who were in large part Muslims keenly aware of developments in the neighbouring countries. At the time of Stalin's death the material progress in these peripheral areas of the Soviet Union populated by Muslims had lessened the tension to such a point that an appeasement could be sought.

At the Twentieth Congress Khrushchev defined (Text X 1) the principal characteristics of the new situation, and drew the consequences for international relations. In the light of his report, of Kuusinen's remarks on India (Text X 1), and of the theoretical articles which spelled out various aspects of the Soviet position (Texts X 2 and X 3), one can see how profound is the rupture with the doctrine of the post-war years, and on certain fundamental points, even with Lenin's ideas. The starting-point for the revisions of the Twentieth Congress was a new evaluation of the global balance of power. Continuing in the path marked out by Stalin in his last work, *Economic Problems of Socialism*, his successors declared that the world situation was characterized by the constant development and irreversible progress of the socialist camp, and also by the no less irreversible decomposition and constant weakening of imperialism. Enfeebled, driven into a defensive position, the imperialist camp could no longer constitute a menace for the countries which had thrown off its domination, who found a safeguard in the very existence of a mighty socialist camp.

According to these Soviet theories, another factor characterized the new era which was beginning at the time of the Twentieth Congress: the creation of an intermediate zone between the two hostile blocs. The role of this 'zone of peace' had already been widely publicized by the voyage of Khrushchev and Bulganin in Asia in 1955, and by the Bandung Conference. It opened a new possibility for the young national states of the East, who could henceforth choose a third path, neutral and independent between the two political poles of the world.

These changes in the world situation led the Soviets to a re-evaluation of the notion of independence. The concept of total independence, both political and economic, was replaced by a more limited concept, that of *formal* or *juridical* independence, which was henceforth considered as the indispensable precondition for liberation from foreign capital. To be sure, the countries which had conquered their sovereignty were still obliged to struggle in order to free themselves from all dependence on foreign capital, first of all by nationalizing foreign corporations. But even in the case of countries which did not proceed in this way (for example, Saudi Arabia) the new doctrine held that they were truly independent, for henceforth they were in a position to prepare the way for economic development which would lead to their enfranchisement. As regards internal economic policies, the Twentieth Congress also made an important concession to governments dominated by the national bourgeoisie in not requiring them to adopt a socialist orientation, but merely recommending that they develop a state capitalist sector in the framework of a rigorous plan. 'There is reason to believe that state capitalism plays a progressive role in the East,'[1] write the authors of one authoritative work. They make a sharp distinction between state capitalism in the East, which 'owes its existence to an anti-imperialist movement and is objectively directed against the expansion of the monopolies in the East', and Western state capitalism, which is *monopolistic*, and hence fundamentally reactionary, because it implies the domination of the monopolies over the state machinery.

In the perspective of this book, the most important doctrinal revision at the Twentieth Congress pertains to the national bourgeoisie. Ever since the Second Comintern Congress it had been an article of faith that, at the stage of the struggle against imperialism, in countries where the proletariat was weak and the peasantry dispersed and ill-organized, an alliance with the bourgeoisie, or even bourgeois leadership of the national movement, could be regarded as objectively progressive. But in Lenin's view, as in that of his successors, this alliance could only be provisional and conditional. Only the Muslim communists of the former Russian empire

[1] *Fundamentals of Marxism-Leninism* (Moscow, Foreign Languages Publishing House, 1961), pp. 511–12.

had proposed that this alliance should be regarded as *durable*, in view of the specificity of colonial problems, and they had been condemned by the Comintern. The theses of the Twentieth Congress bore a distinct resemblance to these theses of the Muslim communists. They postulated that the contradictions between the national bourgeoisie of the newly independent countries and imperialism were infinitely more profound than the contradictions between the national bourgeoisie and the proletariat within a given country. From this the conclusion was drawn that during an unlimited period the national bourgeoisie could transcend its class nature. Henceforth, the collaboration with the national bourgeoisie and the support given to governments led by it were to be *lasting* and *sincere*; lasting, because this collaboration was to continue throughout the whole period during which imperialism still exists, and sincere, to the extent that the problems are envisaged primarily in terms of national interest. The 'National Front' as defined at the Twentieth Congress thus implies that priority should be accorded to the national revolution, the social revolution being postponed until such a time as the common enemy, Western capitalism, has been definitively vanquished. At this point, the bourgeoisie will *perhaps* be frightened when confronted by a proletariat resolved to defend its own interests against those of its allies. But even this eventuality was envisaged only very vaguely at the time of the Twentieth Congress, and the emphasis was definitely on the solidarity created by the struggle against imperialism.

The Chinese did not put forward, at the time of the Twentieth Congress, theoretical formulations as precise as this attributing to the national bourgeoisie political hegemony in the newly independent countries. Nevertheless, on his return from a voyage in Asia and in Europe, in March 1957, Chou En-lai recognized that many Asian and African countries had taken the path to independence and economic development under the leadership of the 'nationalists', and not under that of the communists (see Text X 5). Although he did not pronounce the word 'bourgeois', it is clear that there is here something analogous to the formulations of the Twentieth Congress. But it is characteristic that the class nature of these 'nationalist' movements was not clearly spelled out. For to recognize explicitly the hegemony of the bourgeoisie would have been to cast doubt on the doctrinal authority of Mao Tse-tung, who had written categorically in 1949: 'In the epoch of imperialism, no other class anywhere [with the exception of the proletariat] can lead a genuine revolution to victory.'[1]

To be sure, China, like Russia, is a great power whose leaders are inclined to take into account their diplomatic interests as well as

[1] *The Political Thought of Mao Tse-tung*, p. 235.

their ideological convictions. Mao and his colleagues are therefore quite prepared, in certain cases, to maintain friendly relations with states that are in no wise under the leadership of the proletariat, as the examples of Burma (until 1967), Cambodia, Afghanistan and Pakistan suffice to demonstrate. At the same time, it is only fair to recognize that such compromises with non-proletarian régimes need not be simply a matter of *Realpolitik*, but may also reflect the contradictions between internal and external criteria of what constitutes a revolutionary force.

As regards internal policy, Mao's dictum of 1949 flatly lays down that only a government under the leadership of the proletariat can be genuinely revolutionary. But in Mao's eyes any government that opposes imperialism is objectively playing a revolutionary role on the world scene. Thus, it was recognized in 1959 by the leading Chinese journal of international affairs that not only states dominated by the national bourgeoisie, but even those ruled by monarchies or aristocracies (but not, of course, by the *comprador* bourgeoisie) frequently struggle against imperialism and adopt a foreign policy of peace and independence.[1]

Although the Chinese did not, even at the time of the Twentieth Congress of the C.P.S.U., openly recognize that the national bourgeoisie could also preside over progressive developments *within* the non-European countries, there were occasional hints of a slightly more flexible interpretation. For example, an article on Latin America succeeded in combining realism with political orthodoxy by declaring that the working class 'is in the process of becoming or will shortly become the leading class', and further qualifying this by the statement that the national bourgeoisie plays an 'important role' in the national independence movement and 'has already seized the hegemony in certain important countries'.[2] Obviously, if one takes a long historical view of these developments, the affirmation that the proletariat will 'shortly' assume the leadership of the revolution is compatible with a great deal of tactical flexibility in dealing with the bourgeoisie.

Ultimately more significant than these statements on the tactics to be followed in other Asian and African countries were the changes which took place at this time in the spirit and methods of the Chinese revolution itself. Hitherto, Mao Tse-tung and his comrades had been 'building socialism' by methods basically similar to those of the Soviet Union, with their emphasis on the decisive importance of technical and material factors. Now suddenly Mao Tse-tung put forward the thesis that in China, collectivization must precede mechanization, and pushed ahead with the formation

[1] Ho Fang, 'Yu-kuan tang-ch'ien min-tsu tu-li yün-tung ti chi-ko wen-t'i', *Kuo-chi wen-t'i yen-chiu*, no. 3, 1959, pp. 10–19.

[2] ibid., no. 1, 1959, pp. 10–18.

of cooperatives at a rate in excess of that acceptable to a majority of the Chinese Communist Party.

We cannot consider here in detail the application of these policies.[1] But their general implications are extremely clear. Henceforth, the original Marxist postulate that the technical knowledge and organizing capacity of the workers were indispensable to the success of any genuinely socialist revolution, and the corollary that the 'cities' must lead the 'countryside', were more and more openly discarded not only in fact but in theory. In January 1956 Mao Tse-tung presented to the public his draft twelve-year programme for the development of Chinese agriculture. The very fact of laying down plans in this sector for so long a period, when planning for the economy as a whole, including industry, was still on a five-year basis, indicates a striking shift in priorities from the emphasis on heavy industry which characterized the first five-year plan. Mao's explanations were even more revealing. Thus he declared that 'a spurt must *also* be made in other kinds of work besides agriculture' in order to keep up with the high tide of socialist revolution in the countryside. And the programme itself, although it paid lip service to the principle of working-class leadership, in fact put the cities and the countryside on a basis of strict equality (Text X 4).

In September 1956, at a time when the revolutionary fervour and spirit of class struggle of 1955 had momentarily given way to a period of relaxation and moderation, Mao laid heavy stress on the importance of learning modestly from Soviet experience – as well as hailing the positive contribution of the Twentieth Congress of the Communist Party of the Soviet Union in terms which would today be regarded as worthy only of a revisionist (Text X 5). But in the spring of 1958 radicalism burst forth again in the shape of the 'Great Leap Forward', the people's communes, and the theory of the 'permanent revolution'.[2] At the time, Mao Tse-tung and Liu Shao ch'i appeared to be the joint promoters of these developments, and it was Liu who first enunciated what has been called ever since 'Mao Tse-tung's theory of the permanent revolution' – though it is perhaps significant that he referred to it as the 'Marxist-Leninist theory' (Text X 7). In any case, it is no doubt Liu Shao-ch'i and the majority of the leaders of the party who insisted on the adoption of the resolution of December 1958 redefining and limiting the scope of the theory. And yet, this same resolution strikingly reflects Mao's 'rural' mentality, especially in

[1] For a discussion of the 'high tide' of the cooperative movement in 1955 and its ideological implications, see *The Political Thought of Mao Tse-tung*, pp. 80–82.

[2] For the reasons which lead us to translate 'permanent revolution' rather than 'uninterrupted revolution', see S. Schram, *La 'révolution permanente' en Chine* (Paris, Mouton, 1963).

the statement that people's communes can be set up only somewhat later in the cities, because 'bourgeois ideology' is still fairly prevalent there (Text X 8).

In November 1957, Mao put forward his famous slogan 'The East wind prevails over the West wind'. At the time, this optimistic view was justified largely by the power of the Soviet Union, symbolized by the sputnik which had just been launched.[1] But it is not altogether certain that even then the Chinese did not also interpret the words 'East' and 'West' in a geographic, if not a racial, sense. In July 1958, for example, this slogan was applied to the Middle Eastern crisis in a way which suggests that it referred above all to the expulsion of the Europeans from Asia.[2]

While the Chinese were thus expressing their emotional solidarity with the non-European peoples who had been the victims of colonialism, the Soviet leaders continued their attempts at a Marxist analysis of the problem of the national bourgeoisie. The Twenty-First Congress of the C.P.S.U., while it remained on the whole oriented in the same direction as the Twentieth Congress, was nevertheless characterized by a step backward on the question of the national bourgeoisie. It was stated that the economic development of the backward countries would rapidly lead to a difference of opinion regarding the course to be followed in the future, and that the problem would then be posed in terms of class. The bourgeoisie, which had come to power with the support of a national liberation movement which united all the progressive strata of the population, was obliged at first to follow a democratic line in order to ensure its supremacy over the feudal and big bourgeois elements it had supplanted. During this stage, the national bourgeoisie was obliged to organize the state along democratic lines (though there were exceptions such as Egypt); above all, it was obliged to embark on economic and social policies in conformity with the demands of the masses (planification, steps towards agrarian reform, labour legislation). To this extent, and also by virtue of its continuing struggle against imperialism, the role of the bourgeoisie at the stage of the creation of the national state remains objectively progressive. Nevertheless, one must not forget the fundamental tendencies of the bourgeoisie, inherent in its class nature. Once in power the bourgeoisie cannot accept the aspirations of the proletariat. As these demands find increasingly open expression, the bourgeoisie tries first of all to hamper them by legal methods, and above all by moving progressively towards more authoritarian forms of power which only exacerbate the contradictions in society.

[1] For the text of Mao's declarations in November 1957, see *The Political Thought of Mao Tse-tung*, Text IX K.

[2] See the poem 'Mediterranean Sea, Sea of Our Hearts' in *Hsin Kuan-ch'a*, no. 15, 1958.

Ultimately the bourgeois leaders of the Asian and African countries may even go so far as to accept the support offered by Western capitalism.[1]

In this way, the lasting character of the national front, which had been justified at the Twentieth Congress not only by the guarantee offered by the Soviet camp, but also by a new conception of the road to socialism, was called into question. Khrushchev's report at the Twentieth Congress had indicated that recourse to violence was not inevitable, especially in countries where capitalism was still weak and had no organized means of defence, and that socialism could be reached by the parliamentary path. Some doubt was expressed on this score following the Twenty-First Congress, where the emphasis had been placed on the danger of a reformist interpretation of the idea of a peaceful transition to socialism, which had been interpreted by certain communists as 'the renunciation of all struggle, of all violence, a purely evolutionary movement, without a revolutionary break with the foundations of life in the past, without complications, without class conflict'.[2] Carried to an extreme, this conception implies that leadership of the movement should be assumed by the vanguard of the working class – the Communist Party. But this eventuality remains theoretical and remote, for the foundations of the 'national front' cannot safely be undermined prematurely. The national front should be maintained as long as there is a foreign menace, and as long as the bourgeoisie has not clearly concluded a compromise with the West.

On the tactical level, the Soviet position in 1959 was thus close to that of Mao Tse-tung, who had firmly maintained for more than a decade the two basic principles: *participation* of the bourgeoisie in the revolution, and even in the 'people's dictatorship', but *hegemony* of the proletariat from beginning to end. On the strategic level, on the other hand, an abyss separated the attitudes of the two great communist powers, a gulf attributable above all to the fact that they belong to different historical, geographic, and cultural worlds. For Moscow, imperialism would ultimately be defeated primarily by the socialist camp. Despite the victories of the national movements in the underdeveloped countries, in the final analysis the destinies of these countries continued to depend, in the Soviet view, on changes in the world scene, and above all on the proletariat of the advanced countries of the socialist camp, and on the proletariat of Western Europe and North America. Such a conception, it soon became clear, was not acceptable to China

[1] These Soviet conceptions were developed by G. Levinson in his article 'Natsional'naya Burzhuaziya u Vlasti' in *Sovremennoye Osvoboditel'noye Dvizheniye i Natsional'naya Burzhuaziya* (Prague, 1961), pp. 320–8.

[2] C. Stepanian, 'O Zakonomernostyakh Pererastaniya Sotsializma v Kommunizm', *Kommunist*, no. 14, 1959, pp. 33–47.

either as a former victim of Western domination, or as a great Asian power.

The Moscow Conference of 1960 and the Beginning of an Open Schism in the Communist Bloc

We have already seen that tensions have existed between the Chinese Communist Party and Moscow at least since 1927, and that these tensions were particularly apparent when the communists took power in China in 1949. Although one cannot uncritically accept the version of the events following the Twentieth Congress of the Communist party of the Soviet Union currently propagated by the Chinese, it seems established that beginning in 1956 they criticized in private the way in which 'de-Stalinization' was carried out, if not the whole substance of this policy. Nevertheless, both the Russians and the Chinese took the greatest pains to hide any disagreements which may have existed from the outside world. In the middle of 1959, this attitude changed, and open signs of conflict began to appear. In July 1959 in a speech delivered in Poland, Khrushchev repeated publicly, in violent terms, the criticisms of the communes he had already voiced in private conversations with American visitors. And on 9 September 1959, the Soviet news agency Tass published a declaration regarding the Sino–Indian border conflict which placed the two adversaries on exactly the same plane and urged them to find a peaceful solution to their disagreements.

The Chinese now state that this declaration first revealed the Sino–Soviet conflict to the outside world. They add that, the text having been submitted to them a few hours prior to release, they energetically protested, but the Soviet leaders took no account of their objections and went ahead and published the statement just the same.[1] The position adopted by the Soviets was altogether understandable in the context of Moscow's foreign policy, for which friendship with Nehru's India was an essential objective. At the same time, there is no doubt that this action did in fact violate the principle of class solidarity among communist governments, which were normally expected to support one another in all circumstances against 'bourgeois' governments, even non-aligned Asian bourgeois governments.

The aim of this book is not to analyse the Sino–Soviet conflict as such, to which a large number of studies have already been devoted,[2] but to emphasize the fundamental tendencies inherent in the two great communist powers which cause them to have diver-

[1] It is in their editorial of 27 February 1963 that the Chinese publicly denounced for the first time the Tass declaration; their prior protest is mentioned in an editorial of 2 November 1963. See *Peking Review*, nos. 9 and 45, 1963.

[2] See Bibliography below, p. 379.

gent views of the revolution and of the world. In this perspective, most of the statements of the years 1959 to 1963, which seemed extremely spectacular at the time, have lost much of their interest in comparison with the more precise and detailed texts published since the summer of 1963. Nevertheless, to the extent that their involvement in the conflict also affected the thinking of the Soviets and the Chinese the conflict itself cannot be left out of account altogether.

Since 1959, Sino–Soviet divergences have manifested themselves in three domains:

1. The domain of ideology (problems of war and peace, peaceful transition to socialism, the role of wars of national liberation in our era);

2. The domain of organization (principles governing relations among members of the communist bloc, the leading role of the U.S.S.R. and/or of China); and

3. The domain of 'relations between states' (economic and technical assistance of the Soviet Union to China, problems of frontiers and of the minorities living near the frontiers, foreign policy conflicts).

Needless to say, there is constant overlapping and interaction between these three domains. But more important than these outward issues are the differences in mentality and in vision of the world which underlie the conflict as a whole, and influence all its manifestations.

The divergent perspectives engendered by differing traditions and differing historical situations are clearly reflected in the positions adopted by Moscow and Peking regarding more concrete and practical issues. Thus, for example, as regards the problem of war and peace the Chinese attitude, although it cannot fairly be regarded as 'bellicose', is marked by a certain lack of concern regarding the consequences of an eventual nuclear war which obviously reflects the situation of a vast and populous country which has less reason than others to fear being simply wiped off the map. It is only in this context that one can understand the viewpoint of the editorialist who, after quoting Mao's declarations at the Moscow meeting of 1957 forecasting the destruction of half of humanity in case of war, comments: 'We are optimistic about the future of humanity.'[1] Mao's position, according to which it is men and not atomic bombs that would be the decisive force in any future war, also proceeds from his own experience of guerrilla warfare, in which the role of the individual combatant was indeed decisive. This being the case, Khrushchev was displaying the absence of tact which marked all his dealings with the Chinese when, at the congress of the Rumanian Communist Party in June 1960, he declared that in our day the militia (which was then

[1] See the editorial of 1 September 1963 in *Peking Review*, no. 36, 1963, p. 10.

being emphasized by China in the context of the communes) was nothing but a mass of human flesh.[1]

Similarly, the violent denunciations of Togliatti's attempts to adapt communism to Italian conditions,[2] and more generally the commentaries of the Chinese press on the political situation in Europe or in the United States, reflect a total incomprehension of the reality of advanced industrial society – an incomprehension only natural in minds shaped partly by the experience of a completely different society, and partly by a naïve belief in the letter of the Marxist scriptures.

In reality, the controversies between the Chinese on the one hand and the majority of the other communist parties on the other, on the problems of war and peace or the roads to socialism, are to such an extent a series of unrelated monologues that they are not of much interest. Consequently, we have preferred to choose for the period 1959 to 1963 texts centred on problems such as the adaptation of Marxism to the particular conditions of each country, or technical assistance to the underdeveloped countries, which call into play cultural factors.

It is clear today that the conference of the eighty-one communist and workers' parties held in Moscow in November and December 1960 with the aim of re-establishing the unity of the communist bloc served in fact to permit the crystallization of the existing differences, despite the final statements which attempted to maintain appearances by ambiguous formulas which could be interpreted by everyone according to his own taste. One detailed study of this meeting concludes that, if there were violent clashes on the questions of war and peace, and of the judgement to be expressed regarding Albania and Yugoslavia, in the last analysis the decisive role was played by organizational problems, as has always been the case within the communist universe.[3] At a certain level, this was no doubt true. The Chinese communists clearly had the ambition, as early as 1960, of playing a more and more important role in the leadership of the world communist movement. Being then too weak to lay claim openly to the number one position, they endeavoured to maintain the concept of a united movement with the Soviet Union at its head, and at the same time to avoid the condemnation of 'fractionalism' which would have hampered their own efforts to increase their influence throughout the communist movement as a whole. As disciples of Lenin and Stalin, they understood the importance of the organizational factor

[1] This is, in any case, the way the Chinese summarize his declarations, op. cit., p. 13.

[2] See in particular the *Hung-ch'i* editorial of 4 March 1963, 'Once More on Our Differences with Comrade Togliatti'.

[3] See W. E. Griffith, 'The November 1960 Moscow Meeting: a Preliminary Reconstruction', *China Quarterly*, no. 11, 1962, pp. 38–57.

in a struggle for hegemony such as the one on which they were embarking. So, of course, did the Soviets and their supporters. Even the Italian delegates, who defended the right of each communist party to conduct its affairs in its own way, were shocked by Teng Hsiao-p'ing's open declaration that the Chinese communists had no intention of accepting majority viewpoints which they regarded as erroneous, and would await the verdict of history.[1]

This attitude on the part of the Chinese illustrates the fact that, if they regarded organization as important, they did not make a fetish of organizational principles, which were for them a means rather than an end. The important thing for them was not the form of the world communist movement, but the possibility afforded them to maintain their own freedom of action, and to increase the audience of their own position. 'No one,' declared Luigi Longo, 'may consider himself, by virtue of his own decision, the sole depositary of Marxism-Leninism.'[2] This is exactly what the Chinese claimed, and have continued to claim. At the same time, they maintained that since its Twentieth Congress the Communist Party of the Soviet Union had abandoned, 'in the most obvious manner, the true way of Marxism-Leninism and of the Moscow Declaration' of 1957.[3]

This pretension on Mao's part was no doubt based on the conviction, later to be affirmed openly and passionately, that the peoples of Asia, Africa, and Latin America constitute the only truly revolutionary force in the world today. (In a memorandum to the preparatory commission of the 1960 Moscow conference the Italian delegation denounced the Chinese, without naming them, for holding views of precisely this kind. According to the Italians, certain people were spreading 'sectarian theories' regarding 'a degenerate Europe condemned by the young nations'.)[4] But Chinese national pride was also a decisive factor. This being the case, Maurice Thorez's heavy-handed irony regarding the 'Chinifying of Marxism' (Text XI 1 B) must have provoked very sharp resentment, especially as the name of Mao Tse-tung himself has long been attached to the idea of the 'Sinification' of Marxism.[5]

Not only Thorez's direct attack, but the more vaguely worded passage in the final statement regarding the harmful character of an excessive emphasis on national peculiarities (see Text XI 1 A),

[1] *Interventi della delegazione del P.C.I. alla Conferenza degli 81 Partiti comunisti e operai. (Mosca, novembre 1960)*, Sezione centrale di stampa e propaganda della Direzione del PCI, Rome, 1962, pp. 69–70.

[2] ibid., p. 70.

[3] ibid., p. 48.

[4] ibid., p. 43.

[5] For the *locus classicus*, see *The Political Thought of Mao Tse-tung*, Text II A. As indicated there, the disappearance of the term 'Sinification' is not, as Thorez imagines, a question of translation, but of changes in the Chinese text itself made by Mao in 1951.

constituted so many blows to Chinese pride. It is therefore not surprising that in 1963 the president of the Indian Communist Party, wounded by the attacks of the Chinese, should have taken revenge by replying on this theme, among others (see Text XI 5).

If the Chinese were obliged, at the November 1960 conference, to accept the passage just mentioned condemning too extensive adaptation to national conditions, they succeeded, on the other hand, in eliminating from the condemnation of Yugoslav 'revisionism' the expression 'national communism'. 'They felt,' said Maurice Thorez, 'that this expression contained in reality a condemnation of their own party.'[1]

If, in defending the originality of Mao Tse-tung's contribution to Marxism-Leninism, the Chinese delegates were defending above all the dignity of their own civilization, on the problem of technical assistance there is no doubt that they expressed reactions common to many underdeveloped countries. Despite Maurice Thorez's eloquent plea defending the draft of the paragraph in question (Text XI 1 D), they succeeded in eliminating from the text of the statement a passage declaring that the 'democratic forces of the advanced capitalist countries' should share with the formerly dependent peoples 'their experience and their knowledge', so as to aid these peoples to solve the problems of economic development. The original version cited by Thorez (and no doubt written by the Soviets) suggests, without saying so explicitly, that such technical assistance is indispensable to the non-European countries. In the face of the withdrawal of the Soviet technicians, suddenly decided by Moscow in the previous July, the Chinese were moving towards the idea that each country should rely almost exclusively on its own material and intellectual resources to assure its development. They could therefore not accept the formulation of the draft, and it was finally replaced by a simple reference to the obligation, for the advanced countries, to aid the former colonies, without any precise indication as to the nature of that aid[2] (see the end of our extract from the Statement, Text XI 1 A).

The mixture of nationalist and revolutionary motives which characterizes the action of the Chinese communists is particularly well illustrated by another subject discussed at the Moscow conference: the Sino–Indian dispute. Already on this occasion the Chinese representative put forward the accusation which they did not make in public until three years later, namely that the Tass communiqué of 9 September 1959 constituted a violation of the

[1] See Thorez's report of 15 December 1960, in *Problèmes du Mouvement Communiste International*, p. 51. See also the speech of the Indian delegate Ajoy Ghosh in *The India-China Border Dispute and the Communist Party of India* (New Delhi, Communist Party Publication, July 1963), p. 50, and the passage on Yugoslavia in the text of the Statement, para. VI, p. 39.

[2] Ajoy Ghosh, op. cit., pp. 46–7.

principles of proletarian internationalism and a gift to President Eisenhower on the eve of the talks at Camp David. The Secretary General of the Indian Communist Party, Ajoy Ghosh, replied by emphasizing the positive role played by the Republic of India in the struggle for peace, and the favourable prospects for India's internal development. Summarizing the history of the exchange of views between the Indian and Chinese parties on this question, he complained of the disdainful attitude of the Chinese leaders, who often did not even bother to reply to the messages of the Indian Communist Party, and accused the Chinese of taking no account whatever of the consequences of their actions on political developments within India.[1] For their part, the Soviet leaders had already stigmatized the Chinese attitude towards India, in February 1960, as an example of 'narrow nationalism'.[2]

There is no doubt that these accusations are partly justified, and that the Chinese leaders were inspired, in their conflict with India, by the desire to demonstrate their country's might, and to weaken a rival for the leadership of the Afro-Asian bloc. But at the same time it is clear that in her conflict with India, China also pursues ideological objectives: that of discrediting India not as another Asian great power, but as a bourgeois dictatorship which has falsely given itself progressive airs, and of demonstrating that neutralism, if it does not rest on a close alliance with the socialist countries, is a fraud. The Chinese have not published Teng Hsiao-p'ing's reply to Ajoy Gosh at the Moscow conference, but their attack of 1963 on Dange, the president of the Indian Communist Party, undoubtedly summarizes the essence of their views on this question (see Text XI 4).

As could have been expected from the suspicions of the Chinese towards 'bourgeois' governments in the non-European countries, which are the logical consequence of Mao Tse-tung's ideas regarding the national bourgeoisie, Peking's representatives at the Moscow conference opposed the adoption of the concept of 'national democracy', which was none the less included in the final text of the statement[3] (see Text XI 1 A, which contains the paragraph defining this term). To be sure, the Chinese had already shown in the past, and would show again in the future, that like the Soviets they were often prepared to subordinate the interests of the revolution to the diplomatic interests of their own state. Despite this fact, they preferred to avoid the contradictions which, as we have seen, constantly afflict Soviet analyses of the role of the various classes in the non-European countries, and therefore opposed this concept which appeared to open the door to the theoretical consecration of

[1] See the extract in Text XI 1 C, and also the whole speech in op. cit., pp. 28–52.

[2] *Peking Review*, no. 45, 1963, p. 19 (editorial of 2 November 1963).

[3] Oral information from participants in the meeting.

the leading role of the national bourgeoisie. The Soviets, on the other hand, were attached to this legitimation of their behaviour since the Twentieth Congress. In a word, the Soviets preferred a theory which appeared to be universally applicable, even if, as a result, it had to be confused and contradictory; the Chinese preferred to set forth rigid principles, and then violate them in practice.

As we have already emphasized, this conference of November 1960 saw the emergence of virtually all the themes and attitudes which have since characterized the Sino–Soviet conflict – even though at the time very little filtered through to the outside world. The Twenty-Second Congress of the C.P.S.U. in October 1961 brought little substantial change in the situation, despite the spectacular clash between Khrushchev and Chou En-lai regarding the evaluation of Stalin. It is nevertheless interesting to note, in the new programme of the Soviet Communist Party adopted on that occasion, passages which further develop and accentuate the condemnation of nationalism contained in the Moscow statement of 1960 (see Text XI 2).

Beginning especially in early 1963, the Chinese hurled these accusations of national egoism back at their Soviet comrades with the utmost violence. Once again, their position was characterized by both nationalist and revolutionary passion. On the one hand, they denounced the 'great-nation chauvinism' of the Soviet communists and their efforts to establish among the communist parties 'abnormal patriarchal and feudal relations' incompatible with the dignity of China.[1] At the same time, they proclaimed their support for the national liberation struggles of the peoples of Asia, Africa, and Latin America and denounced the selfishness of the Soviets, who were, according to the Chinese, more concerned with their own security than with the sufferings of others or with their duty of revolutionary solidarity (see Text XI 3).

The Sino-Soviet Rupture

By the summer of 1963, the rupture between Moscow and Peking was open and complete. The negotiations between the Chinese and Soviet Communist Parties had ended in an impasse, and Khrushchev had added insult to injury by choosing the precise moment of their failure to conclude the nuclear test-ban treaty which was regarded by Mao Tse-tung as the symbol and the proof of Soviet–American collusion to dominate the world. On the ideological level, the two sides had already stated their positions in the Chinese 'Proposal Concerning the General Line of the International Communist Movement' of 14 June 1963 (commonly known as the 'letter in 25 points') and the 'Open Letter to Party Organizations and all Communists in the Soviet Union' issued by

[1] See the *Jen-min jih-pao* editorial of 27 February 1963.

the Central Committee of the C.P.S.U. on 14 July. During the ensuing year there was continual verbal escalation of the dispute, of which the most important landmarks were the nine successive Chinese replies to the Soviet Letter of 14 July 1963, and the speeches made at the February 1964 plenum of the Central Committee of the C.P.S.U. For a time, it seemed that the conflict was the dominant factor in the political life of both countries.

But this was only a passing phase, and very soon it became apparent that the Chinese and Soviet leaders were not talking to each other at all, but to their own peoples and their respective partisans in the world communist movement. And although both Moscow and Peking remained bent on mobilizing support for themselves and endeavouring to limit the influence of their rivals, these tactical aims linked to the Sino–Soviet conflict once more came to appear less fundamental than basic preoccupations determined by the traditions and situation of each country. This is particularly obvious in the case of China, where the 'Great Proletarian Cultural Revolution', though it has no doubt been affected by Peking's relations with both Washington and Moscow, is primarily an outgrowth of Chinese internal developments since 1958. It is also true of the Soviet Union, where in recent years there have taken place efforts at ideological renewal only marginally affected by the rivalry with Peking.

The acute phase of the Sino–Soviet conflict was marked by an extraordinarily complex interaction of national and ideological factors, which entirely rule out any attempt to find a single simple explanation. If one were to read only the Chinese editorial 'Apologists of Neo-Colonialism' (Text XII 1) and Suslov's counterblast (Text XII 3), it would seem obvious that we are dealing above all with a clash between two peoples and two cultures. And yet other documents of the same period, as well as more recent developments, show clearly that ideological elements, linked to the respective ages of the Soviet and Chinese revolutions and the situation in the two countries, are likewise of vital importance.

The Chinese text which opens Section XII appears first of all as an attempt to justify a fundamentally nationalist or regionalist position in terms of Marxist strategy. According to the view set forth in this editorial, the gravest error committed by the U.S.S.R. lies in an obstinate refusal to recognize that historical conditions have changed. The reality of the present epoch is said to consist in a shift of the 'storm centres of world revolution' from the Western countries to Asia, Africa and Latin America. (It is suggested that this situation has existed for some time.) To be sure, the Chinese concede with a certain irony that the epicentre may perhaps move back to the West at some future time. But the essential point in their eyes is that, since for the time being the backward countries constitute the decisive link in the revolutionary struggle, this fact should be recognized and efforts concentrated on this sector.

It is clear that for the Chinese, as for the Muslim communists of the Soviet Union in 1920, the Western countries constitute a 'burnt-out revolutionary hearth', and one must therefore re-define the global strategy of revolution. According to the Chinese, if the Soviets refuse to recognize these facts, and if they refuse to re-evaluate the strength of the various revolutionary forces, it is primarily because they are determined to keep for themselves and for the West a monopoly of revolutionary action. It is also because they perpetuate the traditional 'paternalist' attitude of the Western communists, for whom the underdeveloped peoples cannot take charge of their own destiny, and consequently cannot inflict the decisive blows in the world revolutionary struggle, the historic mission of playing such a decisive role belonging to the West alone.

Carrying their argument a step further, the Chinese saw in Khrushchev's policy of peaceful competition a concrete sign of the common interests linking the industrially developed great powers – interests which transcend the divergences between social systems. By postulating that the problem of the revolution today is no longer that of the traditional bipolar imperialism–socialism, but that of the bipolar imperialism–national liberation movement, the Chinese implicitly recognize what the Russian Muslims had endeavoured to justify theoretically, namely that contradictions among classes are less fundamental than the contradiction between imperialism and the countries it has dominated, and in the last analysis the contradiction between the developed and non-developed worlds. To be sure, the Chinese violently denounce the collusion of the Soviet Union with American imperialism, which they attribute to the fact that the Soviet leaders attach less importance to revolutionary principles than to the common interest of all industrial nations in the preservation of the *status quo*. To this unholy alliance they would oppose a homogeneous block of oppressed and underdeveloped countries. But by thus founding their policy on the solidarity of the disinherited, they implicitly recognize the existence of another entity which is the developed world.

Another factor which has contributed to making this debate more passionate is unquestionably that of the clash between white and coloured peoples. We have already seen how Li Ta-chao, as early as 1924, reinterpreted Leninism in this sense (Text VI 11). At the same time, it is important to emphasize what a gross over-simplification is the Soviet charge of 'racism' directed against the Chinese. What Peking was defending in 1963 and 1964 was the dignity of China and of the other Asian and African countries, not only in terms of race but in terms of civilization and revolutionary traditions. This dimension is particularly evident in the opening paragraphs of the editorial 'Defenders of Neo-Colonialism', which is deliberately modelled on Mao's famous 'Report on an Investigation of the Peasant Movement in Hunan', written in 1927.[1] Like this classic text, the editorial begins by calling on all those who claim to be revolutionaries to take a stand for or against a revolutionary phenomenon which does not fit in with orthodox schemas. In 1927 it was the action of the peasantry independently from the urban proletariat; in 1963 it was the national liberation struggles which took precedence over the action of the European proletariat. There is even a parallelism in the language, which is certainly deliberate. The true revolutionaries, it is stated in both texts, should feel that the situation is 'very good indeed' (*hao te hen*), and not echo the opinion of the reactionaries according to whom things are 'in an awful mess' (*tsao te hen*). This passage vividly expresses both Mao Tse-tung's revolutionary passion and his far-reaching ambitions. Having led to victory in China a revolutionary war based on the peasantry, he is now resolved to lead to victory in the same way the whole of the oppressed peoples of the world in their struggle against imperialism.

Although Mao's passionate commitment to revolution, and his intimate involvement with the experience of the Chinese people over the past half century, are a source of strength to him as the leader of China, they also distort his vision of the outside world. Thus he can find no other explanation for the pro-Soviet attitude of the Western European communists save the 'national-chauvinism' of the French Communist Party or Togliatti's revisionist influence. But if the Chinese analysis of this conflict between two worlds at different stages of development is cursory and partisan, there can be no doubt that such a cleavage exists within the communist universe, just as it does in the capitalist universe. This did not prevent Suslov, in his report of February 1964 to the plenum of the Central Committee of the C.P.S.U. (Text XII 3), from presenting the whole thing as merely a malicious invention of Peking. The Soviet leaders, he said, were animated in all circumstances by proletarian internationalism and a spirit of fraternal assistance between communist parties. Apart from this, he pursued the controversy at the lowest possible level, that of 'Chinese racism', and 'neo-Trotskyite deviations'. This text is interesting because it marks an important watershed in the Sino–Soviet conflict; it does not add much to the theoretical discussion.

This is far from being the case of the posthumously published speech of Otto Kuusinen (Text XII 4). To be sure, one might have some doubts as to the significance of a text emanating from an author already dead.[2] Nevertheless, to the extent that Kuusinen was a member of the revolutionary old guard who had succeeded

[1] *The Political Thought of Mao Tse-tung*, pp. 251–2.

[2] This speech, delivered at the plenum of February 1964, was published in *Pravda* only in May, after Kuusinen's death.

in remaining in favour both in Stalin's day and during the subsequent period of de-Stalinization, his position carries considerable weight. In the speech, Kuusinen first dismisses out of hand the whole of the Chinese revolution, because of its dubious class composition. He denounces two basic flaws. First of all, he objects to the role attributed to the bourgeoisie. Despite Mao's efforts to disguise the fact, by formulating his position more and more prudently in his successive writings, it is obvious according to Kuusinen that in China the bourgeoisie participates in the dictatorship on a basis of equality with the other classes, and that it does so not just momentarily, as a result of transient conditions, but by virtue of a theoretical conception of the historical mission of the bourgeoisie, which is conceived by Mao as not radically different from that of the labouring classes.[1]

The other error of the Chinese leaders is, according to Kuusinen, their negative attitude towards the working class, which they regard as less revolutionary than the peasantry and in which they endeavour to destroy class consciousness and replace it by a spirit of blind submission to a quasi-military authority.

Kuusinen's conclusion is that if the policy of the Comintern in China was not always completely correct, it was exceedingly well founded on this decisive point of the class basis of the revolution. Despite a few verbal precautions, this speech practically rehabilitates the line of the International in China, both as regards the explanations given at the time for the catastrophe of 1927, and as regards the perpetual criticisms directed at the Chinese Communist Party during the ensuing years because of its neglect of the cities and of orthodox methods of political struggle (see Text VII 3).

But this text contains something even more remarkable. Carried away by his zeal in denouncing the ideological errors of the Chinese Communist Party, Kuusinen goes to such lengths that he strikes at the very foundation of Leninism itself. In his eyes, the ultimate deviation of Mao and his comrades consists in systematically confusing the dictatorship of the proletariat and the leading role of the communist party, so as to camouflage their own dictatorship as the dictatorship of the proletariat. In fact, as we saw earlier, one of Lenin's fundamental innovations, as compared to Marx's own position, was the idea, formulated in 1902 in *What Is To Be Done?*, that the communist party should not be simply the vanguard of the working class, expressing the will of the workers, but that on the contrary it was the communist party, as a conscious *élite*, which should inject into the proletariat its true will, which the workers were quite incapable of discovering for themselves. In so doing, he opened the door, as Benjamin Schwartz

[1] For Mao's ideas on the participation of the bourgeoisie in the dictatorship, see above, p. 66.

has written, to the divorce between the revolutionary party and the class it is supposed to represent which has characterized the communist movement ever since. And yet it is precisely for their fidelity to Lenin's teaching on this point that Kuusinen denounced the Chinese communists. Never before, neither in the texts setting forth the line of the Twentieth Congress nor in their polemics with the Chinese, had the leaders of the Communist Party of the Soviet Union gone so far in revising Lenin.

Recent Tendencies

Since 1963 Chinese and Soviets have had little really new to say about one another. They have merely spelled out more loudly and more bitterly the criticisms already exchanged against a background of mutual recrimination regarding Vietnam. But this does not mean there has been no change in their respective positions regarding the revolution in the developing countries. In the case of the Soviet Union, new tendencies have emerged in recent years after a period of stagnation following the innovations of 1965 concerning the national bourgeoisie.

It is not difficult to understand the reasons for this ideological pause. Obliged to cope simultaneously with the constantly growing and more explicit demands of the citizens of the Soviet Union, and with the rivalry of Peking, the Soviet government wanted first of all to answer the challenge to its position in the world communist movement by being the first to reach the stage of communism. Although at the Twenty-Second Congress it was proclaimed that all the socialist countries could reach communism simultaneously, it is clear that this was a mere abstract notion. The effort necessary in order that the U.S.S.R. might succeed in carrying out, within twenty years, the programme it had set for itself, required all its energies, and all its resources. The Soviet Union could thus afford to employ little of its capacities for the benefit of the outside world. It is for this reason that the Twenty-Second Congress was unquestionably marked by a turning inward of the U.S.S.R. How could she have devoted her attention to developing revolutionary situations outside the country, in particular in the non-European countries, when her own development towards communism thus occupied all her efforts?

This aspect of the Twenty-Second Congress did not escape the attention of a certain number of communists from Asia, Africa and Latin America, who concluded that henceforth China alone would support their revolutionary movements, whereas the Soviet Union had found a sequel to Stalin's slogan of 'Socialism in One Country' in the idea of 'Communism in One Country'.

At the level of the higher party organs, the ideological line laid down in the Soviet Union, which had been stabilized at the Twentieth Congress, very soon ceased to reflect either Soviet practice or the evolution of certain non-European countries. The increasingly radical political climate and the imperatives of economic development led nearly everywhere to the progressive elimination of the national bourgeoisie in favour of representatives of less favoured groups in society – generally the petty bourgeoisie, the minor civil servants, the well-to-do peasants, etc. To be sure, the concept of *national democracy* put forward at the conference of the eighty-one communist and workers' parties in November 1960 corresponded, at least in the mind of the Soviet leaders, to this new phase. Was the national-democratic state, where the unhampered exercise of the basic freedoms was supposed to permit a rapid development towards socialism, a more adequate definition of the developments taking place in the non-European countries than the theoretical formulations of 1956?

If one looks more closely at the facts, national democracy, at least in its Soviet version (that is to say, proletarian hegemony being considered not as an indispensable condition, but merely as desirable) appears once more as primarily designed to fit Soviet practice based above all on foreign policy imperatives. What had been since 1956 the criterion of a progressive state in Soviet eyes? Very clearly, the essential qualification was a refusal to follow the lead of the Western powers in external relations. It was perpetually the neutralism of a non-European state rather than its internal tendencies that determined the Soviet attitude and hence the ideological judgement regarding this state.

As long as the fundamental problem of the countries of Africa, Asia and Latin America was that of national independence, internal differences were not very much in evidence. But once independence has been achieved, the problems of development lead to a challenge to the ruling groups.[1] In order to save their position, the latter have a choice between a withdrawal to more conservative positions, or an attitude even more radical than that of those who challenge their policy. Henceforth, foreign policy choices no longer correspond infallibly to differences in internal orientation. The first list of national democracies published in Moscow included, together with Indonesia, African countries such as Guinea, Ghana and Mali, as well as Cuba, but it did not include a single country from the Arab East.[2] The first addition to the list was Algeria. Very soon it became evident that this evaluation underestimated the influence of socialism in Cuba, and overestimated the political stability and the prospects for socialism in Indonesia, in Algeria, and in certain African countries. It also failed to take account of

[1] V. I. Pavlov and I. B. Red'kov, 'Gosudarstvo natsional'noy demokratii i perekhod k nekapitalisticheskomu razvitiyu', *Narody Azii i Afriki*, no. 1, 1963, pp. 28–41.

[2] B. Ponomarev, 'O Gosudarstvakh natsional'noy demokratii, *Kommunist*, no. 8, 1961.

the fundamental reforms in the economic and social system carried out in Egypt and Syria. The Soviet government soon came to offer more and more effective support to Nasser. But there was no evidence that these developments in Soviet policy had been incorporated into Soviet theory.

The Twenty-Third Congress of the C.P.S.U., in March and April 1966, did not deal with recent developments in the non-European countries. Nor did it indicate precisely how the U.S.S.R. envisaged the establishment of variants of socialism, comprising genuinely socialist transformations and adapted to the conditions of each country, when this socialism was in fact incarnated by men or groups issued from intermediate strata of society who intend to impose an ideological monopoly which rules out communism. Nevertheless, on the level of political judgements the attitude of the Soviet government is slightly more explicit. As regards Egypt, which has become (with the collapse of the so-called national democratic régimes in Indonesia, Algeria, Ghana, and elsewhere) the stablest country, which has progressed most consistently towards socialism, the Soviet authorities and the C.P.S.U. sometimes express rather clear judgements. Like Khrushchev, his successors consider that Egypt is following a 'non-capitalist path of development', and is 'building socialism'.[1] It must not be forgotten that President Nasser's Party, the Arab Socialist Union, was the explicit beneficiary of the Egyptian Communist Party's decision to dissolve itself, after which its members joined the A.S.U.[2] By inviting a delegation of the A.S.U. to its Twenty-Third Congress as the representative of Egypt, the C.P.S.U. clearly gave its sanction to the ideological shift involved in the dissolution of the Communist Party; implicitly, it accepted the claim of the Arab Socialist Union to an ideological monopoly, despite the A.S.U.'s clear declaration of non-communism.[3]

Does the fact that many theoretical problems were not clearly posed by the speakers at the Twenty-Third Congress imply that the C.P.S.U. is not aware of them, or rather that its position is not altogether clear? The latter hypothesis seems more plausible, for it is important to note that the ideological problems raised by the evolution of the Arab East are by no means ignored in the Soviet

[1] *Pravda*, 14 April 1966; G. Mirskoy, 'Gamal Abdel Nasser', *MEIMO*, no. 7, July 1964, pp. 112–15.

[2] The Egyptian Communist Party decided by a large majority to dissolve itself in January 1965. The news was reported on 25 January 1965 in *Al Ahram.* The Egyptian press devoted a great deal of space to the discussions of the Communist Party at that time. It is not without interest to note that, on the contrary, the Soviet press and even the theoretical journals were completely silent on this point.

[3] It is true that since 1964 Nasser has stated more and more clearly that Egyptian socialism is 'scientific socialism', whereas previously he had rejected this term.

Union. For four years an ample and very important discussion has been going on in Soviet research institutes.[1] At the Institute of the Peoples of Asia and Africa, and above all at the Institute of World Economics and International Relations, specialists on the non-European countries are asking themselves questions about current developments in certain countries, and are raising explicitly the problem of the nature of political power in these countries.

These discussions, of which the scope is often hidden by the fact that they are broken up by regions, focus on a certain number of fundamental points. Among these are such questions as: Does the internal development of certain countries reflect merely the willingness of the groups in power to have recourse to every possible expedient to maintain themselves in power, or does it result from an objectively revolutionary situation? Supposing that such objectively revolutionary situations exist, can they be dealt with by any group whatever, which will in any case be *obliged* to apply socialist solutions, or will development take a socialist direction only if the proletariat and its organizations take charge of the revolutionary movement? What is the link between the nature of political power and the classes in power? Must the building of socialism necessarily be guided by communist ideology, or does the revolutionary situation progressively inflect any ideology towards communism?

Such are the general questions, which seek to assign a precise role to the non-European countries in the course of the world revolution, which raise in new terms the problem of the means to be employed to carry out the revolution in these countries, and which envisage for the first time in such a clear fashion the problem of integrating cultural specificity into the revolutionary process. The Soviet theorists base their analyses on precise examples such as that of Egypt, Syria, or even Algeria. In this connexion, they have raised the problem of military power, of the communist parties of these countries, of the formation of local *élites*, and even – though timidly – of bureaucracy.

Of all these discussions, that regarding military régimes is certainly the furthest advanced and the most curious at the present time. The Soviet theoreticians started from the consideration that in many countries throughout Asia, Africa and Latin America military régimes have taken over power from the national bourgeoisie. Everywhere the military *élites* which dominate these régimes are commonly issued from the same milieux – the intermediate strata which provide the personnel of the national armies – but their political choices are not everywhere identical. On the other hand, the importance of the military has been clearly demonstrated everywhere. From this, the Soviet authors conclude that

[1] See above all the symposium held at the Institute of World Economics and International Relations on this theme in the spring of 1964, of which the verbatim record was published in *MEIMO*, no. 4, 1964, pp. 116–32, and no. 5, pp. 62–82.

though the army may not play a decisive role everywhere, nothing decisive can be done against it. This being the case, how should one evaluate this factor, especially as all the military régimes without exception profess a nationalist and not a communist ideology, and deny the communist party a place in the political system, or even exclude it from the life of the nation?

Taking into account the orientation adopted by certain military régimes, and especially by that of Nasser, the Soviet theorists postulate that in the conditions presently existing in the non-European countries, the army has a tendency to assume the role of a 'vanguard', and to feel itself invested with an historic mission, both as regards the conquest of national independence and as regards economic development. In certain cases, this leads the army to transcend particular interests, including those of the class from which it is issued, and sometimes those of the government, so as to represent the nation as a whole (see Text XII 7). This new analysis, characterized by the fact that it envisages the possibility of a rupture between the interests of the ruling strata and the interests of the milieu from which they have originated, is reinforced by a re-evaluation of the concept of national bourgeoisie.

In 1963, at a time when the Chinese showed themselves not very much inclined to contest the revolutionary qualifications of the urban middle and petty bourgeoisie provided they claimed to be revolutionary, the Soviets emphasized the instability of these groups.[1] Henceforth, the Soviet theorists consider that if, to be sure, the middle and petty bourgeoisie is unstable by *nature*, it is the objective conditions which dictate the attitude it must adopt if it is not to be eliminated from power. Thus the Soviet theorists arrive at the view that in the conditions of the non-European countries the choice of the non-capitalist path of development depends not on the social origins of the groups holding power, nor even on the conditions in which they have taken power, but above all on the real political situation and the political consciousness of the masses.

This leads one to reflect on a problem which Soviet political practice seems to have solved already, at least in certain cases: that of the ideological monopoly of the ruling groups. In general, the ideology of the non-communist one-party régimes of Asia, Africa and Latin America is explicitly anti-communist. What are the local communist parties to do in this case? Keep silent? Or carry on underground work against the régimes in power? The Soviet reply to this question is a hesitant one; the only clear example is once more that of Egypt. The integration of the local Communist Party into the party of President Nasser appears to indicate that in certain circumstances the primacy accorded to the Communist

[1] E. Zhukov, 'Natsional'no-osvoboditel'noye dvizheniye na novom etape' *Kommunist*, 12 August 1963, pp. 23–30.

Party, which has been a constant factor in Soviet theory since Lenin, is called into question. But this case can also be interpreted differently. One can ask oneself if the Soviets do not believe that the integration of the Communist Party into the ruling party will in the end have the result of giving to the latter party, whose ideology remains empirical, the ideological basis it lacks, so that communization from within can be substituted for a struggle from without. Thus the Soviet theorists have sketched out, if not precisely a new conception of the revolution, then at least a new conception of the development of the non-European countries in a revolutionary direction (see Text XII 6).

Apart from these new ideas about the role of various classes and groups in social change, Soviet thinking about the non-European countries in recent years has been marked by another interesting development: the re-appearance of Marx's concept of the Asiatic mode of production. This concept had been explained away as merely an oriental variant of feudalism at the Leningrad conference of 1931, and for thirty years thereafter it was severely banned from the vocabulary of Soviet writers. (Meanwhile, in 1934, it had been re-defined as a variant of slave-holding society rather than of feudalism.) 'For us', wrote S. Oldenburg in 1931,

> there is no such thing as a division of peoples and countries into an Orient and an Occident opposed to one another and which must be studied in a different manner. In our [Soviet] Union, the Orient has the same rights as the Occident and we study it with the same Marxist methodology as the Occident. There was and still is a class struggle in the East as in the West. The history of the Orient has known the same [economic] formations as that of the Occident.[1]

Following the Twentieth Congress of the Communist Party of the Soviet Union in 1956, a number of young Soviet scholars seeking to abandon the rigid dogmatism of the Stalin era in this domain also were tempted by the concept of the Asiatic mode of production, but the anathema of Leningrad continued to weigh heavily on their reflections. Thus, as late as 1964 a communication on rural communes presented at the Orientalists' Congress in Moscow by Gamayunov and Ulianovskiy carefully avoided all reference to Marx's writings on the Asiatic mode of production.[2]

The pioneering role in the rediscovery of this concept was consequently left to Communist scholars in Eastern and Western Europe. Sinologists associated with the French and Hungarian Communist Parties were particularly active in this respect. At first, their writings circulated in mimeographed form; the matter

[1] Quoted by Jan Pečirka, 'Die Sowjetischen Diskussionen über die asiatische Produktionsweise und über die Sklavenhalterformation', *Eirene* III, 1964; translated in *Recherches internationales à la lumière du marxisme*, no. 57–8, 1967, p. 65.

[2] J. Chesneaux, 'Le mode de production asiatique–quelques perspectives de recherche', *La Pensée*, no. 114, April 1964. p. 37.

was first made public by a special issue of *La Pensée* in April 1964.

In itself, it is an excellent thing that this part of Marx's work should no longer be regarded as unmentionable in communist circles, but the way in which the concept of the Asiatic mode of production has been resurrected makes quite clear that many of those involved are not inspired exclusively by scientific considerations. Some actually go so far as to drape themselves in the authority of Marx and Engels in order to suggest that only civilizations shaped by classical Antiquity can in fact have a genuine history of their own, or be regarded as participating in universal history.[1]

To be sure, Marx himself heavily underlined the stagnation of Asian society prior to the impact of the West. But we have seen that his ideas on the subject evolved with the years. More important, an attitude of superiority towards the rest of the world was understandable a century ago, on the part of an observer such as Marx deeply impressed by the spectacle of the mastery of man over nature which was then unfolding for the first time in Europe. It is less excusable today, when we know more about the wealth of other civilizations and the evils of our own. It is difficult, in any case, not to see in this renewed interest in the 'Asiatic mode of production' the counterpart, on the cultural level, of Kuusinen's anti-Chinese remarks on the strategic level. Kuusinen endeavoured to demonstrate that revolutions in non-European countries were only second-class revolutions because they were not carried out by a highly developed proletariat. Similarly, if one affirms that China did not even have either a history or a civilization worthy of the name until the Opium War, it evidently follows that Peking is ill-qualified to assume the leadership of the world revolution.[2]

[1] See in particular Ferenc Tökei, 'Le mode de production asiatique dans l'œuvre de K. Marx et F. Engels', *La Pensée*, no. 114, April 1964, pp. 13, 25, 31 etc.

[2] In the French edition of this book we took pains to point out that not all those communist scholars who have taken an interest in the Asiatic mode of production exploit it politically in this fashion. 'Jean Chesneaux,' we wrote, 'warns against the tendency to exclude from the history of humanity the peoples to whom this category is applied, and even proposes to give it another name, without the geographical reference which "irritates . . . the legitimate pride of some people".' (*La Pensée*, no. 114, April 1964, pp. 40, 51.) Professor Chesneaux none the less felt himself obliged to take up the cudgels on behalf of his comrades, writing that it was laughable to imagine that the purely academic interests of the French, Hungarian, and other European Marxists were in any way inspired by a patronising attitude towards China, since discussions on the subject had in fact begun long before the Sino-Soviet split. See J. Chesneaux, 'Où en est la discussion sur le mode de production asiatique', *La Pensée*, no. 129, October 1966, p. 40.

Whatever the original motives of the precursors in this enterprise, it is impossible to deny the anti-Chinese animus of many of those who refer to the concept of the Asiatic mode of production today. This is particularly the case

Despite the obvious utility of this reasoning, the Soviets were, as already indicated, slower than their European comrades to employ it against the Chinese. The reason is not far to seek: it is for them a two-edged sword. For as we have seen earlier, Marx and Engels considered Russia itself as an oriental despotism. Citing a text of Engels in which Russia is included in this category, Ferenc Tökei seeks to get around the difficulty by observing quaintly that this reference 'has given rise to misunderstandings'.[1] The Soviet writers cannot dismiss the problem quite so lightly, for the concept of the Asiatic mode of production in fact calls into question the whole of their own history. Beginning in the middle of the nineteenth century, Slavophiles and Westernizers in Russia fought over this very problem of whether Russian history was unique, or whether it was rather part of a universal current. Marx had opened a door – narrow to be sure – towards the thesis of uniqueness, and the Populists, after the Slavophiles, defended this claim, in the name of which they opposed capitalism considered as something foreign to Russian history. As a result of this debate, Marxism in Russia has been marked from the beginning by the desire to tear the country away from this temptation to worship its own uniqueness, by showing that it was subject to the laws of unilinear historical development. Throughout his life Lenin was haunted by this problem. He saw Russia as Asiatic and barbarous, but he refused to consider this as a unique trait growing out of the country's development in the margin of world history, rather than as simply the situation at one moment in history. After 1926, with the reflux of revolution in the West, this orientation became even more indispensable. How could the U.S.S.R., vanguard and model of socialist development, have reached her present stage by following a different way from that prescribed by Marx and Engels for the revolution in the societies of the West?

Given these problems, both psychological and political, it is not surprising that the first Soviet writer to come out publicly and emphatically in favour of the use of the concept of the Asiatic mode of production was Eugene Varga, who devoted a whole chapter to the subject in his last work, published at the end of 1964. 'Today, thirty years afterward,' he wrote,

when we evoke the discussion of the question as to whether the Asiatic mode of production is a variant of feudalism, it is very hard to understand the extreme obstinacy with which the existence of the Asiatic

---

of Tökei; it is also true, to a slightly lesser degree, of Roger Garaudy, who has relied extensively on Tökei's writings in his recent book on China. Thus, after saying that there is 'nothing offensive' to the peoples of the Orient in Marx's concept, M. Garaudy goes on to describe all the recent, and in his eyes erroneous, policies of Mao Tse-tung as 'sequels' of the Asiatic mode of production. (R. Garaudy, *Le Problème chinois*, Paris, Seghers, 1967, pp. 23, 104.)

[1] *La Pensée*, no. 114, April 1964, p. 20.

mode of production was denied, and Marx's writings on the subject misinterpreted – despite the fact that in the programme of the Comintern adopted by all the Communist Parties three years earlier, mention was made of countries marked by survivals of the Asiatic mode of production.[1]

The publication of Varga's book marked the beginning of an open discussion in the Soviet Union on this theme, and in May 1965 the Institute of the Peoples of Asia organized a conference on the Asiatic mode of production.[2] Even though the debate was introduced and summed up by two leading adversaries of the concept, G. F. Kim and V. N. Nikiforov, the fact that such a forum had been possible at all is striking evidence of the pressures for change. Thus far, however, the Soviet scholars have remained at the stage of exploring Marx's use of the concept rather than of making any new contribution.

The sceptics, such as Nikiforov, declare that the existence of a peculiar 'Asiatic' mode of production is not borne out by the historical record. In his view, 'the more deeply we penetrate in our research, the more we discern the common character of the essential stages through which humanity has passed in the course of universal history'. There are, to be sure, differences between Europe and Asia, but in Nikiforov's opinion one could just as well speak of the peculiarities of the evolution of the countries of Western Europe as compared to the Orient as the reverse (see Text XIII 4). Others, such as Garushiants, are persuaded that the Asiatic mode of production must be clearly distinguished from slave society and feudalism (see Text XIII 5).

In the background of these academic debates regarding a methodological concept, we can clearly distinguish the echoes of the old controversy between Slavophiles and Westernizers regarding the sense of Russian history. The younger Soviet scholars are attracted by the concept of the Asiatic mode of production because it appears to them to provide an instrument which gives full weight to the uniqueness of specific cases, and at the same time preserves the essence of Marxism, namely the vision of human society evolving through a succession of stages to a higher level. Their older colleagues, who resist the use of this concept in the name of the orthodoxy of the 1930s, take their stand in the tradition of the Westernizers and as such are attached to the idea of a process of development common to all societies.

In the past year or two, it would appear that there has been a

[1] E. Varga, *Ocherki po Problemam Politekonomiki Kapitalizma*, Moscow, Gospolitizdat, 1965, p. 379.

[2] The proceedings were published in 1966 under the title *Obshchee i Osobennoe v Istoricheskom Razvitii Stran Vostok* (The General and the Particular in the Historical Development of the Countries of the East), Moscow, Izdatel'stvo 'Nauka'.

less active interest in the Asiatic mode of production, both in the Soviet Union and among European communists. This new swing of the pendulum can no doubt be explained partly on political grounds. The 'Asiatic' concept is a useful weapon for belabouring the Chinese, but apart from the delicate issue of oriental despotism in Russia, this approach does not fit in well with the current Soviet line attributing a leading role in the non-European countries to the army. For, as we have already seen, support for the army is based on the postulate that no matter what class, group, or institution serves as the agent of economic progress, in the long run economic development will lead to progressive changes in the political and social system. Such an assumption is clearly incompatible with the idea that the societies of Asia and Africa are qualitatively different from those of the West, for in this case the army would reflect their 'Asiatic' character and could hardly serve as the agent of modernization. It is thus not surprising that Professor Kim, who is one of the leading exponents of the new theories regarding the vanguard role of the army, is extremely reticent about the Asiatic mode of production.

Independently of such considerations of political advantage, even those who led the way a few years ago to the re-discovery of Marx's writings on the Asiatic mode of production are showing increasing doubts about the value of the concept. They seized upon it as a forbidden fruit, in a conscious effort to escape from the straitjacket of Stalinist orthodoxy, and also because it provided a convenient ready-made explanation for the peculiarities of Asia and Africa. But quite apart from the tendentious use which is made of the concept by people such as Tökei or Godelier, this new approach soon began to appear quite as rigid and artificial as the arbitrary application of the categories of 'slave-holding society' and 'feudalism' to Chinese history. In a sense, the attitude of the Stalinist period and that of some of the partisans of the Asiatic mode of production proceed from the same assumption, namely that every word Marx wrote is sacred and true. This being the case, the only defence against his ideas on Asian society was to deny their existence; and once they were rediscovered, they necessarily had to be applied. Today, there appears to be developing among Marxist authors in Europe, and also in the Soviet Union, a more independent attitude, involving a fresh study of all Marx's writings and their evaluation in the light of the facts available today.[1]

[1] Thus, in his introduction to the first English translation of the passage on pre-capitalist economic formations from Marx's *Grundrisse der Kritik der Politischen Ökonomie*, E. J. Hobsbawm called for a careful study of this important text, adding that this 'does not mean the automatic acceptance of all Marx's conclusions'. (Karl Marx, *Pre-Capitalist Economic Formations*, translated by Jack Cohen, edited and with an Introduction by E. J. Hobsbawm, London, Lawrence and Wishart, 1964, p. 65.)

It is easy to understand, in any case, in the light both of the content of Marx's own writings and of the use which is made of them today by certain European communists hostile to China, why the Chinese themselves reject the concept of the Asiatic mode of production, and prefer to apply Stalin's unilinear schema. To discern in their own country's past the four epochs of primitive communism, slave-holding society, feudalism and capitalism which Marx found in the history of Europe, is, in a sense, to affirm the full participation of China in universal history. There is here a kind of alienation engendered by the prestige of Europe: even as they reject the pretensions of the Europeans to world leadership, the non-Europeans want to resemble them. Perhaps in time the Chinese will come to have enough confidence in themselves to proclaim openly the uniqueness not only of their culture, but also of the political and economic organization of ancient China. To do so would, however, have the disadvantage of undermining their claim to constitute the vanguard of a worldwide revolution.

The complicated and dialectical interaction between the idea of China's uniqueness and the universality of China's revolutionary role is one of the dominant themes in the current 'Great Proletarian Cultural Revolution'. It is impossible here to give an exhaustive account of this extraordinary upheaval.[1] These recent developments must nevertheless be dealt with at some length, for they are of interest not merely as a new chapter in the political and ideological history of China, but also as a subject of meditation regarding the fate of Marxism in the non-European countries in general.

Mao's aim in launching this movement was that defined in a quotation first published in 1964, but identified as having been written in 1963: to ensure that in the future China does not 'change colour', i.e. alter her political character (see Text XIII 1). Mao's fear that, after his disappearance, his life-work might be undone, appears to have two main roots. On the one hand, he is convinced that China's youth, which has not been tempered like the previous generation in combat against the Japanese and against Chiang Kai-shek, and which has never lived under the oppression of landlords and capitalists, might easily be tempted to abandon the great cause of revolution and think rather of individual comfort and satisfaction. More generally, he believes that everywhere and at all times prosperity involves a risk of *embourgeoisement* – a risk against which it will be necessary to struggle for centuries by a ceaseless effort of indoctrination.

[1] Stuart Schram has endeavoured to retrace the history of this movement in the revised edition of his biography, *Mao Tse-tung*, to be published in 1970 by Penguin Books. On the ideological aspects of the 'cultural revolution', see also the new edition of his *The Political Thought of Mao Tse-tung*, published recently by Penguin Books (and in New York by Frederick A. Praeger).

These motives for Mao's fear that China may 'change colour' were clearly stated in the editorial entitled 'Khrushchev's Phoney Communism and its Lessons for the World', published in July 1964 (see Text XIII 1 for extracts), and also at the congress of the Chinese Youth League held in June 1964. The second reason for Mao's fear was carefully hidden at the time, but may well have been more important. It was his discovery of 'capitalist', 'bureaucratic', and 'revisionist' tendencies among his own close comrades. The radical policies of the 'Great Leap Forward' of 1958–60 had unquestionably been Mao's own, and he had staked all his prestige on their success. When it proved necessary, in the face of catastrophic economic conditions, to modify or abrogate many of these policies, Mao obviously regarded this as a temporary expedient, to be accepted with reluctance. He soon discovered that many of those responsible for the leadership of the government and the economy of the Chinese People's Republic had no sympathy for the idea of a new leap forward, with its emphasis on political zeal rather than on technical competence, and on mass mobilization rather than on rational economic planning. As a result, by the time he launched the slogan of preventing a 'change of colour' in 1963, he was already relying heavily on the People's Liberation Army (under the leadership of Lin Piao since Peng Te-huai's removal in 1959 following his attacks on Mao's policies) as a more faithful and effective instrument than the party for carrying out his own line.

The growing role of the army which has characterized the situation in China since that time is obviously of great political and ideological significance. In a sense, recent events are merely the culmination of a tendency which runs through the whole history of the Chinese Communist movement since Mao led his first little guerrilla band up the Chingkangshan in the winter of 1927. Throughout the ensuing two decades, the Communist Party rebuilt its shattered organization and carried on political work under the protection of the Red Army. Mao's very first experiments with ideological indoctrination and the 'rectification' of incorrect ideas were carried out in the ranks of the army in 1928–9, and much of the political work connected with the massive expansion of communist influence behind the Japanese lines during the years 1937–45 was carried out directly by the army. Thus, while it would not be fair to say that in Mao's practice the Red Army had replaced the Communist Party as the leading force in the revolution, it came to assume a certain symbolic importance of its own as the vanguard of the national and social revolution in China.

Nevertheless, Mao still laid down in 1938 that the Party was to command the gun, and 'the gun must never be allowed to command the Party'.[1] Today, although this sentence still appears in

[1] *The Political Thought of Mao Tse-tung*, p. 289.

the Red Guards' bible, *Quotations from Chairman Mao*,[1] it has been repeatedly violated in pactice.

During the early stages of the cultural revolution, and especially in the period from February to May 1966, this movement appeared as a paradoxical combination of rational and irrational elements. A careful reading of the innumerable articles by workers and technicians regarding the application of Mao Tse-tung's thought to science and production left the impression that what was in fact being inculcated were a certain number of pragmatic and experimental attitudes indispensable to progress. At the time, the contradiction between the language of the Mao cult and its rational kernel appeared to reflect the complex nature of Mao's own personality and of the reality with which he had to deal. It has now been officially revealed that this phase during which the cultural revolution pursued relatively constructive aims was precisely the phase when Liu Shao-ch'i and his allies in the party leadership had captured control of the movement and were shaping it to their own purposes.[2] When Mao Tse-tung regained command, in the middle of May 1966, he oriented the 'cultural revolution' in a quite different direction.

The course of the 'cultural revolution' in the ensuing three years can be viewed in many perspectives, among which two of the most important are defined by the institutional changes involved, and by the transformation Mao is endeavouring to carry out in the mentality and habits of the Chinese people. Although it is possible to separate them for purposes of analysis, these two aspects of the 'cultural revolution' are, of course, closely interrelated, since in Mao's view the bureaucratic methods of leadership employed in the past are largely responsible for the failure to transform the thinking of the masses. Let us consider first the institutional context, which is stressed in the extracts from Chinese ideological writings of the past three years contained in this volume.

In order to smash the resistance of his peers, Mao sponsored the creation of the Red Guards and entrusted them with the task of 'rebellion' against the Party leadership. By a singular irony, the Mao text which serves as an ideological justification for this policy originally attributed to Stalin the sentiment there expressed: 'In the last analysis, all the truths of Marxism can be summed in one sentence: to rebel is justified.'[3] While Stalin, too, mercilessly

[1] *Quotations from Chairman Mao Tse-tung* (Peking, Foreign Languages Press, 1966), p. 102.

[2] See the Circular of the Central Committee of the Chinese Communist Party dated 16 May 1966, only published a year later, and the accompanying *People's Daily* editorial, as translated in *Peking Review*, no. 21, 1967, pp. 6–12.

[3] This quotation is from Mao's speech at Yenan on the occasion of Stalin's sixtieth birthday in 1939; for a full translation, see *The Political Thought of Mao Tse-tung*, Text X G. When a brief passage was reprinted in the Peking press in

purged the Party leadership and bureaucracy of opponents, real or imagined, he did this with the aid of another apparatus, the secret police. Nothing could have been further from his methods and mentality than to mobilize millions of adolescents and encourage them to terrorize the local Party secretaries.

As already indicated, Mao justified this assault on the Party by the need to find a method for extirpating once and for all the bureaucratic tendencies which had manifested themselves in China even under his leadership, and for preventing their re-emergence in the future. This is one of the main themes in the 'Decision of the Central Committee of the Chinese Communist Party concerning the Great Proletarian Cultural Revolution' adopted on 8 August 1966, with its emphasis on action by the masses and its utopian echoes of the Paris Commune (see Text XIII 7 for extracts).

These policies of encouraging 'rebellion' against all organs of authority could not be maintained indefinitely in their pure form without producing complete anarchy. And Mao had too long shown an instinctive understanding of the importance of organization as a political weapon to fall victim to the cult of untrammelled mass spontaneity professed by certain of his disciples in the West. In January 1967 the 'cultural revolution' therefore moved into a new stage: that of the 'seizure of power'.[1] This took a form of great theoretical interest. In a series of provinces and municipalities provisional authorities were founded on the basis of the 'three-in-one alliance' of 'leading members of revolutionary mass organizations [such as the Red Guards], leading members of local People's Liberation Army units and revolutionary [i.e. pro-Mao] leading cadres of party and government organizations'.[2] These provisional organs were to take over all power, within their respective spheres of action, from both the former government and party hierarchies.

This process was finally carried to a conclusion only in the autumn of 1968, a year and a half after Mao had launched the 'seizure of power'. Meanwhile, despite frequent fluctuations in one direction or the other, there had been a trend towards the partial rehabilitation of the Party. In the summer of 1969, it is still not clear whether this rehabilitation is purely verbal, or whether the Party as an institution is once more reasserting itself to some extent as a

August 1966, it was not indicated that Mao had originally characterized this idea as a lesson learned from Stalin.

[1] For the call to seize power see the *People's Daily* editorial of 22 January 1967, translated in *Peking Review*, no. 5, 1967, pp. 7–9. Chou En-lai, in a speech of the same date not generally published, declared that this undertaking marked 'a new stage' in the cultural revolution; he traced its origins to Mao's decision, earlier in January, to broadcast a message from the 'revolutionary rebels' of Shanghai calling for a counter-attack against the 'bourgeois reactionary line'. *Hsin Pei-ta*, 23 January 1967, p. 1.

[2] For this formulation, and in general for the theoretical justification of the 'great alliance' for the 'seizure of power', see Text XIII 8.

force in the Chinese political system, as the proceedings of the recently-held congress tend to suggest. One thing is, however, definitely established. The Party as it existed prior to 1966 has become nothing more than a supplier of trained political specialists, whose expertise may be useful but who must be constantly watched and controlled by the army and by the new militants who have emerged in the course of the cultural revolution. There has been a shift in emphasis (illustrated by the *Red Flag* editorials of February 1967 and October 1968 which constitute respectively Text XIII 8 and Text XIII 10) from a direct challenge to the authority of the Party to the regeneration of the Party from within, but the criterion of whether or not one is a good communist remains not status in the Party but absolute fidelity to the teachings of Chairman Mao.

Thus, despite the constant talk of participation by the masses, the result of the 'seizure of power' is not spontaneous mass democracy, but the domination of Chinese political life by a charismatic leader relying above all on the army. Both Mao's own role and that of the army are of fundamental significance in assessing the ideas and practices which go under the name of Marxism-Leninism in China today. The predominance of the army is not merely an obvious fact; it has been elevated to the level of a theoretical principle. 'The great Chinese People's Liberation Army,' we read in an editorial of 30 March 1968, 'is the main pillar of the dictatorship of the proletariat' (See Text XIII 9).

Even more singular in a sense than the direct intervention of the army in all aspects of political and social activity is the obsessive presence in every nook and cranny of existence of a figure who is the object of a cult which has some parallels with that of Stalin, and with traditional Chinese attitudes towards the emperor, but is not adequately defined by either of these analogies. The parallel with Stalin is to be found not only in the use of violence to purge the apparatus of disloyal elements, but in the tendency to discover in today's adversaries traitors of forty years' standing. The differences lie, apart from Mao's reliance on the army to a greater extent than on the secret police, in the fact that he has set himself deliberately above the Party. This is a point of the highest theoretical importance. That the Party as a collective body is the repository of all authority and of all truth is the very keystone of the arch of Leninism. Even Stalin, though, in fact, he terrorized his comrades of the Party with the aid of the police and of his own personal secretariat, had always claimed to be merely the mandatory of the Party, ruling in the Party's name. In China today, this relationship has been stood on its head not only in practice, but in theory. It is Mao as an individual, by virtue of his superior grasp of Marxist theory and his historical role as the leader of the Chinese revolution, who is the source of authority and of truth. Other persons and organizations, including the Party, enjoy legitimate authority only to the extent that they apply his thought and obey his instructions.

The ultimate expression of Mao's new conceptions regarding the structure of the political system and the locus of legitimacy is to be found in the Party constitution adopted in draft form by the 12th Plenum of the Central Committee of the Chinese Communist Party in October 1968, and ratified by the Ninth Party Congress on 14 April 1969.[1] This document, said to have been drawn up under the direct guidance of Chairman Mao, reflects in many respects the personalization of authority which has characterized his thinking since he declared in 1939: 'If we did not have a Stalin, who would give the orders?'[2]

Perhaps the most striking illustration of this is the paragraph naming Lin Piao as Mao's successor. This passage has been widely discussed as a clue to the most likely outcome of the power struggle in China, but its ideological implications have been largely neglected. They are nothing less than startling. For the choice of a leader, like any other aspect of Party policy, is normally the prerogative of the Central Committee. By imposing in advance a decision which should properly be taken only after his death, and thus tying the hands of the Party's collective leadership in the future, Mao has indicated once more that for him, the Party as an organization is entirely subordinate to his own charisma and unique historical vision. The same viewpoint is evident in the provision of the new constitution which allows individual Party members to appeal over the heads of their immediate superiors not merely to the Central Committee, but to the Chairman (Mao Tse-tung) in person.

These attitudes are evident in every text emanating from Peking. Thus, in February 1967 it was stated, 'The current seizure of power from the handful of persons within the Party who are in authority and taking the capitalist road is not effected by dismissal and reorganization from above [i.e., by the Party organization itself], but from below by the mass movement called for and supported by Chairman Mao himself.' Or again, 'The proletarian revolutionary line that Chairman Mao represents is the highest authority in the great proletarian cultural revolution. All provisional organs of power that carry out this correct line in directing the struggle to seize power should have authority and do have it as a matter of course.' (See Text XIII 8.) It is, moreover, made abundantly clear that 'authority' really means authority, which exercises a stern dictatorship over all dissenters. Presumably those who enjoy such authority know from inner conviction that they

[1] For the text see *Peking Review*, no. 18, 1969, pp. 36-9.

[2] See *The Political Thought of Mao Tse-tung*, p. 427. For further reflections on this theme, see S. Schram, 'The Party in Chinese Communist Ideology', *China Quarterly*, no. 38, 1969.

are acting in harmony with Mao's correct line, just as those predestined to be saved in Calvin's scheme of things know they are acting in accordance with God's will – but if there is any doubt as to who is a true disciple, Chairman Mao himself will assuredly not fail to make his judgement known. The same viewpoint was reaffirmed in October 1968, when it was explained that Mao had deliberately tested communists in 'the great tempest of the turbulent and extremely complicated revolutionary movement' in order to 'ferret out the counter-revolutionaries' and permit the emergence of a new Party leadership at all levels wielded by those who 'are loyal to Chairman Mao, to Mao Tse-tung's Thought and to Chairman Mao's proletarian revolutionary line' (see Text XIII 10). Although it is stated that the numerous 'rebel fighters with proletarian consciousness' who have emerged in the course of the cultural revolution come 'from among the revolutionary masses, primarily the labouring masses, the workers, peasants and soldiers', the class criterion is manifestly less important than the ideological criterion of loyalty to Chairman Mao.

The parallel with the emperor, who was the fountainhead both of authority and of ideological orthodoxy, and the mediator between the Chinese nation and its historical destiny, is also suggestive. But Mao Tse-tung has now quite eclipsed all his predecessors in the intensity of his cult. It is impossible to grasp this point except from examples. Two will suffice. First, from the 'Message Saluting Chairman Mao Tse-tung' adopted at the rally to found the Peking Municipal Revolutionary Committee on 20 April 1967:

In the midst of our great struggle against and vigorous criticism and repudiation of the top Party person in authority taking the capitalist road [Liu Shao-ch'i] we proletarian revolutionaries of the capital, with great elation, report to you, the reddest red sun in our hearts, the exciting news that the Peking Municipal Revolutionary Committee has been set up. This is another paean of victory for your brilliant Thought soaring to the skies! This is another great victory for the proletarian revolutionary line you represent!

On this grandest festival of proletarian revolutionaries we cheer and sing, in one voice from thousands of hearts: Long live Chairman Mao! A long, long life to Chairman Mao!

Chairman Mao! When we think back over the inspiring course of the Chinese revolution words cannot express our boundless loyalty to you, neither song nor music is expressive enough to sing your praise, oceans are not vast enough to contain our boundless respect and love for you.[1]

And another example, from the editorial of *Liberation Army Daily* hailing the decision to issue to every member of the People's Liberation Army a badge with a portrait of Chairman Mao, and another with a quotation from his works:

[1] *Peking Review*, no. 18, 1967, p. 8.

Wearing shining badges with a profile of Chairman Mao and badges with a quotation from his works, we will be able at any moment to see the glorious image of our most respected and beloved leader Chairman Mao and constantly take to heart his good teachings. Having Chairman Mao with us, we will have immense wisdom and strength. We do not fear hidden shoals and we dare to climb a mountain of swords and brave a sea of flames and advance from victory to victory in the revolutionary direction indicated by our great helmsman, Chairman Mao.[1]

This fetishism of the leader's image is quite in harmony with the fetishism of his words, as contained in the little red-bound volume of *Quotations from Chairman Mao*. Not only are these used for the reading in unison of selected passages, reminiscent of a presbyterian service, which has become a regular feature of life in China since the autumn of 1966. The book itself is regarded as a kind of talisman, which is carried upon the person twenty-four hours a day and displayed on occasion as a warning to 'demons' and 'monsters'.

These extraordinary new developments of the Mao cult can, of course, be explained partly by the genuine attachment of the majority of the Chinese people to Mao Tse-tung, who led them to victory and appears to many of them as the symbol of China's rebirth as a modern nation. It is quite obvious, too, that Mao Tse-tung and his supporters have deliberately exploited the prestige of the charismatic leader as the only sufficient weapon at their disposal for countering the control of Liu Shao-ch'i and Teng Hsiao-p'ing over the organization. To probe further into this aspect of Mao's role would lead us into domains of collective psychology which are outside the scope of this book and of the competence of the authors. But however obsessive Mao's presence in China today, his image has not completely swallowed up the other aspect of the cultural revolution – the aim of transforming the mentality of the Chinese people and teaching them to think and act for themselves.

One of the first innovations in this domain was the putting forward, in the summer of 1966, of the slogan of a 'proletarian literature'. This term was used long ago in the Soviet Union to signify either the discovery and encouragement of writers issued from the proletariat and the peasantry, or the writing of works dealing with the life of the proletariat and adapted to the mentality of the proletariat. In the first sense the idea was condemned by Lenin as early as 1919; Stalin liquidated *Proletkult* in the second sense a decade later. Mao's line, laid down in 1942 in his talks at the Yenan Forum on Art and Literature, has always been that literature should be written for the masses, to serve their needs. This is the interpretation that was given to his views during the period when Liu Shao-ch'i and the other Party leaders now accused of attempting to 'restore capitalism' ran the cultural revolution.

[1] *Peking Review*, no. 21, 1967, p. 13.

But when Mao himself took over in May 1966, tendencies soon emerged which went even beyond those in the Soviet Union in the years immediately following the October Revolution. It was not merely that workers and peasants with literary talent should be encouraged to *become* writers; in line with the general tendency to belittle the role of experts in every field as 'reactionary bourgeois authorities', it was suggested that any worker or peasant could create works of literature. Thus a shipyard worker was quoted as saying in July 1966:

> We workers, peasants and soldiers must be and, without question, are able to be the masters of culture. We are participants in the three great revolutionary movements of class struggle, the struggle for production, and scientific experiment. Compared with others, we workers, peasants and soldiers are in the most favourable position to create literary and art works reflecting our life and struggles. Only in 1958 was I able to discard the designation of illiterate, but since 1959, I have been writing poems. I am a workman in a heat-treating shop. Those bourgeois 'poets' treated us workers with disdain, and never wrote any poems to praise us workers in the heat-treating shop. So I determined to write them myself. I wrote my first poem in 1959 and my worker colleagues were elated. They said: That's really good! It puts strength into us! So, in the past few years I have written nearly 300 poems. I must arm myself with Chairman Mao's *Talks* to seize hold of all cultural positions, to fight hard for the creation of proletarian literature and art.[1]

At the same time, in the name of proletarian culture, Mao's position regarding the selective assimilation of cultural values both from China's past and from foreign countries was largely repudiated. 'We are Marxist historicists,' Mao wrote in 1938; 'we must not mutilate history. From Confucius to Sun Yat-sen we must sum it up critically, and we must constitute ourselves the heirs of all that is precious in this past.'[2] Regarding learning from abroad he declared in 1940: 'We must absorb whatever we find useful today, not only from the present socialist or new-democratic cultures of other nations, but also from the older cultures of foreign countries, such as those of the various capitalist countries in the age of enlightenment.'[3]

Although lip service is still occasionally paid to the principle of selective absorption of elements from abroad and from China's past, Mao's ideas of thirty years ago have been largely forgotten in the present zeal to 'smash the old and set up the new'. At the same time, the Chinese have turned inside out Mao's thesis, put forward in the same speech of 1938, about the 'Sinification of Marxism'. Then Mao had declared that what he called 'abstract' Marxism – in other words, the general principles laid down in the writings of

[1] *Peking Review*, no. 29, 1966, pp. 4–5.
[2] *The Political Thought of Mao Tse-tung*, p. 172.
[3] ibid., p. 357.

Marx, Engels, and Lenin – was not merely useless but non-existent until it had been adapted to the concrete conditions in each country.[1] In 1945, as we have already seen, Liu Shao-ch'i hailed Mao as the theoretical genius who had already carried out this tremendous task of the 'Sinification of Marxism'.[2] Today, instead of recognizing that each people must assimilate Marxism in its own way, Mao has claimed for his own thought the universality he previously denied to Marx. Thus, even as they carry out a 'cultural revolution' which aims to make all things new, the Chinese have reverted to the conception of China as the centre of the world and the mentor of less-favoured peoples.

If we seek for a single concept which will provide the key to all of the recent developments in China, it is no doubt to be found in Mao's unwavering faith in the revolutionary capacities of the peasantry. Just as guerrilla warfare in the countryside opened the way to victory over the Kuomintang substantially without the participation of the urban working class, so the transformation and regeneration of Chinese society can begin in the countryside and spread from there to the cities. The revolutionary virtues of the Chinese peasants are such that they do not require the leadership either of the Party, as the emanation of the urban proletariat, or of more advanced countries such as the Soviet Union. All that they need is the guidance of the 'great leader, great teacher, great supreme commander and great helmsman', who will write upon their poverty and blankness the newest and most beautiful ideas,[3] and thus inspire them to act spontaneously as the builders of the new society and the vanguard of the historical process.

It would be frivolous and unfair to look upon these conceptions as simply the expression of the vanity and megalomania of an ageing leader, and to ignore the genuine need for a 'cultural revolution' in China. As we have stressed above, both the intellectual traditions and the social system of pre-revolutionary China had conditioned the masses of the population to the passive acceptance of authority, and there is no doubt that in all too many instances the Party bureaucrat was slipping into the role of the former scholar-official as the man of education whose word was to be accepted without question. But there remain grounds for doubt as to whether Mao's current methods will contribute to a real spirit of initiative among the masses, or whether the type of mass mobilization which is being carried on is compatible with modernization and economic development.

One of the most striking illustrations of the ambiguous tendencies of current policies is to be found in the decision of December 1968

[1] For the classic text, see *The Political Thought of Mao Tse-tung*, p. 172.

[2] See above p. 64, and the corresponding text, pp. 259–61.

[3] For Mao's 'poor and blank' hypothesis, see *The Political Thought of Mao Tse-tung*, pp. 101–3, 351–2.

to send idle young people from the cities to be re-educated by the poor peasants.[1] This is presented as a way of pursuing Marx's utopian goal of the abolition of the differences between town and countryside, but by suggesting that 'proletarian consciousness' can best be instilled into the sons of urban workers on the farms and not in the factories, Mao is in fact repudiating Marx, Lenin, and Soviet experience, all of which treat the interaction between town and countryside as a one-way street in which workers and intellectuals from the cities combat 'rural idiocy' instead of surrendering to it.

[1] On these new policies and their implications, see *The Political Thought of Mao Tse-tung*, pp. 110, 137.

CONCLUSION

We have traced the successive stages in the acclimatization of Marxism to Asia over the past century. We have seen how a form of thought which originally grew out of Marx's reflections on the destiny of European society has been transformed into a vehicle of Chinese nationalism. The practical consequences of these developments are immense and unpredictable, but that is not our concern here. Let us rather conclude with a few observations on the fate of Marxism today.

If one looks at the outward reality in which the doctrines forming the subject of this book are incarnated – what used to be called the 'socialist camp', and might now be loosely defined as those régimes and movements claiming to derive a substantial part of their inspiration from Lenin and the Russian revolution – the first impression is that current developments are merely the logical culmination of what has gone before. Are not European and Asian communists arguing, as they have been since the Second Comintern Congress, about the relative weight of the industrially developed nations and the world's 'countryside' in the revolution as a whole? Does not Mao, like Li Ta-chao, denounce the pretension of the West to cultural superiority, and proclaim that ultimate victory belongs to the peoples of Asia, Africa, and Latin America because they constitute the overwhelming majority of the world's population? And do not the Soviets retort by using the familiar argument, rooted in Marxist orthodoxy, according to which leadership belongs to the working class, and therefore to the advanced nations which possess a significant proletariat?

When we first undertook four years ago, in the introduction to the French edition of this book, to sum up the lessons of the half-century-old dialogue between European and Asian interpreters of Marxism, it seemed to us that despite the current sharp conflict the ultimate tendency was towards greater uniformity. We tended to think that, although the peoples of the underdeveloped countries were driven by their impatience with existing conditions to transform Marx's teaching in the direction of a greater emphasis on the role of the human will as compared to objective reality, in the long run they would return to a more orthodox interpretation. This seemed to be borne out by the example of the Soviet Union. 'The criticisms which the Soviets are today hurling at the Chinese', we wrote then, 'are, *mutatis mutandis*, the same ones which the socialists of Western Europe directed at them half a century ago, when they dared to carry out a socialist revolution in such an "Asiatic" and backward country as Russia. Having arrived at a level of economic development comparable to that of Western Europe at that time, the heirs of Lenin turn into neo-Kautskians, and excommunicate in the name of Lenin those who follow his example.' From this we ventured to draw the conclusion that a similar path would most likely be followed by all those who had embarked on revolution in the name of Marx, whatever their starting-point. 'Perhaps,' we wrote, 'in twenty or thirty years the ideologists in Peking will denounce the heresy of those who claim to create communist parties in the African jungle, where (as everyone knows) there is no proletariat. When that day comes, Marx will truly have had the last word.'

Despite the shattering of the 'socialist camp' and the multiplication of ideological perspectives, it still seems to us today that there is a certain underlying unity within this diversity. But the central axis along which communist régimes and movements of all tendencies are advancing now appears as radically different from that which we thought it possible to discern four years ago. Far from being characterized by the triumph of Marx's economic and social determinism, the evolution of communism today increasingly brings to the fore a theory which dissociates the task of carrying out the revolution not only from the proletariat, but from any class basis whatsoever.

The most remarkable example of this is no doubt furnished by the ideas propagated today in Cuba. Although professing their attachment to Marx, Fidel Castro and his authorized interpreters, such as Régis Debray, have replaced the proletariat not, as did Mao, by the peasantry, but in the first instance by a handful of individuals whose 'proletarian' character derives not from their social origins, nor even from the fact that they have been reshaped by a correct theory, but from their youthful vitality, skill in handling weapons, and isolation from the corrupting atmosphere of the cities. In this view, the revolutionary vocation depends primarily on a combination of geographical and biological qualities. On the one hand, 'the mountains proletarianize bourgeoisie and peasants, the city may bourgeoisify even the proletariat'.[1] On the other hand, 'there exists a profound link in Latin America between biology and ideology, wherever armed struggle is on the order of the day. However absurd or shocking this link may appear, it is none the less decisive. An elderly man, accustomed to the atmosphere of the city, has difficulty in adapting himself to the mountains, or to a lesser extent even to clandestine activity in the cities. . . . A

[1] Régis Debray, *Révolution dans la révolution* (Paris, Maspéro, 1967), p. 78.

perfect Marxist-Leninist education is not, in the first instance, an indispensable condition.'[1]

Although Lenin, as we have seen, launched a trend towards élitism by shifting the accent from the proletariat to the Party as the instrument of the revolution, these ideas of the Cubans are accompanied by an extreme emphasis on the role of the leader and his little band of comrades-in-arms that smacks more of Blanqui, not to say of Nietzsche, than of the Leninist tradition. In this respect, Debray has revised Lenin in the opposite direction from Mao, towards an even greater stress on the educated minority instead of towards a populist faith in the peasant masses. But in other ways there is convergence between the ideological tendencies of the Chinese and of the Cubans. For both, Marxism can be summed up to a large extent in two postulates: revolution must be carried out in the name of the disinherited, who are baptized 'proletarian' without any reference to their precise social origin; and this revolution must be carried out – at least in the beginning – not *by* the masses but *for* the masses.

The idea that revolution is simply the revolt of the oppressed, whoever they may be, against their oppressors, is in fact widely shared by other Asian revolutionaries, and lies at the heart of the whole debate about the strategy and tactics of world revolution. A corollary of this proposition, which is taken as a matter of course both by Mao Tse-tung and by the Cubans, is that the desire and capacity to make revolution are directly proportional to the degree of misery suffered by a given people or social category, and have little to do with their role in the productive process. To say that, in reasoning thus, Mao, Castro and the others have merely carried to its logical extreme Lenin's accentuation of the voluntarist element in Marxism at the expense of its determinist element is in fact to minimize the break which these ideas represent with the very essence of Marxism and with the whole history of the Communist movement. In fact the rupture goes much deeper, and involves not merely discarding a certain number of Marxist axioms judged (as Liu Shao-ch'i said in praising Mao in 1945 – see Text IX 1) 'obsolete' or not adapted to Chinese conditions, but a frontal attack on Marx's most fundamental aims and beliefs.

Though Marx was a bitter political enemy of the bourgeoisie, he had the profoundest respect for the material and technical accomplishments of bourgeois society in his own age, and regarded capitalism as infinitely more progressive than feudalism. We have seen that this positive and optimistic attitude towards the ultimate consequences of capitalist development was carried over in his evaluation of the effects of the British rule in India. Today we encounter among revolutionaries in Asia, Africa and Latin America

[1] ibid., pp. 107–8. Note the parallel between these ideas and the emphasis on 'vigour' as a criterion for selecting new Party leaders in Text XIII 10.

not only a total hostility towards the 'imperialists' and all those who profit from imperialist exploitation of the non-European countries, but a virtual denial that the capitalist and imperialist phase in world history has contributed anything positive either economically, scientifically, culturally or otherwise. This involves in fact the complete abandonment of the whole logic of Marxism, which implies that, while the proletariat will smash the bourgeois state machine, it will at the same time build upon the cultural and technical heritage of the bourgeoisie.

Meanwhile, as we have already observed, Marxism in the Soviet Union is undergoing a decline less spectacular but none the less real. Soviet theorists today hail the revolutionary character of military régimes created by the petty bourgeoisie and the well-to-do peasantry who have imposed the domination of a single party having no links whatever with the working class. They assure us that these régimes are not the emanation of the *milieu* from which their leaders originated, and that the army is a national institution which transcends classes because historical circumstances confer on it a leading function. In so doing, they display, to be sure, a great deal of realism in recognizing the situation which has taken shape in many underdeveloped countries. By the same token, Soviet theory tends to base itself on concrete situations, and to disregard any link between these situations and class relationships. Such an attitude appears to correspond rather to the necessity of justifying diplomatic actions than to a rigorous theoretical analysis. But it would be superficial to conclude that only considerations of opportunism and diplomatic manoeuvring are involved. For Marxism is everywhere being revised today, in directions which are less contradictory than they appear at first sight, and in fact there are parallels between these Soviet conceptions and the Chinese and Cuban attitudes already mentioned.

As regards the non-European countries, it is clear that the Soviets are no more inclined than the Cubans or the Chinese to attribute, as did Marx, a decisive importance to social classes as the central fact in any political analysis. On the contrary, although the word 'proletariat' is on everyone's lips, the tendency is to substitute for the working class (and in some instances even for its 'vanguard', the Communist Party) a variety of forces of which the social basis plays no great role. First place among these non-class or super-class forces belongs, of course, to the army, which is considered both as the key element in the political system and the most coherent force for replacing a weak or non-existent proletariat.

Similarly, Soviets and Chinese agree in their evaluation of the revolutionary potential of the proletariat of the advanced countries, though they disagree in the conclusions they draw from this analysis. Both are convinced of the profoundly ingrained reformist tendencies of the Western proletariat, and its total unwillingness to indulge in revolutionary struggle. The Soviets continue to place their hopes in an eventual rebirth of revolutionary spirit in the West, whereas the Chinese, despite occasional references to student militancy in Europe and America, do not appear to see any real prospect that the 'epicentre of world revolutionary storms' will move back to the highly-developed industrial countries in the near future.

Thus, while the Chinese attitude appears relatively consistent, Soviet thinking is characterized by the contradiction between a nostalgic attachment to Marxist orthodoxy in Europe, and the complete abandonment of the role of classes when dealing with non-European societies. Perhaps the Soviet theorists hope that this contradiction will one day be resolved when the non-European countries have attained a level of development similar to that of Russia in 1917, and when as a result their class structures are more in conformity with traditional Marxist analysis. But it is rather strange for the heirs of Marx to imagine that the methods of analysis of the founder of scientific socialism fail to apply to a whole historical epoch.

In any case, when one considers both the various theories which call themselves Marxist, and the realities of the world today, it would seem that the only alternative lies in a choice between a scholastic Marxism which has nothing to do with revolution and a revolution which has nothing in common with Marxism. Never, in the course of the past century, has the name of Marx been so widely invoked; never has this name served to justify so many ideas and actions totally foreign to the genius of Marx.

Hélène Carrère d'Encausse
Stuart R. Schram

PART 2. Texts

SECTION I: MARX AND THE SECOND INTERNATIONAL

1. The Consequences of British Rule in India

This text is composed of extracts from two articles by Marx, entitled 'The British Rule in India' and 'The Future Results of the British Rule in India', written respectively on 10 June and 22 July 1853 for the *New York Daily Tribune*. We have also added one sentence on the same theme from Marx's letter of 14 June 1853 to Engels. Marx here developed for the first time his ideas on 'oriental despotism'.[1]

I share not the opinion of those who believe in a golden age of Hindustan. . . .

There cannot, however, remain any doubt but that the misery inflicted by the British on Hindustan is of an essentially different and infinitely more intensive kind than all Hindustan had to suffer before. . . .

All the civil wars, invasions, revolutions, conquests, famines, strangely complex, rapid and destructive as the successive action in Hindustan may appear, did not go deeper than its surface. England has broken down the entire framework of Indian society, without any symptoms of reconstitution yet appearing. This loss of his old world, with no gain of a new one, imparts a particular kind of melancholy to the present misery of the Hindu, and separates Hindustan, ruled by Britain, from all its ancient traditions, and from the whole of its past history.

There have been in Asia, generally, from immemorial times, but three departments of Government: that of Finance, or the plunder of the interior; that of War, or the plunder of the exterior; and, finally, the department of Public Works. Climate and territorial conditions, especially the vast tracts of desert, extending from the Sahara, through Arabia, Persia, India and Tartary, to the most elevated Asiatic highlands, constituted artificial irrigation by canals and waterworks the basis of Oriental agriculture. . . . This prime necessity of an economical and common use of water, which, in the Occident, drove private enterprise to voluntary association, as in Flanders and Italy, necessitated, in the Orient where civilization was too low and the territorial extent too vast to call into life voluntary association, the interference of the centralizing power of Government. . . .

Now, the British in East India accepted from their predecessors

[1] SOURCE: K. Marx and F. Engels, *On Colonialism* (Moscow, Foreign Languages Publishing House), pp. 32–9, 83–90 *passim*.

the departments of finance and of war, but they have neglected entirely that of public works. Hence the deterioration of an agriculture which is not capable of being conducted on the British principle of free competition, of *laissez-faire* and *laissez-aller*. But in Asiatic empires we are quite accustomed to see agriculture deteriorating under one government and reviving again under some other government. . . . Thus the oppression and neglect of agriculture, bad as it is, could not be looked upon as the final blow dealt to Indian society by the British intruder, had it not been attended by a circumstance of quite different importance, a novelty in the annals of the whole Asiatic world. However changing the political aspect of India's past must appear, its social condition has remained unaltered since its remotest antiquity, until the first decennium of the nineteenth century. The hand-loom and the spinning-wheel, producing their regular myriads of spinners and weavers, were the pivots of the structure of that society. From immemorial times, Europe received the admirable textures of Indian labour, sending in return for them her precious metals. . . .

It was the British intruder who broke up the Indian hand-loom and destroyed the spinning-wheel. England began with driving the Indian cottons from the European market; it then introduced twist into Hindustan and in the end inundated the very mother country of cotton with cottons. . . .

These two circumstances – the Hindu, on the one hand, leaving, like all Oriental peoples, to the Central Government the care of the great public works, the prime condition of his agriculture and commerce, dispersed, on the other hand, over the surface of the country, and agglomerated in small centres by the domestic union of agricultural and manufacturing pursuits – these two circumstances had brought about, since the remotest times, a social system of particular features – the so-called *village system*, which gave to each of these small unions their independent organization and distinct life. . . .

The break-up of these primitive stereotype forms was the condition *sine qua non* of Europeanization.[1]

These small stereotype forms of social organism have been to the greater part dissolved, and are disappearing, not so much through the brutal interference of the British tax-gatherer and the British soldier, as to the working of English steam and English free trade. Those family-communities were based on domestic industry, in that peculiar combination of hand-weaving, hand-spinning and hand-tilling agriculture which gave them self-supporting power. English interference having placed the spinner in Lancashire and the weaver in Bengal, or sweeping away both Hindu spinner and weaver, dissolved these small semi-barbarian, semi-civilized communities, by blowing up their economical basis, and thus produced

[1] Sentence taken from Marx's letter of 14 June 1853.

the greatest, and, to speak the truth, the only *social* revolution ever heard of in Asia.

Now, sickening as it must be to human feeling to witness those myriads of industrious patriarchal and inoffensive social organizations disorganized and dissolved into their units, thrown into a sea of woes, and their individual members losing at the same time their ancient form of civilization and their hereditary means of subsistence, we must not forget that these idyllic village communities, inoffensive though they may appear, had always been the solid foundation of Oriental despotism, that they restrained the human mind within the smallest possible compass, making it the unresisting tool of superstition, enslaving it beneath traditional rules, depriving it of all grandeur and historical energies. We must not forget the barbarian egotism which, concentrating on some miserable patch of land, had quietly witnessed the ruin of empires, the perpetration of unspeakable cruelties, the massacre of the population of large towns, with no other consideration bestowed upon them than on natural events, itself the helpless prey of any aggressor who deigned to notice it at all. We must not forget that this undignified, stagnatory, and vegetative life, that this passive sort of existence evoked on the other part, in contradistinction, wild, aimless, unbounded forces of destruction, and rendered murder itself a religious rite in Hindustan. We must not forget that these little communities were contaminated by distinctions of caste and by slavery, that they subjugated man to external circumstances instead of elevating man to be the sovereign of circumstances, that they transformed a self-developing social state into never changing natural destiny, and thus brought about a brutalizing worship of nature, exhibiting its degradation in the fact that man, the sovereign of nature, fell down on his knees in adoration of Hanuman, the monkey, and Sabbala, the cow.

England, it is true, in causing a social revolution in Hindustan, was actuated only by the vilest interests, and was stupid in her manner of enforcing them. But that is not the question. The question is, can mankind fulfil its destiny without a fundamental revolution in the social state of Asia? If not, whatever may have been the crimes of England she was the unconscious tool of history in bringing about that revolution.

England has to fulfil a double mission in India: one destructive, the other regenerating – the annihilation of old Asiatic society, and the laying of the material foundations of Western society in Asia.

Arabs, Turks, Tartars, Moguls, who had successively overrun India, soon became *Hinduized*, the barbarian conquerors being, by an eternal law of history, conquered themselves by the superior civilization of their subjects. The British were the first conquerors superior, and, therefore, inaccessible to Hindu civilization. They destroyed it by breaking up the native communities, by uprooting the native industry, and by levelling all that was great and elevated in the native society. The historic pages of their rule in India report hardly anything beyond that destruction. The work of regeneration hardly transpires through a heap of ruins. Nevertheless it has begun.

The political unity of India, more consolidated, and extending farther than it ever did under the Great Moguls, was the first condition of its regeneration. That unity, imposed by the British sword, will now be strengthened and perpetuated by the electric telegraph. The native army, organized and trained by the British drill-sergeant, was the *sine qua non* of Indian self-emancipation, and of India ceasing to be the prey for the first foreign intruder. The free press, introduced for the first time into Asiatic society, and managed principally by the common offspring of Hindus and Europeans, is a new and powerful agent of reconstruction. The *zemindari* and *ryotwari* themselves, abominable as they are, involve two distinct forms of private property in land – the great desideratum of Asiatic society. From the Indian natives, reluctantly and sparingly educated at Calcutta, under English superintendence, a fresh class is springing up, endowed with the requirements for government and imbued with European science. Steam has brought India into regular and rapid communication with Europe, has connected its chief ports with those of the whole south-eastern ocean, and has revindicated it from the isolated position which was the prime law of its stagnation. The day is not far distant when, by a combination of railways and steam vessels, the distance between England and India, measured by time, will be shortened to eight days, and when that once fabulous country will thus be actually annexed to the Western world. . . .

Modern industry, resulting from the railway system, will dissolve the hereditary divisions of labour, upon which rest the Indian castes, those decisive impediments to Indian progress and Indian power.

All the English bourgeoisie may be forced to do will neither emancipate nor materially mend the social condition of the mass of the people, depending not only on the development of the productive powers, but on their appropriation by the people. But what they will not fail to do is to lay down the material premises for both. Has the bourgeoisie ever done more? Has it ever effected a progress without dragging individuals and peoples through blood and dirt, through misery and degradation?

The Indians will not reap the fruits of the new elements of society scattered among them by the British bourgeoisie, till in Great Britain itself the now ruling classes shall have been supplanted by the industrial proletariat, or till the Hindus themselves shall have grown strong enough to throw off the English yoke altogether. At all events, we may safely expect to see, at a more or less remote period, the regeneration of that great and interesting country, whose gentle natives are, to use the expression of Prince Saltykov, even in the most inferior classes, '*plus fins et plus adroits que les Italiens*', whose submission even is counterbalanced by a certain calm nobility, who, notwithstanding their natural languor, have astonished the British officers by their bravery, whose country has been the source of our languages, our religions, and who represent the type of the ancient German in the Jat and the type of the ancient Greek in the Brahmin.

The devastating effects of English industry, when contemplated with regard to India, a country as vast as Europe, and containing 150 millions of acres, are palpable and confounding. But we must not forget that they are only the organic results of the whole system of production as it is now constituted. . . . The bourgeois period of history has to create the material basis of the new world – on the one hand the universal intercourse founded upon the mutual dependency of mankind, and the means of that intercourse; on the other hand the development of the productive powers of man and the transformation of material production into a scientific domination of natural agencies. . . .

When a great social revolution shall have mastered the results of the bourgeois epoch, the market of the world and the modern powers of production, and subjected them to the common control of the most advanced peoples, then only will human progress cease to resemble that hideous pagan idol, who would not drink the nectar but from the skulls of the slain.

2. *Revolution in China and in Europe*

In these extracts from an article of the same title written on 20 May 1853 for the *New York Daily Tribune*, Marx suggests already that revolutionary upheavals in Asia can have important repercussions in Europe.[1]

A most profound yet fantastic speculator on the principles which govern the movements of Humanity,[2] was wont to extol as one of the ruling secrets of nature, what he called the law of the contact of extremes. . . .

Whether the 'contact of extremes' be such a universal principle or not, a striking illustration of it may be seen in the effect the Chinese revolution seems likely to exercise upon the civilized world. It may seem a very strange, and a very paradoxical assertion that the next uprising of the people of Europe, and their next movement for republican freedom and economy of government, may depend more probably on what is now passing in the Celestial Empire – the very opposite of Europe – than on any other political cause that now exists – more even than on the menaces of Russia and the consequent likelihood of a general European war. But yet it is no paradox, as all

[1] SOURCE: K. Marx and F. Engels, *On Colonialism*, pp. 15–23 *passim*.
[2] Hegel.

may understand by attentively considering the circumstances of the case.

Whatever be the social causes, and whatever religious, dynastic, or national shape they may assume, that have brought about the chronic rebellions subsisting in China for about ten years past, and now gathered together in one formidable revolution, the occasion of this outbreak has unquestionably been afforded by the English cannon forcing upon China that soporific drug called opium. Before the British arms the authority of the Manchu dynasty fell to pieces; the superstitious faith in the eternity of the Celestial Empire broke down; the barbarous and hermetic isolation from the civilized world was infringed; and an opening was made for that intercourse which has since proceeded so rapidly under the golden attractions of California and Australia. At the same time the silver coin of the Empire, its lifeblood began to be drained away to the British East Indies. . . .

. . . Complete isolation was the prime condition of the preservation of old China. That isolation having come to a violent end by the medium of England, dissolution must follow as surely as that of any mummy carefully preserved in a hermetically sealed coffin, whenever it is brought into contact with the open air. Now, England having brought about the revolution of China, the question is how that revolution will in time react on England, and through England on Europe. This question is not difficult of solution.

The attention of our readers has often been called to the unparalleled growth of British manufactures since 1850. Amid the most surprising prosperity, it has not been difficult to point out the clear symptoms of an approaching industrial crisis. Notwithstanding California and Australia, notwithstanding the immense and unprecedented emigration, there must ever, without any particular accident, in due time arrive a moment when the extension of the markets is unable to keep pace with the extension of British manufactures, and this disproportion must bring about a new crisis with the same certainty as it has done in the past. But, if one of the great markets suddenly becomes contracted, the arrival of the crisis is necessarily accelerated thereby. Now, the Chinese rebellion must, for the time being, have precisely this effect upon England. . . .

Under these circumstances, as the greater part of the regular commercial circle has already been run through by British trade, it may safely be augured that the Chinese revolution will throw the spark into the overloaded mine of the present industrial system and cause the explosion of the long-prepared general crisis, which, spreading abroad, will be closely followed by political revolutions on the Continent. It would be a curious spectacle, that of China sending disorder into the Western World while the Western powers, by English, French and American war-steamers, are conveying 'order' to Shanghai, Nanking, and the mouths of the Great Canal. . . .

3. Revolution in the Mother Country and Revolution in the Colonies

This brief extract from a letter of 10 December 1869 from Marx to Engels has often been cited in polemics within the socialist movement, in the course of the past half century, regarding the possibility that the colonial peoples can play an active role, and even take the initiative, in world revolution.[1]

. . . Quite apart from all the 'international' and 'humane' phrases about *justice for Ireland*, which may be taken as a matter of course in the Council of the International, it is in the direct and absolute interest of the *English working class to get rid of their present connexion with Ireland.* This is my deepest conviction, for reasons which in part I cannot indicate to the English workers themselves. I long believed that it would be possible to overthrow the Irish régime through *English working class ascendancy*. I have always defended this viewpoint in the *New York Tribune*. More thorough study has now convinced me of the exact opposite. The *English working class* will never accomplish anything *before it has got rid of Ireland.* The lever must be applied in Ireland. This is why the Irish question is so important for the social movement in general.

4. Class Collaboration in Dependent Countries, on the Basis of the Polish Example

Extracts from the series of articles entitled 'The Polish Debate in Frankfurt', attributed to Marx at the time of their publication, but in fact written by Engels. The following passages are from the article of 19 August 1848.[2]

The partition of Poland was realized thanks to the alliance of the great feudal aristocracy in Poland with the three powers carrying out the partition. . . .

The consequence, already in the case of the first partition, was quite naturally to bring about an alliance of all the other classes, that is of the nobility, of the urban bourgeoisie, and in part of the peasants, directed both against the oppressors of Poland and against the great aristocracy of the country itself. The constitution of 1791 shows how well the Poles understood, even at that time, that their independence from foreign powers was indissolubly linked to

[1] SOURCE: *Der Briefwechsel zwischen Friedrich Engels und Karl Marx, 1844 bis 1883*, edited by August Bebel and Eduard Bernstein (Stuttgart, Dietz Verlag, 1913), vol. IV, pp. 225–6. Like all of Marx's correspondence with Engels, this letter is studded with expressions in English. The words in italics appear in English in the German text.

[2] SOURCE: *Aus dem literarischen Nachlass von Karl Marx, Friedrich Engels und Ferdinand Lassalle*, edited by Franz Mehring (Stuttgart, Dietz Verlag, 1902), vol. III, p. 149.

the overthrow of the aristocracy and to agrarian reform within the country.

The great agricultural countries between the Baltic and the Black Sea can free themselves from patriarchal-feudal barbarism only through an agrarian revolution which will transform the peasants from their condition of serfdom or of subjection to the corvée into the free owners of the land – a revolution which will be exactly the same as the French revolution of 1789 in the countryside. The Polish nation has the merit of having been the first among all its agricultural neighbour peoples to proclaim this. . . .

Since the very day when they were first subjugated, the Poles began to engage in revolutionary activity, thus binding their oppressors even more tightly to counter-revolution. They obliged their oppressors to maintain patriarchal-feudal conditions not only in Poland, but in the other countries subject to their domination. Especially since the Krakow uprising of 1846, the struggle for Polish independence has become at the same time the struggle of agrarian democracy – the only one possible in Eastern Europe – against patriarchal-feudal absolutism.

So long, therefore, as we help to oppress Poland, so long as we chain part of Poland to Germany, we will ourselves be chained to Russia and to Russian policy, and we will be incapable of radically smashing patriarchal-feudal absolutism in our own country. The re-establishment of a democratic Poland is the first condition for the re-establishment of a democratic Germany.

5. The Role of the Peasants in the Revolution, on the Basis of the French Example

Extracts from Marx's book *The 18th Brumaire of Louis Bonaparte*, published for the first time in 1852. The passages in italic were removed by Marx[1] in preparing the second edition of 1869.[2]

The economic development of small peasant holdings brought about a fundamental upheaval in the relations of the peasantry with the other classes of society. Under Napoleon [I], the division of the land into peasant small holdings merely carried to completion in the countryside the system of free competition by big industry then getting under way in the cities. *The very privileged treatment enjoyed by the peasant class was in the interest of the new bourgeois society. This newly created class was the universal extension of the bourgeois system beyond the gates of the cities, its realization on a national scale.* It constituted an omnipresent protest against the landed aristocracy which had just been overthrown. *If the peasants enjoyed*

[1] For interesting indications regarding the history of these textual changes see H. Mayer's article in *Cahiers de l'I.S.E.A.* (*série* S. 2), pp. 101–2.

[2] SOURCE: Marx and Engels, *Werke*, vol. 8 (Berlin, Dietz Verlag, 1960), pp. 201–4.

a privileged treatment, it was because more than any other class they constituted a basis for an offensive against the restoration of the feudal lords. The roots which peasant small holding put down into the soil of France deprived feudalism of all nourishment. Its fences constituted the natural rampart of the bourgeoisie against any *coup de main* of its former masters. But during the nineteenth century, the usurer in the cities replaced the feudal lords, the mortgage replaced feudal land rights, and bourgeois capital replaced aristocratic landed property. The peasant's small holding is no longer anything but the pretext which allows capitalism to draw profit, interest and rent from the land, and to leave to the peasant himself the problem of how to get himself a salary. . . . Consequently, the interest of the peasant is no longer, as under Napoleon, in conformity but in contradiction with the interests of the bourgeoisie and of capital. They therefore find their natural ally and guide in the urban proletariat, whose task is the overthrow of the bourgeois order. . . .

All the 'Napoleonic ideas' are the ideas of the small holding which is not yet developed and still has the freshness of youth. They are an absurdity for the small holding which has outlived its time. They are nothing but the hallucinations of its agony, words which transform themselves into phrases, spirits which transform themselves into ghosts. But the parody of imperialism was necessary to free the mass of the French nation from the weight of tradition and to make manifest in all its purity the opposition which exists between the state power and society. With the progressive ruin of the peasant small holding the whole state edifice built upon it collapses. The political centralization required by modern society can only be edified on the ruins of the military and bureaucratic governmental apparatus constructed in the past in order to struggle against feudalism. . . . *In losing hope in the Napoleonic restoration, the French peasant loses faith in his small holding, overthrows the whole state apparatus built on that small holding, and thus the proletarian revolution obtains the chorus without which, in all peasant countries, its solo becomes a swan song.* . . .

6. *People's War in China*

Extracts from Engels's article 'Persia and China', written on 22 May 1857 for the *New York Daily Tribune*.[1]

There is evidently a different spirit among the Chinese now to what they showed in the war of 1840 to 1842.[2] Then, the people were quiet; they left the Emperor's soldiers to fight the invaders, and submitted after a defeat with Eastern fatalism to the power of the enemy. But now, at least in the southern provinces, to which the

[1] SOURCE: K. Marx and F. Engels, *On Colonialism*, pp. 123–8 *passim*.

[2] i.e. the Opium War.

contest has so far been confined, the mass of the people take an active, nay, a fanatical part in the struggle against the foreigners. They poison the bread of the European community at Hong Kong by wholesale, and with the coolest premeditation. . . . They kidnap and kill every foreigner within their reach. . . . The piratical policy of the British Government has caused this universal outbreak of all Chinese against all foreigners, and marked it as a war of extermination.

. . . Civilization-mongers who throw hot shell on a defenceless city and add rape to murder may call the system cowardly, barbarous, atrocious; but what matters it to the Chinese if it be only successful? Since the British treat them as barbarians, they cannot deny to them the full benefit of their barbarism. . . .

In short, instead of moralizing on the horrible atrocities of the Chinese, as the chivalrous English press does, we had better recognize that this is a war *pro aris et focis*, a popular war for the maintenance of Chinese nationality, with all its overbearing prejudice, stupidity, learned ignorance and pedantic barbarism if you like, but yet a popular war. And in a popular war the means used by the insurgent nation cannot be measured by the commonly recognized rules of regular warfare, nor by any other abstract standard, but by the degree of civilization only attained by that insurgent nation. . . .

One thing is certain, that the death-hour of old China is rapidly drawing nigh. . . . The very fanaticism of the southern Chinese in their struggle against foreigners seems to mark a consciousness of the supreme danger in which old China is placed; and before many years pass away, we shall have to witness the death-struggle of the oldest empire in the world, and the opening day of a new era for all Asia.

7. *What the European Workers Think*

Extract from a letter from Engels to Kautsky, dated 12 September 1882.[1]

. . . You ask me what the English workers think of colonial policy. Well, exactly the same as they think about politics in general; the same as the bourgeois think. There is no workers' party here, you see, there are only Conservatives and Liberal-Radicals, and the workers joyfully share in the feast of England's monopoly of the world market and the colonies. In my opinion, the colonies proper, i.e. the countries occupied by a European population – Canada, the Cape, Australia – will all become independent. On the other hand, the countries inhabited by a native population, which are simply subjugated – India, Algeria, the Dutch, Portuguese and Spanish possessions – must be taken over for the time being by the proletariat and led as rapidly as possible towards independence. How

[1] SOURCE: *Friedrich Engels' Briefwechsel mit Karl Kautsky* (Vienna, Danubia Verlag, 1955), p. 63; translation adapted from *On Colonialism*, pp. 340–41.

this process will develop is difficult to say. India will, perhaps, or even very probably, make a revolution, and as a proletariat which is in the process of emancipating itself cannot conduct any colonial wars, this revolution would have to be allowed to run its course. It would not pass off without all sorts of destruction, of course, but that sort of thing is inseparable from all revolutions. The same thing might happen elsewhere, for example in Algeria or Egypt, and that would certainly be the best *for us*. We shall have enough to do at home. Once Europe is reorganized, and North America, that will furnish such colossal power and such an example that the semi-civilized countries will of themselves follow in their wake; economic needs in themselves will see to that. But as to what social and political phases these countries will then have to pass through before they likewise arrive at socialist organization, I think we can today advance only rather idle hypotheses. One thing alone is certain: the victorious proletariat can force no blessings of any kind upon any foreign nation without undermining its own victory by so doing. Which of course by no means excludes defensive wars of various kinds. . . .

8. Colonial Policy at the International Socialist Congress of Amsterdam (14–20 August 1904)

It is in his report drawn up for this Congress that the Dutch social democrat Van Kol set forth for the first time the idea that the socialists should not limit themselves to asking for the abolition of the colonies, but rather should advance a 'positive colonial policy'. The other *rapporteur* on this question, the Englishman Hyndman, adopted, on the contrary, an attitude of admiration for the non-European civilizations which is rather exceptional for the period and scarcely compatible with the spirit of Marx.[1]

VAN KOL'S REPORT

. . . The tendency towards colonial expansion is universal; it is a consequence of the development of capitalist society. . . .

Capitalism leads to imperialism and it, in turn, inevitably encourages militarism, which ruins the peoples and sucks the marrow from their bones. . . .

And in spite of all that, will it be necessary to condemn every colonial possession, in every case, and at all times and in all places?

The new needs which will make themselves felt after the victory of the working class and its economic emancipation will make the possession of colonies necessary, even under the future socialist system of government.

[1] SOURCE: *Congrès socialiste international d'Amsterdam des 14–20 août 1904.* Rapports et Projets des Résolutions sur les questions de l'ordre du jour par le Secrétariat socialiste international. Brussels, 1904, pp. 36–82 *passim.*

Modern countries will no longer be able to get along without countries furnishing certain raw materials and tropical products indispensable to industry and the needs of humanity, and this will be the case as long as they cannot be procured by the exchange of products of native industry and commerce.[1]

Even the socialist society of the future will therefore have to define its colonial policy, regulating the relations of the countries which have reached a level on the scale of economic development superior to that of the backward races. . . .

. . . Can we abandon half the globe to the caprice of peoples still in their infancy, who leave the enormous wealth of the subsoil undeveloped and the most fertile parts of our planet uncultivated? Or shall we have to intervene in the interest of all humanity so that the earth which is the property of the human race may furnish all its inhabitants with a means of existence? Must we not understand by socialization of the means of production that the means of living and working belong to everyone? . . .

The hypothesis of Karl Marx that certain countries will be able, at least in part, to bypass the capitalist period in their economic development has not been realized; the primitive peoples will reach civilization only by bearing this cross. It is therefore our duty not to hinder the development of capitalism, an indispensable chain in the history of humanity; we can even favour its appearance while trying to alleviate the pains of childbirth. . . .

. . . We socialists, free of any racial or colour prejudice, keep in our heart a limitless hope in the future of these so-called 'inferior races'. What they are now, we have formerly been; what we have become, they can become in a future perhaps closer than many think because the evolution of humanity moves at an ever quicker pace. The time will come when the hot belt of the globe will be inhabited by yellow or black races who will no longer feel inferior to the whites and who will no longer need our tutelage, being capable of guiding themselves. . . .

. . . But all that is a question of the far-off future. For a long time to come we shall have to protect ourselves against backward forms of production, and from now on the workers of the civilized countries will have to secure themselves against the deadly competition of colonial labour.

HYNDMAN'S REPORT

. . . India is the greatest and most populous empire which has ever been under the control of a nation. Reasonably governed, it would, at present, be one of the most powerful and influential lands in the world. Arts, great literature, great monuments, great industrial works and great military bravery, great laws, great financiers and great legislators shed lustre on its long annals, alongside terrible

[1] Quoted from a draft resolution proposed by Van Kol.

events, comparable to those which were frequent in Europe at the same periods.... Our mission has been to destroy all this greatness and this prosperity and to reduce the inhabitants of the English territories to absolute poverty.

This is a hideous crime. Socialism itself is less important for western Europe than the prevention of this large-scale atrocity. As an Englishman and as a member of a family which has lived in our islands for centuries, I call upon this international Congress to denounce before the civilized world, the statesmen and the nation guilty of this infamy. I beg them to send to the inhabitants of India the heart-felt wishes of the delegates of the workers of all the nations here assembled, with the wish that they may liberate themselves finally in any way possible from the horrors of the most criminal tyranny which has ever afflicted humanity.

But India furnishes only the most striking example of the ignominy of modern capitalism in the colonies. I do not say that the English are worse than the others. Not the least in the world. They have only had the first opportunities and pursue the same system on a larger scale than rival nations. . . .

9. The Stuttgart Congress (1907)

This Congress saw the first great debate on the ideas outlined three years earlier in the Van Kol report to the Amsterdam Congress.[1]

Third Committee

DAVID (Germany): I call for the vote of a resolution stating that the socialist congress accepts the principle of colonization on the grounds that the occupation and exploitation of the entire world are indispensable for the well-being of humanity, but it is of course understood as well that the resolution must also criticize the management of present-day capitalism. We must get out of the realm of words. Europe needs colonies. It does not even have enough of them. Without colonies, we should be comparable, from an economic standpoint, to China.

LEDEBOUR (Germany): Citizen David has neglected the main question, for any colonial policy . . . is necessarily capitalistic because the exploitation of colonies is a result of capitalism itself. David fancies that these abominations can be avoided. . . . This is a fundamental mistake. . . . I consider, on the contrary, that the present colonial policy is the inevitable result of capitalism, and it is only by the resistance of those who are exploited that one will be able to a certain extent to diminish the brutalities that we all deplore. But in the colonies one can hardly count on the force of resistance of the exploited. This is almost completely lacking in the

[1] SOURCE: *VIIe Congrès socialiste international tenu à Stuttgart du 16 au 24 août 1907.* Compte rendu analytique publié par le Secrétariat du Bureau socialiste international, Brussels, Veuve Désiré Brismée, 1908, pp. 216–28, 284–322 *passim.*

native population. Contrary to David's opinion, I think that we must put at the head of our resolution that we do not expect any progress in civilization from capitalistic colonial policy, and as we are, in principle, adversaries of any exploitation and oppression in our own country, we must likewise combat, in principle, an exploitation and an oppression which are prevalent to an even greater extent in the colonies.

TERWAGNE (Belgium): In the name of the minority of the committee and of my party, I recommend that the following introduction be added to the resolution: 'The Congress does not condemn in principle and for all time, every colonial policy; under a socialist régime, colonization can be a work of civilization.'

ROUANET (France): I think it is false to consider colonization as a purely capitalistic phenomenon. Colonization is a historical fact as well. For this reason I support Terwagne's resolution. It is possible, starting immediately, to obtain considerable improvements in the colonies. . . . I find that it is all too easy to blame everything on capitalism and to saddle it with all the crimes of colonization. This is not a capitalistic but a historical phenomenon. . . .

The peoples of the civilized European and American countries find themselves before enormous expanses. Should they or should they not use these expanses to better the economic existence of their countries? I answer in the affirmative. In this case, it is necessary to examine the question of colonization, even if it be bourgeois colonization.

DAVID (Germany): I move that the draft resolution be preceded by the following text:

> The Congress, noting that socialism needs the productive forces of the entire globe, destined to be put at the disposal of humanity and to raise peoples of all colours and languages to the highest culture, sees in the colonizing idea, considered in this respect, an integral element of the universal aim of civilization pursued by the socialist movement.

TERWAGNE (Belgium): For us Belgians the question is as follows: 'Shall we leave the Congo in the state in which it is, or else do we want to better conditions there?'. . . . Do not close the door to the future! If from one day to the next the product of the colonies was suppressed, industry would be seriously damaged. It is therefore logical that men turn to account all the riches of the globe, whatever may be the places in which they are situated. . . . I therefore recommend the amendment which I introduced and which was, moreover, in the original draft of the text proposed by Van Kol.

Chairman VAN KOL: What Terwagne has just said is correct. The first draft of my resolution had the following clause as an introduction:

The Congress, while noting that in general the utility and the necessity of colonies, in particular for the working class, is greatly exaggerated, does not condemn in principle and for all time, every colonial policy; under a socialist régime, colonization can be a work of civilization.

On second thoughts, I move that this clause be reinstated. . . .

I now propose to move a vote.

The original Van Kol resolution is adopted by a large majority. Van Kol's additional clause is adopted by 18 votes to 10. The text adopted by the majority of the Committee is therefore worded as follows:

Draft Resolution

The Congress, while noting that in general the utility and the necessity of colonies, in particular for the working class, is greatly exaggerated, does not condemn in principle and for all time, every colonial policy; under a socialist régime, colonization can be a work of civilization.

Reaffirming its resolutions of Paris (1900) and of Amsterdam (1904), the Congress rejects the present colonization which, being intrinsically capitalistic, has no other objective than to conquer countries and to subjugate peoples in order to exploit them mercilessly for the profit of a very small minority, all the while increasing the burden of the proletarians of the mother country.

Enemy of all exploitation of man by man, defender of all the oppressed without distinction of race, the Congress condemns this policy of robbery and conquest, this shameless application of the right of the strongest, which tramples on the rights of conquered peoples, and further notes that colonial policy increases the danger of international complications and of wars between colonizing countries. . . . The Congress declares that the socialist representatives have the duty to oppose unconditionally in all the parliaments this régime of unbridled exploitation and serfdom, which is prevalent in all the existing colonies, by insisting on reforms to better the lot of the natives, by seeing to the maintenance of their rights, by preventing all forms of exploitation and enslavement, and by working, by all the means at their disposal, to educate these peoples for independence.

Third Plenary Meeting
Chairmanship of Citizen Singer

THE CHAIRMAN: . . . The Colonial Committee has finished its work and has transmitted a resolution to us. . . . The minority of the committee has also given me a resolution which is signed by the citizens Ledebour, Wurm, Delaporte, Bracke and Karski. Here it is:

(1) Strike out paragraph I in the majority resolution.
(2) Replace this paragraph by the following text:

The Congress is of the opinion that capitalist colonial policy, by its very essence, leads inevitably to the enslavement, forced labour or extermination of the native populations in the colonial domain.

The civilizing mission claimed by capitalist society is only used as a pretext to cover its thirst for exploitation and conquest. Only socialist society will be able to offer to all peoples the possibility of fully developing their civilization.

VAN KOL (Holland): . . . A large majority of the Committee adopted a resolution which, in my opinion, abandons a purely negative point of view, and which calls for a socialist colonial policy. The resolution of the minority, on the contrary, reveals a sombre spirit of despair and doubt.

. . . We Dutch are one of the oldest colonial peoples, but as a result of our efforts, killing, torture, and plundering are no longer daily occurrences in the Dutch colonies. Ledebour's plans for the future are purely utopian. Doesn't he know that the colonial policy of tomorrow will always be peaceful, and will be carried out according to humanitarian principles? The colonial question is the great problem which will dominate modern history. It is therefore necessary to create a socialist colonial policy.

Ever since the existence of humanity there have been colonies, and I think there still will be for long centuries. . . . I merely ask Ledebour whether, under the present régime, he has the courage to give up the colonies. He will tell me then what he will do with the overpopulation of Europe, in what country the people who want to emigrate will be able to find a living, if it isn't in the colonies? What will Ledebour do with the growing produce of European industry if he doesn't want to find new outlets in the colonies?

And does he, as a social democrat, want to abandon his duty to work for the improvement of the backward peoples? . . . We must point out the path to follow in order to diminish the exploitation of the natives in the colonies, to increase the degree of their civilization, to give them the rights which we ask for. It is the duty of the Congress to see to it that the millions of unhappy natives can hope for a better future, thanks to the practical work of all the socialists. (*'Very good' from the Dutch benches and from a few English benches.*)

BERNSTEIN (Germany): I am in favour of the majority resolution. . . . The growing force of socialism in certain countries also increases the responsibility of our groups. This is why we cannot maintain our purely negative viewpoint with regard to the colonies. . . . We must reject the utopian idea, the result of which would be the abandonment of the colonies. The final consequence of this conception would be to give the United States back to the Indians (*agitation*). The colonies are there, they must be taken care of, and I consider that a certain tutelage of the civilized peoples over the uncivilized peoples is a necessity. This has been recognized by numerous socialists, in particular by Lassalle and by Marx, and the latter especially in the third volume of his *Capital* where I read the following sentence: 'The earth does not belong to a single people but to humanity, and each people should manage it to the advantage of humanity'....

Other international Congresses have recognized this fact. This is why I consider that we must take a stand on the grounds of real facts and we must pit a socialist colonial policy against the capitalist colonial policy. A great part of our economy is based on the acquisition of colonial products, products which the natives hardly put to use. For all these reasons, we must adopt the majority resolution.

DAVID (Germany): I ask you to accept the majority resolution.... When the minority states that it is not possible to improve the present colonial policy, that it is a misfortune for the native peoples in all circumstances, then the minority, if it wants to be logical, must ask for the suppression of the colonies. ('*Quite right*'.) Ledebour interrupts me and tells me that this is indeed his intention. If this is the case, let our English comrades, supporters of the Ledebour resolution, let our French comrades who support it as well, propose in their respective parliaments the relinquishment of the colonies! If those who adhere to this point of view had the power to do so, they ought to give the colonies back to the natives. What would then become of the colonies? It would not be humane feelings which would triumph. It would be barbarism. ('*Very good*' *from certain benches*.) ... The colonies too must go through the stage of capitalism as well and one can no more there than here jump both feet together from barbarism into socialism. ('*Very good*'.)

KARSKI[1] (Germany): . . . David has recognized the right of one nation to put another nation in tutelage. What such a tutelage is worth we Poles know, we who have had as tutors the Tsar of Russia and the Prussian government. ('*Very good*'.) It is a question here of a confusion of expression, which is due less to bourgeois influence than to the influence of the petty nobility. In stating that every people must go through capitalism, David invokes the authority of Marx. I contest this interpretation. Marx says that where there is a beginning of capitalist development the peoples must go through this evolution completely, but he never stated that all peoples must go through a capitalist stage.... I think that for a socialist there are still other civilizations than capitalist or European civilization. We have no right to praise our civilization so much and to impose it upon the Asiatic peoples who possess a culture much more ancient than ours and perhaps much more refined. (*Bravos*.) David further asserted that the colonies would return to barbarism if they were abandoned to themselves. This assertion seems dubious to me, especially as regards India. I imagine a completely different kind of evolution there. One can perfectly well understand the main-

[1] Pseudonym of J. Marchlewski (see p. 189).

tenance of European culture there, without this implying that the Europeans dominate by the force of their bayonets. I therefore urge you to vote for the minority resolution.

KAUTSKY (Germany): . . . How is it that the idea of a socialist colonial policy finds so many supporters in this circle when it seems to me, in reality, that this idea is based on a logical contradiction? I attribute this fact to the following: the idea was so new that there has been no time to deliberate regarding its real meaning. Until now we have never heard of a socialist colonial policy. . . .

It is said that we have a civilizing policy to carry out, and that we must go to the backward tribes in order to play the part of the educators and counsellors of these primitive peoples. I agree completely. I approve of what was said on this subject by Bernstein. We have every interest in seeing these primitive peoples attain a superior culture, but what I contest is that it is necessary in order to reach this goal to practice a colonial policy, that it is necessary to conquer and to dominate. I could even say that a colonial policy is the opposite of a civilizing policy. ('*Very good*'.)

It is a very widespread error that backward peoples are adversaries of the civilization brought to them by more civilized peoples. Experience shows, on the contrary, that wherever one shows oneself benevolent to the savages, they willingly accept the instruments and help of a superior civilization.

But if one comes in order to dominate them, to oppress them, to bring them into subjection, when they must put themselves under the tutelage of a despotism, even benevolent, they lost all confidence; they then reject, along with foreign domination, foreign culture, and the result is combat and devastation. We see that wherever colonial policy is practised, the result is not to uplift but to degrade the peoples! The socialist system of government could change nothing of that. It would also have to consider the colonies as foreign bodies. It would also find itself obliged to create a foreign domination. If we want to exercise a civilizing influence on these primitive peoples, it is imperative that we gain their confidence, and we shall gain this confidence only when we give them their freedom. (*Bravos.*)

Bernstein has tried to make us believe that this policy of conquest has been a natural necessity. I was very much surprised to hear him defend here this theory according to which there are two groups of people, one which is destined to dominate and the other to be dominated, that there are peoples incapable of administering their own affairs, peoples composed of grown-up children. This is only a variation on the old theme which is the justification of all despotisms and according to which there are some who come into the world with spurs on their heels and others with a saddle on their back, so that the former may consider the latter as their mounts. . . .

Bernstein invokes Marx quite wrongly. Certainly Marx declared that the earth belonged to humanity. But humanity does not as yet today have a colonial policy. Marx did not say that the earth belongs to the capitalist nations. ('*Very good*'.)

VAN KOL (*rapporteur*): . . . Why should we not help the workers of other continents, as we help the workers of Europe? In Europe the gigantic forces of capitalism are facing us. Why not then combat the capitalism which has developed outside Europe? Nowhere can we make greater and easier conquests than in these far-off continents. . . . Kautsky stated that we must try to gain the confidence of the natives. But how does he want to gain this confidence of thousands of men of other colours, if he doesn't want to do anything for them? ('*Very good*'.) We in Holland have the duty and the right to communicate to our comrades of other countries the results of our own experience. We Dutch socialists have won the confidence of thousands of Javanese, but the inhabitants of West Africa know nothing of German social democracy because, until now, the latter has not fulfilled its duty towards the natives. If you want to win the confidence of the natives, you must actively intervene in the colonial question. Our friend went even further when he gave us his opinion of the industrial development of the colonies. He advised us to send machines and tools to Africa. That is a bookish theory. Does he want to civilize the country in this way? If we send a machine to the Negroes of central Africa, do you know what they will do? Very probably they will execute a war dance around our European product (*hilarity*) and it is also probable that the number of their innumerable gods will be increased by one (*further hilarity*). Perhaps he will also ask us to send Europeans knowing how to run the machines. What the natives will do with them I do not know. Perhaps too Kautsky and I could join theory with practice and accompany the machines to the black continent. But I am also convinced that the natives will not be satisfied with smashing them. It could even be possible that they skin us alive or else that they eat us and then . . . (rubbing his stomach) I strongly fear, as my corporal development somewhat exceeds that of Kautsky, that I would be given the preference by my Negro friends. (*Hilarity*.) If we Europeans went to Africa with our European machines, we would be the victims of our expedition. We must, on the contrary, have arms in hand in order eventually to defend ourselves, even if Kautsky calls this imperialism. ('*Very good*' *from some benches*.)

SECTION II: LENIN AND HIS CONTEMPORARIES PRIOR TO THE FOUNDING OF THE THIRD INTERNATIONAL

1. The Stuttgart Congress as Seen by Lenin

Extracts from an article published in November 1907, in which Lenin summed up the debates of the Stuttgart Congress, which he had just attended.[1]

This is not the first time that international congresses have considered the colonial question. Until now their resolutions have unswervingly condemned bourgeois colonial policy as a policy of plunder and violence. On this occasion, however, the Congress Commission was so constituted that opportunist elements led by the Dutchman Van Kol had the upper hand in it. A clause was inserted in the draft resolution, saying that the Congress did not in principle condemn all colonial policy, as under a socialist régime a colonial policy could play a civilizing role. A minority in the Commission (Ledebour from Germany, the Polish and Russian Social Democrats, and many others) protested vigorously against entertaining any such thought. The matter was put before the Congress and the forces behind the two trends proved to be so nearly equal in numbers that a remarkably heated quarrel ensued.

The opportunists threw in their lot with Van Kol. David and Bernstein spoke for the majority of the German delegation, urging acceptance of 'a socialist colonial policy' and attacking the radicals for the pointlessness of their objections, their failure to appreciate the importance of reforms, their lack of a practical colonial programme, etc. They were opposed also by Kautsky, who felt obliged to request the Congress to come out *against* the majority of the German delegation. He noted rightly that there was no question of abandoning the struggle for reforms; this had been stated perfectly plainly in other parts of the resolution which had given rise to no argument. The question was whether we should make concessions to the modern practice of bourgeois pillage and violence. What had been tabled for discussion by the Congress was present-day colonial policy, and this policy was based on downright enslavement of primitive people: the bourgeoisie was introducing virtual slavery into the colonies and subjecting the native populations to untold indignities and violence, 'civilizing' them by the spread of alcohol and syphilis. In such a situation, socialists were

[1] SOURCE: Lenin, *Polnoye Sobraniye Sochinenii*, vol. XVI, pp. 67–71.

expected to mouth evasive phrases about the possibility of recognizing colonial policy in principle! That would really mean deserting to the bourgeois point of view. It would mean a decisive step towards subordinating the proletariat to bourgeois ideology and bourgeois imperialism, which, particularly at the moment, was arrogantly rearing its head.

The Commission's proposal was defeated in Congress by 128 votes to 108 with ten abstentions (Switzerland). It should be noted that in the voting at Stuttgart, nations were for the first time allotted different numbers of votes, ranging from 20 (for the big nations, including Russia) down to 2 (Luxembourg). The total votes polled by the small nations which either do not pursue, or are victims of, a colonial policy exceeded the votes of states where even the proletariat has to some extent been infected with the passion for conquest.

This voting on the colonial question is of very great importance. Firstly, it clearly revealed in its true light that socialist opportunism that falls under the spell of bourgeois blandishments. And secondly, it uncovered a particular negative feature in the European workers' movement, one capable of doing no small damage to the cause of the proletariat and, for that reason, worth serious attention. Marx frequently referred to a certain very significant saying of Sismondi's to the effect that the proletarians of the ancient world lived at the expense of society whereas modern society lives at the expense of the proletarians.

The class of non-working have-nots is incapable of overthrowing the exploiters. Only the proletarian class, which maintains the whole of society, has the power to bring about social revolution. And so, as a result of an expensive colonial policy the European proletariat has *partly* reached a situation where it is *not* its work that maintains the whole of society but that of practically enslaved natives of the colonies. The British bourgeoisie, for example, extracts more profits out of the tens and hundreds of millions of people in India and other colonies than out of the British workers. In certain countries these circumstances create the material and economic basis for infecting the proletariat of one country or another with colonial chauvinism. Of course, this may perhaps be only a temporary phenomenon, but one must nevertheless clearly recognize the evil and understand its causes so as to be able to unite the proletariat of all countries to combat such opportunism. This struggle is bound to end in victory, as the percentage of 'privileged' nations among the capitalist nations is constantly diminishing.

2. *Inflammable Materials in World Politics*

Extracts from an article by Lenin written under this title in 1908, under the influence of the events which followed the Russian defeat of 1905 by the Japanese, the Russian revolution of 1905, the revolution in Persia, and the 'Young Turk' revolution. Lenin saw in these developments the signs of a forthcoming awakening of the oppressed peoples.[1]

The revolutionary movement in various European and Asian states has recently made itself so felt that we are beginning to see emerging a new, incomparably higher stage in the international proletarian struggle. . . .

In Turkey, the revolutionary movement in the army, led by the 'Young Turks', has triumphed. True, this victory is only a half-victory, or even less, for Turkey's Nicholas II has so far got by on a mere promise to re-establish the celebrated Turkish Constitution. But such half-victories in a revolution, such hasty concessions forced from the established power, are the surest guarantee of new moves in the civil war that will be considerably more decisive, sterner, and involve broader masses of people. The school of civil war is not without advantage for the peoples. It is a hard school and the full course *inevitably* involves the counter-revolution winning victories, infuriated reactionaries wreaking wild havoc, and the established power taking savage reprisals against the insurgents, etc. . . . But only confirmed pedants and doddering mummies can lament the entry of the peoples into this school of torment; this school teaches the oppressed masses how to wage civil war and make the revolution victorious; it concentrates in the masses of modern slaves that hatred which downtrodden, crude and ignorant slaves have ever carried within their breasts, and which leads to the greatest historical exploits by slaves who have recognized the shame of their slavery. . . .

In laying their colonialist hands on the Asian countries, the Europeans succeeded in nerving one of them, Japan, for great military victories which have ensured her autonomous national development. There is no doubt that the plunder of India by the English, which has been going on for centuries, and the current struggle of these 'advanced' Europeans against Persian and Indian democracy, *will nerve* millions, tens of millions of proletarians in Asia, to wage a victorious struggle (like that of the Japanese) against their oppressors. The politically-conscious European worker already has Asian comrades, and their number will grow, not daily but hourly. . . .

This step forward that the whole of international socialism has taken, together with sharpening of the revolutionary-democratic struggle in Asia, puts the Russian revolution in a special and particularly difficult situation. The Russian revolution has a great international ally both in Europe and in Asia, but at the same time *and for this very reason* it has not only a national, Russian enemy but also an *international* enemy. Reaction against the mounting struggle of the proletariat is inevitable in all capitalist countries, and this

[1] SOURCE: Lenin, *Polnoye Sobraniye Sochinenii*, vol. XVII, pp. 174–83.

reaction is uniting the bourgeois governments throughout the world against every popular movement, against every revolution in Asia and, above all, in Europe.

3. *Democracy and Populism in China*

In this extract from an article of the same title written in 1912, Lenin analyses the essential characteristics of the system established in China following the revolution of 1911. As regards social forces, he emphasizes the role of the peasantry; on the cultural level he underscores the influence of the West.[1]

The article by Sun Yat-sen, President-ad-interim of the Chinese Republic, which we take from the Brussels socialist newspaper, *Le Peuple*, is of quite exceptional interest to us Russians.

There is a saying that 'the onlooker sees the game best'. Sun Yat-sen is an extremely interesting 'onlooker', for although he is a man of European education he seems completely uninformed about Russia. And yet here we have this man of European education, this spokesman of the militant and victorious Chinese democracy that has won a republic, confronting us – quite independently of Russia, Russian experience and Russian literature – with purely Russian questions. Though a leading Chinese democrat, he reasons exactly like a Russian one. He and the Russian populist are so much alike that their fundamental ideas are identical and they have a good number of expressions in common.

The onlooker sees the game best. The platform of great Chinese democracy – for this is just what Sun Yat-sen's article is – compels us, and provides us with a convenient opportunity, to re-examine in the light of recent world events the question of the relationship between democracy and populism in present-day bourgeois revolutions in Asia. . . .

Comparison invites itself between the President-ad-interim of the Republic in wild, inert, Asiatic China and various other presidents of republics in Europe, America, and countries with a high level of culture. . . .

Here we see this Asiatic republican President-ad-interim as a revolutionary democrat, imbued with that nobility and heroism peculiar to a rising rather than a declining class, a class which does not fear the future but believes in it and fights selflessly for it; a class which hates the past and knows how to cast off its dead decay that stifles every living thing; a class which does not persist in trying to preserve and resurrect the past in order to protect its privileges. . . .

Well then? Does this, then, mean that the materialist West has decayed and that light shines only from the mystic and religious East? No, on the contrary. It means that the East has committed itself to the Western path, that further *hundreds and hundreds of*

[1] SOURCE: Lenin, *Polnoye Sobraniye Sochinenii*, vol. XXI, pp. 401–7.

millions of people will from now on join in the struggle for the ideals for which the West has striven. It is the Western bourgeoisie which has decayed and is face-to-face with its grave-digger, the proletariat. Meanwhile in Asia there *yet remains* a bourgeoisie capable of representing sincere, militant and consistent democracy, a worthy successor to the great prophets and great men of the end of the eighteenth century in France.

The main representative, or main social support, of this Asian bourgeoisie which is still capable of historically progressive action, is the peasant. And side by side with him there is a liberal bourgeoisie, whose leaders, men like Yüan Shih-k'ai, are above all capable of treachery. . . .

Chinese democracy could not have overthrown the old order in China and taken over the republic without the immense spiritual and revolutionary enthusiasm of the masses. Such enthusiasm involves and arouses most sincere sympathy for the situation of the working masses, and the most burning hatred towards their oppressors and exploiters. But in Europe and America, from which the progressive Chinese, *all* Chinese who have experienced this enthusiasm, have borrowed their emancipatory ideas, liberation *from* the bourgeoisie, i.e. socialism, is now the immediate goal. This inevitably arouses sympathy among Chinese democrats for socialism, their *subjective* socialism. . . .

4. Backward Europe and Advanced Asia

Extracts from an article written by Lenin under this title in 1913, in which he develops the theme that the bourgeoisie is still capable of playing a progressive role in Asia.[1]

The comparison appears paradoxical. Who does not know that Europe is advanced and Asia backward? However, the words which form the title of this article contain a bitter truth.

In civilized and advanced Europe, with its highly developed technology, its rich and varied culture and its constitutions, the moment in history has been reached when the dominant bourgeoisie, fearing the growing and increasingly powerful proletariat, is supporting everything that is outdated, moribund and medieval. The obsolescent bourgeoisie is allying itself with all the obsolete or obsolescent forces in an attempt to preserve the tottering system of wage-slavery.

In advanced Europe . . . , the proletariat alone . . . maintains and spreads implacable hostility towards backwardness, savagery, privilege, slavery, and the humiliation of one man by another.

In 'advanced' Europe . . . , the proletariat *alone* is the *advanced* class. . . .

One could hardly quote a more striking example of this rotten-

[1] SOURCE: Lenin, *Polnoye Sobraniye Sochinenii*, vol. XXIII, pp. 166–7.

ness of the *entire* European bourgeoisie than the support it gives to *reaction* in Asia in aid of the selfish interests of financiers and capitalist swindlers.

Throughout Asia a mighty democratic movement is growing, spreading and gaining in strength. The bourgeoisie there *still* sides with the people against reaction. *Hundreds* of millions of people are awakening into life, light and freedom. What enthusiasm this universal movement is evoking in the hearts of all conscious workers, who know that the road to collectivism lies through democracy! How full of sympathy all honest democrats are towards young Asia!

And what of 'advanced' Europe? She is plundering China and helping the enemies of democracy, the enemies of China's freedom! . . .

But the whole of young Asia, that is to say the hundreds of millions of working people in Asia, has a trusty ally in the proletariat of all the civilized countries. No force in the world can prevent its victory, which will liberate both the peoples of Europe and the peoples of Asia.

5. *Theses on Socialist Revolution and the Right of Nations to Self-Determination*

These theses, written during the war (in 1916), develop the ideas set forth by Lenin in 1914 in *The Right of Nations to Self-Determination*, placing them this time in a colonial perspective and not merely in the perspective of the problem as it existed in Europe.[1]

. . . Victorious socialism must of necessity institute full democracy and, therefore, establish not only complete equality of rights between nations but also the right of the oppressed nations to self-determination, i.e. the right to free political separation. . . .

The strengthening of national oppression under imperialism makes it imperative for Social Democracy not to renounce what the bourgeoisie calls the 'utopian' struggle for the freedom of nations to secede but, on the contrary, to make more extensive use of the conflicts which arise in this field *too* as grounds for mass action and for revolutionary demonstrations against the bourgeoisie.

The proletariat of the oppressor nations must not limit itself to the kind of general, stereotyped phrases that any bourgeois pacifist might repeat against annexations and in favour of the equality of nations in general. . . . The proletariat cannot but fight against the use of force to make oppressed nations remain within the boundaries of a particular state; in other words it must fight for the right of self-determination. The proletariat must demand free political separation, for the colonies and the nations oppressed by 'its own nation'.

[1] SOURCE: Lenin, *Polnoye Sobraniye Sochinenii*, vol. XXVII, pp. 252–66.

. . . The socialists of the oppressed nations, on the other hand, should in particular defend and bring about complete and unconditional unity, including organizational unity, of the workers of the oppressed nation and those of the oppressor nation. Without this it is impossible to defend the independent policy of the proletariat and its class solidarity with the proletariat of other countries in face of all the various manoeuvres, betrayals and tricks of the bourgeoisie. For the bourgeoisie of the oppressed nations persistently distorts national-liberation slogans in order to deceive the workers; . . . it uses these slogans in order to enter into reactionary agreements with the bourgeoisie of the dominant nations. . . .

In this connexion, countries should be classified into three main types:

First, the advanced capitalist countries of Western Europe and the United States. Here bourgeois progressive national movements have long since ended. Each of the 'great' nations is oppressing other nations in the colonies and within its own frontiers. The tasks of the proletariat here in the dominant nations are precisely the same as those of the proletariat in England in the nineteenth-century *vis-à-vis* Ireland.

Secondly, Eastern Europe: Austria, the Balkans and particularly Russia. . . . Here there exists the especially difficult and particularly important task of unifying the class struggle of the workers of the oppressed nations and those of the oppressor nations.

Thirdly, the semi-colonial countries such as China, Persia, Turkey, and all of the colonies with their total population of some 1,000 million. Here, bourgeois-democratic movements either have hardly begun, or are far from coming to an end. Socialists must not only demand the unconditional, irreversible and immediate liberation of the colonies (and in its political expression this demand means purely and simply a recognition of the right to self-determination); socialists must also give most resolute support to the more revolutionary elements in the bourgeois-democratic movements of national liberation in these countries and assist their uprising, – or, if need be, their revolutionary war, – *against* the imperialist powers which oppress them. . . .

6. *Imperialism, the Highest Stage of Capitalism*

Extracts from Lenin's celebrated work, published in 1917, in which he explains the collapse of Social Democracy in the advanced countries by the corrupting effects of the colonial system.[1]

. . . Consequently, we are passing through a peculiar period in world colonial policy, which is very closely linked with 'the latest stage in the development of capitalism', namely finance capital. It is essential, for this reason, first of all to study the known facts in greater detail so as to be able to distinguish more clearly how this

[1] SOURCE: Lenin, *Polnoye Sobraniye Sochinenii,* vol. XXVII, pp. 374–6, 402, 404.

period differs from previous ones and what the present situation is. . . .

At the high point of free enterprise in Britain, between 1840 and 1860, the country's leading bourgeois politicians were *opposed to* colonial policy and considered the liberation of the colonies, their complete detachment from Britain, as something both desirable and inevitable. In an article on 'Modern British Imperialism' published in 1898, M. Beer showed that in 1852 Disraeli, a politician favourably disposed, to say the least, towards imperialist policy, stated: 'The colonies are millstones about our necks.' But at the end of the nineteenth century the men of the moment were Cecil Rhodes and Joseph Chamberlain, who openly advocated imperialism and pursued their colonialist policy with the utmost cynicism!

It is of some interest that even at that time the connexion between the, so to speak, purely economic and the socio-political roots of contemporary imperialism was clear to these leading politicians of the British bourgeoisie. Chamberlain preached that imperialism was 'a true, wise and economic policy', indicating particularly the competition Britain was then encountering on the world market from Germany, America and Belgium. Salvation lies in monopolies, – said the capitalists as they established their cartels, syndicates and trusts. Salvation lies in monopolies, – replied the political leaders of the bourgeoisie as they hurried to lay their hands on those parts of the world that had still not been shared out. According to his close friend, the journalist Stead, Cecil Rhodes spoke to him in 1895 about his imperialist ideas as follows: 'Yesterday I was in London's East End (a working-class quarter) and attended a meeting held by some unemployed men. I listened to some wild speeches, which amounted simply to the cry, "Give us bread! Bread!" On returning home and thinking over what I had seen, I was more than ever convinced of the importance of imperialism. . . . My dearest wish is to see the social problem solved: that is to say that in order to save the forty million inhabitants of the United Kingdom from bloody civil war, we colonial politicians must conquer new lands to take our excess population and to provide new outlets for the goods produced in our factories and mines. The Empire, as I have always said, is a question of bread and butter. If you do not want civil war, you must become imperialists.'[1]

. . . Imperialism . . . makes it economically possible to bribe the upper strata of the proletariat; in so doing, it fosters, shapes and reinforces opportunism. But what should not be forgotten are the forces that are lined up in opposition to imperialism in general and opportunism in particular, – forces which, of course, the social-liberal Hobson is not inclined to see. . . .

[1] *Die Neue Zeit*, XVI, 1, 1898, p. 304.

Schulze-Gaevernitz's description of 'British Imperialism' shows us the same parasitical traits. Between 1865 and 1898 Britain's national income practically doubled, whilst over the same period income 'from abroad' increased ninefold. If the 'merit' of imperialism lies in 'training the Negro to habits of industry' (and it cannot be managed without coercion) then its 'danger' is that 'Europe will put the burden of physical labour, – at first agricultural and mining work, and later heavier industrial labour too, – on the shoulders of the coloured races and will itself settle into the role of employer, thus perhaps preparing the way for the economic, and later the political, emancipation of the coloured and dark-skinned races'. . . .

One characteristic of imperialism connected with the features just described is the decline in emigration from the imperialist countries and the increase in immigration (the arrival of workers and their resettlement) into these countries by workers from the more backward countries where wages are lower. . . . Among the workers too, imperialism tends to create privileged categories and to detach them from the broad mass of the proletariat. . . .

7. *The Crisis of Social Democracy*

Extracts from the pamphlet published by Rosa Luxemburg in 1916 under the pseudonym of 'Junius', in which she replied to the theories put forward by Lenin in 1914 in *The Right of Nations to Self-Determination* and to the attacks he had made on her there.[1]

. . . International socialism recognizes the right of free, independent nations, with equal rights. But socialism alone can create such nations; only socialism can turn the right to self-determination into reality. This slogan of socialism is like all its others, not an apology for existing conditions, but a guide-post, a spur for the revolutionary, regenerative, active policy of the proletariat. So long as capitalist states exist, i.e. so long as imperialistic world policies determine and shape the inner and outer life of the nations, the right of national self-determination has nothing whatever in common with the way in which this principle is applied either in war or in peace.

One can go even further, and say that, in general, in the present imperialistic milieu there can be no more wars of national self-defence. Every socialist policy that fails to take account of this determining historic milieu . . . is built upon sand. . . .

The train of events that led to the present war did not begin in

[1] SOURCE: *The Crisis in the German Social-Democracy* (The 'Junius' Pamphlet). By Rosa Luxemburg (New York, The Socialist Publication Society, 1919), pp. 95–127 *passim*; translation corrected and completed on the basis of *Die Krise der Sozialdemokratie* (Juniusbrochüre), von Rosa Luxemburg. Mit einer Einleitung von Clara Zetkin (Berlin, Verlag 'Rote Fahne', 1919), pp. 71–95 *passim*.

July 1914, but reaches back for decades. Thread after thread was woven together with the inexorability of a natural development, until the dense net of imperialist world politics had encircled the five continents, constituting a huge historical complex of events, whose roots reach deep down into the Plutonic deeps of economic change. . . .

Imperialist politics is not the work of any one state or of any group of states. It is the product of a particular stage of maturity in the world development of capital, an innately international phenomenon, an indivisible whole, that can be grasped only in all its reciprocal relations, and from which no nation can hold aloof at will. . . .

. . . The fact that today all modern capitalist states have colonial possessions that will, even though a war may have begun as a 'war of national defence', be drawn into the conflict, if only for purely military reasons, the fact that each belligerent will strive to occupy the colonial possessions of its adversary, or at least to create disturbances there – as illustrated by England's seizure of the German colonies, and the attempts to unleash a 'holy war' in the English and French colonies – this fact automatically turns every war into an imperialistic world conflagration. . . .

Thus it is always the historic milieu of modern imperialism that determines the character of war in the individual countries, and because of this milieu *wars of national self-defence are today no longer possible*. . . .

But the imperialist bestiality raging today in Europe has had another effect, that has brought to the 'civilized world' no horror-stricken eyes, no agonized heart: *the mass destruction of the European proletariat*. Never has a war exterminated whole nations; never, within the past century, has it swept over all of the great and ancient civilized lands of Europe. Millions of human lives were destroyed in the Vosges, in the Ardennes, in Belgium, in Poland, in the Carpathians and on the Save, millions were hopelessly crippled. But nine-tenths of these millions come from the ranks of the working people of the cities and the farms. It is our strength, our hope that is being mowed down there day after day like grass before the scythe of death. It is the best, the most intelligent, the most thoroughly schooled forces of international socialism, the bearers of the holiest traditions and of the boldest heroism of the modern labour movement, the vanguard of the whole world proletariat, the workers of England, France, Belgium, Germany and Russia who are being gagged and butchered in masses. It is precisely the workers of the advanced capitalist countries who have the historic mission to carry out the socialist transformation. Only from Europe, only from the oldest capitalist nations, can the signal come, when the hour is ripe, for the social revolution that will free humanity. Only the English, French, Belgian, German, Russian and Italian workers, together, can lead the army of the exploited and enslaved of the five continents. They alone, when the time comes, can call capitalism to account for centuries of crimes committed against all the primitive peoples, and for its work of destruction around the globe; they alone can exact revenge. But for the advance and victory of socialism, we need a strong, ready, well-trained proletariat, masses whose strength lies in intellectual culture as well as in numbers. And these very masses are being decimated by the World War. . . . The fruit of decades of sacrifices and generations of toil is annihilated in a few short weeks, the choicest troops of the international proletariat are torn out by the life roots.

The blood-letting of the June butchery laid low the French labour movement for a decade and a half. The blood-letting of the Commune again threw it back for more than a decade. What is happening now is a mass carnage such as the world has never seen before, and which is reducing the labouring population in all of the leading civilized nations to the women, the aged, and the maimed; a blood-letting that threatens to bleed white the European labour movement. Another such war, and the prospects of socialism will be buried under the ruins heaped up by imperialistic barbarism. . . .

8. The Junius Pamphlet

Extracts from Lenin's reply to the preceding text.[1]

At last a social-democratic pamphlet on the problems of the war has come out in Germany, illegally, and without making any alterations to suit the evil censorship of the Junkers! The author, who clearly belongs to the 'Left-Radical' wing of the party, uses the pen-name Junius (which in Latin means junior) and has called the pamphlet 'The Crisis of Social-Democracy'. . . .

The first false point Junius makes is to be found in the fifth thesis in the 'International' section: 'During the era of unbridled imperialism national wars are no longer possible. National interests serve only as a means of deception in order to put the working popular masses at the service of their mortal enemy – imperialism. . . .' The beginning of the fifth thesis, which ends with this statement, labels the present war an imperialist war. Possibly this general negation of national wars is either an oversight or an accidental exaggeration in stressing the perfectly correct notion that the *present* war is an imperialist war and not a national one. But because this may equally not be the case, since various social democrats have made the same mistake of denying the possibility of any kind of national war whilst refuting the false proposition that the *present* war is a national one, this mistake must not go unnoted.

[1] SOURCE: Lenin, *Polnoye Sobraniye Sochinenii*, vol. XXX, pp. 1–9 *passim*.

Junius is quite right to stress the decisive influence of the 'imperialist setting' of the *present* war and to say that behind Serbia stands Russia, and 'behind Serbian nationalism stands Russian imperialism'. . . . This is indisputable, so far as the *present* war is concerned. . . .

But it would be a mistake to exaggerate this truth at all, to deviate from the Marxist obligation to be specific, and to extend one's assessment of the *present* war to all possible wars while imperialism exists, and to ignore the national movements against imperialism. . . .

National wars waged by colonies and semi-colonies in the imperialist era are not only probable but *inevitable*. Some 1,000 million people, or *more than half* of the world's population, live in the colonies and semi-colonies (China, Turkey, Persia). Here, national-liberation movements are either already very powerful or are growing and maturing. Every war is the continuation of politics by other means. The continuation of the policy of national liberation by the colonies will *inevitably* lead them to wage national wars *against* imperialism. These wars *may* lead to an imperialist war between the present 'great' imperialist powers, but on the other hand they may not, there being many factors in play here. . . .

We have dwelt at length on the false proposition that 'national wars are no longer possible', not merely because it is patently false from the theoretical point of view. . . . Indeed this mistake is very harmful also in its practical and political aspects: it gives rise to . . . outright, reactionary indifference to national movements. Such an attitude of indifference turns to chauvinism when members of the 'great' European nations, i.e. the nations oppressing the mass of small and colonial peoples, declare with an air of seeming wisdom: 'National wars are no longer possible!' National wars against the imperialist powers are not only possible and probable; they are inevitable, *progressive and revolutionary*, though, of course, if they are to *succeed*, they will require either a concerted effort by vast numbers of people in the oppressed countries . . . , or else a *particularly* favourable combination of circumstances in the international situation (for example that the imperialist powers be paralysed and unable to intervene through exhaustion, or through mutual antagonism, etc.), or a *simultaneous* uprising by the proletariat in one of the great powers against the bourgeoisie (the last-mentioned case really comes first as the most desirable and favourable for the victory of the proletariat).

9. *The Irish Rebellion of 1916*

These extracts from an article written by Lenin in 1916 under the title 'Summing up of a Discussion on Self-Determination' show how far he still was at that time from attributing to Asia the same weight as to Europe.[1]

[1] SOURCE: Lenin, *Polnoye Sobraniye Sochinenii*, vol. XXX, pp. 52–4.

Our theses were written before this rebellion, which must serve as a testing-ground for our theoretical views.

The views of the opponents of self-determination lead to the conclusion that the viability of small nations oppressed by imperialism is already exhausted, that they are incapable of playing any role against imperialism, and that there is nothing to be gained by supporting their purely national aspirations, etc. The experience of the imperialist war of 1914–16 provides *actual facts* which refute conclusions of this sort.

The war proved to be a period of crisis for the Western European nations and for imperialism as a whole. Every crisis spurns the conventional, tears down façades, sweeps away the obsolete and uncovers underlying motives and forces. What has it uncovered from the point of view of the movement of oppressed nations? In the colonies it has revealed a number of attempted rebellions which the oppressor nations naturally did everything possible to conceal by means of their military censorship. It is known, however, that in Singapore the British brutally suppressed a mutiny among their Indian troops; also that there were attempted uprisings in French Annam and the German Cameroons . . . ; and that in Europe there was, on the one hand, a rebellion in Ireland which the 'peace-loving' English, who had not dared to extend conscripted national service to the Irish, put down by means of executions, and, on the other hand, the Austrian Government passed sentence of death on the deputies of the Czech Diet 'for treason', and sent whole Czech regiments before the firing squad for the same 'crime'.

This list is, of course, very far from complete. It nevertheless demonstrates that, *because of* the crisis of imperialism, the flames of national rebellion have flared up *both* in the colonies and in Europe, and that national sympathies and antipathies have made themselves felt in spite of Draconian threats and repressive measures. . . .

On 9 May 1916, the *Berner Tagwacht*, the organ of the Zimmerwald socialists and also of certain Leftists, published an article on the Irish rebellion. . . . The rebellion was stated to have been nothing more or less than a 'putsch' since, so it said, 'the Irish question was an agrarian question', the peasants had been appeased by reforms, and the nationalist movement was now but 'a purely urban, petty-bourgeois movement which, despite the great commotion it had caused, did not represent very much socially'. . . .

The Irish national movement . . . manifested itself in street battles fought by a section of the urban petty bourgeoisie *and a section of the workers* after a lengthy period of mass agitation, demonstrations, suppressions of newspapers, etc. Anyone who can call *such* a rebellion a 'putsch' is either a diehard reactionary or a doctrinaire, hopelessly incapable of picturing social revolution as a living phenomenon.

To think that social revolution is *conceivable* without revolts by small nations in the colonies and in Europe, without revolutionary outbursts by a section of the petty bourgeoisie *with all its prejudices*, and without the politically naïve proletarian and semi-proletarian masses moving against oppression by the landlords, the church, the monarchy, and against national oppression, etc., – such thinking means *repudiating social revolution*. It is as though one army formed up in one place and said, 'We are for socialism,' and another formed up somewhere else and said, 'We are for imperialism,' and this was what one called social revolution! Only someone holding so pedantic and ridiculous a view could dream of vilifying the Irish rebellion by calling it a 'putsch'.

If anyone expects a 'pure' social revolution, he will never live to see it. He is a revolutionary in word only and does not understand what true revolution is. . . .

The socialist revolution in Europe *cannot be other than* an outburst of mass struggle by all oppressed and discontented people of every kind. . . .

The struggle of the oppressed nations *in Europe*, a struggle capable of going as far as insurrection and street fighting, of breaking the iron discipline of the army and of a state of siege, will 'aggravate the revolutionary crisis in Europe' infinitely more than a far more developed rebellion in a distant colony. The blow struck against the power of the English imperialist bourgeoisie by the rebellion in Ireland is a hundred times more significant politically than a blow of the same force struck in Asia or Africa. . . .

10. *Stalin: 'Do Not Forget the East'*

Extracts from an article by Stalin published under this title in 1918 in the organ of the Commissariat for Nationalities (*Zhizn' Natsional'nostei*), in which the non-Russian communists were just beginning at that time to develop their own ideas regarding the revolution. Despite its title, this text appears primarily as a warning by Stalin against certain 'oriental' tendencies of his non-Russian comrades.[1]

At a time when the revolutionary spirit is developing in Europe . . . all eyes are naturally on the West. It is here, in the West, that the chains of imperialism, which were forged in Europe and which are strangling the whole world, must first be broken. It is here first of all that the new socialist life must be vigorously developed. At such a time, one involuntarily tends to forget the backward East with its hundreds of millions of people enslaved by imperialism. However, the East must not be forgotten for a single moment, for it represents the 'inexhaustible' source of supply and the 'most reliable' rearguard of world imperialism. . . .

The duty of communism is to shatter the centuries-long slumber of the oppressed peoples of the East, to imbue the workers and

[1] SOURCE: Stalin, *Sochineniya*, vol. IV, pp. 171–3.

peasants of these countries with the liberating spirit of revolution, and to rouse them to fight imperialism and to deprive world imperialism of its 'most reliable' rearguard and 'inexhaustible' source of supply.

Failing this, the ultimate victory of socialism, its complete victory over imperialism, is unthinkable.

SECTION III: THE SECOND CONGRESS OF THE COMMUNIST INTERNATIONAL

1. Extracts from Lenin's Report on the International Situation and the Basic Tasks of the Communist International

In this report, presented on 19 July 1920 at the first session of the Congress, Lenin put forward for the first time the idea of forming peasant Soviets, or Soviets of toilers, in the backward countries where there did not yet exist an urban proletariat. This idea did not appear in the draft of his theses on the national and colonial question (see Text III 3); he developed it at greater length in his report on the same question (Text III 4).[1]

Our comrade, the Chairman, has said that this Congress can deservedly be called a World Congress. I think he is right, particularly because we have among us quite a number of representatives of the revolutionary movement of the colonies and backward countries. This is only a small beginning, but it is important that this start has been made. At this Congress a union is taking place between the revolutionary proletarians of the capitalist, advanced countries, and the revolutionary masses of those countries where there is no proletariat or practically no proletariat, namely the oppressed masses of the colonies and the Eastern countries. It depends on us – and I am convinced that we will do it – to consolidate that union. World imperialism cannot but fall when the revolutionary onslaught of the exploited and oppressed workers in each country, overcoming the resistance of petty-bourgeois elements and the influence of the paltry upper crust of labour aristocrats, joins forces with the revolutionary onslaught of hundreds of millions of people who have hitherto remained beyond the bounds of history and have been regarded only as the object of history.

The imperialist war has helped the revolution: the bourgeoisie has withdrawn soldiers from the colonies, from the backward countries and from their isolated life, to take part in this imperialist war. The British bourgeoisie impressed upon the soldiers from India the idea that it was the duty of Indian peasants to defend Great Britain against Germany; the French bourgeoisie impressed upon the soldiers from the French colonies that it was the duty of black men to defend France. They taught them how to handle firearms. This is an extremely useful skill and we might thank the bourgeoisie very much for it on behalf of all the Russian workers and peasants, and particularly on behalf of the entire Red Army. The imperialist war has drawn the dependent peoples into world history. And

[1] SOURCE: Lenin, *Polnoye Sobraniye Sochinenii*, vol. XLI, pp. 233–5.

one of our most important tasks now is to think how to lay the foundation for organizing the establishment of the Soviet movement in the *non*-capitalist countries. Soviets are possible there; they will not be workers' Soviets but peasants' Soviets or working-people's Soviets. . . .

A start has been made on establishing the Soviet movement throughout the East. . . . The idea that the exploited must rise up against their exploiters and establish their own Soviets is not too complicated. After our experience, after the two and a half years that the Soviet Republic has existed in Russia, and after the First Congress of the Third International, this idea is becoming accessible to hundreds of millions of people oppressed by the exploiters throughout the whole world. If today in Russia we are often obliged to make compromises, and to temporize, since we are weaker than the international imperialists, we know, nevertheless, that the masses whose interests we are defending number one and a quarter thousand million. We are still hampered by obstacles, prejudices and ignorance, which with every hour that passes are receding into the past; but the further we advance, the more we genuinely represent and defend this 70 per cent of the world's population, this mass of working and exploited people. . . .

2. *Summary of Speeches by Lenin and Roy in the Commission on the National and Colonial Question*

The session of the Commission on the National and Colonial Question was the scene of a direct clash between Lenin and M. N. Roy, the Indian delegate, who had prepared a series of 'Supplementary Theses' on the same question. This debate, which took place both on the tactical level (collaboration with the bourgeoisie) and on the strategic level (importance of Asia in the world revolution), ended in a compromise which led to the modification of both series of theses (see below Texts III 3 and III 4).[1]

ROY: It was in the 1880s that the nationalist movement in India began to assume more or less definite shape and found its expression in the national Congress.

In the course of its development, this movement extended its influence to large circles of student youth and the middle classes, but the nationalists' call to struggle for India's independence found no response among the popular masses.

The popular masses of India are not fired with a national spirit. They are exclusively interested in problems of an economic and social nature. The situation of the population of India is difficult in the extreme.

Since the establishment of British capitalism in India, the 80 per cent of the population which lives by agrarian work has lost its

[1] SOURCE: *Vestnik Vtorogo Kongressa Kommunisticheskogo Internatsionala*, no. 1, 27 July 1920, pp. 1–2.

property and has been transformed into hired labour. These millions of people live in poverty. Although they are engaged in working the land, they are starving, as everything that they produce is exported. These tens of millions of people have no interest whatsoever in bourgeois-nationalist slogans; only one slogan – 'land to the tillers' – can interest them.

Compared with the rural proletariat, the industrial proletariat in India is small in number. It numbers only 5 million workers. The trade union movement is spreading rapidly among these workers. Recently a strike movement has developed strongly among the working class of India. The first significant strike took place in 1906. It was held by railwaymen and amounted to a veritable insurrection.

The elements exist in India for creating a powerful Communist Party. But as far as the broad popular masses are concerned, the revolutionary movement in India has nothing in common with the national-liberation movement.

Basing himself on this analysis, Comrade Roy came to the conclusion that the point in paragraph 11 of the theses on the national question that dealt with the duty of all communist parties to support bourgeois-democratic liberation movements in the Eastern countries should be deleted. In India the Communist International should assist the creation and development of the communist movement alone, and the Communist Party in India should occupy itself exclusively with organizing the broad popular masses to fight for their own class interests.

Comrade Roy defends the idea that the fate of the revolutionary movement in Europe depends entirely on the course of the revolution in the East. Without the victory of the revolution in the Eastern countries, the communist movement in the West would come to nothing. World capitalism draws its main resources and income from the colonies, principally from those in Asia. If it comes to the worst, the European capitalists can give the workers the full surplus value from their efforts and in this way win them over to their side, having killed their revolutionary aspirations. And these same capitalists will continue to exploit Asia, with the help of the proletariat. Such an outcome would suit the capitalists very well. This being so, it is essential that we divert our energies into developing and elevating the revolutionary movement in the East, and accept as our fundamental thesis that the fate of world communism depends on the victory of communism in the East. . . .

Comrade Lenin . . . contested Comrade Roy's view. In Russia we supported the liberation movement of the liberals when it acted against tsarism. The Indian communists must support the bourgeois-democratic movement,[1] without merging with it. Comrade

[1] The text here says 'bourgeois-communist movement', but this is clearly a printer's error.

Roy goes too far when he asserts that the fate of the West depends exclusively on the degree of development and the strength of the revolutionary movement in the Eastern countries. In spite of the fact that the proletariat in India numbers 5 million and there are 37 million landless peasants, the Indian communists have not yet succeeded in creating a Communist Party in their country. This fact alone shows that Comrade Roy's views are to a large extent unfounded.

3. Lenin's Theses on the National and Colonial Questions

Here we give extracts from the theses on these questions prepared by Lenin in his capacity as *rapporteur*. The text which appears here is that adopted by the Congress after the changes decided on in commission; the variants between this version and Lenin's original draft are indicated in the notes.[1]

4. . . . Closer union between the proletarians and the working masses of all nations and countries for joint revolutionary struggle to overthrow the landlords and the bourgeoisie must be made the cornerstone of the Communist International's policy on the national and colonial questions. For this union alone can guarantee victory over capitalism, without which the abolition of national oppression and inequality is impossible.

5. The world political situation has now put the dictatorship of the proletariat on the agenda, and all developments in world politics are inevitably focusing around one central point, namely the struggle of the world bourgeoisie against the Soviet Russian Republic, which should[2] unfailingly group around itself, on the one hand, the Soviet movements of the advanced workers of all countries, and, on the other, all the national-liberation movements in the colonies and among the oppressed nationalities, who are learning from bitter experience that their only salvation lies in *an alliance with the revolutionary proletariat and in*[3] the triumph of Soviet power over world imperialism.

6. Consequently, one cannot limit oneself at present to mere recognition or proclamation of the need for closer union between the working people of various nations; what is essential is to pursue a policy designed to achieve the closest alliance of all national and colonial liberation movements with Soviet Russia, determining what forms this alliance should take according to the degree of development attained by the communist movement among the proletariat of each country, or by the *revolutionary-liberation movement*[4] in backward countries or among backward nationalities.

[1] SOURCE: *Protokoly Vtorogo Kongressa* (Moscow, 1934), pp. 491–6. For the original text by Lenin, see *Polnoye Sobraniye Sochinenii*, vol. XLI, pp. 163–8.

[2] Lenin wrote simply 'which is grouping'.

[3] The words in italic were added by the Commission.

[4] As explained in the Introduction, the most important change made in

7. Federation is a transitional form leading to the complete unity of the working people of different nations. Federation has already shown its suitability in practice both in the relations of the R.S.F.S.R. with other Soviet republics (the Hungarian, Finnish and Latvian in the past, and the Azerbaidjan and the Ukrainian at present) and in relations inside the R.S.F.S.R. itself with regard to nationalities which previously enjoyed neither statehood nor autonomy. . . .

8. . . . Recognizing federation as a form of transition towards complete unity, we must strive for ever closer federal unity. . . .

11. In respect of more backward states and nations, where feudal or patriarchal and patriarchal-peasant relations predominate, it is particularly important to bear in mind *the following points*:[1]

(A) All communist parties *must give practical assistance to the revolutionary-liberation movements*[2] in these countries; *moreover, the form that such aid is to take should be discussed with the Communist Party of the particular country, if such a party exists*.[3] The obligation to render the most active assistance rests in the first instance with the workers of the country on which the backward nation is colonially and financially dependent.

(B) It is necessary to struggle against the reactionary and medieval influence of the clergy, the *Christian missions*[4] and other similar elements.

(C) It is necessary to struggle against Pan-Islamism, *the Pan-Asian movement*[5] and similar trends which attempt to combine the liberation struggle against European and American imperialism with the reinforcement *of Turkish and Japanese imperialism, of the nobility, big land-owners, the clergy, etc.*[6]

(D) It is particularly necessary to give special support to the peasant movement in backward countries against the landlords, against large-scale land-proprietorship, and against all manifes-

---

Lenin's theses by the Commission consisted in replacing throughout 'bourgeois-democratic' by 'revolutionary'. The original draft read here 'bourgeois-democratic liberation movement of the workers and peasants', instead of 'revolutionary-liberation movement'.

[1] The addition of the words 'the following points' resulted in a certain number of purely stylistic changes in points A to F of paragraph 11 which are entirely without interest for our purposes.

[2] Here again 'bourgeois-democratic liberation movements' have become 'revolutionary-liberation movements'.

[3] The passage in italic was added by the Commission.

[4] This whole sentence was recast, but the only modification of substance was the addition of the Christian missions to the list of reactionary influences to be struggled against.

[5] Added by the Commission.

[6] In Lenin's original draft, the words in italic were replaced by: '. . . the reinforcement of the positions of the khans, of the land owners, of the mollahs, etc.'.

tations or survivals of feudalism; it is essential to try to make the peasant movement most revolutionary in character *by uniting the peasants and all the exploited, wherever possible, into Soviets, and thereby*[1] achieving the closest possible union between the Western European communist proletariat and the revolutionary peasant movement in the East, in the colonies and the backward countries generally.

(E) It is necessary to struggle determinedly against the tendency to paint *not genuinely communist revolutionary-liberation trends in the backward countries*[2] in communist colours; the Communist International is obliged to support *revolutionary*[3] movements in colonial and backward countries only on condition that, in these backward countries, the elements of future proletarian parties, which will be communist in more than name, are banded together and trained to be aware of their special tasks, namely those of the struggle against the bourgeois democratic movements within their own nations; the Communist International must enter into *temporary arrangements, even alliances,*[4] with the bourgeois democrats in the colonies and backward countries, but should not merge with them, and should maintain at all costs the independence of the proletarian movement even in its most embryonic form.

(F) It is necessary to explain constantly and to expose to the broadest working masses of all countries and nations, and especially to the backward ones, the deception systematically practised, with the assistance of *the privileged classes of the oppressed countries,*[5] by the imperialist powers, who, under the guise of creating politically independent states, bring into being states that are completely dependent upon them economically, financially and militarily. *The Zionist enterprise in Palestine provides a striking example of the deception of the working masses of an oppressed nation brought about jointly by the imperialism of the Entente and by the bourgeoisie of the nation in question. . . .*[6] Under present-day international conditions there is no salvation for dependent and weak nations except in a union of Soviet republics.

12. The age-old oppression of colonial and weak nationalities by the imperialist powers has left the working masses of the oppressed

[1] Lenin had added the idea of forming Soviets as an afterthought, on the proofs of his theses, at the end of point D. The Commission moved this idea to the middle of the sentence, and changed 'Soviets of toilers' into 'Soviets of peasants and of all the exploited'.

[2] The words in italic replace 'bourgeois-democratic liberation trends'.

[3] As usual, 'revolutionary movements' were originally 'bourgeois-democratic national movements'.

[4] Lenin wrote simply, 'conclude a temporary alliance'.

[5] This hostile reference to the indigenous bourgeoisie, added by the Commission, is evidently in accord with Roy's ideas.

[6] This whole passage against Zionism, of which we give only about half here, was absent from Lenin's original draft.

countries not only with hatred but distrust of the oppressor nations in general, the proletariat of these nations included. The despicable betrayal of socialism by the majority of the official leaders of this proletariat in 1914–19, when the social chauvinists passed off their defence of the 'right' of their 'own' bourgeoisie to oppress colonies and fleece financially-dependent countries as 'defending the fatherland', was bound to deepen this perfectly legitimate distrust.[1] These prejudices are bound to die out very slowly, for distrust and national prejudices can disappear only after imperialism and capitalism have been eradicated from the advanced countries, and after the whole foundation of the economic life of the backward countries has been radically changed. Hence it is the duty of the entire politically-conscious communist proletariat of all countries to treat with particular caution and attention the survivals of national sentiment in countries and among nationalities which have been longest oppressed; it is also their duty to make certain concessions in order to see to it that this distrust and these prejudices are dispelled more quickly. Unless the proletariat, followed by the working masses in all countries and nations throughout the world, voluntarily strive to achieve alliance and unity, complete victory over capitalism cannot be won.

4. *Extracts from the Debates in Plenary Session, 26–8 July 1920*

As emphasized in the Introduction, the debates on the national and colonial question at the Second Congress of the International constituted a decisive stage in the development of revolutionary tactics adapted to the non-European countries. As compared to the discussion in the Commission (Text III 2), the chief novelty here is the appearance, in addition to Roy's asiocentrism and Lenin's relatively balanced position, of an extreme europocentric position defended by the Italian Serrati.[2]

[1] Here the Commission eliminated the following passage, which appeared in Lenin's original draft: 'On the other hand, the more backward a country is, the stronger in it are small agricultural production, patriarchalism and ignorance, which inevitably cause the deepest of petty-bourgeois prejudices, viz., the prejudices of national egoism and national narrowness, to become particularly strong and tenacious.' This sentence, although perfectly in harmony with the spirit of Marx's writings on Asiatic society, was hardly compatible with the advice given by Lenin a few lines further on, regarding the obligation for European revolutionaries to show great tact in dealing with 'survivals of national sentiment' in the former colonial and dependent countries. Today the Soviet leaders seem to attach more weight to what Lenin eliminated from his theses than to what he retained. (See below, Text X 3.)

[2] SOURCE: For Lenin's report, we have followed as usual the most recent edition of his works: *Polnoye Sobraniye Sochinenii*, vol. 41, pp. 241–7. Our translation of his report is taken, with a few minor corrections, from the *Selected Works* (London, Lawrence and Wishart, 1938), vol. X, pp. 239–44. Roy's supplementary theses are printed as given in *Theses of the Communist International* complete. As adopted by the Second Congress held in Moscow, August 1920 (London, Communist Party of Great Britain, 1921). For Roy's speech and his

LENIN (Report on the national and colonial question): What is the most important, the fundamental idea contained in our theses? The distinction between oppressed nations and oppressing nations. Unlike the Second International and bourgeois democracy, we emphasize this distinction. . . .

The characteristic feature of imperialism is that the whole world, as we see, is at present divided into a large number of oppressed nations and an insignificant number of oppressing nations possessing colossal wealth and powerful military forces. The overwhelming majority of the population of the world, numbering more than a billion, in all probability a billion and a quarter, if we take the total population of the world at one and three-quarter billion, i.e., about 70 per cent of the population of the world, belongs to the oppressed nations, which are either in a state of direct dependence or belong to the outlying colonial states such as Persia, Turkey and China, or else, after being conquered by the armies of a big imperialist power, have been forced into dependence upon it by treaties. This distinction, the idea of dividing the nations into oppressing and oppressed nations, runs like a thread through all the theses, not only the first theses which appeared over my name and which were published earlier, but also through Comrade Roy's theses. The latter were written mainly from the point of view of the situation in India and among other large nationalities which are oppressed by Great Britain, and this is what makes them very important for us.

The second leading idea in our theses is that in the present world situation, after the imperialist war, the mutual relations between the nations, the whole world system of states, are determined by the struggle waged by a small group of imperialist nations against the Soviet movement and the Soviet states, at the head of which stands Soviet Russia. . . .

Thirdly, I would like particularly to emphasize the question of the bourgeois-democratic movement in backward countries. It was this question that gave rise to some disagreement. We argued about

---

further remarks in the course of the debate, we follow the English version of the proceedings of the Congress. The remainder of our text has been established after a comparison of all the existing versions, namely:

English edition: *The Second Congress of the Communist International.* Proceedings . . . (Moscow, Publishing Office of the Communist International, 1920), p. 595.

German edition: *Der zweite Kongress der Kommunistischen Internationale.* Protokolle der Verhandlungen . . . (Verlag der Kommunistischen Internationale. Auslieferungsstelle für Deutschland, Carl Hoym Nachf. Louis Cahnbley, Hamburg, 1921), p. 798.

Russian editions: *Vtoroy Kongress Kominterna.* Stenograficheskiy otchet (Moscow, 1921) and *Protokoly Kongressov Kommunisticheskogo Internatsionala.* Vtoroy Kongress (Moscow, 1934).

French edition: *IIème Congrès de la IIIème Internationale communiste.* Compte-rendu sténographique (Petrograd, Editions de l'Internationale Communiste, 1921), p. 628.

whether it would be correct, in principle and in theory, to declare that the Communist International and the communist parties should support the bourgeois-democratic movement in backward countries. As a result of this discussion we unanimously decided to speak of the nationalist-revolutionary movement instead of the 'bourgeois-democratic' movement. There is not the slightest doubt that every nationalist movement can only be a bourgeois-democratic movement, for the bulk of the population in backward countries are peasants who represent bourgeois-capitalist relations. It would be utopian to think that proletarian parties, if indeed they can arise in such countries, could pursue communist tactics and a communist policy in these backward countries without having definite relations with the peasant movement and without effectively supporting it. But it was argued that if we speak about the bourgeois-democratic movement all distinction between reformist and revolutionary movements will be obliterated; whereas in recent times this distinction has been fully and clearly revealed in the backward and colonial countries, for the imperialist bourgeoisie is trying with all its might to implant the reformist movement also among the oppressed nations. A certain *rapprochement* has been brought about between the bourgeoisie of the exploiting countries and those of the colonial countries, so that very often, even in the majority of cases, perhaps, where the bourgeoisie of the oppressed countries does support the national movement, it simultaneously works in harmony with the imperialist bourgeoisie, i.e. it joins the latter in fighting against all revolutionary movements and revolutionary classes. In the commission this was proved irrefutably, and we came to the conclusion that the only correct thing to do was to take this distinction into consideration and nearly everywhere to substitute the term 'nationalist-revolutionary' for the term 'bourgeois-democratic'. The meaning of this change is that we communists should, and will, support bourgeois liberation movements in the colonial countries only when these movements are really revolutionary, when the representatives of these movements do not hinder us in training and organizing the peasants and the broad masses of the exploited in a revolutionary spirit. Even if these conditions do not exist, the communists in these countries must fight against the reformist bourgeoisie, among which we include the heroes of the Second International. Reformist parties already exist in colonial countries, and sometimes their representatives call themselves social democrats and socialists. The above-mentioned distinction has now been drawn in all the theses, and I think that, thanks to this, our point of view has been formulated much more precisely.

I would like next to make a few remarks concerning Peasants' Soviets. The practical work carried on by the Russian communists in the colonies which formerly belonged to tsarism, in backward countries like Turkestan and others, confronted us with the question of how to apply communist tactics and policy amidst pre-capitalist conditions; for the most important characteristic feature of these countries is that pre-capitalist relations still predominate in them, and, therefore, a purely proletarian movement is out of the question in them. In those countries there is almost no industrial proletariat. Nevertheless, even there we have undertaken and had to undertake the role of leader. Our work revealed to us that in those countries we have to overcome colossal difficulties; but the practical results of our work also revealed to us that, notwithstanding these difficulties, it is possible to rouse among the masses a striving for independent political thought and independent political activity, even where there is almost no proletariat. This work was more difficult for us than for the comrades in West European countries, because the proletariat in Russia is overwhelmed with state work. It is quite understandable that peasants who are in a state of semi-feudal dependence can fully appreciate the idea of Soviet organization and put it into practice. It is also clear that the oppressed masses, who are not only exploited by merchant capital, but also by feudal rulers, and by the state, on a feudal basis, can wield this weapon, this form of organization, even in the conditions under which they live. The idea of Soviet organization is a simple one and can be applied, not only to proletarian, but also to peasant, feudal and semi-feudal relations. Our experience in this sphere is not yet very considerable; but the debates which took place in the Commission, in which several representatives of colonial countries participated, proved irrefutably that it is necessary to indicate in the theses of the Communist International that Peasants' Soviets, Soviets of the exploited, are a useful weapon, not only for capitalist countries, but also for countries in which pre-capitalist relations exist; and we must say that it is the bounden duty of the communist parties, and of those elements which are associated with them, to carry on propaganda in favour of the idea of Peasants' Soviets, of Toilers' Soviets everywhere, in backward countries and in colonies; in those countries, also, they must strive to create Soviets of the Toiling People as far as conditions will allow.

This opens up for us a very interesting and important sphere of practical work. Our general experience in this respect is not particularly large as yet; but little by little we shall accumulate an increasing amount of material. There can be no argument about the fact that the proletariat of the advanced countries can and must assist the backward toiling masses, and that the development of the backward countries can emerge from its present stage when the victorious proletariat of the Soviet republics stretches out a helping hand to these masses.

A rather lively debate on this question took place in the Commission, not only in connexion with the theses which I signed, but still more in connexion with Comrade Roy's theses, which Comrade Roy will defend here, and to which certain amendments were unanimously adopted.

The question was presented in the following way: can we recognize as correct the assertion that the capitalist stage of development of national economy is inevitable for those backward nations which are now liberating themselves and among which a movement along the road of progress is now, after the war, observed? We reply to this question in the negative. If the revolutionary, victorious proletariat carries on systematic propaganda among them, and if the Soviet governments render them all the assistance they possibly can, it will be wrong to assume that the capitalist stage of development is inevitable for the backward nationalities. In all colonies and backward countries, we must not only form independent cadres of fighters, we must not only form party organizations, we must not only immediately carry on propaganda in favour of organizing Peasants' Soviets and strive to adapt them to pre-capitalist conditions; the Communist International must lay down, and give the theoretical grounds for, the proposition that, with the aid of the proletariat of the most advanced countries, the backward countries may pass to the Soviet system and, after passing through a definite stage of development, to communism, without passing through the capitalist stage of development....

I would also like to mention the importance of the revolutionary work of the communist parties, not only in their own countries but also in the colonies, and especially among the troops which the exploiting nations employ to hold the peoples of their colonies in subjection.

Comrade Quelch of the British Socialist Party spoke of this in our Commission. He stated that the rank-and-file English worker would consider it treachery to help the enslaved peoples in their revolt against British rule. It is true that the jingo and chauvinist-minded labour aristocracy in England and America represents a very great danger to socialism, that it is the strongest support of the Second International, and that here we have to deal with the worst treachery of those leaders and workers who belong to the bourgeois International. The Second International also discussed the colonial question. The Basle Manifesto also spoke of it quite plainly. The parties of the Second International promised to behave in a revolutionary way, but we see no real revolutionary work and help for the exploited and oppressed peoples in their revolts against the oppressing nations from the parties of the Second International, nor I believe, from the majority of the parties which have left the Second International and wish to join the Third International....

ROY: Comrades, as a representative of British India I have submitted to the Congress and to the Commission certain supplementary theses which should be made public here, in view of the fact that they have not been published. I will now read them.

1. To determine more especially the relation of the Communist International to the revolutionary movements in the countries dominated by capitalist imperialism, for instance, in China and India, is one of the most important questions before the Second Congress of the Third International. The history of the world revolution has come to a period when a proper understanding of this relation is indispensable. The great European War and its result has shown clearly that the masses of non-European subjected countries are inseparably connected with the proletarian movement in Europe, as a consequence of the centralism of world capitalism; for instance, the sending of colonial troops and huge armies of workers to the battle front during the war, etc.

2. *One of the main sources from which European capitalism draws its chief strength is to be found in the colonial possessions and dependencies.*[1] Without the control of the extensive markets and vast fields of exploitation in the colonies, the capitalist powers of Europe cannot maintain their existence even for a short time. England, the stronghold of imperialism, has been suffering from overproduction since more than a century ago. But for the extensive colonial possessions acquired for the sale of her surplus products and as a source of raw materials for her ever-growing industries, the capitalist structure of England would have been crushed under its own weight long ago. By enslaving the hundreds of millions of inhabitants of Asia and Africa, English imperialism succeeds so far in keeping the British proletariat under the domination of the bourgeoisie.

3. Extra profit gained in the colonies is the mainstay of modern capitalism, *and so long as the latter is not deprived of this source of extra profit it will not be easy for the European working class to overthrow the capitalist order.*[2] Thanks to the possibility of the extensive and intensive exploitation of human labour and natural resources in the colonies, the capitalist nations of Europe are trying, not without success, to recover from their present bankruptcy. By exploiting the masses in the colonies, European imperialism will be in a position to give concession after concession to the labour aristocracy at home. Whilst on the one hand, European imperialism seeks to lower the

[1] Instead of the sentence in italic, Roy originally wrote: 'European capitalism draws its chief strength less from the industrial countries of Europe than from its colonial possessions.' (In as much as only the final version of Roy's theses is available in English, and one must rely for his original draft on the Russian and German translations, this and the following variants can be indicated only approximately, but the general sense of the modifications is clear enough.)

[2] This is the most important change made in Roy's theses in commission. Roy's original draft stated categorically: 'The European working class will not succeed in overthrowing the capitalist order until this source has been definitively cut off.'

standard of living of the home proletariat by bringing into competition the productions of the lower-paid workers in subject countries; on the other hand, it will not hesitate to go to the extent of sacrificing the entire surplus value in the home country so long as it continues to gain huge super-profits in the colonies.

4. The breaking up of the colonial empire, together with a proletarian revolution in the home country, will overthrow the capitalist system in Europe. Consequently, the Communist International must widen the sphere of its activities. It must establish relations with those revolutionary forces that are working for the overthrow of imperialism in the countries subjected politically and economically. These two forces must be coordinated if the final success of the world revolution is to be guaranteed.

5. The Communist International is the concentrated will of the world revolutionary proletariat. Its mission is to organize the working class of the whole world for the overthrow of the capitalist order and the establishment of communism. The Third International is a fighting body which must assume the task of combining the revolutionary forces of all the countries of the world. Dominated as it was by a group of politicians, permeated with bourgeois ideas, the Second International failed to appreciate the importance of the colonial question. For them the world did not exist outside of Europe. They could not see the necessity of coordinating the revolutionary movement of Europe with those in the non-European countries. Instead of giving moral and material help to the revolutionary movement in the colonies, the members of the Second International themselves became imperialists.

6. Foreign imperialism, imposed on the Eastern peoples *prevented them from developing, socially and economically, side by side with their fellows in Europe and America.*[1] Owing to the imperialist policy of preventing industrial development in the colonies, a proletarian class, in the strict sense of the word, could not come into existence there until recently. Skilled craft industries were destroyed to make room for the products of the centralized industries in the imperialist countries; consequently a majority of the population was driven to the land to produce food grains and raw materials for export to foreign lands. On the other hand, there followed a rapid concentration of land in the hands of the big land-owners, of financial capitalists and the State, thus creating a huge landless peasantry. The great bulk of the population was kept in a state of illiteracy. As a result of this policy, the spirit of revolt, latent in every subject people, found its expression only through the small, educated middle class.

Foreign domination has obstructed the free development of the

[1] The original draft read here: '. . . has unquestionably handicapped their social and economic development and prevented them from reaching the level of Europe and America.'

social forces, therefore its overthrow is the first step towards a revolution in the colonies. So to help overthrow the foreign rule in the colonies is not to endorse the nationalist aspirations of the native bourgeoisie, but to open the way to the smothered proletariat there.

7. There are to be found in the dependent countries two distinct movements which every day grow further apart from each other. One is the bourgeois democratic nationalist movement, with a programme of political independence under the bourgeois order, and the other is the mass action of the poor and ignorant peasants and workers for their liberation from all forms of exploitation. The former endeavours to control the latter, and often succeeds to a certain extent, but the Communist International and the parties affected must struggle against such control and help to develop class-consciousness in the working masses of the colonies. For the overthrow of foreign capitalism, which is the first step towards revolution in the colonies, *the cooperation of the bourgeois nationalist revolutionary elements is useful.*[1]

But the first and most necessary task is the formation of communist parties which will organize the peasants and workers and lead them to the revolution and to the establishment of Soviet Republics. Thus the masses in the backward countries may reach communism, not through capitalist development, but led by the class-conscious proletariat of the advanced capitalist countries.

8. The real strength of the liberation movements in the colonies is no longer confined to the narrow circle of bourgeois democratic nationalists. In most of the colonies there already exist organized revolutionary parties which strive to be in close connexion with the working masses. (The relation of the Communist International with the revolutionary movement in the colonies should be realized through the mediums of these parties or groups, because they were the vanguard of the working class in their respective countries.) They are not very large today but they reflect the aspirations of the masses, and the latter will follow them to the revolution. The communist parties of the different imperialist countries must work in conjunction with these proletarian parties of the colonies, and through them give all moral and material support to the revolutionary movement in general.

9. The revolution in the colonies is not going to be a communist revolution in its first stages. But if from the outset the leadership is in the hands of a communist vanguard, the revolutionary masses will not be led astray, but may go ahead through the successive periods of development of revolutionary experience. Indeed, it would be extremely erroneous in many of the oriental countries to try to

[1] Here Roy wrote simply: 'The first step towards revolution in the colonies must be the overthrow of foreign capitalism.' Any idea of collaboration with the bourgeois nationalists was thus absent from his theses.

solve the agrarian problem according to pure communist principles. In its first stages, the revolution in the colonies must be carried on with a programme which will include many petty bourgeois reforms, such as division of land, etc. But from this it does not follow at all that the leadership of the revolution will have to be surrendered to the bourgeois democrats. On the contrary, the proletarian parties must carry on vigorous and systematic propaganda of the Soviet idea and organize the peasants' and workers' Soviets as soon as possible. These Soviets will work in cooperation with the Soviet Republics in the advanced capitalist countries for the ultimate overthrow of the capitalist order throughout the world.

Certain of the alterations which the Commission has made in my theses have been accepted by me. I draw the special attention of the Congress to these most important questions. I am most pleased that I have the opportunity for the first time to take part in the serious discussion of the colonial question at the Congress of the revolutionary proletariat. Until the present time, the European parties did not pay sufficient attention to this question; they were too busy with their own affairs and ignored the colonial questions. At the same time, these questions are of great importance for the international movement. . . .

. . . A new movement among the exploited masses has started in India, which has spread rapidly and found expression in a gigantic strike movement. This mass movement is not controlled by the revolutionary nationalists, but is developing independently, in spite of the fact that the nationalists are endeavouring to make use of it for their own purposes. This movement of the masses is of a revolutionary character, although it cannot be said that the workers and peasants constituting it are class-conscious. . . . This stage of the revolutionary movement of the masses opens a new field of activity for the Communist International, and it is only a question of finding the proper methods for gathering the fruits of that activity. Naturally a revolution started by the masses in that stage will not be a communist revolution, for revolutionary nationalism will be in the foreground. But at any rate this revolutionary nationalism is going to lead to the downfall of European imperialism, which would be of enormous significance for the European proletariat. I conclude my speech with an urgent appeal to the delegates of the Congress in no wise to reject that support which the colonial peoples are now offering the revolutionary proletariat. . . .

SULTAN-ZADÉ: . . . [There exists in the East] a highly-charged atmosphere, and the next storm of the national revolution in these countries may, given the extreme weakness of the bourgeoisie, transform itself rapidly into a social revolution. This situation is on the whole that of most of the colonial countries of Asia. Does it perhaps follow that the destiny of world communism depends on the triumph of the social revolution in the East, as Comrade Roy claims? Naturally not. And yet a number of comrades, especially those from Turkestan, fall into this error. . . . Let us suppose that the communist revolution begins today in India. Will the workers of that country be able to resist the onslaught of the bourgeoisie without the aid of a great revolutionary movement in England and in all Europe? Assuredly not. The experience of the Persian and Chinese revolutions demonstrates this. If the Turkish and Persian revolutionaries are now throwing down the gauntlet to almighty England, it is not because they have become stronger, but because of the weakness of the world imperialist robbers. The revolution which threatens in the West has shaken the East to its foundations and thereby strengthened the revolutionaries of Persia and Turkey. The epoch of the world revolution is open.

The passage in the theses proposing that we support the bourgeois-democratic movement in the backward countries appears to me to be valid only for countries in which this movement is barely getting under way. On the contrary, in countries where we have an experience of ten years or more, and in those such as Persia where bourgeois democracy is the foundation and the mainstay of the existing political power, the application of such tactics would mean pushing the masses towards the counter-revolution. In such cases our task is to create and to support a purely communist movement, opposed to the bourgeois-democratic movements. Any other evaluation of the facts could produce disastrous results. . . .

MARING: . . . In my opinion, there is no question on our agenda of such great importance for the future development of the world revolution as the national and colonial question.

. . . It suffices to note that in Java alone there are 200 large sugar refineries employing a numerous proletariat, to understand that these Eastern countries also have a certain importance for the revolution. . . . The peasants are the proprietors of their land, but in reality they are completely proletarianized, being obliged to rent part of their land to European capital, and being totally exploited by the privileged classes of Java. As a result, being unable to earn a living as peasants, they are obliged to go and work in the sugar refineries. When one stops to think that there is now in Java a proletariat of one million, with an average income of half a ducat per day, that the cost of living is rising there, too, and that a majority of the Javanese cannot even eat rice once a day throughout the year, one realizes that the situation there is altogether ripe for revolutionary propaganda. . . .

. . . I give these few facts here simply because I have the impression that with a few exceptions, this Congress of the Third International has not thoroughly grasped either the great importance of the Eastern question. . . .

. . . I now come to my second point, and I begin by stating that I see no difference whatever between the theses of Comrade Lenin and those of Comrade Roy. Their meaning is identical. The difference lies solely in finding the correct attitude towards the relations between revolutionary nationalist movements and socialist movements in the backward countries and in the colonies. In practice, this difficulty does not exist. It is unquestionably necessary to collaborate with the revolutionary nationalist elements, and we are neglecting half our task if we reject this movement, if we behave like doctrinaire Marxists. . . .

. . . I have only one last plea. Comrade Reed said yesterday that the Negroes should come here to familiarize themselves with conditions in Russia. I propose that the Communist International provide the means so that the leaders of the Far East can spend half a year here and attend a few courses in communism, so that they may properly understand what is going on here and so that they may create a Soviet organization and carry out communist work in the colonies. I ask this because I am convinced that Moscow and Petrograd constitute a new Mecca for the East, and that the capitalist governments will do everything to prevent our communist Hadjis from going there. We must provide the opportunity here in Russia for the Eastern revolutionaries to acquire a theoretical training, so that the Far East may become an active participant in the Communist International.

ZINOVIEV: I propose that we vote for and against the theses, and that we send the amendments back to the Commission. I hope that the Commission will arrive at unanimous conclusions, but if there should be divergences, they would be submitted to the Congress.

SERRATI: I had the intention of making a speech: I now prefer to limit myself to a brief statement explaining my vote. I find in the theses on the national and colonial question presented to the Congress by Comrades Lenin and Roy not only some contradictions, but also, and above all, a grave danger for the position of the communist proletariat in the advanced countries, which should remain clearly hostile to all forms of class collaboration, especially in a pre-revolutionary period.

The definition of a 'backward country' is too vague and imprecise to avoid lending itself to chauvinist interpretations.

In general, no act of national liberation carried out by bourgeois-democratic groups – even if methods of insurrection are employed – is a revolutionary act. It is carried out either on behalf of a national imperialism in the process of formation, or in the context of the struggle of the capitalist imperialism of one state against the state which dominated the country in the first place. National liberation can never be revolutionary if the proletariat does not participate in it. Class struggle, even in the so-called backward countries, can be carried out only in maintaining absolutely the independence of the proletariat from all exploiters, even from these bourgeois democrats who call themselves 'revolutionary nationalists'.

The genuine liberation of the oppressed peoples can be carried out only by the proletarian revolution and the Soviet régime, and not by a temporary and accidental alliance of the communist parties with bourgeois parties which are said to be revolutionary.

Such alliances can, on the contrary, lead only to the weakening of the class consciousness of the proletariat, above all in the countries which as yet are scarcely accustomed to the struggle against capitalism.

The insufficient clarity of the theses hides the danger of giving arms to the pseudo-revolutionary chauvinism of Western Europe against truly communist international action.

For these reasons, I declare that I shall abstain from voting.

WIJNCUP: This is an unheard-of development. . . . Comrade Serrati, who took no part in the discussion and did not present his arguments, as he could and should have done, now informs us that these excellent theses are counter-revolutionary. . . .

ROY: Serrati says that Lenin's theses and mine are counter-revolutionary.

SERRATI: No, no.

ROY: I am sure that no proletarian can regard the assistance rendered to the oppressed peoples in this struggle against foreign oppression as being reactionary. Every national revolution in a backward country is a step in advance. It is unscientific to distinguish the various forms of revolution. Every revolution is one of the varieties of the social revolution. The peoples of the exploited countries, whose economic and political evolution has been hampered, must pass through the stages which the European peoples have passed long ago. One who regards it as reactionary to aid these people in their national struggle is himself reactionary and the advocate of imperialism.

I protest against Serrati's declaration, and request that it not be inserted in the proceedings.

SERRATI: . . . Comrade Roy did not understand my declaration. I say that he did not understand it, for I think I expressed myself clearly enough. I was trying to say that the theses as they have been presented are not sufficiently clear, and that they can lend themselves to chauvinist and nationalist interpretations. If I had thought that it was a matter of adopting counter-revolutionary theses, dear

Comrade Roy, I am sufficiently honest and frank to vote against them, and there would have been no harm in the fact that, at a communist Congress, someone voted against a proposition that had been formulated.

Comrade Roy says that every revolution has a social character, but this is the argument that was put out during the war by all the intermediaries and accomplices of the bourgeoisie. They told us: 'Revolutionary war is a socialist war; you must participate in it.' And we replied: 'No, we will not participate in it.'

. . . I had the intention of proposing a resolution regarding the order of the day, and I did not do so because I thought that it was not possible to have a reasonably objective discussion. I wanted to present the following order of the day:

The Congress sends its most fraternal salutations to the peoples who are suffering from the oppression of the imperialist states. It expresses its entire and active sympathy for their struggle against the exploiters, and it declares that, in its struggle against capitalist oppression, the proletariat has the right to take advantage of national insurrections in order to transform them finally into a social revolution.

My idea here is very simple. Instead of saying that the Communist Party and the proletariat may, in certain cases, under certain circumstances and with certain guarantees, unite with the petty-bourgeois movement, I say no. The working class can take advantage of a petty-bourgeois revolutionary movement in the interest of the social revolution. But it must not, above all in the backward countries, support the bourgeoisie, for otherwise it runs the risk of losing its class position and its class orientation, and the masses can lose their class orientation more easily in the backward countries than in the advanced countries, for in these countries the proletariat does not yet have a firm class consciousness, and blindly follows its leaders. . . .

ZINOVIEV: The theses on the national and colonial questions are put to a vote. . . . (*The theses are adopted unanimously, with three abstentions. Applause.*)

SECTION IV: THE PROBLEM OF A COLONIAL REVOLUTION IN THE LIGHT OF RUSSIAN EXPERIENCE

1. The Second Congress of the Communist Organizations of the Peoples of the East

The First Congress of the Muslim communist organizations, which met in Moscow in November 1918, largely on Stalin's initiative, had created a 'Central Bureau of the Muslim Organizations of the Russian Communist Party' (*Musburo*), which was supposed to shape and coordinate the activity of the Muslim organizations in conformity with the general line of the Russian Communist Party. The Muslim Bureau rapidly evolved in the direction of a specifically Muslim communism, and the divergences between the leadership of the Russian Communist Party and the *Musburo* were already in evidence at the time of the Second Congress of the Communist Organizations of the Peoples of the East, as can be seen from the two texts which follow.

A Lenin's Report[1]

. . . The Russian Bolsheviks have succeeded in making a breach in the old imperialism, and taking upon themselves the extremely difficult but extremely noble task of laying new paths of revolution, but you, the representatives of the working masses of the East, have before you an even bigger and newer task. . . . The socialist revolution will not be merely, or mainly, the struggle of the revolutionary proletariat of each country against its own bourgeoisie – no, it will be the struggle of all colonies and countries oppressed by imperialism, of all dependent countries, against international imperialism. Describing the approach of the universal socialist revolution in our Party Programme which was adopted last March, we said that the civil war of the working people against the imperialists and exploiters in all the advanced countries is beginning to be combined with national wars against international imperialism. This is confirmed by the course of the revolution and will continue to be confirmed more and more. And it will be the same in the East.

We know that in the East the popular masses will arise to act independently, to create a new life, because these hundreds of millions of people belong to nations that are dependent and underprivileged, nations which until now have been objects of international imperialist policy, and have existed only as fertilizing agents for capitalist culture and civilization. . . . The majority who had hitherto remained completely outside the scope of historical

[1] SOURCE: Lenin, *Polnoye Sobraniye Sochinenii*, vol. XXXIX, pp. 318–30 *passim*.

progress because they could not constitute an independent revolutionary force ceased, as we know, to play such a passive role at the beginning of the twentieth century. We know that after 1905 revolutions followed in Turkey, Persia and China, and a revolutionary movement developed in India. The imperialist war also contributed to the growth of the revolutionary movement, because the imperialists had to bring whole colonial regiments into their struggle in Europe. The imperialist war aroused the East also and drew its peoples into international politics. Britain and France armed the colonial peoples and helped them to become familiar with military equipment and sophisticated machinery. And they will now make use of this knowledge against their imperialist masters. . . .

Most of the Eastern peoples are in a worse situation than Russia – the most backward country in Europe; but we succeeded in uniting the Russian peasants and workers in our struggle against feudal survivals and capitalism, and if our struggle succeeded so easily, it was because the peasants and workers united against capitalism and feudalism. . . .

You now face a task which has not confronted communists anywhere in the whole world until now: relying on general communist theory and practice, you must adapt yourselves to specific conditions of a sort not met with in European countries; you must learn to apply that theory and practice to a situation in which peasants form the bulk of the population, and in which the object is to struggle against medieval survivals, not against capitalism.

It is self-evident that final victory can be won by the proletariat of all the advanced countries of the world alone, and we Russians are starting something which the British, French or German proletariat will consolidate; but we see that they cannot be victorious without the assistance of the working masses of all the oppressed colonial peoples, the Eastern peoples first and foremost. We must realize that in isolation the vanguard cannot achieve the transition to communism.

B Resolution on the Eastern Question[1]

1. The Congress considers that without the participation of the East – a definite social and economic power – the problems of the world social revolution cannot be solved.

2. The Russian Communist Party (Bolsheviks), which by virtue of its international status at present occupies the position of leader of the world communist movement, must take specific and genuine measures to bring revolution to the East.

3. The Communist Party's revolutionary work in the East must proceed in two directions: the one stems from the Party's basic

[1] SOURCE: *Zhizn' Natsional'nostey*, no. 46 (54): 20 December 1919 and no. 47 (55): 27 December 1919.

class-revolutionary programme, which enjoins it gradually to create communist parties – sections of the Third Communist International – in the Eastern countries; the other is determined by the political and, of course, historical, social and economic situation of the present moment in the East, which makes it necessary for it to give support for a certain length of time to local national movements aiming at the overthrow of the power of Western-European imperialism, always provided that these movements do not conflict with the world proletariat's class-revolutionary aspiration to overthrow world imperialism.

4. To achieve these aims, it is essential immediately to take most earnest and thorough steps to organize Party work and anti-imperialist propaganda in the East.

5. This work must be directed by the central organ of the communist organizations of the peoples of the East, which should set up regional branches and executive departments and itself work directly under the leadership of the Central Committee of the Russian Communist Party.

6. In order to concentrate all this revolutionary energy which is to be transmitted to the East, where it will be absorbed into the system and awaken the revolutionary instinct, revolutionary work in the East must be centralized in the already existing or potential Soviet eastern republics (Turkestan, Kirghizia and others). . . .

7. To these ends it is essential to work out immediately the particular form of union and the kind of relationship to be established between these republics as they become the focal point of the revolution in the East.

8. . . . The Congress considers first and foremost that the following particular measures should be undertaken urgently:

(i) that the training of Party and Soviet workers for the East be accelerated;
(ii) that a body of Soviet orientalists be established in the East;
(iii) that an eastern, international, working-class Red Army be established, as part of the international Red Army;
(iv) that the training of Red Army commanders be intensified. . . .

2. *Extracts from the Debates at the Baku Congress (1920)*[1]

ZINOVIEV: . . . We consider this Congress a major historical event for it demonstrates that not only are the advanced workers and toiling peasants of Europe and America now awake, but we have all lived to see the awakening no longer of isolated individuals but of tens, hundreds of thousands, even millions of workers of the peoples of the East, who constitute the greater part of the world's

[1] SOURCE: *Perviy S'yezd Narodov Vostoka*, Baku, 1–8 Sentyabrya 1920 g. Stenograficheskiy Otchet (Petrograd, 1920), pp. 31–179 *passim*.

population and are therefore alone capable of finally settling the tussle between labour and capital. . . .

Comrades, our Moscow Congress debated the question: can a socialist revolution take place in the countries of the Far East before these countries have passed through a capitalist stage? You know that the view existed for a long time that each country has first to pass through a capitalist stage, that large factories must be set up and big property-owners emerge, and that the workers must of necessity gravitate into towns, and only then would it be possible to raise the question of socialism. We think now that this is not the case. As soon as even one country has broken free from the chains of capitalism, as Russia has done, as soon as the workers have put forward the question of proletarian revolution, we are enabled to say that China, India, Turkey, Persia and Armenia can and should also begin a direct struggle to establish a Soviet system. The workers of Europe will assume power, naturally not to plunder Turkey, Persia and other countries but to help them. This being so, these countries can and ought now to prepare for a Soviet revolution, for the abolition from their countries of the division between riches and poverty, in order to create a State founded on labour and conclude a firm alliance with the organized workers of the whole world.

In this connexion we put the following question to you: what form will the State take; what form of organization will there be in the East? We have reached the conclusion that we must create Soviets, even where there are no urban workers. In these cases we can create States of peasant toilers' Soviets. Not mock 'Soviets' like the ones one is sometimes shown in Turkey, but real ones, where every toiling peasant has the right to vote. . . .

We appeal not only to those who are of communist persuasion but also to non-Party people. There exist two currents. One is very swift, tumultuous and powerful: this is the current of workers' proletarian communist struggle in Russia and Germany, France and Italy, which is everywhere expanding; but there is another current, which is not yet strong enough and which now and then zigzags – this is the movement of the oppressed nationalities, which have not yet chosen their course, and which do not yet know exactly what they want but feel that their backs are breaking under drudgery and their necks being weighed down by the yoke of French and British capitalism.

We want these two movements to come closer and closer together and we want the latter one to rid itself of its nationalist prejudices, and we also want them to merge into a tumultuous and mighty current which, like the sea, will sweep away all obstacles in its path and purge the earth of all the evil from which we have suffered for so long. It is for this reason that I say to you: we patiently support groups that are not yet at one with us and on certain issues are even against us – in Turkey, for example, as you know, comrades, the Soviet Government supports Kemal. . . .

The movement that Kemal leads wishes to free the 'sacred' person of the Caliph from the hands of his enemies. . . . Is this a communist attitude? No. We respect the religious disposition of the masses; we also know how to re-educate the masses. This needs many years of work. We approach with caution the religious beliefs of the working masses of the East and of other countries. . . . You must dispel and shatter this faith in the Sultan and you must establish genuine Soviets. The Russian peasants used also to have great faith in the Tsar. However, when genuine popular revolution erupted, practically nothing remained of this faith in the Tsar. The same will happen in Turkey and throughout the East when genuine truly peasant revolution breaks out. The people then will rapidly lose their faith in the Sultan and in their overlords. We repeat, therefore, that the policy pursued by the present popular government in Turkey is not that of the Communist International, not our policy. At the same time we state that we are prepared to assist every revolutionary struggle against the British government. . . .

The great significance of the revolution that is beginning in the East does not lie in asking messieurs the British imperialists to leave the feast and then allowing rich Turks to settle their feet very comfortably on the table. No, we want to ask all of the rich most politely to take their dirty feet off the table, so that we shall no longer be dominated by easy living, charlatanism, insults against the people, and idleness, but that the work-grimed hands of the working man shall run the world.

(*Stormy applause.*)

We therefore say frankly and determinedly to the non-Party people present that pan-Islamism and Mohammedanism and all such tendencies are not in our line. We have quite a different policy. . . .

Comrades, when the East really starts to move, not only Russia but the whole of Europe will seem but a small corner in the vast panorama. Real revolution will break out only when we are joined by the 800 million inhabitants of Asia, and by the African continent, and when we see hundreds of millions of people on the move. . . . We are not concealing anything from you, but tell you clearly where we differ in our views with the representatives of the present national movement and where we are at one with them. We tell you: the national movement's aim is to help the East to rid itself of British imperialism. We have a no less important aim of our own, which is to help the workers of the East in their struggle against the rich, to help them here and now to build their own communist organizations, to explain to them what communism is, to prepare them for the real workers' revolution, for real equality and for the liberation of mankind from all oppression. . . .

Comrades! Brothers! The time has now come when you can begin to organize a genuine, popular, holy war against the bandits and oppressors. The Communist International appeals today to the peoples of the East and says to them: 'Brothers, we summon you to a holy war primarily against British imperialism!'

(*Thunderous applause, continuing shouts of 'Hurrah'. The members of the Congress stand and brandish weapons. For a long time the speaker is unable to continue. . . . Shouts of, 'We give our word.'*)

May today's announcement be heard in London, Paris, and all cities where capitalists are still in power. May they hear the solemn oath of the representatives of tens of millions of workers of the East, that in the East the power of the oppressors – the British – and the capitalist yoke oppressing the workers of the East shall be no more!

Long live the fraternal alliance of the peoples of the East with the Communist International! May capitalism perish! Long live the empire of labour!

(*Burst of applause.*

Voices: 'Long live the renaissance of the East!' Shouts of 'Hurrah!' Applause. . . . Voices: 'Long live the unifiers of the East, our honoured leaders, our beloved Red Army!')

RADEK: . . . And when we hand on to you, comrades, the banner of the joint struggle against our common enemy, we know perfectly well that together with you we shall create a culture a hundred times better than the one created by the slave-owners of the West. The East, oppressed under the yoke of the capitalists and property-owners, has developed a philosophy of long-suffering. We appeal, comrades, to the fighting instincts which animated the peoples of the East in the past, when they marched against Europe under their great conquering leaders. We know, comrades, that our opponents will say that we are invoking the memory of Genghis-Khan and the great conquering Muslim Caliphs. But we are convinced that it was not with the object of conquest or of turning Europe into a cemetery that yesterday you drew your daggers and revolvers; you drew them in order to create a new culture along with the workers of the whole world – the culture of the free worker. And this is why, when the European capitalists say that they are threatened by a new wave of barbarism, a new horde of Huns, we reply: Long live the Red East which, together with the workers of Europe, will create a new culture under the banner of communism!

(*Stormy applause.*)

NARBUTABEKOV: . . . There exist two worlds: the Western world and the Eastern world. You are aware that in the course of its historical development over many centuries the West has several times changed its form of government, beginning with the most despotic forms and ending with liberal ones in a democratic republic, whereas in the East the form of government has not changed. Russia is the first of the European powers to put forward a new form of government, the form of Soviet power. Comrades, the Eastern world and the Western world are in this respect diametrically opposed. The East is in a special situation as much from the psychological, cultural, economic and religious point of view as from that of its social structure and customs, and these peculiarities must be borne in mind. . . .

We people of the East . . . have faith in our ideological guides and the leaders of the world proletariat – comrades Lenin, Trotsky, Zinoviev and others, but all the same we must state at this Congress what we want, and the voice of the Muslim workers and the peoples of the East must be heard. If it is heard, then the state power will find it easier to fulfil its tasks and aims in implementing the great principles of social revolution in the East. We demand genuine realization of the principles of freedom, equality and brotherhood in fact and not merely on paper. . . . Everyone knows that the East is utterly different from the West and its interests are different – thus rigid application of the ideas of communism will meet with resistance in the East. And so, if we want the four hundred millions in the Muslim world to adopt the Soviet system, some special criterion will have to be applied in their case. . . .

We Turkestanis state that we have never before seen either Comrade Zinoviev or Comrade Radek or the other leaders of the revolution. They should come and see for themselves what is happening in our country, what exactly the local authorities, whose policies drive the working masses away from the Soviet power, are up to. I feel it my duty as a delegate to say this, precisely because I am staunchly behind the policy of the Soviet power. . . .

I therefore affirm that the Soviet power could not find at present a better ally than the working masses of the East. For three years now the Western European proletariat has failed to give any active support in response to the appeals of our comrades, the best leaders of the world revolution. . . .

Without further delay, therefore, the East must be properly organized, in accordance with its religious, human, social and economic circumstances. There is no other way open to the Soviet power.

(*Applause.*)

We Turkestanis state that since the first movement of the October Revolution the Turkestani working masses have been as wedded to the Soviet power as our Russian comrades. In shedding our blood on the Turkestan fronts against the enemies of the

Soviet power, we bound up our lives closely with the working masses of the whole of Russia, and the accusations of chauvinist tendencies made against Turkestani leaders must be dropped, for our workers have proved the contrary in shedding their blood. . . .

There is no question of counter-revolution, even less of chauvinism, for we ourselves, we representatives of our working peoples, combat our narrow, nationalist tendencies; we, the first revolutionaries of Turkestan, fear neither the Ulemas nor the mullahs' black hundreds. We were the first to raise our banner against them (*applause*), and we will keep it raised to the end: it will be either death or victory. I tell you, comrades, that our Turkestani masses have to fight on two fronts. On the one hand against the evil mullahs at home, and on the other against the narrow, nationalist little movements of local Europeans. Neither Comrade Zinoviev nor Comrade Lenin nor Comrade Trotsky knows the true situation in Turkestan, and what has been going on in Turkestan these past three years. We must speak out frankly and paint a true picture of the state of affairs in Turkestan, and then the eyes of our leaders will be opened. They will come to Turkestan and put matters straight. . . .

We say: remove your counter-revolutionaries, remove your alien elements who spread national discord, and remove your colonizers working behind the mask of communism!

(*Tumultuous applause and shouts of* '*Bravo*'.)

Comrades, I shall not speak at great length, but I shall simply remind you of the sacred words of our world leader, Comrade Lenin, that he is alone and that we must all help him in every way.

You have his famous words before you and you keep them in your hearts, and, having heard them, no one could say that the Soviet power wishes us any ill. Among the number of their representatives there are, perhaps, provocateurs and demagogues, but these must be ruthlessly eliminated, just as you eliminated the counter-revolutionaries. . . .

In November 1917, the Council of Peoples' Commissars addressed a special appeal bearing the signature of Comrade Lenin himself to all Muslim workers in Russia and the East. This historic appeal . . . contains the following words: 'Henceforth your beliefs and customs, your national and cultural institutions are declared free and inviolable. . . . This is your right. You must be masters in your own country. You must organize your life after your own manner and custom.'

Can we reject the Soviet power after such words?

Then along come Muslims and tell us that our beliefs are being trampled upon, that we are not allowed to pray or to bury our dead according to our rites and religion. What is the meaning of this? This is purely and simply what is meant by spreading counter-revolution among the working masses.

Perhaps this is also going on in other places. . . .

Long live our leaders, the leaders of the world proletariat – comrades Lenin, Trotsky, Zinoviev and others! . . .

PAVLOVIČ: The Third International, that is to say the communists of the whole world, sets itself the basic task of explaining the simple truth that as long as the yellow and black races are oppressed, as long as European mercenaries continue to kill Turks, Persians, Arabs, Egyptians and so forth, the European worker is unable to throw off his own chains and will remain the capitalists' slave. This is why the Third International calls on the European workers to fight for the liberation of the East. . . .

Comrades, we must not forget the simple truth that the peoples of the East shall not be able to achieve their freedom without joining forces with the proletariat of all countries. . . .

If the Eastern peoples wish to have on their side the sympathy of the international proletariat, they must also fight for Soviet power and the principles proclaimed by Soviet Russia. . . .

The example of Poland, whose bourgeois and land-owning representatives have for decades lamented the partition of the old Republic and written fervent articles about respecting the national rights of peoples; and the example of bourgeois Poland which is now behaving like a butcher towards the national minorities on its own territory and playing the gendarme for international capitalism in its struggle against the workers and peasants of Russia . . . together with a whole list of other similar facts, go to show that the establishment of national eastern states in which power left the hands of expelled aliens only to pass into those of indigenous capitalists and land-owners would not constitute a great step forward in trying to improve the situation of the popular masses.

. . . The popular masses must rise up against their indigenous and foreign oppressors. If the national revolutionary movement were to lead only to the establishment of new, strong states in the East ruled by their own local bourgeoisie, by Indian, Persian or other such parliaments – ten years from now we would have a new, terrible world war compared with which all the horrors of the 1914–18 war would pale into insignificance. . . . The revolutionary national movement will improve the lot of the popular masses only when it becomes one of the decisive stages towards a profound and broad socialist movement. . . .

RYSKULOV: . . . The East offers at present perfectly favourable conditions for the introduction of the revolutionary movement and for drawing the working masses into the socialist movement. . . .

The socialist movement in the West may be communist in character, but we in the East can certainly not count on having a purely communist movement. The movement in the East will assume a petty-bourgeois nature, and will be a movement for national self-determination and for unification of the East. But this movement will certainly turn into a social, agrarian movement. . . .

(*Applause.*)

At present the movement in the East, in those countries where the revolutionary organizations and the workers' organizations are weak, is of course national and bourgeois in character. It is led by supporters of petty-bourgeois revolution and democracy. . . . This movement, which at the outset is more united and more powerful, will, naturally, be of great service to us, for it opposes the Entente and world capitalism, and this greatly helps us.

Naturally, the Third International and the Communist Party must support this movement, but at the same time it must be said that it is not this movement that will finally liberate the working masses. The liberation of the working masses can come about only through social revolution. Therefore, even if we see that, though fighting against capitalism, the petty-bourgeois revolutionaries of the East have nothing in common with communism and strive persistently to set up their own national autonomous republics, such republics will be autonomous in name only, and none of them will ever be truly independent and autonomous. For they will line up either on the side of the bourgeoisie and the capitalists or on the side of the world proletariat – there is no alternative between the two. . . . The workers of the East have only one choice, namely to organize themselves as soon as possible under the banner of the Communist International and by its slogans, carry out an agrarian revolution with all speed, and take both land and power into their own hands. This is their only answer, the only way, the only means of genuinely implementing the right of peoples to self-determination and of bringing about their true liberation from the yoke of world capital.

(*Applause.*)

BELA KUN: . . . Whereas in the West, Soviet power is an expression of the dictatorship of the proletariat, in those countries of the East where there is no industrial working class, it will be an expression of the dictatorship of the impoverished peasantry. It goes without saying that where there are factories with however small a number of better-educated and more skilled industrial workers, these workers will become the leaders of the poor people in the countryside. . . .

I should like in a very few words to refute the ignorant view that peoples who have not passed through the capitalist stage of development and hence through the stage of bourgeois democracy must go through this entire evolution before achieving a Soviet system. This view is argued for the sole purpose of keeping the poor peasantry of the East longer under the authority of the emirs, pashas, beys and foreign colonizers. . . .

We also hear the objection that 'the peoples of the East are not advanced enough to look after their own affairs; they need to pass through the school of bourgeois democracy and to learn how to govern themselves'. Only imperialist colonizers use this argument.

In everyday language this means, 'Just have patience, you poor Muslims, until the pashas, beys, speculators and money-lenders see fit to teach you how to take their land and their power from them.'

3. Sultan Galiev: 'Social Revolution and the East'

This text was written in 1919 by Sultan Galiev, the leader of the Tatar communists, who was then a member of the Russian Communist Party, during the period when he collaborated most actively with the Soviet power. It was published in the organ of the Commissariat for Nationalities.[1]

. . . The Soviet system as an expression of communism is the antithesis of bourgeois-capitalist statehood. The two systems can neither live peaceably side by side nor coexist. They can only temporarily bear each other, only up to the moment when one side gains even a slight advantage over the other, when it is bound to launch an attack upon the momentarily weaker opponent.

Because of this immutable and fundamental law of development of social revolution, the Russian revolution, from the moment of its inception, was bound to begin developing into a world revolution: otherwise, the Soviets in Russia would have been but a small island amid the raging sea of imperialism, menaced with being obliterated at any moment by the scourge of rampant world imperialism.

The leaders of the October Revolution understood this situation very well and tried to steer the revolution on to a universal, international course. They could not have done otherwise, or else the social revolution in Russia would have lost all intrinsic meaning. From a tactical point of view, however, this was a misdirected course for the revolution to take. Though seeming outwardly correct in certain isolated manifestations (the Spartakist movement in Germany, the Hungarian revolution, etc.), it was, taken overall, one-sided. The imbalance resulted from the fact that the attention of the leaders of the revolution was almost entirely focused on the West. It seemed to them that to transform the October Revolution into a world socialist revolution all that was necessary was mechanically to impart the energy of the Russian revolution to the West, namely to the part of the globe where contradictions between the class interests of the proletariat and the bourgeoisie

[1] SOURCE: *Zhizn' Natsional'nostey*, 38 (46):5 October 1919; 39 (47): 12 October 1919; 42 (50): 2 November 1919.

appeared to be sharpest and most evident, and where, therefore, the ground seemed most favourable for the development of class revolution.

The East, however, with its one and a half thousand million people enslaved by the Western European bourgeoisie, has been almost completely overlooked from this point of view. The tide of the main process of development of the international class struggle has bypassed the East and the problem of 'bringing revolution to the East' has existed only for a few individuals who bulked no larger than a drop of water in the raging sea of revolution.

Ignorance of the East and consequent fear of it are responsible for the fact that the idea that the East could participate in the international revolution has been clearly discredited.

But it was incorrect to give the international socialist revolution an exclusively Western orientation.

It is true that the states of Western Europe, and their ally America, are countries in which all the material and 'moral' forces of international imperialism are concentrated, and in this respect they would appear to be the main battleground where we should launch our general offensive against that imperialism – but we could not state with any confidence that the Western European proletariat alone is strong enough to wreck the Western European bourgeoisie, for the simple reason that the latter is an international, world bourgeoisie and that its destruction calls for the concerted revolutionary will and energy of the whole international proletariat, including the proletariat of the East.

By taking action against international imperialism through the Western European proletariat alone, we have left it full freedom of action and manoeuvre in the East. So long as international imperialism in the shape of the Entente retains the East as a colony where it is absolute master of the entire natural wealth, it is assured of a favourable outcome of all isolated economic clashes with the metropolitan working masses, for it is perfectly able in this situation to 'shut their mouths' by agreeing to meet their economic demands.

The way in which we waited in vain for assistance from the West during the first two years of revolution in Russia eloquently confirms this proposition.

But even if the Western European worker were to succeed in defeating his local bourgeoisie, we should inevitably clash with the East, as the Western European bourgeoisie, like its fellow in adversity – the Russian bourgeoisie – would set about concentrating all its forces on its 'borderlands', primarily in the East. To crush social revolution in Western Europe, it would have no hesitation in exploiting the East's age-old national and class hatred against the West as the originator of imperialist oppression, and in organizing the Negroes to march on Europe.

Not only do we admit this to be possible, but we are convinced of it, as two years' experience of the Russian proletariat's struggle against the Russian bourgeoisie has taught us a great deal on this subject.

If one considers the East from an economic and social standpoint, one sees that it is almost entirely subject to exploitation by Western European capital, providing the main source of supply for its industry, and thus represents for us very highly 'inflammable' revolutionary material. . . .

4. *Safarov: 'The East and Communism'*

G. Safarov was sent to Turkestan by Lenin in 1919 to investigate the conflicts between the Muslims and the Russians, whether Bolsheviks or not. He presented the conclusions which he had drawn from his experience at the Tenth Congress of the Russian Communist Party in March 1920, and also in a work containing reflections of a general character on the problems of the East from which we have extracted the following text.[1]

. . . The bourgeoisie in the backward Eastern countries is incapable of waging a consistent struggle to the very end against feudalism and imperialism. It can *only begin* this struggle. This does not mean . . . that immediate sovietization of all Eastern countries struggling for national liberation is possible and necessary.

It means that in the period of fierce struggle between the dictatorship of the proletariat and world imperialism *the national movement in the East can triumph only in alliance with the proletarian Soviet republics* in the West. Federation is the form of alliance for advanced and backward nations *on a Soviet basis*. It is a sufficiently flexible and elastic form to accommodate all the diversity of historical conditions in the development of the various countries. But it is a form which presupposes a certain degree of *revolutionary maturity* in the units joining in federation. So long as the semi-proletarian and peasant masses of the backward countries blindly follow the local bourgeoisie and even feudal elements, there can be no question of their coming forward with a plan of action of their own. Moreover, given that the working masses are weakly organized, and given the existence of an insignificant minority who are capable of taking initiatives yet are only slightly linked with the masses, it is necessary to be deliberately wary of *revolutionary adventurism*. . . . Overestimating the true balance of forces can lead to playing dangerously into the hands of international imperialism. The support given to the feudal Küchük Khan of Gilan in Persia in 1920 can be quoted as an instance of this.

In the East, it is *Soviet diplomacy* primarily that should pave the way for the Communist International. . . . The agreements between the R.S.F.S.R. and Bukhara, Khiva, Afghanistan, Persia

[1] SOURCE: G. Safarov, *Problemy Vostoka* (Petrograd, 1922), pp. 170–83 *passim.*

and Turkey show that in spite of the imperialists' insane agitation against Soviet Russia, the peoples of the Near and Middle East have understood the need to unite with the Workers' and Peasants' Soviet Republic to protect their national liberty and independence. . . .

The 'Turkestanis' are Kirghiz, Uzbek and Turkmen semi-proletarians. There is more revolutionary significance in them than in all your Scheidemanns and Noskes. . . .

The strongest and most organized enemy of the proletarian revolution in the East is world imperialism. To fight against it is the paramount and fundamental task, the first and inevitable stage of the *social* revolution, since imperialism is the principal obstacle to the revolutionary development of the East. *The national movement among the oppressed nations passes through the same historical stages as the nations themselves in the course of their development*: at first, it is patriarchal-feudal elements who play a large part in it, and then these give way to an alliance between feudal elements and representatives of big finance and commercial capital, and at length the leadership passes into the more democratic hands of the artisan, commercial and industrial bourgeoisie, and only then does it pass into the hands of semi-proletarian elements, who usher in the agrarian-peasant revolution. . . .

Conditions exist in all the Eastern countries for *agrarian-peasant* revolution. . . . Raising the *agricultural* productive forces in Turkey, in Persia, Turkestan, Kashgar, Dzungaria and in India is the fundamental precondition for the genuine emancipation of these countries. However, it must be emphasized that only *the development of proletarian revolution in Europe* makes the victory of agrarian-peasant revolution in the East possible. If the indigenous bourgeoisie of the Eastern Muslim countries cannot rid itself of medieval prejudices, the *peasant* masses are even less able to take up an independent position in the struggle for national and social liberation. The imperialist system of States has no place for peasant republics. Numerically insignificant cadres of local proletarians and semi-proletarian urban and rural elements *can carry with them* broad peasant masses into the battle against imperialism and feudal elements, but this requires an *international revolutionary situation* which would enable them to ally themselves with the proletariat of the advanced countries. It is precisely from this point of view that the very existence of the R.S.F.S.R. is of considerable revolutionary importance for all Eastern countries. This international alliance of workers from West and East has already been accomplished within the R.S.F.S.R. in a Soviet form, and the peripheral eastern Soviet republics serve as a bridge linking the Western proletarian revolution with the Eastern peasant revolution. The construction of Soviets within the territory of the former tsarist 'empire' has shown in practice the validity of the

Soviet as a form for organizing working masses at the most varied stages of development. . . .

In the backward East in particular, universal suffrage laws and formal 'liberties' are not what is required for organizing working masses who have for centuries suffered under feudal dictatorship and spiritual obscurantism and who remain to this day fettered by patriarchal-feudal bonds. A dictatorial 'despotic intervention' by the progressive revolutionary vanguard is essential in order to remove from power all predatory and exploiting elements. . . .

There cannot be a special 'Eastern communism'. Petty-bourgeois 'populist' utopianism in the East inevitably takes the form of democratized pan-Turkism, which is inimical to the interests of the proletariat. But the existence of the international proletarian revolution calls for *a special revolutionary approach* to the problems of the East. . . .

National revolution, Soviet semi-proletarian peasant revolution, and the federative alliance of the peasant Soviet Eastern Republics with the proletarian Republics of the West – these are the historical stages of the revolutionary movement in the East.

5. *National Factors in Building the Party and the State*

The first open and important discussions regarding the national question took place at the Twelfth Congress of the Russian Communist Party in April 1923. They dealt primarily with the means which should be employed to struggle against local nationalisms. Stalin's report, of which we give extracts here, tended to substitute for the idea which had hitherto been prevalent, namely that the local nationalisms were a reaction against great-Russian chauvinism, the idea that such nationalisms represented an independent phenomenon of exceptional gravity.[1]

. . . A group of comrades, led by Bukharin and Rakovsky, has overemphasized the importance of the national question; they have exaggerated it and have allowed it to obscure the social question – that of working-class power.

Moreover, it is clear to us as communists that the basis of all our work is our effort to strengthen the power of the workers, and only then do we face that other question, a very important one but subordinate to the first, namely the national question. We are told one must not offend the other nationalities. This is perfectly correct and I agree one must not offend them. But to deduce from this a new theory that the Great-Russian proletariat must be put in an inferior position *vis-à-vis* the formerly suppressed nations is absurd. . . . Moreover it is clear that the political basis of proletarian dictatorship lies primarily and chiefly in the central, industrial regions and not the border regions, which are peasant countries. . . .

[1] SOURCE: *Dvenadtsatiy S'yezd Rossiiskoiy Kommunisticheskoiy Partii* (*b*), *17/25 aprelya 1923 g.* (Moscow, 1923), pp. 596–8.

It should be remembered that, apart from the right of peoples to self-determination, there also exists the right of the working class to consolidate its power, and the right of self-determination is subordinate to this latter right. There are cases when the right to self-determination comes into conflict with this other superior right – this right of the working class, having come to power, to consolidate that power. In such cases – and this should be said bluntly – the right of self-determination cannot and must not be a barrier preventing the working class from exercising its right to dictatorship. The former must give way to the latter. Such was the case, for instance, in 1920 when, in the interests of defending the working-class power, we were obliged to march on Warsaw.

The second question concerns local chauvinism and Great-Russian chauvinism. We have had speeches here from Comrade Rakovsky and particularly from Comrade Bukharin, and the latter proposed that the clause about the harmfulness of local chauvinism be deleted. There is no point, he inferred, in concerning ourselves about a little worm like local chauvinism when we are faced with a 'Goliath' like Great-Russian chauvinism. . . .

The whole Congress has seen for itself that local, Georgian, Bashkir and other chauvinism exists, and that it must be fought.

Russian communists cannot fight against Tatar, Georgian or Bashkir chauvinism, because if a Russian communist were to undertake the difficult task of fighting against Tatar or Georgian chauvinism, his struggle would be judged as one waged by a Great-Russian chauvinist against the Tatars or the Georgians. This would confuse the whole issue. Only the Georgian, Tatar and similar communists can fight against Georgian, Tatar and other chauvinism; only the Georgian communists can successfully fight against Georgian nationalism or chauvinism. This is the duty of the non-Russian communists. This is why it is necessary to note in the theses the double task of the Russian communists (their struggle against Great-Russian chauvinism) and of the non-Russian communists (their struggle against anti-Armenian, anti-Tatar and anti-Russian chauvinism).

6. *Stalin's Report on the Affair of Sultan Galiev*

At the Fourth Enlarged Conference of the Central Committee of the Russian Communist Party in June 1923, the orientation adopted at the Twelfth Congress took a more precise form with the condemnation of the 'national deviations' of Sultan Galiev, who was accused of creating an illegal organization in the Northern Caucasus, and of having planned to create an International of the Turkish peoples. The Turkestani delegates Ikramov and Khodzhanov attempted, for their part, to rehabilitate the idea that there was a link between the local nationalisms and the 'colonialist attitude' of the Bolshevik authorities.[1]

[1] SOURCE: Stalin, *Sochineniya*, vol. V, pp. 301–12.

. . . Khodzhanov spoke well, in my opinion. Ikramov did not speak badly either. But I must mention one passage in the speeches made by these comrades which gives food for thought. Both of them said that there was no difference between the Turkestan of today and tsarist Turkestan; only the signboard had been changed and Turkestan had remained as it had been under the Tsar. Comrades, if that was not a slip of the tongue, if it was a considered statement and if it was said wittingly, it must be said that in that case the Basmachi[1] are right and we are wrong. If Turkestan is in fact a colony as it was in tsarist times, then the Basmachi are right and it is not we who should be trying Sultan Galiev but he who should be trying us for tolerating the existence of a colony within the orbit of the Soviet régime. . . .

Now, a word about the 'leftists' and rightists. Do such things exist in the regional and republican communist organizations? Of course they do. One cannot deny it.

What are the sins of the rightists? They are that the rightists are not and cannot be an antidote or a sound bulwark against the nationalist tendencies that are developing and gaining in strength in connexion with the NEP. . . . .

It should be borne in mind that our communist organizations in the border areas in the republics and regions can develop and stand on their own feet and become true internationalist Marxist cadres only if they overcome nationalism. Nationalism is the chief ideological obstacle preventing the formation of Marxist cadres and a Marxist vanguard in the border areas and the republics. . . .

It is only under the cover of nationalism that various bourgeois influences, including Menshevik influences, can penetrate our organizations in the border areas. . . .

But the 'leftists' in the border areas are not less guilty, but perhaps even more guilty. If the communist organizations in the border areas cannot grow stronger and develop into genuine Marxist cadres unless they overcome nationalism, then these cadres themselves can become mass organizations and rally the majority of the working masses around themselves only by learning to be sufficiently flexible to attract into our State institutions all national elements with any sort of loyalty, by making concessions to them; these organizations should learn to strike a balance between a determined struggle against nationalism in the party and an equally determined struggle to attract into the work of the Soviets all more or less loyal elements among the local populace, the intellectuals, and so on. . . .

If the rightists threaten, with their susceptibility to nationalism, to hinder the growth of our communist cadres in the border areas,

[1] The Basmachi were a nationalist movement of the Muslims of Central Asia which carried on armed resistance against Soviet power. Although growing progressively weaker, the movement lasted from 1919 to 1930.

the 'leftists' threaten by their infatuation with a simplified and hasty 'communism' to isolate our party from the peasantry and from broad strata of the local population.

Which of these dangers is the greater?

If comrades with 'leftist' inclinations are thinking of continuing to pursue locally their policy of artificially splitting the population; and if they think that the Russian model can be mechanically transplanted into a specific national milieu regardless of particular customs and circumstances; if they think that in fighting against nationalism everything that is national should be thrown overboard all at once; in short, if the 'leftist' communists in the border areas think they can remain unchecked, I must say that of the two dangers the 'leftist' one could prove the more serious. . . .

7. Stalin on the National Question

Extracts from lectures on the principles of Leninism delivered at the beginning of April 1924 at Sverdlovsk University.[1]

Leninism . . . recognizes revolutionary potentialities within the national-liberation movement of the oppressed countries and sees the possibility of using them for the overthrow of the common enemy, imperialism. . . .

Hence the need for the proletariat of the 'dominant' nations to give support, resolute and active support, to the national-liberation movement of the oppressed and dependent peoples.

Of course, this does not mean that the proletariat should support *every* national movement, no matter where or when, in every separate, specific case. Their aim should be to support those national movements that are directed at weakening and overthrowing imperialism, not at strengthening and preserving it. Cases occur when national movements in certain oppressed countries come into conflict with the interests of the development of the proletarian movement. Obviously there can be no question of support in such cases. The question of the rights of nations is not an isolated or self-contained problem but a part of the general question of the proletarian revolution; it is subordinate to the whole and must be considered from the point of view of the whole. During the 1840s Marx favoured the national movement of the Poles and Hungarians and opposed the national movement of the Czechs and Southern Slavs. Why? Because the Czechs and Southern Slavs were at that time 'reactionary peoples', 'Russian outposts' in Europe, outposts of absolutism, whereas the Poles and the Hungarians were 'revolutionary peoples' struggling against absolutism: also because support for the national movement of the Czechs and Southern Slavs at that time meant indirect support

[1] SOURCE: Stalin, *Sochineniya*, vol. VI, pp. 142–5.

for Tsarism, the most dangerous enemy of the revolutionary movement in Europe.

'The various demands of democracy' – to quote Lenin – 'including the right of self-determination, are not an absolute but an integral small *particle* of the whole *world* democratic (nowadays socialist) movement. It is possible that in certain particular cases the part may conflict with the whole, in which event it must be rejected.'[1]

. . . The same must be said of the revolutionary nature of national movements in general. The undoubted revolutionary nature of the vast majority of national movements is as relative and singular as is the potentially reactionary nature of certain other national movements. The revolutionary character of a national movement in conditions of imperialist oppression does not necessarily imply that the movement contains proletarian elements, or that it has a revolutionary or republican programme, or that it has a democratic basis. The struggle of the Emir of Afghanistan for the independence of Afghanistan is objectively a *revolutionary* struggle, in spite of the monarchistic cast of the views of the Emir and his associates since it weakens, disunites and undermines imperialism. . . . For the same reasons, the struggle of the Egyptian merchants and bourgeois intellectuals for the independence of Egypt is objectively a *revolutionary* struggle, in spite of the bourgeois origins and bourgeois title of the leaders of the Egyptian national movement, and in spite of the fact that they are opposed to socialism; but by contrast the struggle of the British 'Labour' government to maintain Egypt's state of dependence is, for the same reasons, a *reactionary* struggle, despite the proletarian origins and proletarian title of the members of that government and despite the fact that they are 'in favour of' socialism. And I need hardly mention the national movement in other, larger, colonial and dependent countries like India and China, whose every step on the road to liberation, even if it runs counter to the demands of formal democracy, is a sledge-hammer blow struck against imperialism, i.e. unquestionably a *revolutionary* step. . . .

[1] Lenin, *Polnoye Sobraniye Sochinenii*, vol. XXX, p. 39. This passage appears in the article from which we have extracted Text II 9.

SECTION V: THE INTERNATIONAL AND REVOLUTION IN THE EAST, 1921–4

1. The Third Congress of the International as seen by M. N. Roy

Full text of Roy's protest against the way in which the Eastern question was 'liquidated' at the Third Congress, on 12 July 1921.[1]

I have been allowed five minutes for my report. As this theme cannot be dealt with adequately even in an hour, I wish to employ these five minutes for an energetic protest.

The way in which the Eastern question has been dealt with at this Congress is purely opportunist, and is worthy rather of a Congress of the Second International. It is absolutely impossible to draw any practical conclusions whatever from the few sentences which the Eastern delegations have been allowed to speak.

I protest against this method of liquidating the Eastern question. It was put on the agenda at a session of the Executive Committee. But during the whole Congress, no attention whatever was accorded to this question. A session finally took place yesterday in commission, but it was a pitiful affair. Not a single representative of the European and American delegations was present. This commission, which had not even been formally constituted as a result of the disorder which reigns at this Congress, decided to adopt no theoretical resolution regarding the Eastern question. This decision is absolutely erroneous, and should not be maintained. I therefore call upon the Congress to adopt a decision to the effect that the Eastern question should be entrusted to a duly constituted commission and treated with the seriousness which it merits.

2. The Fourth Congress of the Communist International

Extracts from the debates and from the theses of this Congress, which took place in November and December 1922.[2]

[1] SOURCE: *Protokoll des Dritten Kongresses der Kommunistischen Internationale*, Moskau, 22. Juni bis 12. Juli 1921 (Verlag der Kommunistischen Internationale, Auslieferungstelle für Deutschland, Carl Hoym Nachf. Louis Cahnbley, Hamburg, 1921), p. 1018.

[2] SOURCE: *Protokoll des Vierten Kongresses der Kommunistischen Internationale*, Petrograd-Moskau vom 5. November bis 5. Dezember 1922 (Moscow, 1923, Verlag der Kommunistischen Internationale, Auslieferungsstelle: Verlag Carl Hoym Nachf. Louis Cahnbley, Hamburg), pp. 187–9, 590–98, 620–21, 627–34, 1035–44. Our translation of the theses is adapted from that in Jane Degras, *The Communist International 1919–1943*, Documents, vol. I, pp. 384–93 *passim*.

A Extracts from the Debates

TAN MALAKA: . . . The decision of the Second Congress of the Communist International means in practice that we, too, must establish a united front with revolutionary nationalism. We must recognize that in our country too the united front is necessary. At the same time, it will be a united front not with the Social Democrats, but with the revolutionary nationalists. The nationalists employ diverse tactics against imperialism, such as boycotts and the war of liberation of the Muslims, or Pan-Islamism. . . .

I must recognize that the boycott is by no means a communist method, but in view of the military and political yoke to which we are subjected in the East, it is one of our most effective arms. The experience of the past three years shows us that in 1919 the boycott of the Egyptian peoples against English imperialism, like the great Chinese boycott of 1919–20, was crowned with success. . . . We know that the boycott is not our method of struggle. It can be the method of the petty bourgeoisie or of the nationalist bourgeoisie. We can even go further and say that the boycott represents support given to indigenous capitalism. But we have also seen that following the campaign of boycott in India 18,000 leaders still remain in prison, and that the boycott movement engendered a very revolutionary atmosphere, to such an extent that the English government was obliged to ask for the military support of Japan in case this movement degenerated into an open armed insurrection. . . .

As for Pan-Islamism, it is a long story. First of all, I should like to speak of our experience in the [Dutch East] Indies, where we worked with the Muslims. In Java we had a big association, to which many poor peasants belonged, called the 'Sarekat Islam' ('Islamic League'), and which had, between 1912 and 1916, perhaps a million members, perhaps as many as three or four millions. This was a very large popular organization, which appeared spontaneously, and which was extremely revolutionary. Down to 1921 we collaborated with it. Our party, which then had 13,000 members, went into this popular association and carried out propaganda there. In 1921, we succeeded in getting our programme adopted by the 'Sarekat Islam'. The Islamic League also carried out propaganda in the villages for the slogans 'Control of Production' and 'All power to the poor peasants, all power to the proletarians'. Thus the 'Sarekat Islam' carried out the same propaganda as our Communist Party, except that often it was expressed in different terms. But in 1921 a scission took place, as a result of clumsy criticism directed at the leaders of the 'Sarekat Islam'. The government exploited this scission through the intermediary of its agents in the 'Sarekat Islam'; it also exploited the slogan of the Second Congress of the Communist International regarding the struggle against Pan-Islamism. . . . It said to the simple peasants:

'You see, the communists not only want to carry out a scission in your ranks, they want to annihilate your religion.' This was too much for a simple Muslim peasant. The peasant said to himself: 'I have lost everything in this world. Must I lose my place in heaven as well? This won't do!' The agents of the government very skilfully exploited this frame of mind, and we therefore had a scission. (*Chairman Marchlewski: Your time is up!*) I have come from the Indies, and I travelled forty days to get here! (*Applause.*) The members of 'Sarekat Islam' believe in our propaganda and are with us (to use a familiar expression) with their stomachs, but their hearts rest attached to 'Sarekat Islam', to their heaven. For we cannot give them heaven. That is why they have boycotted our meetings, and we were not in a position to carry out any kind of propaganda whatsoever.

Early last year, we tried to re-establish the link with 'Sarekat Islam'. We said at our Congress of last December that the Muslims of the Caucasus and of the other countries which collaborate with the Soviets and fight against international capitalism have a better understanding of their religion, and we also said that if they wanted to carry out propaganda for their religion they could do it not in the meetings but in church. . . .

Last March a general strike broke out, and the Muslim workers needed us, for we had the railway workers with us. The leaders of the 'Sarekat Islam' said to us: 'If you want to work with us, you must help us too.' We naturally went with them, and we said: 'It is true, your God is powerful, but your God has said that the railway workers were even more powerful on this earth. (*Applause.*) The railway workers are God's executive committee on this earth.' (*Laughter.*) But the question is still not settled, for if we have another scission, the agents of the government will surely bring up the question of Pan-Islamism again. That is why this question is extremely topical.

Just what does Pan-Islamism mean? Formerly it had an historical signification, namely that Islam should conquer the whole world sword in hand. . . . At present Pan-Islamism has in fact a quite different meaning. It corresponds to the national liberation struggle, for Islam is everything for the Muslim. It is not only his religion, it is his state, his economy, his nourishment and all the rest. Thus Pan-Islamism now means the fraternity of all the Muslim peoples, the liberation struggle not only of the Arab people, but of the Hindu and Javanese peoples, and of all the other oppressed Muslim peoples. This fraternity now means a liberation struggle directed not only against Dutch capitalism, but against English, French, and Italian capitalism, against the capitalism of the whole world. That is what Pan-Islamism means today in the Indies, among the oppressed colonial peoples; it is in these terms that they have secretly propagated it, namely as a struggle against the various imperialist powers in the world. There is here a new task for all of us. Just as we wish to support national wars, we also wish to support the war of liberation of the 250 millions of extremely active and extremely combative Muslims against the imperialist powers. That is why I ask you once again: 'Should we support such Pan-Islamism as this?' I have said my say. (*Loud applause.*)

ROY: . . . The theses adopted by the Second Congress of the Communist International drew the conclusion that the national movement in the colonial and semi-colonial countries was objectively, fundamentally a revolutionary struggle, and as such a part of the great world revolutionary struggle. It was therefore decided that the communist parties of the Western countries, and in particular of the imperialist countries, should do all in their power to develop this liberation movement. . . . Very few understood at that time how varied were the regions and the peoples embraced by this general term of 'colonial and semi-colonial countries', and how they represented in fact every type of social development, and every type of political and industrial backwardness. We thought that, simply because they were all politically, economically, and socially backward, we could lump them all together, and deal with this problem as though it were a general problem. But this was a mistake. We know today that the Eastern countries cannot be taken as a homogeneous whole, neither politically, economically, nor socially. This Eastern question therefore represents for the Communist International a question of greater complexity than the struggle in the West – assuming that the International is prepared to take it seriously. The social character of the movement in the Western countries is uniform; this is not the case in the East.

The Eastern countries can be divided into three categories. First of all, the countries in which capitalism has reached a fairly high level of development. There, not only has the import of capital from the great capitalist centres resulted in the development of industry, but indigenous capitalism has come to maturity, thus favouring the appearance of a bourgeoisie endowed with well-developed class consciousness, and of its counterpart, a proletariat which also develops its class consciousness and finds itself engaged in economic struggles which gradually pass over to the political stage. Secondly, the countries in which capitalist development has begun, but is still at a rather low level, and in which feudalism remains the backbone of society. Then we have the third level, where primitive relations still predominate, where the feudal patriarchate still constitutes the whole of the social order. . . .

Today we find ourselves before a concrete problem: how can we encourage the development of the revolutionary movement in these countries? For despite the differences just indicated, we are confronted in all of them with a revolutionary movement. But since their social structure is different, the nature of the revolutionary movement also differs, from which it follows that the programme and tactics of revolution must likewise vary. . . .

. . . In countries in which capitalism is relatively developed, the upper stratum of the bourgeoisie, that is to say, the portion of the bourgeoisie which already has what we could call a certain basis in the country, which has invested considerable capital and created an industry, finds it more advantageous to take advantage of the protection of imperialism. For when the great social movement began at the end of the war, and developed into a revolutionary tempest, not only foreign imperialism, but also the indigenous bourgeoisie, felt itself to be threatened by this eventuality. . . . The industrial development carried out by the bourgeoisie requires peace and order, which are maintained in most of these countries by foreign imperialism. When this peace and order are endangered, and there is a possibility of an upheaval and of a revolutionary upsurge, a compromise with imperialist domination becomes more acceptable to the indigenous bourgeoisie. . . .

If we consider the second group of colonial countries, where the dominant elements in society are commercial and usurious capital, feudal bureaucracy and feudal militarism, and where these elements provide the leaders of the national movement, such a policy of compromise with imperialism has likewise been put into practice, but has not given as satisfactory results as in the countries of the first category. For it is not so easy to conciliate the interests of the feudal bureaucracy and of the feudal lords with those of the colonial power as it is to conciliate those of the imperialists and those of the indigenous bourgeoisie. Hence we see that in the course of the past year, the national struggle in Turkey has forged ahead of all the other colonial struggles.

But the recent events in Turkey also show us the weakness of this situation, for we know that a national struggle cannot give rise to a national sentiment of a political character so long as the economic destiny of the people in question is linked to a feudal-patriarchal system. So long as there is no bourgeoisie to take over the leadership of society, the national struggle with all its revolutionary possibilities cannot develop freely. . . . The bourgeoisie becomes a revolutionary factor when it raises the standard of revolt against backward and obsolete social forms, that is to say, when the struggle is directed primarily against the feudal order, with the bourgeoisie leading the people. In such circumstances, the bourgeoisie is the vanguard of the revolution.

But the same cannot be said of the new bourgeoisie in the Eastern countries, or at least of the greater part of this bourgeoisie. Although in these countries the bourgeoisie leads the struggle, it does not direct the struggle against feudalism. It carries on the struggle of a weak, underdeveloped and oppressed bourgeoisie against a powerful and highly developed bourgeoisie. Instead of a class struggle, this struggle is, so to speak, a struggle between competitors, and therefore contains possibilities of compromise. . . .

. . . Is there another social factor capable of intervening in this struggle, and of wresting the leadership from those who have thus far been directing it?

In the countries where capitalism is sufficiently developed, we find that such a social factor is already beginning to manifest itself. A proletarian class is in the process of being created there, and in countries where capitalism has begun oppressing the peasantry, this gives birth to a large mass of poor landless workers. This mass progressively joins in a combat which is not purely economic, but which is daily taking on a more political character. . . .

The existence of . . . communist parties in the Eastern countries and their historical role become more significant when we envisage the question from another standpoint. Unfortunately, the bourgeoisie has come a bit too late to the colonial and semi-colonial countries, some hundred and fifty years too late. It is in no wise inclined to play the role of liberator because it can and will go only so far, but no further. Consequently, the nationalist revolutionary movement, in these countries where millions and millions of human beings aspire to national liberation, and want to free themselves economically and politically from imperialism, . . . cannot achieve victory under the leadership of the bourgeoisie. . . .

Thus we see that these communist parties are necessary, even if for the moment they are merely cells. . . .

. . . The dislocation of capitalist equilibrium in Europe forces imperialism to seek new markets, in order to restore the equilibrium of world capitalism. It hopes to find these markets in the colonial countries, by furthering the industrial development of countries such as India and China. . . .

It may be objected that this is impossible, for the interest of imperialism lies in keeping the colonial countries in an economically backward state, in order to sell them the manufactured products of the mother country. Yes, but this is a completely mechanical way of looking at things. . . .

. . . Side by side with the united front of the workers of the Western countries, we must organize an anti-colonialist united front in the colonial and semi-colonial countries. . . . The organization of this front, as has been demonstrated by the experience of the past two years, cannot be carried out under the leadership of the bourgeois parties. We must therefore develop our parties in these countries, in order to take charge of the leadership and the organization of this front. . . .

SAFAROV: In spite of the decisions of the Second Congress of the Communist International, the communist parties of the imperialist countries have done extraordinarily little to deal with the national and colonial questions. . . .

The French party, despite the considerable revolutionary movement in the French colonies, has only a study group on colonial problems, instead of a properly organized centre to direct this very important branch of its activity.

Worse still, the flag of communism is used to hide chauvinist ideas foreign and hostile to proletarian internationalism.

The Section of Sidi-bel-Abbès has given a brilliant demonstration of this.

Protesting against the appeal of the Communist International to the French colonies, these comrades – if one can call them comrades, for they are not comrades but petty bourgeois – these citizens say. . . .

[*Here Safarov reads the first paragraph of Text V 3,* see p. 196–8 below.]

Here is the viewpoint of these so-called communists.

These people are altogether convinced that the Communist International and its Executive Committee want the good people of Sidi-bel-Abbès to be eaten by cannibals.

We are not so harsh as this, we are not so terroristic, and these good people of Sidi-bel-Abbès and of the Federation of Algeria can be reassured: it is not a matter of cannibalism, it is merely a matter of the national and colonial question.

It must be declared once and for all that the conceptions which existed before the war in the Second International cannot be tolerated. . . .

RADEK: . . . Our thesis was: the exploited East must defend itself against international capitalism, and it will defend itself. This implies support to the exploited East. In reality, not only are the Eastern peoples not led by communists, but in most cases they are not even led by bourgeois revolutionaries. These Eastern peoples are still led by representatives of the dying feudal cliques, in the person of officers and functionaries. The support we give to the Eastern peoples thus raises the question of our relations with these leading elements. . . .

. . . We do not regret for a moment that we said to the Turkish communists: your first duty, once you have organized yourselves in an independent party, will be to support the national liberation movement. The whole future of the Turkish people is at stake. It is a question of whether the latter can free itself, or whether it will become the slave of world capitalism. . . . Today we say to the Turkish communists, in spite of the repression to which they are subjected, do not forget the near future behind the present. The task of the defence of Turkish independence, which is of great revolutionary importance, is not yet finished. You must defend yourselves against the repression, return blow for blow, but you must also understand that the time has not yet come for the final struggle for emancipation, and that you still have a long road to travel, side by side with the revolutionary bourgeois elements. . . .

A few words on the reports which have been presented and on the statements which have been made here on the situation and the activity of the communist parties in the East.

As always, I begin by saying: Comrades, do not see things in too rosy a light, do not overestimate your forces. When the Chinese comrade comes and tells us: we have taken root all over China, I must say to him, honoured comrade, it is not a bad thing to feel strong enough, when one undertakes a piece of work, to carry it through successfully, but one must also see things as they are. . . . The comrades who are working in Canton and Shanghai have not had much success in establishing links with the masses of the workers. . . . Many of them shut themselves up in their chambers to study Marx and Lenin just as formerly one studied Confucius. Comrades, you must understand that in China neither the question of the triumph of socialism, nor that of a Soviet republic is on the order of the day. Unfortunately, in China even the question of national unity and of a united national republic is not yet historically on the order of the day. . . . Practically, in the great trade union movement in the Indies, in this great wave of strikes, we play no role as yet. . . . We have not yet taken the first step as a real workers' party. All this means that 'It's a long way to Tipperary'. If our comrades complain that we do not take much interest in their work, I must reply that the interest aroused by a party depends on its acts. . . .

B Theses on the Eastern question adopted by the Fourth Comintern Congress

. . . To the extent that capitalism in the colonial countries arises on feudal foundations, and develops in distorted and incomplete transitional forms, which give predominance to commercial and usurious capital (the Muslim East, China), the differentiation of bourgeois democracy from the feudal-bureaucratic and feudal-agrarian elements frequently proceeds in a devious and protracted manner. . . .

That is why the ruling classes among the colonial and semi-colonial peoples are unable and unwilling to lead the struggle against imperialism in so far as that struggle assumes the form of a revolutionary mass movement. Only where feudal-patriarchal relations are not sufficiently disintegrated to separate the indigenous aristocracy completely from the masses – as, for example, among nomads and semi-nomads – can the representatives of these upper strata come forward as active leaders in the struggle against imperialist oppression (Mesopotamia, Mongolia, Morocco). . . .

The objective tasks of the colonial revolution go beyond the limits of bourgeois democracy if only because a decisive victory for this revolution is incompatible with the rule of world imperialism. At first, the indigenous bourgeoisie and intelligentsia are the pioneers of the colonial revolutionary movements, but as the proletarian and semi-proletarian peasant masses are drawn in, the big bourgeois and bourgeois-agrarian elements begin to turn away from the movement in proportion as the social interests of the lower classes of the people come to the forefront. There is a long struggle ahead of the young proletariat of the colonies, a struggle covering an entire historical epoch, against imperialist exploitation and their own ruling classes, who are trying to monopolize and keep to themselves all the advantages of industrial and cultural development, while keeping the broad working masses firmly in their former 'prehistoric' condition.

This struggle for influence over the peasant masses must serve the indigenous proletariat as training for the role of political leadership. Only when they have mastered this job and won influence over the social strata nearest to them will they be in a position to come out against bourgeois democracy which, in the conditions prevailing in the backward East, is far more hypocritical in character than it is in the West. . . .

The workers' movement in the colonial and semi-colonial countries must first of all win for itself the position of an independent revolutionary factor in the anti-imperialist front as a whole. Only when its importance as an independent factor is recognized and its political independence secured, are temporary agreements with bourgeois democracy permissible and necessary. . . .

Every Communist Party of the countries possessing colonies must take over the task of organising systematic moral and material assistance for the proletarian and revolutionary movement in the colonies. The pseudo-socialist tendencies towards colonialism of some categories of well-paid European workers in the colonies must be firmly and stubbornly combated. European communist workers in the colonies must try to organize the indigenous proletariat and win their confidence by concrete economic demands (raising the wages of native workers to that of European workers, labour protection, social insurance, etc.). The creation of separate European communist organizations in the colonies (Egypt, Algiers), is a concealed form of colonialism and only helps imperialist interests. The creation of communist organizations on this national basis is incompatible with the principles of proletarian internationalism.

3. *Letter from the Communists of Sidi-bel-Abbès*

This letter was cited at the Fourth and Fifth Congresses of the International as showing the 'colonialist' spirit of certain Western communists (see in particular the intervention of Safarov, Text V 2, p. 193 above), but it has never been published in full. Thanks to the kindness of Mr Jules Humbert-Droz and of the Institute of Social History in Amsterdam, we are able to give large excerpts of it here. The communists of Sidi-bel-Abbès made known their position as a reaction to an appeal launched in May 1922 by the Executive Committee of the International concerning the nationalist movement in French North Africa. (For extracts see Jane Degras, *The Communist International*, vol. I, pp. 352–3.) The letter is dated 27 June 1922. It was transmitted to Frossard, then secretary-general of the French Communist Party, on 10 July 1922, from Montpellier.[1]

. . . The colonial question is characterized by its absolute and necessary lack of unity: in Egypt, Tripolitania, Syria, Tunisia, Algeria, Morocco, Sudan, Senegal, Madagascar, Indochina, the West Indies, etc. . . ., the question arises under totally different conditions because there are oppressed peoples who are, as of now, ready for sovereignty and others which are not; there are peoples in tutelage which are, as of now, capable of governing themselves alone, and others which as yet are not; and if communist duty orders that liberty be given to the former, it even more imperiously orders that the latter not be abandoned to their miserable fate, it strongly orders that we serve them as humane and disinterested preceptors. If an Egyptian sovereignty is necessary, a sovereignty of cannibals is undesirable; if a Gandhi can become a head of state, a Batouala cannot. . . .

. . . The communist section of Sidi-bel-Abbès cannot accept the underlying idea of the above-mentioned appeal of Moscow, because the 'revolt of the Algerian Muslim masses', which is spoken of in Paragraph five, would at the present time, that is to say before any victorious revolution in the mother country, be a dangerous folly of which the Algerian federations of the Communist Party, who have above all a Marxist sense of situations, do not wish to make themselves accomplices before the judgement of communist history. Indeed, the Algerian communist federations proclaim that any revolutionary movement must mark a step forward in the historical development of humanity towards progress and not a reaction towards a political, economic and social stage already condemned by history. Now, a victorious revolt of the Muslim masses of Algeria which would not be posterior to a similar victorious revolt of the proletarian masses of the mother country, would inevitably bring Algeria back to a régime close to feudality,

[1] SOURCE: Humbert-Droz Archives, International Institute of Social History (Amsterdam).

a result which cannot be the objective of a communist action.

In Paragraph twelve of the *Moscow appeal*, when it is stated: 'The French proletariat . . . will assure the victory of the colonial revolution,' the communist section of Sidi-bel-Abbès replies: 'Yes, but when the French proletariat is able to keep this promise, that is to say, when it has shown us the example of its victorious revolution.'

In Paragraph thirteen, when it is stated: 'The struggle for the liberation of Algeria will cease only when the slaves have triumphed,' the section of Sidi-bel-Abbès replies: 'Granted! But we warn you that you will certainly, in the case of a premature Arab sovereignty, have to liberate communist slaves from the yoke of Muslim feudalism. As Algerians we know these slaves so well, these Muslim slaves of today, that we can assert that their triumph will not do away with slavery at all. It will only change poles. We even assert that slavery will be amplified, because the fact of possessing slaves, in the strict sense of the word, is a Muslim tradition in Algeria.'

In short, to sum up its opinion on the question, the communist section of Sidi-bel-Abbès can do no better than to repeat the order of the day which it voted at its session of 22 April 1922, and of which the text follows. . . .

Considering,
1. That the natives of North Africa are, for the most part, composed of Arabs resistant to the economic, social, intellectual and moral evolution indispensable to individuals in order to form an autonomous state capable of reaching communist perfection;
2. That the Muslims refuse education for women . . .;
3. That they have neither technicians, nor equipment, nor workers capable of developing the soil and sub-soil of North Africa;
4. That the native proletarians are above all exploited by their bourgeois co-religionists, by their religious leaders . . ., by their landed proprietors . . .;
5. That the Arab bourgeoisie professes nationalist and feudal principles . . .;
6. That the nationalist Arab bourgeoisie, just as in the case of sovereign Poland, would take advantage of their independence to pursue a feudal policy of oppression towards the native masses of the countryside;
For these reasons,
The communist section of Sidi-bel-Abbès considers that the liberation of the native proletariat of North Africa will be the fruit only of the revolution in the mother country, and that the best way in which to 'aid . . . every liberating movement' in our colony is not to 'abandon' this colony, as it is stated in the [eighth][1] condition of admission to the Third International, but on the contrary to remain there, on condition that the Communist Party . . . multiplies its propaganda in favour of trade-unionism, communism and the cooperative system, in order to

[1] This refers to the 21 conditions defined at the Second Congress of the Comintern.

create in the whole country a state of mind and a social framework which will perhaps be able, when communism triumphs in France, to facilitate its establishment in North Africa. . . .

4. Lenin: 'Better Fewer, But Better'

Extracts from Lenin's last article, dictated in February 1923 a few weeks before the stroke which put an end to all literary and political activity during the last months of his life. The revolutions in the West had been put down, and the capitalist system seemed to have been consolidated in Europe for an indefinite period. Lenin concluded from this that the destiny of the Russian revolution would depend, at least for a time, on revolutionary developments in the East.[1]

. . The existing system of international relationships is such that a European state, Germany, is enslaved by the victor states. Moreover a number of states, some of the oldest in the West, are, as a result of their victory, in a position to make some slight concessions to their oppressed classes – concessions which, though paltry, nevertheless hold back the revolutionary movement in those countries and create some semblance of 'class peace'. . . .

At the present time we are thus confronted with the question – shall we be able to hold on with our small-scale and very small-scale peasant production, with our country in its present dilapidated state, until the Western European capitalist countries complete their development towards socialism? But they are not completing this development as we previously expected they would. They are completing it not through a steady 'maturing' of socialism, but through the exploitation of some states by others, through the exploitation of the first of the states to be defeated in the imperialist war combined with the exploitation of the whole of the East. On the other hand, it was precisely in consequence of that first imperialist war that the East was once and for all drawn into the world revolutionary movement. . . .

Can we stave off the impending conflict with these imperialist countries? Can we hope that the internal antagonisms and conflicts between the prosperous imperialist countries of the East will again give us a respite as they did once before on the first occasion, when the crusade of the Western European counter-revolution in support of the Russian counter-revolution broke down as a result of the antagonisms in the camp of the Western and Eastern counter-revolutionaries, in that of the Eastern and Western exploiters and that of Japan and the U.S.A.?

I feel that this question requires the reply that the issue depends upon too many factors, and that the outcome of the struggle as a whole can be forecast only because, in the final analysis, the vast majority of the world's population is being educated and trained for the struggle by capitalism itself.

[1] SOURCE: Lenin, *Polnoye Sobraniye Sochinenii*, vol. XLV, pp. 402–4.

Ultimately, the outcome of the struggle will be settled by the fact that Russia, India, China, etc., constitute the vast majority of the world's population. And it is this majority of the population which, during the past few years, has been drawn into the struggle for emancipation with extraordinary rapidity; in this respect there cannot be the slightest doubt concerning the final outcome of the world struggle. In this sense, the complete victory of socialism is absolutely assured.

But what interests us is not this inevitable complete victory of socialism. What interests us is the tactics which we, the Russian Communist Party, we, the Russian Soviet power, should pursue to prevent the Western European counter-revolutionary states from crushing us. So that we may be assured of our survival until the next military conflict between the counter-revolutionary imperialist West and the revolutionary and nationalist East, between the most civilized states in the world and the states that are backward as the oriental states are; though these latter comprise the majority, this majority must have time to become civilized. We, too, are not sufficiently civilized to be able to pass straight on to socialism, although we do possess the political prerequisites for this. . . .

5. *Extracts from the Debates of the Fifth Comintern Congress*

This Congress, which met in July 1924, was called upon to approve tactics of more and more intimate cooperation with the nationalists in the non-European countries. It was also the scene of extremely violent attacks against the colonialist deviations of the French and British Communist Parties.[1]

NGUYEN AI QUOC[2]: I am here in order to draw the attention of the International untiringly to the fact that colonies exist and to point out to it that, apart from having to solve the problem of the future of the colonies, it faces a danger in the colonies. It seems to me that comrades have not thoroughly grasped the idea that the destiny of the world proletariat, and especially of that of the colonizing countries, is closely bound up with the destiny of the oppressed classes in the colonies. This being so, I shall make use of every available opportunity and, if necessary, seek such opportunities in order to awaken you to the colonial question. . . .

Forgive me for being so bold, Comrades, but I feel obliged to tell you that, on hearing the speeches of comrades from the metropolitan countries, I gained the impression that they all wanted to kill the serpent by beating its tail. All of you know that at present

[1] SOURCE: *Pyatiy Vsemirniy Kongress Kommunisticheskogo Internatsionala. Stenograficheskiy Otchet* (Moscow, 1925), pp. 218–19, 592–9, 607–12, 964–5.

[2] As noted in the Introduction, this was the pseudonym used at the time by Ho Chi Minh.

the poison and vital capacity of the imperialist viper are concentrated in the colonies rather than in the metropolitan countries. The colonies provide raw materials for its factories. The colonies supply soldiers for its army. The colonies will serve it as a mainstay of counter-revolution. And yet you, in speaking of the revolution, neglect the colonies! . . .

Why, in the question of the revolution, do you not match your tactics to your forces? Why do you not balance your forces and propaganda against those of the enemy with whom you wish to fight and whom you wish to defeat? Why do you neglect the colonies at a time when capitalism is relying on them for its defence and to fight against you? . . .

In discussing the possibility of and the means for accomplishing the revolution, and in drawing up your plan for the coming war, you British and French comrades and also you comrades from other parties have completely lost sight of this extraordinarily important strategic point. This is why I say to you with all the strength I can muster, 'Take care!'

MANUILSKY: We have noticed recently among the broad working masses in a number of countries a tendency to establish workers' and peasants' parties with a comparatively radical programme of struggle against imperialism. Two such instances, for example, are the creation of a workers' and peasants' party in the Dutch Indies, notably in Java, and the formation of the Kuomintang Party in China. . . .

What should be the attitude of the communist sections of the countries concerned towards parties of this sort? What specific organizational forms should their common revolutionary front take in the struggle against imperialist oppression? . . .

Our sections are thus faced with a twofold danger: either that of nihilistically ignoring new phenomena of this kind which are revolutionizing the East or of straying from the proletarian path on to the path of vulgar collaboration with the petty bourgeoisie. . . . Moreover, for us it is not merely a question of revolutionary cooperation with parties of this sort where they already exist but of whether communists in countries where the economic structure is poorly developed should themselves assume the initiative and create such parties. This question is approached in a state of extreme fear and funk, and this leads to our letting the leadership of the national-liberation movement out of our grasp and ceding it to nationalistic indigenous elements. . . .

There is a second type of error, that is connected with certain social-imperialist survivals. . . . Sad as it may be, it must be noted that views of this sort find a certain response in the minds of isolated politically incompetent party members. About a year ago the Comintern made an appeal to colonial slaves, calling on them to rebel against their masters. When this appeal reached one of the communist sections of the French Communist Party in Algeria – at Sidi-bel-Abbès – that section passed a resolution condemning the Comintern for making such an appeal to people of a different race who were exploited by French imperialism. . . .

I would ask our French comrades: have these men, who are perhaps good Frenchmen but extremely bad communists, been removed from the Party? And I would further ask our French comrades where are the documents in which the French Communist Party publicly proclaimed the slogan for the separation of the colonies? (*Sellier interjects: 'In the Party Programme.'*) Where are the acts by which you have supported the separation of your colonies from French imperialism? You French comrades have at present in France 800,000 native workers. I ask you, what have you done to organize these workers, to make them into cadres of revolutionary agitators for us in the colonies? There are 250,000 black soldiers in your army. Do you think you will be able to bring about social revolution if tomorrow these 250,000 are on the other side of the fence? Will your working class be capable of victory in even a single strike if the bourgeoisie has these black reserves which it can hurl at will against your heroic proletariat? Have you spread anti-imperialist propaganda among these black soldiers? (*From the French seats: 'Yes, yes, yes.'*)

No, I do not know of a single serious document on the subject. I know that an energetic struggle is needed to change the Party's frame of mind. I shall quote you a fact that perhaps seems unimportant but is extremely indicative of the psychology of our parties. At the Lyons Congress the Comintern made an appeal to the French workers and the colonial peoples. In publishing this appeal the editors of *l'Humanité*, the Party's central organ, circumspectly omitted from the text the words 'and to the colonial peoples'. Can the Party, in this frame of mind, conduct energetic propaganda among the natives? I wish with all my heart that the French Communist Party would return, on this question at least, to the Jaurès tradition. . . .

Our British comrades are even more deserving of reproach for their passivity in the matter of colonial propaganda. . . .

ROY: . . . We must first of all ask ourselves the following question: has the Communist International succeeded in establishing a link with the national bourgeoisie in the colonial countries? No, it has not, with the exception of a few instances in the semi-colonial countries, where a so-called national state exists. In these cases it has been possible, of course, to establish friendly diplomatic relations between the Soviet government and these national states. But we are not concerned with this aspect here. What we are now talking about is the relations between the Communist International, that is the revolutionary proletariat of the Western capitalist countries, and the revolutionary popular movement of the Eastern countries. If we wish to understand the reasons for our failure . . . we must examine the social nature of this movement. . . .

I must now clarify one point. . . . It might appear that I support the view that Bukharin put forward under the name of 'self-determination of the working masses, not of nationalities'.[1] This is not so. It has already been established (and the Second Comintern Congress made it sufficiently clear) that the Communist International recognizes the historical necessity of proclaiming the right of oppressed nationalities to self-determination. But in proclaiming this, we are obliged to explain how and by what means these diverse oppressed nationalities will be able to realize their right to self-determination. When we recognize that the right to self-determination belongs to the nationalities and not to the working masses, this does not mean that we consign this right in fact to the bourgeoisie or the upper classes of the oppressed nationalities as opposed to the working masses. It is quite correct to say that just as the upper classes of the oppressed peoples are not alone in possessing the right to self-determination, so too the proletariat or the working masses have no monopoly over this right. . . . It is necessary to establish which of these classes, which of these social strata, has the greater objective potential for waging the struggle all the way through to complete victory. . . .

Comrades, the very frequent bloody clashes that take place in India are a form of peasant rebellion, rebellion by the exploited peasantry against indigenous land-ownership. Just as in the cities we see the Indian proletariat rebelling against local capitalism, in the same way we encounter revolts in the villages by the exploited peasants against Indian landlords. Two years ago these clashes were not so fierce. The great discontent among the peasants and the working class occasioned by wartime and post-war conditions has been mobilized by the bourgeoisie, which organized the great national movement of 1920–22. At first the bourgeoisie did not understand the real significance of the revolutionary forces which, to its great disappointment, it found itself to be leading. As soon as

[1] At the Eighth Congress of the Russian Communist Party in March 1919, Bukharin did in fact propose the formula of 'self-determination of the labouring classes of each nationality', in opposition to the self-determination of the bourgeoisie. But he applied this idea above all to the relations between Soviet Russia and neighbouring countries such as Poland. On the other hand, with reference to the 'Hottentots, Bushmen, Negroes and Hindus' he recognized that the Bolsheviks had nothing to lose in putting forward the slogan of 'the right of the nations to self-determination' – though this did not prevent Lenin from attacking him sharply because of the abstract character of his views and his refusal to look in the face the problem of self-determination as it presented itself in the former Russian empire. See *Vos'moy S'yezd RKP (b)*. Protokoly (Moscow, 1959), pp. 46–8, 52–6.

these revolutionary forces began to assume a dangerous form, the bourgeoisie at once renounced all forms of revolutionary mass action. Had it not done so, the history of British imperialism would have taken an entirely different course. So revolutionary and powerful was the popular movement that, if it had not been sabotaged by the nationalistic bourgeoisie, the edifice of British imperialism would long since have collapsed. . . .

Surely, then, we cannot continue to insist on a formula which holds that the colonial bourgeoisie is an objectively revolutionary force which we should support and with which we should establish relations? This would be an utterly ridiculous stand to take. . . .

MANUILSKY: I want, first of all, to spend some time considering the mistakes made by Comrade Roy, whose concepts undoubtedly reflect the influence of nihilist theory on the national question. . . . He recommends that in defining its attitude towards self-determination for the colonial peoples the Comintern should take into account which class it is that will bring about this self-determination. Comrade Bukharin earlier tried to put the self-determination of the workers in the place of the self-determination of nations. But Comrade Bukharin at least limited his concept to Europe, where social relations have reached a high degree of development. But when Comrade Roy now tries to extend such a formula to the colonial countries, he is making a far graver mistake than many of us made at the Eighth Party Congress.[1] Marx, in a letter written to Engels at the height of the Austro-Prussian war, had already savagely derided this kind of national nihilism.[2]

[1] See previous note for the Eighth Congress.

[2] Reference to a letter by Marx dated 20 June 1866, in which he told Engels about a debate in the Council of the International during which certain French representatives had declared that nations were 'outworn prejudices'. 'The English', wrote Marx, 'laughed heartily when I began my speech by observing that our friend Lafargue . . ., who had abolished nationalities, spoke to us in "French", i.e. in a language which nine-tenths of the audience did not understand. I added that, quite unconsciously, he seemed to understand by the negation of nationalities their absorption into the French model nation' (*Briefwechsel* III, p. 328).

SECTION VI: CHINESE COMMUNISM FROM THE ORIGINS TO 1927

1. Ch'en Tu-hsiu: 'Patriotism and Consciousness of Self'

Extracts from an article written in 1914 by one of the two founding fathers of the Chinese Communist Party, who was then a partisan of Western-style democracy.[1]

In our world the minds of men are governed solely by two factors: emotion and knowledge. . . .

In present-day China, minds are in confusion and one can speak neither of emotion nor of knowledge. It is due to the absence of emotion that public security and common danger are considered as having nothing to do with the happiness or misfortune of each individual. *This I call lack of patriotism.* It is due to lack of knowledge that one understands neither others nor oneself. *That I call lack of consciousness of self. If the citizens lack patriotism, their state should normally perish; but if the citizens lack consciousness of self, their state is equally jeopardized. If the citizens lack both patriotism and consciousness of self, then the existence of their state becomes simply impossible.* Alas! Have our fellow countrymen fallen so low?

Patriotism is an essential element in setting up a state – this is an idea often expressed by the Europeans, and which has been transmitted to China by Japan. The Chinese language also includes the so-called doctrine of allegiance to one's prince and love for one's state. But in the Chinese view of the state, or national community, what is translated as patriotism is identical with allegiance to the prince. Hence the state or national community in question is the great enterprise brought successfully through all difficulties by the ancestor of the prince and which is transmitted by him to his descendants. As for the people, their role is merely to sacrifice themselves for the builders of this enterprise, from which they derive not the slightest liberty, nor right, nor happiness. This is the political system which existed everywhere in Europe before the appearance of constitutional government, and which our China has kept unchanged since ancient times. The modern conception of the state in Europe and in America is that of an organization whose members cooperate in the search for the security and happiness of the citizens; the rights of the people are inscribed in the constitution. . . . The European view of the state is very different from that which prevails in our country. *Consequently, what they call*

[1] SOURCE: *Chia-yin tsa-chih*, vol. I, no. 4, 10 November 1914.

patriotism has a name similar to what we use in Chinese, but the reality is different.

Once the meaning of the state has thus been cleared up, one is able to say that we Chinese are not patriots. One can also say that there have never as yet been any patriots among us; one can even go so far as to say that we Chinese have never as yet set up a state. What does that mean? *It means that we Chinese have never as yet had an organization which undertook to cooperate in seeking our happiness and our interest, similar to what the Europeans and the Americans call a state at the present time.* . . . Those who, since ancient times, have been called in our country 'state builders', and of whom there are in all several dozen, have never sought our happiness and our interest; on the contrary, they have been harmful beings who did violence to our happiness and our interest.

Patriotism belongs to the domain of emotion. Consciousness of self belongs to the domain of knowledge. What does the patriot love?[1] *He loves the organization which guarantees our rights and which seeks to increase our happiness. What is he conscious of, he who is endowed with consciousness of self? He is conscious of the aims of his state and the situation in which this state finds itself. Consequently, to love one's state without knowing its aims is vain; to love one's state without knowing its situation is dangerous.*[2] *Whether vain or dangerous, the two errors are similar.*

Those who love their state without knowing its aims are people like the citizens of Germany, Austria or Japan. And yet are not Germany, Austria and Japan what are called constitutional states? . . . Finally one arrives at today's bloody Great War. . . . Trying to embellish it, they say that they are fighting for the German people. In fact they are fighting in favour of the extravagant ambitions of the Kaiser, with his pretensions to a divine right monarchy, that's all. . . . The Germans are fighting to strike a blow at the liberty of others. . . . This is imperialism. Patriotism is the ideology of self-defence; its goal is the happiness and interest of the citizens.

The countries in which the citizens do not know the situation of their state, but nevertheless love it, are countries such as Korea, Turkey, Japan, Mexico and China. . . .

. . . Those who fear the danger of the partition of China among the great powers, who worry about the loss of our state and consider that if China is not saved it will fall to the level of India or Korea, are people who have good sentiments but whose ideas are erroneous. If one carefully examines the situation of our country

[1] The Chinese term for 'patriot', *ai-kuo-che*, means literally 'he who loves his country (or state)'. As a result, in many instances Ch'en Tu-hsiu's argument can be rendered accurately only by a paraphrase; here, for example, a more precise translation would be: 'What does he love, he who loves his state?'

[2] Here there is a deliberate parallel with a passage from the Confucian *Analects*, Book II, Chapter 15.

and the mentality of its inhabitants, by what means can one avoid a partition? I do not see at all what is so redoubtable in being slaves without a country. . . . *Today the misfortunes of our country do not lie solely in its government.* If one takes into consideration all the aspects of the problem, is the knowledge of our people sufficient to build a state in the twentieth century? If we don't give way to empty bragging, one cannot help having doubts. . . . If one judges with complete objectivity, how could our fellow citizens possibly desire to lose their state and to become slaves? Yet if one examines political conditions carefully, then, if by being impetuous and hot-headed, we arrived at such an extremity as the loss of our state and its partition among the great powers, these would not be things either which we should fear nor which should cause us to lament. *The state is that which defends the rights of the people and seeks to increase the happiness of the people. When this is not so, it is neither glorious to maintain one's state nor regrettable to lose it. . . . When the state is really not able to protect the people and to deserve their love, the patriotism of the people in question is then rejected bv their consciousness of self and eliminated.*

2. *Li Ta-chao: 'Pessimism and Consciousness of Self'*

Extracts from a letter to the editor of *Chia-yin tsa-chih*, protesting against Ch'en Tu-hsiu's article. As emphasized in the introduction, Li Ta-chao came to Leninism from a much more nationalist position than Ch'en Tu-hsiu; this is reflected here in the value he attaches to the state.[1]

I have re-read many times Mr [Ch'en] Tu-hsiu's article, published in number 4 of your estimable review and entitled 'Patriotism and Consciousness of Self', which has made me infinitely sad. . . . Forgetting to take into consideration my incompetence, I would like to set forth here the implicit meaning of Mr Tu-hsiu's words and to explain them. . . . The difference between a good and a bad state has given rise to very involved controversies among all the ancient and modern thinkers. Aristotle, Plato, Hegel and the others have praised the virtues of the state and have adorned it with the greatest perfection. The school of natural law considers it as a necessary evil, while the advocates of anarchism do not even admit the state and want to overthrow it completely and by every means. . . . Because the state is an entity which is indispensable for our existence and our survival, it is certainly excessive to call it an evil. As for the purpose of the state, the spirit of Eastern and Western political customs is naturally not the same. In this respect, the characteristic trait of the Orient is that one serves another on bended knee. The distinctive feature of the Occident is that everyone abides in mutual peace. Because customs and the teachings of

[1] SOURCE: *Chia-yin tsa-chih*, vol. I, no. 8, 10 August 1915.

the sages have these spiritual particularities as a basis, there is no doubt that politics are also elaborated on the basis of these particularities. But the fusion of oriental and occidental cultures and the evolution of the political habits peculiar to each one depend on the efforts of pioneers which one cannot hope to see materialize at a moment's notice. It is in this way that our nation must really become conscious of itself. The significance of consciousness of self *lies in advancing the spirit which devotes itself to the construction of the state; it lies in seeking a state worthy of being loved and in loving it. It is not fitting to renounce one's state and not love it because it is not worthy of being loved. Still less is it advisable, because our people have not yet benefited from a state worthy of being loved, to neglect the one we have, thus finding ourselves in the position of a people without a state and putting ourselves in the position of those who are incapable of creating a state worthy of being loved. For it is men who create the state; we are the ones who dominate the immensity of the universe; the universe allows us to exist, we people of the same species, and admits that we may be capable of creating a state. Why should we be the only ones incapable of doing so? If we do not underestimate ourselves, we have only to rely on the strength of our consciousness of self and to advance with all our might towards the goal defined by our will, without losing time to ask when we shall reach it.* As far as the advancement or the ruin of the state, the dispersion or the growth of a people are concerned, history teaches us that natural convulsions, vast and limitless currents, bring grandeur and decadence to the dynasties, and that these are apparently not confined to any given [ruling] family nor to any given race. The ambitious projects of the emperors of the Ch'in and of the Yüan dynasty, the enterprises of domination of Persia or Rome, at the time of their flowering, were marked by an abundance of achievements and a great glory which certainly did not fail to dazzle the world at that epoch. And yet after a very short time, the natural environment having remained the same, the affairs of men had completely changed. The old traces of the heroes who dominated the world had been completely lost amongst broken stones and towers in ruin. They had vanished like smoke, and one can no longer identify them. Those who reigned over vast empires, where are they now? *Thus since antiquity there has been no state which has not finally perished, and as long as it has not perished, there is no state which is not worthy of being loved. If one asserts that only if one has a state like that of England, France, Russia or America can one love it, it is the same as saying that these states, which did not originally come into being at the same time as the universe, are simply free gifts from heaven. In reality, at the outset the foundations of the state are laid by men, and the building of the state thereafter does not fail to depend upon the patriotic spirit of the citizens to extend its greatness and glory until it is finally complete. If one has a state and if one loves it, it will begin, without any doubt, to be established. But if one has a state and if one is not interested in it, how can one speak of patriotism?*

Furthermore, to say that although the peoples of Korea, Turkey, Mexico and even China, have a state they should not necessarily love it, implies that these peoples can even congratulate themselves for having gained something when Korea was annexed by Japan, Turkey partitioned among several countries and Mexico bound to the United States. To say that our country, growing weaker like those just mentioned, no longer has any choice, means that the best way for it to extricate itself is to wait peacefully for its downfall, to let the others cut it up, to subordinate itself to Russia or to obey Japan, to let itself be directed entirely by the orders and threats of the mighty. If that can be accepted with pleasure, what is there left to be feared in the world? Personally, I really cannot understand what happiness or advantage we could have in willingly accepting the condition of slaves without a country, when our state still possesses its body, although it be battered. It is surely not this which Mr Tu-hsiu calls consciousness of self.

A bad state makes its people miserable, and there are some like ferocious tigers who make them really suffer, and in this case it is altogether appropriate to try to find a way of salvation. But if one affirms that the situation of the inhabitants of such a state proves even more tragic than that of a people which has lost its state, one uses, blinded by one's emotion, an exaggeratedly pessimistic language. The sufferings which result from a bad state are only a temporary phenomenon. It is not a calamity comparable to the loss of one's state, which cannot be repaired for all eternity. . . .

3. Li Ta-chao: 'The Luminous Asiatic Youth Movement'

Extracts from an article with the same title dated 30 April 1920, which illustrates the internationalist phase through which Li Ta-chao passed immediately after the October Revolution and the First World War.[1]

The existing youth movements of the different Asiatic peoples are all movements from darkness towards the light.

Although from an exterior and formal point of view there are differences and even on certain points mutual clashes between the Chinese youth movement against the great powers, the Japanese youth movement for universal suffrage and in favour of labour, and the Korean youth movement in favour of autonomy, as regards their spirit and their real nature all these movements are animated by the same spirit, and they are all moving forward in the same direction.

The reform movements of Asiatic youth already have similar origins, and are headed in the same direction. Asiatic youth must therefore break down the boundaries between races and between states, it must completely reject all the hostilities and barriers

[1] SOURCE: *Li Ta-chao hsüan-chi* (Jen-min Ch'u-pan-she, Peking, 1962), pp. 327–9.

which have been imposed on us by the dominant classes, break them all in order to open a path of light along which to lead our dear brothers, in the bright light of sincerity, to establish an atmosphere of mutual confidence, to discuss a common strategy for reform and to create a common reform movement. It absolutely cannot allow itself to be deceived, provoked into conflict, separated or blinded again by these privileged classes. Chinese youth must conclude a great alliance with the youth of all of Asia on the basis of a reform policy for all of Asia, and create a great unified movement.

If we set apart Asia in this way, it is not because we want to draw boundaries between the yellow and white races; it is simply to evoke the part of the world in which we live and to make it a region of reform. The Russian youth of the Far East should be included as well among Asiatic youth.

It is an undeniable fact that the centre of power in Asia is concentrated in the militarism and the capitalistic aggressiveness of Japan. It is likewise a self-evident truth that the emancipation movement, the reform movement, the luminous movement of Asiatic youth must naturally begin by demolishing militarism and capitalistic aggressiveness inside Asia. . . .

The Japanese say that the Chinese student movement is an anti-Japanese movement. We can certainly not accept this viewpoint. The Chinese say that the Chinese student movement is a patriotic movement. We cannot accept this either. We love the working class, the common people and the youth of Japan with the same sincerity with which we love the working class, the common people and the youth of our own country and other countries. We do not consider that the state possesses any principle whatsoever which deserves being loved. We consider that to go and kill people and to appropriate their territory in the name of patriotism is an act of piracy, an act contrary to humanity and reason. We only admit that the Chinese student movement is a movement of resistance against the great powers.

Recently the Russian workers' and peasants' government proclaimed that it was giving up all the rights usurped from China by the Romanov dynasty. Chinese youth deeply admires such a great spirit. But if we are grateful, it is certainly not simply because we have recovered some material advantages; it is because, in this world of great powers, it has been able to show its humanistic and universal spirit that we grant it our respect. If one day the Japanese people proclaimed that it would recognize the freedom of the Korean people, our joy and our admiration would be ten times greater than for the message addressed to China by the workers' and peasants' government. For such a spirit would be as great as the spirit of the Russians; the influence of such a fact on the life of humanity would be even greater.

We are convinced that all of humanity possesses the right to work and the right to existence. All that is required is a reform of economic organization, in order that everywhere on earth people's work and existence may be secured. Then we can all set to work peacefully, and there will be no mutual conflict but only cooperation, no hostility but only friendship.

The entire world is luminous!

All the members of humanity are brothers!

May all our Asiatic youth do its utmost!

4. Ch'en Tu-hsiu: 'The Monument to von Ketteler'

Extracts from an article written by Ch'en Tu-hsiu in 1918, illustrating his hostile attitude towards the Boxers at a time when he was still in his Westernizing phase.[1]

Why was it necessary to build this monument as an apology to Germany? Because the Boxers for no reason had killed the German minister, Mr von Ketteler, and the united armies of all the countries demolished the city of Peking in order to force China to build a monument on the spot where von Ketteler had been killed, and refused to end their military action until this was done. How shameful it was for China! How detestable the Boxers were! . . .

. . . The Boxers were the crystallization of all the superstitions and heterodox doctrines of the whole society; as a result, as soon as they opened their mouths, they said that they had received a mandate from the Supreme Deity [of Taoism] to exterminate the foreigners. . . .

Although Confucius does not speak of spirits, he does not categorically deny their existence. Moreover, the main idea of the *Spring and Autumn Annals* is none other than to 'respect one's prince and to drive out the barbarians'. Doesn't the slogan of the Boxers, 'Support the Ch'ing and exterminate the foreigners', express exactly the same idea?

The last of the . . . causes [of the Boxer movement] is the conservative party with its hostility towards the new studies and its falsely high idea of itself. . . . People of this kind don't even know what occidental culture is. They conserve the old ideas handed down from one century to another, concerning the preservation of our national essence. . . . In their opinion, the moral principles and the rules of conduct taught by great China's ancient sages still shine with the same supreme perfection; and hence, of what account are these barbarians from different foreign countries? . . .

At the present time there are two paths in the world. One of them is the luminous path of science and atheism which leads towards the republic; the other is the dark path of superstition and theocracy which leads towards despotism. If the people of our

[1] SOURCE: *Hsin Ch'ing-nien*, vol. V, no. 5, 15 October 1918, pp. 481–90.

country do not want the Boxer movement to appear again, if they do not want shameful monuments like von Ketteler's to be erected any longer, which path, all things considered, would it be better to choose?

5. Ch'en Tu-hsiu: 'Salute to the Spirit of the Hunanese'

Even before he assimilated Leninism, Ch'en Tu-hsiu was by no means indifferent to the fate of his country, despite his Westernizing ideas. This is amply demonstrated by this salute to the inhabitants of Mao Tse-tung's native province, whose warlike qualities aroused Ch'en's admiration.[1]

What is the spirit of the Hunanese? 'The Chinese State could not perish unless all the Hunanese were dead. . . .'

This fighting spirit of the Hunanese is not at all . . . a piece of empty boasting, but is really demonstrated by history. Wang Ch'uan-shan,[2] who lived a little more than two centuries ago, was a scholar who struggled under such very difficult conditions! How Tseng Kuo-fan, Lo Tse-nan and others of the same group who lived a few score years ago, were scholars who 'took fortresses by storm' and 'fought to the death'! Huang K'e-ch'iang,[3] leading a column of Hunanese soldiers, experienced all sorts of difficulties and defended Hanyang against a large force of the Ch'ings. Ts'ai Kung-p'o,[4] although he was sick, himself led 2,000 Hunanese soldiers with insufficient ammunition and engaged a battle to the death with 100,000 soldiers of Yüan Shih-k'ai. What resolute and indomitable soldiers they were! . . .

The life of an individual does not exceed a hundred years at most, and whether it be long or short is not a very great issue, for this is not the true life. What is the great issue? What is the true life? The true life is the eternal life of the individual as it is prolonged in society. This kind of immortal and imperishable life is the great issue as far as the life of the individual is concerned; and whether there are or are not individuals in society in possession of this kind of immortality is a great issue for society.

A short story of Mrs Olive Schreiner contains the following sentences: 'Have you seen how grasshoppers cross a river? The first goes down the bank of the river and is carried away by the water, then a second comes too, and a third, and a fourth; and finally their dead bodies rise to the surface of the water, forming a bridge on which the others cross.' It is not those who pass who constitute our true life; it is this bridge which constitutes our real life, our immortal life! . . .

One could not say that Wang Ch'uan-shan, Tseng Kuo-fan, Lo

[1] SOURCE: *T'i-yü chou-pao t'e-k'an* (Changsha, May 1920).
[2] Wang Fu-chih.
[3] Huang Hsing.
[4] Ts'ai Ao. On Wang, Huang, and Ts'ai, see above, the Introduction.

Tse-nan, Huang K'e-ch'iang and Ts'ai Kung-p'o are completely dead people, for their lives, in so far as they form a bridge, still remain. When we salute the spirit of the Hunanese, we salute their fighting spirit, we salute the spirit with which they struggle to build a bridge. We salute the bridge they are building, which will be much larger and much more beautiful than that built by Wang Ch'uan-shan, Tseng Kuo-fan, Lo Tse-nan, Huang K'e-ch'iang and Ts'ai Kung-p'o.

6. *Ts'ai Ho-sen on Proletarian Revolution in China*

This text consists of extracts from a letter which Mao Tse-tung's intimate friend Ts'ai Ho-sen sent to Ch'en Tu-hsiu on 11 February 1921. It was written in Montargis, where Ts'ai was then studying the French language and assimilating the revolutionary ideas current in France in the company of other 'work and study' students.[1]

. . . The revolutionary doctrine of Marx is entirely based on the theory of objective necessity. Since the revolution is necessary, why must we conscious proletarians also go and rouse the consciousness of the other members of the same class?

1. Because, having become conscious ourselves of the origins of our sufferings (which do not originate in destiny but exclusively in the system of private property), our existence becomes even more intolerable to us;
2. Because we have a feeling of sympathy for the members of our class who suffer in the same way as we do;
3. If we wait for it to come about by the spontaneous development of things, the time will be very long, and the sacrifices will be extremely numerous; nobody knows how many proletarians will die each day from causes connected directly or indirectly with misery, or directly or indirectly with war. . . .

For these three reasons, we proletarians have long refused to tolerate suffering . . . or to quell our anger. How can one, in these circumstances, go on talking about whether the economic conditions for revolution are ripe or not?

However, if we make plans for our proletarian revolution, we must, before the revolution, undertake a great movement of economic transformation. How can this movement be undertaken? Our proletarian socialist party must organize, in all the big cities, the unemployed of our class, the lowest stratum of the poor who have no resources, and its first step must be to demand publicly of governments of the North and South 'the right to existence' and the 'right to work', to oblige the government to borrow investment credits from the banks of the five great powers. The second step will lie in requiring the right of supervision of the utilization of the investment credits. The third step will consist

[1] SOURCE: *Tu-hsiu wen-ts'un* (Shanghai, 1922), vol. IV, pp. 295–8.

in demanding a right of control over industry and government.

Mr [Ch'en] Tu-hsiu! At the present time the English, French, American and Italian labour movements are only at the beginning of the third step and have not yet reached their objective. If we are intelligent and resolute, we shall certainly be able, in a very short period, to leap past the labour movements of Europe and America. . . . I am deeply convinced that the three concrete steps suggested above constitute the only course for the socialist movement and social reform in China. If we continue to wrangle and our movement consequently ends in bankruptcy, in the space of four or five years capitalism will certainly develop by leaps and bounds. Rather than waiting for the militarists and financial magnates to form a league with the five great powers in order to strengthen capitalism in China, better that the proletariat first establish its domination over the others in order to obtain benefits and avoid misfortunes for itself. For, of the three factors necessary for production, China has two but lacks the third (it has the labour force and the raw materials, but it lacks capital). The destiny of the entire country thus lies in the hands of the five great capitalist countries. If we proletarians do not at once elaborate plans for dominating the others, we shall be dominated by them, and we shall have to sit and wait for the coming of capitalism without being able to do anything about it. And then, it will be necessary to wait for the social revolution to take place within the five great powers before being able to make a revolution ourselves. This idea makes us unbearably sad, it really is not worthwhile, it really does not pay.

Sir! The liberation of labour is absolutely not the concern of a single place, a single state, or a single people, but a world-wide social question. Marxian socialism is an international socialism. We absolutely do not want to take on a regional or national coloration. The class war in China is the international class war. To say that because China has no big bourgeoisie, the class war is useless, is to forget the economic position of China on the international level, to forget that foreign capitalists have long been the masters of the Chinese proletarians. Likewise, to say that the class war in China is the war of the immense majority of workers against a few pitiful capitalists of our own country, is also to forget the economic position of China on the international level, is also to forget that foreign capitalists have long been the masters of the Chinese proletarians. Consequently, I consider that the class war in China is an international class war. The few capitalists who have appeared in China, as well as the capitalist class to come, are nothing other than an appendix of the capitalist class of the five great powers. I consider that our country as a whole, with the exception of an insignificant handful of militarists, financial magnates and capitalists, if it is not solely composed of proletarians, is made up of petty bourgeois. Now, the petty bourgeois are candidates for the proletariat. Just see how many bourgeois families in China at the present time can eat properly and educate their children and do not experience misery. Therefore, in my opinion, all of China is a proletarian country (the big bourgeois are extremely few in number, the majority is composed of proletarians in the full sense of the word, the others being semi-proletarians or middle-class families). Consequently, the capitalist class of China is the capitalist class of the five great powers (to which also belong the very small number of militarists, financial magnates, and capitalists of our own country), and the class war in China is an international class war.

7. Extracts from Zinoviev's Speech at the First Congress of the Communist and Revolutionary Organizations of the Far East

It is at this Congress, which met first in Moscow and then in Petrograd in January 1922, that the representatives of the Chinese Communist Party learned the tactics of collaboration with the bourgeois nationalists.[1]

. . . Within the boundaries of Europe, all imperialist rivalry is more or less ended. The focal points of imperialist competition are presently moving towards Asia. Precisely for this reason, the Far Eastern problem is becoming a thousand times more topical than ever in the past. It is becoming *the* great question, the axis of world politics as a whole, and also the axis of the whole liberation movement of the proletariat and the oppressed peoples. . . .

The Communist International has written on its banner world revolution, not simply European revolution. The European revolution is only a small part, a tiny spot on the map of world revolution. We are extremely well aware that it is our task to assure proper cooperation and coordination of the forces of your working class with those of the working class of America and Europe.

Nevertheless, the initiative lies in your hands, and it will depend largely on you to what extent we succeed in establishing proper coordination of the interest of the proletariat on the one hand, and on the other hand of the non-proletarian oppressed masses and peoples of the Far East, for whom the chief aim at the present time is national liberation and national independence. The eloquence that we hear here is as yet not communist but national-revolutionary eloquence. Will we succeed in uniting this immense current of the constantly growing national-revolutionary movement

[1] SOURCE: *Der Erste Kongress der Kommunistischen und Revolutionären Organisationen des Fernen Ostens*, Moskau, Januar 1922 (Verlag der Kommunistischen Internationale, Auslieferungsstelle für Deutschland, Carl Hoym Nachf. Louis Cahnbley, Hamburg, 1922), pp. 18–36 *passim*.

with the much more powerful general current of the proletarian movement, which pursues purely communist aims? Such unity is necessary and inevitable. . . .

. . . We are neither doctrinaires nor sectarians. We do not renounce the fundamental ideas of communism, and will not renounce them. We shall propagate communism everywhere, even where we are only a little handful, but at the same time we shall live and work shoulder to shoulder with the many millions of the masses who live and struggle on our sinful earth. We will advise our comrades, the Chinese, Korean and Japanese communists, who for the time being are still a little group, not to stand apart, not to look down on those 'sinners' and 'publicans' who have not yet become communists, but to make their way into the deepest depths, among those millions of people who are struggling in China, among those people who for the moment are struggling for national independence and liberation. This is necessary, for history has now raised the question in very definite form. . . .

8. Li Ta-chao: 'The October Revolution and the Chinese People'

Opening passages of an article with the same title written by Li Ta-chao in November 1922.[1]

In the flames of the October Revolution was born the state and government of the worker and peasant masses. It is the fatherland of the worker and peasant masses of the entire world, their pioneer, their great central bastion.

The slogan launched by the October Revolution calls for the overthrow of world capitalism and imperialism. With this slogan, it calls the proletarians of the entire world to unite and join the front of the world-wide revolution.

Those who are subjected to capitalist oppression are, at the class level, the proletariat, and at the international level, the weak and small nations. For the past century, the Chinese people have been subjected to the trampling and the depredations of the forces of the aggressive imperialism armed by the developed capitalism of Europe and America, and it has fallen into the state of those who are weak and vanquished. The toiling popular masses of our country, suffering from two or several kinds of oppression, have suddenly heard the call of the October Revolution: 'Overthrow world capitalism', 'Overthrow world imperialism'. In our ears this voice resounds . . . in an exceptionally significant way.

This October Revolution, which is of great historical significance, must be commemorated not only by the toiling popular masses, but by all the people of the national states which, like China, are victims of oppression. They must all become profoundly conscious of their own responsibilities; they must, without hesitating,

[1] SOURCE: *Li Ta-chao hsüan-chi*, pp. 401–2.

quickly join together in a 'united democratic front', create a popular government, and resist international capitalism, for this also constitutes part of the work of the world revolution. . . .

9. Ts'ai Ho-sen: 'Congratulations to the Turkish Nationalist Party on Their Victory'

Extracts from an article published in September 1922 emphasizing the solidarity between China and Turkey, considered as the two most eminent representatives of the oppressed countries of the East.[1]

For the past century, of the great and ancient countries which have come under the oppression of international imperialism, there are none which have suffered as much as Turkey and China. The Turkish question and the Chinese question are what are called the Near Eastern question and the Far Eastern question. These two regions have become, on the one hand, the centres of the wars and pillage of international imperialism, cruel and insatiable; and, on the other hand, the zone in which the oppressed peoples which make up more than a third of humanity suffer the most and are the most martyred.

Before 1914, the misdeeds of the imperialist great powers in Turkey were exactly like those committed in China: armed aggressions, partition of territory, extortion of indemnities, control of public finances, extraterritoriality, fomentation of internal divisions and disorders. Moreover, in many places they created an atmosphere in which the Muslims who rose to resist the atrocities and oppression of Christianity – that invisible instrument of imperialism – were slandered as uncivilized and xenophobic peoples. . . .

Under these conditions, Turkey fell, from 1914 to 1918, into the bloody whirlpool of the imperialist world war. When the war was over, Turkey, in the wake of Germany, was mutilated by the imperialism of the Allies. . . .

In August 1920, the allied states imposed on Turkey the cruel Treaty of Sèvres, which deprived it of two-thirds of its territory and one-half of its population. . . .

These circumstances brought on a bloody four-year war and a great resistance of the popular masses which were living in unbearable conditions. General Kemal, a great man endowed with a great revolutionary spirit, led his nationalist party and started an insurrection in Ankara, where he organized a new government and a new national army. He fought with the Greek army in the west, the English army in the east, the French army in the south; he won one battle after the other, and Turkey, which had been on the verge of death, found itself in a new situation.

On what force, on what tactic, could Kemal's nationalist party

[1] SOURCE: *Hsiang-tao*, vol. I, no. 3, 27 September 1922, pp. 20–22.

rely to defeat international imperialism in such a situation of defeat, ruin and mutilation? First of all, it relied on the force of the popular masses of an oppressed people. Secondly, it changed the philo-imperialist foreign policy of all the former political parties – a policy consisting of counting on the wolf for protection from the tiger and relying on the tiger for protection from the wolf – and resolutely and firmly joined forces with the good friend of the oppressed peoples of the entire world, Soviet Russia. Since the appearance of Soviet Russia in 1917, not only have the oppressed peoples of the whole world lost a particularly terrifying demon, but they have gained a protecting star particularly worthy of confidence; as a result, the destiny of the oppressed peoples of the entire world has undergone a change. . . .

What should the oppressed peoples of the Far East think of this? In particular, what should be the opinion of the Chinese Nationalist Party [Kuomintang], which has struggled along for thirty years, which has suffered to an exceptional degree from the hatred and oppression of international imperialism, and which is, moreover, in the same situation as the Turkish Nationalist Party [Kuomintang]?

My 400 million down-trodden brothers, have you seen what has happened? The Turkish people, which like us is subjected to the oppression of international imperialism, has already overcome it! Their nationalist party has already led them along the path of great victories! We admire them, and even more than that, we want to imitate their great example. Let us rise quickly to incite our revolutionary party to lead us to unite with Soviet Russia, in order to overthrow international imperialist oppression in China! We must not feign to be deaf and blind. Now everywhere in the Near East, the down-trodden peoples clamorously and ardently wish for the victory of Turkey! Consequently, we 400 million brothers, oppressed by international imperialism, should also manifest our warm sympathy and good wishes. We should all cry: Long live the victory of the oppressed Turkish people! Long live the union of the oppressed peoples of the world with Soviet Russia! Long live the liberation of the oppressed peoples of the whole world!

10. Kao Chün-yü: 'The Chinese People Must Join the Workers of the West in Opposing the Atrocities Inflicted on Germany by French Imperialism'

Extracts from an article published in the organ of the Chinese Communist Party a few days after the French occupation of the Ruhr in January 1923, showing the instinctive sympathy of the Chinese communists for Germany, presented as another 'weak and small country', which, like the countries of Asia, was a victim of the depredations of the Entente.[1]

[1] SOURCE: *Hsiang-tao*, vol. I, no. 18, 31 January 1923, pp. 143–4.

After having experienced greater and lesser dismemberments during the five years which have elapsed since the Great War, Germany has become more or less a colony of all the robber states. Recently French imperialism, particularly obstinate and reactionary, still further increased its already unprecedented atrocities and sent soldiers to occupy the Ruhr with the objective of again dismembering Germany on a large scale and laying its hands on a great coal-producing region. How angry this affair makes us! At the same time, these acts of France prompt us all – the popular masses of China and not only the workers – to side with Germany, which is oppressed like us, and this for two reasons.

First of all . . . the present French atrocities clearly show us that aggression and pillage are the objectives of the imperialist states. The treaties that they sign with small and weak countries are only pretexts for imposing obligations on their partners, while the imperialist states can violate the treaties as much as they want and act outside the limits which they have imposed. . . . Secondly, the objective of the present act of pillage by France is to detach a great coal-producing district. Now, this affair is not only closely tied to the German national economy, but also has rather strong links with the various weak and small peoples of the East. For if France succeeds in detaching the Ruhr, this will constitute a financial contribution to the French bourgeoisie which will allow France to progress more quickly in becoming an imperialist state equipped with a great industry and even more capable of aggression. Consequently, this does not only constitute a loss for the German people; it also constitutes a danger for all the weak and small peoples of the world.

We weak and small peoples of the whole world stand together on one side, sharing common advantages and drawbacks; we stand on the side opposite from the imperialist states. After the present French atrocities against Germany, we understand this idea even more clearly. Having understood that all the peoples from smaller and weaker nations are on one side and share common advantages and drawbacks, we must then unite to oppose all the imperialist states, and it is even more necessary not to deprive ourselves of the aid of Soviet Russia which has united closely with the working class and the weak and small peoples of the world, and which struggles for their interests.

Our most important task is to unite all the weak and small peoples with Soviet Russia, in order to resist imperialism together, but such an undertaking can succeed only at the price of great efforts. Today we should immediately show our indignation and our resistance in face of the French atrocities. . . .

The revolutionary workers of France have very heroically opposed the imperialism of their own country, and the leader of their struggle – Comrade Cachin, the Communist chief – was arrested as a result. . . .

Our friends the Western workers have already unanimously shown their support for the German people and their resistance to French atrocities. . . . Let our friends, the workers of the whole country, as well as all organized groups among the people, quickly show that we unanimously oppose, with our friends the Western workers, the present atrocities of France against Germany!

11. Li Ta-chao: 'The Racial Question'

Extracts from the notes taken by a member of the audience at a lecture given by Li Ta-chao before the political club of the students at Peking University on 13 May 1924.[1]

Race, nation and citizens. If we are going to deal with the racial question, we must begin by making a distinction between 'race', 'nation', and 'citizens'. What do we mean by 'citizens'? The meaning of this word originates in political and juridical concepts. Thus all those who participate in a common life which has taken form under the same political system, without regard to their racial or national similarities or differences, are called citizens. What does 'nation' mean? National differences are a result of historical and cultural particularities. Thus all citizens who participate in a common history and culture, whether they be united or not from a political and juridical point of view, can be considered as belonging to a same nation. For example, even though the people of Taiwan are today subjected to the Japanese government, their history and culture are similar to ours, and therefore they cannot be separated from the Chinese nation. As for knowing what 'race' means, one must pay even less attention to political and juridical unity, as well as to similarities and differences in history and culture. Race is a concept which belongs uniquely to the domain of ethnography, and which arises from the examination of biological characteristics.

The relations between race and nation. Among the various different races a feeling of 'being different' springs into existence naturally. This is the racial instinct. . . . At the present time, one can see that the clashes between nations are marked by racial differences, and one can therefore see the relationship which exists between nation and race. . . .

The European conception of the world. As far as their culture is concerned, Europeans consider that nothing could be added to

[1] SOURCE: *Hsin Min-kuo*, vol. I, no. 6.

Christianity; as for their vision of the world, only the white world exists for them. According to the Frenchman Théodore Jouffroy, if one considers the problem of the capacity of savages to progress towards civilization in the future, one ought to distinguish between three systems: (1) Christianity; (2) Islam; and (3) Brahminism. It is only Christianity which is progressive, which is unceasingly in transformation and can adapt itself to the tendencies of the present-day world. If one compares the two others to Christianity, they are lazy, backward and unprogressive. . . . If, during a long period, new elements do not appear in Christianity, at length the world will become a world of Christian nations. At the present time, Germany, France and England make use of their national characteristics, which can be designated as science, philosophy, and concrete applications, in order to induce cultural progress. One can consider them as the precursors of a European culture, and that in the future it will be possible to put an end to all wars within Europe. This judgement is drawn from history, but Jouffroy's conclusion, according to which the world is entirely a world of white people, is perhaps exaggerated.[1]

In as much as white men are the pioneers of culture, they consider that the coloured peoples belong to the lower classes, and they themselves hold the higher positions. Consequently, on the international scale the racial problem becomes a class problem. That is to say, antagonistic classes have taken form in the world. It can be foreseen with certitude that, in the future, racial struggles will inevitably break out, and these struggles will take the form of wars between white and coloured men and will merge with the 'class struggle'! One can find the proof of this in the Russian revolution. White people participated in the Russian revolution, but coloured people of the oppressed classes also took part in it. Their common objective was to oppose the whites of the oppressive classes; one can here see the 'class struggle' of the coloured people of the lower classes against the white people of the upper classes already roughly represented, and this is only a beginning.

In 1910 the Englishman Putnam Weale wrote a book entitled *Contest of Colours*. . . . According to Weale's investigations, the various races are divided up as follows:

[1] See T. Jouffroy, *Mélanges Philosophiques* (Paris, Hachette, 1860), chapter VI, 'The Present State of Humanity'. Let us quote this charming statement of Jouffroy: 'The conduct of Russia and England towards the Asiatics is an admirable thing and proves the superiority of Christian civilization' (p. 85); stating that Christian civilization, in turn, is directed by France, England and Germany, he adds: 'There exists between them an alliance . . . majestically holy, for its effect is the improvement of humanity, and Providence seems to have entrusted them with the destinies of the world' (p. 95).

WHITES	
Europe	453,500,000
North America	85,000,000
Australia	6,000,000
South America	20,000,000
Africa	1,500,000
To which are added half-breeds	40,000,000
Total	606,000,000

YELLOW, BROWN AND BLACK RACES	
Asia	947,000,000
Africa	140,000,000
The Pacific Islands	2,000,000
North America	10,000,000
Total	1,099,000,000

If we compare the numerical strength of the white race to the numerical strength of the yellow, brown and black races, the latter are superior to the former. If we infer from the preceding paragraph that, in the future, racial struggles will necessarily appear at the same time as class struggles, it can be foreseen, on the basis of the numerical comparison just made, that the coloured races will be victorious. In 1850 the Frenchman Gobineau published *On Racial Inequality*, the essential argument of which is that, the races being different, there are inevitably those which are superior and those which are inferior. He is of the opinion that the most superior of all are the Aryans, the Germanic peoples constituting the supreme representatives of the Aryan race. But he has a kind of pessimistic theory according to which the superior races in general are going to decline, for in the future when the majority, composed of inferior races, unites to fight against the superior races, the latter will inevitably be defeated and the former will be victorious. And this too is perfectly logical. Moreover, many historians acknowledge the validity of this doctrine. . . .

The ideals represented by the different nations lead to clashes and explosions, and then wars break out. For war is nothing other than the symbol of the lack of harmony between the ideals of each nation. As a result, the strength and the weakness of ideals must express themselves in victory and defeat. The truth of yesterday can be erroneous today. Obviously war is the decisive struggle between truth and falsehood; thus victory is the triumph of truth over error. Therefore victory is not dependent upon Heaven, but upon a binding principle: Truth must triumph. Thus, from victory and defeat in wars, one can estimate the noble or base quality of the spirit of a nation and its particularities. This is the theory of war elaborated by Victor Cousin, but one can also evoke it to elucidate the racial problem.

Since the leader of our revolution, Mr Sun Yat-sen, put forward the Three People's Principles – the welfare of the people being the objective, nationalism (the essential of the three principles) being the means of realizing this objective, and democracy being the method of putting into application the welfare of the people – there is a certain change in the manner of explaining nationalism in the Chinese national-revolutionary movement. . . . And when the Kuomintang held its national Congress last year in Canton, there was yet another new interpretation of nationalism. This interpretation makes a distinction between two aspects, the external aspect and the internal aspect. In the present-day world the Chinese nation wants to be independent and to withstand the invasion and oppression of any other nations. This is the external aspect. At the same time, peoples of diverse nationalities living in different economic conditions within the country want to realize their liberation, self-determination and independence; that is the internal aspect. Now that the nationalism of the Kuomintang has undergone this reinterpretation, its meaning is new and even more universally valid.

Gentlemen, you can all see from the foregoing theories that this new meaning of nationalism is very closely related to the racial question. At the same time it can be seen how important it is to give our attention to the preparations of our Chinese nation for its participation in the class war against the other nations of the world. Everyone, or almost everyone, considers that the contribution of our Chinese nation to the world is ancient and great, but impotent. Today I would like to ask you a question: Is it condemned finally to continuing on in this old and great impotence without being able to revive once more? No! Since the movement of May 4th we have already become conscious of the motives of this national resurrection. But I want to ask another question: All things considered, is this nation capable of coming to life again? The critical moment has come, everything depends on how we fight, and on the efforts we make! If we can see to it that a new culture and new blood are injected into our nation day after day, then it will be the moment of a true renewal and a true resurrection. . . . We must all advance courageously with all our force, we must once again appear on the stage of the nations to display our national characteristics, we must once again in the history of our nation and in the history of the world clearly manifest our national spirit! This has been my idea in dealing with this racial question before you today, Gentlemen. I hope that everyone will make an effort in this direction!

12. Ch'en Tu-hsiu: 'Two Mistaken Ideas That We Have About the Boxers'

Extracts from an article in which the Leninist Ch'en Tu-hsiu of 1924 denounces as erroneous ideas which he himself had set forth six years earlier (see Text VI 4, pp. 210–11 above).[1]

The Boxers constitute an important fact in the modern history of China. In reality their importance is no less than that of the revolution of 1911, but people, in general, not only underestimate their importance, but also entertain two mistaken ideas about them.

The first mistaken idea consists in detesting the Boxers as barbaric xenophobes. They see only the xenophobia of the Boxers; they do not see the causes of the appearance of the Boxers' xenophobia – the fact that, since the Opium War, all of China has had to suffer the bloody odour of the oppression of foreign soldiers, diplomats and missionaries! . . . They see only the fact that the Boxers injured the lives and property of a few foreigners; they do not see how the military and commercial invasion of China by imperialism has caused the Chinese innumerable losses in lives and property! . . . They accuse the Boxers of being superstitious and retrograde, because they called on people to support the Ch'ing and exterminate the foreigners and to rely on theocracy; they for get that present-day China is governed, as in the past, by the three forms of the spiritual civilization of the Orient: ancestral ethics, feudal government and theocracy! There is no doubt that the Boxers were superstitious, backward and barbaric; but the entire world (China included, of course) is still living in backward, superstitious and barbaric conditions; how can one, therefore, condemn only the Boxers, especially as these Boxers' movement had the significance of a national resistance movement? Rather than hating the barbaric xenophobia of the Boxers, we prefer to hate the culture of militarists, bureaucrats, disloyal merchants, university professors and journalists who fawn on the foreigners at the present time.

The second mistaken idea consists in considering that the affair of the Boxers was the crime of a minority, and that the great powers should not punish the entire Chinese people because of a minority, by imposing on them the burden of heavy indemnities. They have not seen that when the great powers invaded China it was directed against the whole of our people and not against a minority. This violent invasion of the great powers created the violent resistance of the Boxers, and this resistance also expressed the consciousness and the interests of the entire people and certainly was not ascribable to the accidental action of a minority. . . . Our entire people suffers from foreign oppression, and if, in truth,

[1] SOURCE: *Hsiang-tao,* no. 81, 3 September 1924, pp. 645–6.

there had only been a minority of Boxers unwilling to submit to it, this would be a supreme disgrace for our entire people! If those who took part in the Boxer movement constitute a minority among our people, those who participated in the revolution of 1911 and the May 4th movement were also a minority among the people. . . .

It is fortunate that there was a minority of barbaric Boxers to save part of the reputation of the Chinese people!

I myself have lived through the barbarity of the Boxers, their backward and superstitious character, the atmosphere of terror which they created. I have read the diplomatic and commercial history of China over the past eighty years, and I finally cannot refuse to recognize that the Boxer affair is the great and tragic prologue to the history of the Chinese national revolution.

13. Li Ta-chao: 'Marx's Point of View regarding the Chinese National Revolution'

Extracts from Li Ta-chao's commentaries on an article by Marx which appears earlier in this anthology (Text I 2, pp. 119–21 above). Li's observations were accompanied by a complete translation of Marx's article, which had recently been republished in communist periodicals in France, the United States, etc.[1]

Having read this article of Marx, we should understand very clearly that, in theory and in practice, the Chinese national revolution is a part of the world revolution. In the world revolutionary movement the positions occupied by China and England are the most important. For England is the representative of European industry on the world market, and China is an important market for the sale of the merchandise of English imperialistic capitalism. The expansion of the Chinese national revolution means, therefore, the contraction of the market of English imperialistic capitalism; it can make the general crisis imminent and speed up the explosion of the world revolution. This oppression of China by English imperialism created the Chinese revolution, and then the Chinese revolution replies to England by its influence, and through England it replies to Europe, thus creating the chain reaction leading from the English revolution to the European revolution, and finally even to the world revolution. At the time of Marx, that is to say at the time of the Taiping rebellion, this was the case, and today at a time when the anti-imperialist movement has broken out all over China, it is still the case; until the day when the world revolution will have been completed, this will always be the case. However, this tie appears more clearly every day, and the tendency of the Chinese revolution to accelerate the world revolution becomes more pressing each day, that is all.

[1] SOURCE: *Li Ta-chao hsüan-chi*, pp. 553–5.

Since the Taiping rebellion, the main tide of the national-revolutionary movement in China has always risen in an imposing way, without stopping even a single little instant. The oppression of the Chinese people by imperialism has not stopped growing day by day and, as a result, the revolutionary movement of the Chinese people has likewise not stopped becoming more intense every day. And now what is happening? Are the imperialists continuing to behave as before? No, now it is a hundred times worse than before.... Everywhere there are bloody traces of the massacre of the Chinese popular masses by the forces of their so-called 'order', and everywhere too there is the struggle of the Chinese popular masses to resist the great powers. For the only answer to oppression is resistance, the only way to return the favour of the 'order' by which they repress us is the agitation by which we offer them resistance, that is to say, revolution. In accordance with the rule of etiquette, 'Propriety requires reciprocity', this agitation must obligatorily be transported to Europe, to all the imperialist countries. Marx said it very well, if the imperialists come and meddle unreasonably in the movement of the Chinese popular masses, this interference can have no other result than to make the Chinese revolutionary movement more enraged every day; it can only limit even more each day the commerce of the great powers in China. One can calculate that seventy-three years have already passed since Marx wrote this article. The Chinese revolutionary movement has become more widespread every day and the European crisis has become more imminent every day. During the last two years, the development of the political parties of the Chinese proletariat and of the English proletariat has really progressed with giant strides. In the competition among the proletarian revolutionary movements of all the peoples of the world, they are the ones who have made the most progress. Today, at the same moment as the national-revolutionary movement is spreading all over China, the English workers have called a great unprecedented strike in which several millions of men are taking part. It is truly as they say: 'The Copper Mountain topples down in the east, and the bells of Loyang answer it in the west.' Isn't it like this that the 'order' brought to China by the warships of the English capitalist class is sent back from China in the shape of agitation? Isn't it like this that the spark of the Chinese revolution has already penetrated into the overcharged mine of the European industrial system, so as to give birth to a great explosion in the future? This . . . will be demonstrated by the impending revolution.

14. Stalin on the Chinese Question, 1925–7

Extracts from Stalin's articles and speeches illustrating his successive positions on the Chinese question.

A Speech delivered at a meeting of students of the Communist University of the Toilers of the East (C.U.T.E.) on 18 May 1925[1]

. . . The distinctive feature of the colonies and dependent countries at the present time is that there no longer exists a single, all-embracing colonial East. . . .

In countries where the national bourgeoisie has as yet no grounds for splitting into a revolutionary party and a compromising party, like in Morocco, the task of communist elements is to take all steps to create a united national front against imperialism. In such countries communist elements can be grouped into a single party only in the course of the struggle against imperialism, especially after a victorious revolutionary war against imperialism.

In countries like Egypt or China, where the national bourgeoisie is already split into a revolutionary party and a compromising party, but where the compromising section of the bourgeoisie is as yet unable to ally itself with imperialism, communists can no longer set themselves the task of forming a united national front against imperialism. Communists in these countries must pass from a united national front policy to the policy of a revolutionary bloc of the workers and the petty bourgeoisie. This bloc, in these countries, can take the form of a single party, a workers' and peasants' party of the Kuomintang type,[2] provided, however, that this special kind of party does in fact represent a bloc of two forces – the Communist Party and the party of the revolutionary petty bourgeoisie. The tasks of this bloc are to expose the half-heartedness and ambivalence of the national bourgeoisie and to wage a determined struggle against imperialism. Such a dual party is necessary and suitable . . . provided that it does not restrict the Communist Party's freedom to carry out agitation and propaganda work, that it does not hinder proletarians from rallying around the Communist Party, and that it facilitates effective leadership of the revolutionary movement by the Communist Party. . . .

The situation is somewhat different in countries like India. The fundamental and new feature in the conditions of life of colonies like India is that not only has the national bourgeoisie split into a revolutionary party and a compromising party but, what is more important, that the compromising section of this bourgeoisie has already largely succeeded in coming to an understanding with imperialism. Fearing revolution more than imperialism, and more concerned with its money-bags than with the interests of its own

[1] SOURCE: In as much as this text was modified in the collected edition of Stalin's works, we here take as our source the text published in *Pravda* on 22 May 1925.

[2] The words 'of the Kuomintang type' were omitted in the present edition.

country, this section of the bourgeoisie, the richest and most influential section, is going over completely into the camp of the sworn enemies of the revolution and is allying itself with imperialism against the workers and peasants of its own country. It will be impossible for the revolution to triumph unless this bloc is smashed. But in order to smash it, fire must be concentrated on the compromising national bourgeoisie, its treachery exposed, the toiling masses freed from its influence and the necessary conditions systematically prepared for establishing the hegemony of the proletariat. . . . The task is to create a revolutionary anti-imperialist bloc and to ensure within this bloc the hegemony of the proletariat. This bloc must not take the form of a single workers' and peasants' party.

B The Perspectives of the Chinese Revolution

Extracts from Stalin's speech before the Chinese commission of the Central Executive Committee of the Communist International, 30 November 1926.[1]

. . . Lenin was right in saying that whereas formerly, before the advent of the era of world revolution, the national-liberation movement was part of the general democratic movement, it is now, after the victory of the Soviet revolution in Russia and the onset of the era of world revolution, part of the world proletarian revolution. . . .[2]

I think that the future revolutionary government in China will generally resemble in character the kind of government that was being talked about in our country in 1905, that is to say something in the nature of a democratic dictatorship of the proletariat and peasantry, but with the difference that it will be first and foremost an anti-imperialistic government.

It will be a government of transition towards the non-capitalist or, more accurately, socialist development of China.

That is the direction in which the revolution in China should go. . . .

C Reply to the Students of Sun Yat-sen University

Extracts from Stalin's conversation with the students of the Sun Yat-sen University in Moscow, 13 May 1927.[3]

. . . *Question:* Is there not a contradiction between your assessment of the Kuomintang (see speech at the students' meeting of the Communist University of the Toilers of the East [C.U.T.E.] of 18 May 1925, Text VI 14A, p. 226 above) as a bloc of two forces – the

[1] SOURCE: Stalin, *Sochineniya*, vol. VIII, pp. 365–6.

[2] See above, Text IV 7 and the accompanying note, p. 186.

[3] SOURCE: Stalin, *Sochineniya*, vol. IX, pp. 245–51.

Communist Party and the petty bourgeoisie – and the assessment made in the Comintern's resolution on the Kuomintang which saw it as a bloc of four classes which includes the big bourgeoisie?

Would it be possible for the Chinese Communist Party to belong to the Kuomintang if there were a dictatorship of the proletariat in China?

Answer:. . . I must say that I do not see any contradiction between these two definitions of the Kuomintang. I do not see any, because what we are dealing with here is two definitions of the Kuomintang from different points of view, neither of which can be called incorrect, as they are both correct.

When I spoke in 1925 of the Kuomintang as a party consisting of a bloc of the workers and peasants, I had absolutely no intention of describing the *actual* state of affairs in the Kuomintang, or of describing which classes in *actual fact* adhered to the Kuomintang in 1925. In speaking then of the Kuomintang, I was looking at it only as a *type* of structure of a people's revolutionary party in the oppressed Eastern countries, particularly in such countries as China and India; as a *type* of structure for a people's revolutionary party which *must* be based on a revolutionary bloc of the workers and the urban and rural petty bourgeoisie. I stated clearly at the time that 'in such countries, communists *must pass* from a *united national front* policy to a policy of a *revolutionary bloc* of the workers and the petty bourgeoisie'. . . .

What I had in mind, therefore, was not the present but the *future* of people's revolutionary parties in general, and of the Kuomintang in particular. And in this I was absolutely right, for organizations like the Kuomintang can have a future only if they strive to base themselves on a bloc of the workers and the petty bourgeoisie, and by the petty bourgeoisie one must mean principally the *peasantry*, which constitutes the *basic* force of the petty bourgeoisie in the capitalistically backward countries.

The Comintern was actually interested in another aspect of the problem. At its seventh expanded plenary session it considered the Kuomintang not from the point of view of its future, of what it should become, but of its *present*, the *existing* situation within the Kuomintang and of the particular classes that were linked to it *in actual fact* in 1926. And the Comintern was absolutely right when it stated that at that particular time, *when there was as yet no split in the Kuomintang*, the Kuomintang was in fact a bloc of the workers, the petty bourgeoisie (urban and rural) and the national bourgeoisie. . . .

But since the Comintern did not confine itself to the *actual state of affairs* in 1926 but also touched on the Kuomintang's *future*, it was bound to state that this bloc was only a temporary one and that it would be replaced in the near future by a bloc of the proletariat and the petty bourgeoisie. . . .

Would it be possible for the Chinese Communist Party to belong to the Kuomintang if there were a dictatorship of the proletariat in China?

I think this would be inexpedient and, for that reason, impossible. It would be inexpedient not only if there were a dictatorship of the proletariat but also if Soviets of workers' and peasants' deputies were formed. For what does the formation of Soviets of workers' and peasants' deputies in China signify? It means the creation of a dual power. It means a power struggle between the Kuomintang and the Soviets. The formation of workers' and peasants' Soviets constitutes a preparation for the transition from the bourgeois-democratic revolution to the proletarian, the socialist revolution. Can such preparation be undertaken under the leadership of *two* parties belonging to one and the same revolutionary-democratic party? No, it can not. The history of revolutions teaches us that preparation for the dictatorship of the proletariat and transition to the socialist revolution can be carried out only under the leadership of a *single* party, the Communist Party....

Therefore, not only when there is a dictatorship of the proletariat but even prior to such a dictatorship, in the process of the formation of Soviets of workers' and peasants' deputies, the Communist Party will have to withdraw from the Kuomintang in order to conduct the preparations for a Chinese October under its own exclusive leadership. . . .

D The Stages in the Chinese Revolution

Extracts from Stalin's speech at the Plenum of the Central Committee and of the Central Control Commission of the Communist Party of the Soviet Union, 1 August 1927.[1]

. . . What are the stages of the Chinese revolution?

In my opinion there should be three:

The first is that of the revolution of an all-national *united* front, that of the Canton period, when the revolution was directed principally against foreign imperialism and when the national bourgeoisie supported the revolutionary movement;

The second stage is the bourgeois-democratic revolution, after the national troops reached the Yangtse, when the national bourgeoisie deserted the revolution and the agrarian movement expanded into a mighty revolution of tens of millions of peasants (the Chinese revolution is at present at the second stage of its development);

The third stage is that of the Soviet revolution, which has not yet arrived but which will come. . . .

What is the characteristic feature of the first stage of the Chinese revolution?

[1] SOURCE: Stalin, *Sochineniya*, vol. X, pp. 14–35.

The characteristic feature of the first stage of the Chinese revolution is, firstly, that it was a revolution of an all-national united front, and, secondly, that it was chiefly directed against foreign imperialist oppression (the Hong Kong strike, etc.). . . .

Is it true that the first stage of a colonial revolution must be of precisely this nature? I think it is. In the 'Supplementary Theses' of the Second Comintern Congress, which dealt with the revolution in China and India, it is explicitly stated that in these countries 'foreign domination is continuously retarding the free development of social life', and that '*the first step* of a revolution in the colonies must therefore be to overthrow foreign capitalism'.[1]

One characteristic feature of the Chinese revolution is that it has taken this 'first step', has passed this first stage in its development, namely the period of agrarian revolution. . . .

Let us now turn to the second stage of the Chinese revolution.

If the first stage was marked by the fact that the spearhead of the revolution was levelled chiefly at foreign imperialism, the distinguishing mark of the second stage is that the revolution's spearhead is aimed mainly at internal enemies, primarily at the feudal landlords and the feudal régime. . . .

What was the communists' task at the second stage of the revolution in China, when the centre of the revolutionary movement had obviously switched from Canton to Wuhan and when a counter-revolutionary centre was established in Nanking, parallel with the revolutionary centre in Wuhan?

The task consisted in making the fullest use of the chance of openly organizing the party, the proletariat (trade unions), the peasantry (peasant unions) and the revolution in general.

It consisted in pushing the Wuhan Kuomintangites to the Left, towards the agrarian revolution.

It consisted in converting the Wuhan Kuomintang into the centre of the fight against counter-revolution and the nucleus of the future revolutionary-democratic dictatorship of the proletariat and peasantry. . . .

The opposition is gloating that the alliance with the Wuhan Kuomintang proved short-lived, and it states, moreover, that the Comintern did not warn the Chinese communists of the possible collapse of the Wuhan Kuomintang. . . . It would appear that the opposition thinks that alliances with the national bourgeoisie in colonial countries should be long-lasting. But only those who have lost the last vestiges of Leninism can think this way. . . .

15. Trotsky on the Four-Class Bloc

Extract from Trotsky's speech at the Eighth Plenum of the Executive Committee of the Communist International, in May 1927, in which he

[1] See Roy's supplementary theses, Text III 4, pp. 160–63 above. (The italics here are Stalin's.)

expressed himself ironically on the 'Four-Class Bloc' which was Stalin's principal theoretical contribution to the debate on the Chinese revolution.[1]

> Just what does it mean after all – four-class bloc? Did you ever encounter this expression before in the Marxist literature? If the bourgeoisie leads the oppressed strata of the people under the bourgeois banner, and in so leading them seizes political power for itself, that is no bloc, but the political exploitation of the oppressed classes by the bourgeoisie. The development of nationalism in the backward countries is likewise progressive. But its progressive character is conditioned not by the economic *cooperation* of the classes, but by the *exploitation* of the proletariat and the peasantry by the bourgeoisie. He who speaks not of class struggle, but of class cooperation, in order to characterize capitalist progress, is no Marxist, but a prophet of pacifist day-dreams. He who speaks of the four-class bloc in order to exalt the progressive character of the political exploitation of the proletariat and the peasantry by the bourgeoisie has nothing whatever to do with Marxism. . . .

[1] SOURCE: *Die Chinesische Frage auf dem 8. Plenum der Executive der Kommunistischen Internationale*, May 1927 (Hamburg-Berlin, Verlag Carl Hoym Nachf., 1928), p. 38.

SECTION VII: THE COMINTERN AND REVOLUTION IN THE COLONIES, 1928–34

1. The Colonial Problem at the Sixth Congress of the International

The Sixth Congress met in 1928 after the policy recommended by the leadership of the Comintern had led to utter failure in China. Apart from the cynical attempt to shift the responsibility for Stalin's errors to the leaders of the Chinese Communist Party, the documents of this congress already reflect the ideological authoritarianism of the Stalinist epoch, at the time when the idea of 'Socialism in One Country' was beginning to guide Russian policy.[1]

A Extracts from the Debates

BUKHARIN (Report on the international situation and the tasks of the International): . . . We have had a broad discussion on basic principles with our opposition regarding the question of the Chinese revolution. We are once again in a position to throw light retrospectively on certain basic problems of the Chinese revolution. As everyone knows, the Chinese Communist Party has suffered a grave defeat. This is an undeniable fact. We can legitimately ask ourselves whether this defeat is not the result of the adoption by the Communist International of erroneous tactics in the Chinese revolution. Perhaps it was really not appropriate to constitute a bloc with the bourgeoisie, perhaps this was the capital sin, the basic error which determined all the others and which, progressively, led to the defeat of the Chinese revolution. . . .

In general, the error was situated not in the basic tactical line, but in the political acts carried out and in the line adopted in practice in China. (1) In the early period of the Chinese revolution, in the period of collaboration with the Kuomintang, the error consisted in a lack of independence on the part of our Party, in insufficient criticism of the Kuomintang by our Party; at times our Party transformed itself from the ally of the Kuomintang into a mere appendix. (2) The error lay in the fact that our Chinese Party did not understand the change in the objective situation, the transition from one stage to another. Thus, for example, during a

[1] SOURCE: *Sechster Weltkongress der Kommunistischen Internationale*, Moskau 17 Juli–1. September 1928. Protokoll (Hamburg-Berlin, Verlag Carl Hoym Nachf., 1928), vol. I, p. 143, vol. III, pp. 266–8, and vol. IV, *passim*. For the translation of the theses, we have followed, with some corrections, that in *The Revolutionary Movement in the Colonies* (London, Modern Books, 1929), pp. 7–35 *passim*. The remarks of Narayan (pseudonym of S. Tagore), which are not included in the German version of the proceedings, are taken from *International Press Correspondence* no. 66, 25 September 1928, p. 1203.

certain time it was possible to march side by side with the national-revolutionary bourgeoisie, but at a certain stage, it was necessary to foresee the changes that would take place in the near future. . . . (3) Because of this error, our party sometimes played the role of an obstacle to the mass movement, to the agrarian revolution, and to the workers' movement. These were fateful errors, which naturally contributed to the defeat of the Chinese Communist Party and of the Chinese proletariat. After a series of defeats, the Party corrected its opportunist errors; as a matter of fact, it corrected them rather energetically. But this time, too, certain comrades fell, as often happens, into the opposite extreme. They did not prepare the insurrection seriously enough, and unquestionably manifested putschist tendencies; they fell into adventurism of the worst kind. . . .

We see in the present situation of the Chinese revolution the conclusion of a long period during which the revolutionary waves rose very high, and the beginning of a period during which the principal task is to group the masses, accumulate our forces, and prepare for a mighty new revolutionary upsurge. . . .

In India, the possibility of a long period during which the Hindu bourgeoisie would play an equally revolutionary role is totally excluded. Naturally this does not apply to the different petty-bourgeois parties or to the terrorist organizations which exist in India. I am speaking of the principal cadres of the bourgeoisie, of the Swarajist Party.[1]

I am not in a position to give an economic analysis of the situation in India, but I must point out that I do not share the viewpoint of those who claim that India has ceased to be a colonial country, and that we are witnessing a process of decolonization there. That would be a one-sided assertion. On the contrary, after a period of concessions by the imperialists, British imperialism has recently intensified its colonial yoke over India in general, and the Hindu bourgeoisie in particular. This obliges the Swarajist Party to oppose British imperialism once more. It therefore carries on activities of opposition. But it is a long way from this to armed struggle. As soon as the masses intervene, the Swarajist Party will turn to British imperialism and conclude an agreement with it. By the intervention of the masses, I mean an intervention in which the latter would propagate their own independent radical slogans, such as the confiscation of the land or radical slogans regarding the defence of the workers' interests. . . .

BUNTING (South Africa): I have read the draft programme of the Communist International; it declares that there are two essential revolutionary forces: the 'proletariat' of the capitalist mother countries, and the 'masses' of the colonies. I venture to protest

[1] i.e. the Congress Party of Gandhi and Nehru.

against this bold distinction. Our workers are not simply 'masses', they are proletarians, quite as authentic as any proletarians in the world.

The draft programme attributes to the colonies the sole task of rebelling against imperialism. . . . In the draft programme, and also in Comrade Bukharin's speech, there is no reference whatever to the colonial proletariat as such, to the class strength of these colonial workers. As a class they are condemned to inaction.

Is not this distinction between European 'proletariat' and colonial 'masses' of the same order as the treatment meted out to the black workers by our 'labour aristocracy'?

NARAYAN (India): . . . . As a matter of fact, one of the most characteristic features of the draft programme is the stress laid upon the colonial side of the proletarian revolution. But precisely this colonial aspect of the world revolution, as formulated in the programme, confronts us with certain difficulties.

Take, for example, that section in the first chapter of the draft programme where we find the statement '. . . that the colonial movements of the proletariat should march under the leadership of the revolutionary proletarian movement in the imperialist home countries'. This means that the proletarian movement in India should march under the leadership of the British Communist Party, or that the Javanese communist movement should march under the leadership of the Dutch Communist Party. Nobody will deny that in the organic structure of British imperialism, India and England are closely connected with each other, and for the same reason the Communist Parties of India and Britain are organically linked up with each other for carrying out the proletarian revolution in these two countries, but this on no account means the subordination of the colonial party to the leadership of the party of the imperialist home country.

Later on [in the programme] it is said that the colonies and semi-colonies are of importance in this transitional period for the reason that they represent the world rural districts in relation to the industrial countries which are the world towns. I think that this formulation is also not a very happy one. If we say that the colonies and semi-colonies are world villages, it means that there is no capitalist development at all. This is far from being true in India. But the implication is also that, if there is any capitalist development, it should be hindered and smothered, and that the colonies and semi-colonies should be kept to supply raw materials to the industrial West. I am quite sure that there is no such intention on the part of the Communist International, but the faulty formulation gives rise to very shady implications. . . .

The sixth chapter of the draft programme declares with regard to the Communist Parties in the colonial and semi-colonial countries:

Temporary agreements with the national bourgeoisie may be made only in so far as they will not hamper the revolutionary organization of the workers and peasants and are genuinely fighting against imperialism.

I consider this formulation to be fundamentally wrong. After our experience in India in 1922, when the bourgeoisie betrayed the great mass movement, which shook India from one end to the other, it is high time now to formulate it more clearly to show that the bourgeoisie can never fight imperialism genuinely. . . .

Even partial alliance with the bourgeoisie means the abandonment of the slogan of agrarian revolution, which means the virtual abolition of revolutionary struggle in the colonial countries, especially in such a predominantly agricultural country as India.

PADI[1] (Indonesia): In the name of our delegation, I wish to make a few remarks on Comrade Kuusinen's theses. . . .

It is said in Paragraph 12 of Comrade Kuusinen's theses: 'The most important task in this respect is the union of the forces of the revolutionary movement of the white workers with the class movement of the coloured workers, the formation of a revolutionary united front with that part of the indigenous national movement which truly carries on a revolutionary liberation struggle against imperialism.'

To show how difficult it is to carry out this task, let us take for example the relations between the white workers and the coloured workers in Indonesia – an example which, in our opinion, applies equally well to the American Negroes. The white (Dutch) workers, employed in Indonesia, are for the most part foremen, mechanics, and metallurgical workers. They constitute a well-paid group of workers whose average salary is higher than that of the indigenous workers. The white workers earn at least 100 to 300 florins a month . . .; in addition, they receive enormous bonuses of from 1000 to 3000 florins a year. The indigenous workers (skilled workers) and coolies get only 20 or 25 florins a month, without any other privileges. . . .

The class differentiation between the white and coloured workers in the colonies gives rise to a colossal hatred. This is deliberately encouraged by the Dutch imperialists, in order that they may carry on their policy of 'divide and rule', as is proved by numerous murders of white workers on the tobacco, rubber and sugar plantations. . . .

We have little hope of forming a revolutionary united front between white and coloured workers, as the critical situation in Indonesia shows. This is why we recommend to the Congress that it instruct our parties in Western Europe to carry on propaganda among the white workers in order to urge them not to go to the colonies. . . .

[1] Pseudonym of Alimin Prawirodirdjo.

B Extracts from the Programme of the International

Against the powerful concentrated forces of finance capital the two main revolutionary forces are assembling: *the workers of the capitalist countries* and *the popular masses of the colonies*, oppressed by foreign capital, and who march under the leadership and hegemony of the international revolutionary proletarian movement. . . .

The international revolution of the proletariat comprises a series of diverse and unsynchronized processes: pure proletarian revolutions; revolutions of a bourgeois-democratic type, which turn into proletarian revolutions; wars of national liberation; colonial revolutions. It is only at the end of its development that this revolutionary process leads to the world dictatorship of the proletariat.

The unevenness of the development of capitalism, accentuated in the epoch of imperialism, has given rise to differences in the degree of maturity and to manifold particular conditions of the revolutionary process in individual countries. The historically absolutely necessary consequences of these circumstances are the multiplicity of the paths and the differences in tempo in the seizure of power by the proletariat, as well as the inevitability of certain transitional stages to the proletarian dictatorship in a series of countries. As a result, the building of socialism likewise takes on diverse forms in individual countries.

The manifold conditions and paths of the transition to proletarian dictatorship in the various countries can be reduced schematically to the following three types:

Highly developed capitalist countries (the United States, Germany, England, etc.). . . . In these countries the chief political demand of the programme is for the direct transition to the dictatorship of the proletariat. . . .

Countries at an intermediate level of capitalist development (Spain, Portugal, Poland, Hungary, the Balkan countries etc.). . . . In many of these countries a more or less rapid transformation of the bourgeois-democratic revolution into the socialist revolution is possible; in others, there may be types of proletarian revolutions with broad tasks of a bourgeois-democratic nature. . . .

Colonial and semi-colonial countries (China, India, etc.) and independent countries (Argentina, Brazil, etc.) with the beginnings of an industry, or in certain cases even with a substantial development of industry, though for the most part to a degree insufficient for building socialism independently; with a predominance of medieval feudal relations, or of the 'Asiatic mode of production', both in the economy and in the political superstructure; finally, with the concentration of the decisive industrial, commercial and banking enterprises, and of the most important means of transportation, the latifundia, plantations etc. in the hands of foreign imperialist groups. In such countries decisive importance attaches to the struggle against feudalism, against pre-capitalist forms of exploitation, as well as to a thoroughgoing agrarian revolution by the peasantry and to the struggle against foreign imperialism and for national independence. Here the transition to the proletarian dictatorship is possible as a rule only through a series of preparatory steps, as the result of a whole period in which the bourgeois-democratic revolution is transformed into the socialist revolution. The successful building of socialism is possible in most of these countries only with the direct support of the countries of the proletarian dictatorship.

In even more backward countries (for example, in some parts of Africa), where there are virtually no wage workers, or even none at all, where the majority of the population lives in tribal conditions and survivals of the old clan order still persist, where there is practically no national bourgeoisie and foreign imperialism appears in the first instance as an armed conqueror, who robs the inhabitants of the land – in such countries the fight for national independence is the main task. Victorious national uprisings can, in such countries, open the way to socialism, bypassing the capitalist stage, provided the countries of proletarian dictatorship grant effective help. . . .

From the standpoint of the struggle against imperialism and of the conquest of power by the working class, the colonial revolutions and national liberation movements play an exceedingly great role. In the period of transition, the colonies and semi-colonies are important also because they represent the villages of the world, as contrasted with the industrial countries, which play the role of the cities of the world in the international economy. Hence the question of the organization of the international socialist economy, and of the proper combination of industry and agriculture, becomes in large measure the question of the relations to the former colonies of imperialism. The establishment of a fraternal fighting alliance with the toiling masses of the colonies is therefore one of the chief tasks of the world industrial proletariat, in its capacity of leader who exercises hegemony in the struggle against imperialism. . . .

C Theses on the Revolutionary Movement in the Colonies and Semi-Colonies

The toiling masses of the colonies struggling against imperialist slavery represent a most powerful auxiliary force of the socialist world revolution. The colonial countries at the present time constitute for world imperialism the most dangerous sector of their front. The revolutionary liberation movements of the colonies and semi-colonies more and more rally around the banner of the Soviet Union, convincing themselves by bitter experience that there is no salvation for them except through alliance with the revolutionary proletariat, and through the victory of the world proletarian revolution over world imperialism. The proletariat of the U.S.S.R., and the workers' movement in the capitalist countries, headed by the Communist International in their turn are supporting and will more and more effectively support in deeds the liberation struggle of all the colonial and other dependent peoples; they are the only sure bulwark of the colonial peoples in their struggle for final liberation from the yoke of imperialism. Furthermore, the alliance with the U.S.S.R. and with the revolutionary proletariat of the imperialist countries, creates for the toiling masses of the people of China, India and all other colonial and semi-colonial countries, the possibility of an independent, free, economic and cultural development, avoiding the stage of the domination of the capitalist system or even the development of capitalist relations in general....

The bourgeois democratic revolution in the colonies is distinguished from the bourgeois democratic revolution in an independent country chiefly in that it is organically bound up with the national liberation struggle against imperialist domination. The national factor exerts considerable influence on the revolutionary process in all colonies, as well as in those semi-colonies where imperialist enslavement already appears in its naked form, leading to the revolt of the mass of the people. On the one hand, national oppression hastens the ripening of the revolutionary crisis, strengthens the dissatisfaction of the masses of workers and peasants, facilitates their mobilization and endows the revolutionary mass revolts with the elemental force and character of a genuine popular revolution. On the other hand, the national factor is able to influence not only the movement of the working class and peasantry, but also the attitude of all the remaining classes, modifying its form during the process of revolution. Above all, the poor urban petty-bourgeoisie, together with the petty-bourgeois intelligentsia, is during the first period to a very considerable extent brought under the influence of the active revolutionary forces; secondly, the position of the colonial bourgeoisie in the bourgeois-democratic revolution is still for the most part an ambiguous one, and its vacillations in accordance with the course of the revolution are even more considerable than in the bourgeoisie of an independent country (e.g. the Russian bourgeoisie in 1905–17)....

Along with the national liberation struggle, the agrarian revolution constitutes the axis of the bourgeois-democratic revolution in the chief colonial countries. Consequently communists must follow with the greatest attention the development of the agrarian crisis and the intensification of class contradictions in the village, they must from the very beginning give a consciously-revolutionary direction to the dissatisfaction of the workers and to the incipient peasant movement....

It is absolutely essential that the communist parties in these countries should from the very beginning demarcate themselves in the most clear-cut fashion, both politically and organizationally, from all the petty-bourgeois groups and parties. In so far as the needs of the revolutionary struggle demand it, a temporary cooperation is permissible, and in certain circumstances even a temporary union between the Communist Party and the national revolutionary movement, provided that the latter is a genuine revolutionary movement, that it genuinely struggles against the ruling power and that its representatives do not put obstacles in the way of the communists educating and organizing in a revolutionary sense the peasants and broad masses of the exploited. In every such cooperation, however, it is essential to take the most careful precautions in order that this cooperation does not degenerate into a fusion of the communist movement with the bourgeois-revolutionary movement. . . .

2. *Trotsky: 'Summary and Perspectives of the Chinese Revolution. Its Lessons for the Countries of the Orient and for the Whole of the Comintern'*

Extracts from Trotsky's criticism of the draft programme of the Communist International as it was distributed prior to the Sixth Congress. Trotsky wrote these observations in exile and sent them to the Congress, where they were given only very limited circulation in manuscript form. The third part of Trotsky's critique has the title indicated above. In it, Trotsky develops his ideas about the impossibility of any serious or lasting cooperation with the bourgeoisie in the underdeveloped countries, and about the incapacity of the peasantry to engage in autonomous revolutionary action.[1]

. . . The draft programme states: 'Temporary agreements [with the national bourgeoisie of colonial countries] are admissible only in so far as the bourgeoisie does not obstruct the revolutionary organization of the workers and peasants and wages a genuine struggle against imperialism.' . . .

The sole 'condition' for every agreement with the bourgeoisie, for each separate, practical, and expedient agreement adapted to each given case, consists in not allowing either the organizations or the banners to become mixed directly or indirectly for a single day or a single hour; it consists in distinguishing between the Red and the Blue, and in not believing for an instant in the capacity or readiness of the bourgeoisie either to lead a *genuine* struggle against imperialism or *not to obstruct* the workers and peasants. For practical and expedient agreements we have absolutely no use for such a condition as the one cited above. On the contrary, it could only cause us harm, running counter to the general line of our struggle

[1] SOURCE: Leon Trotsky, *The Third International after Lenin* (New York, Pioneer Publishers, 1936), pp. 167–226 *passim*.

against capitalism, which is not suspended even during the brief period of an 'agreement'. As was said long ago, purely practical agreements, such as do not bind us in the least and do not oblige us to anything politically, can be concluded with the devil himself, if that is advantageous at a given moment. But it would be absurd in such a case to demand that the devil should *generally* become converted to Christianity, and that he use his horns not against workers and peasants but exclusively for pious deeds. In presenting such conditions we act in reality as the devil's advocates, and beg him to let us become his godfathers. . . .

Lenin really taught us to differentiate rigidly between an oppressed and oppressor bourgeois nation. From this follow conclusions of exceptional importance. For instance, our attitude towards a war between an imperialist and a colonial country. For a pacifist, such a war is a war like any other. For a communist, a war of a colonial nation against an imperialist nation is a bourgeois revolutionary war. Lenin thus *raised* the national liberation movements, the colonial insurrections, and wars of the oppressed nations, to the level of the bourgeois democratic revolutions, in particular, to that of the Russian revolution of 1905. But Lenin did not at all place the wars for national liberation *above* bourgeois democratic revolutions. . . .

Lenin insisted on a distinction between an oppressed bourgeois nation and a bourgeois oppressor nation. But Lenin nowhere raised and never could raise the question as if the bourgeoisie of a colonial or a semi-colonial country in an epoch of struggle for national liberation must be more progressive and more revolutionary than the bourgeoisie of a non-colonial country in the epoch of the democratic revolution. . . .

To present matters as if there must inevitably flow from the fact of colonial oppression the revolutionary character of a national bourgeoisie is to reproduce inside out the fundamental error of Menshevism, which held that the revolutionary nature of the Russian bourgeoisie must flow from the oppression of feudalism and the autocracy. . . .

For a Marxist it was clear even prior to the Chinese events of the last three years – and today it should be clear even to the blind – that foreign imperialism, as a direct factor in the internal life of China, renders the Chinese Miliukovs and Chinese Kerenskys in the final analysis even more vile than their Russian prototypes. It is not for nothing that the very first manifesto issued by our party proclaimed that the farther East we go, the lower and viler becomes the bourgeoisie, the greater are the tasks that fall upon the proletariat. This historical 'law' fully applies to China as well. . . .

Large and middle-scale landed estates (such as obtain in China) are most closely interlinked with city capital, including foreign capital. There is no caste of feudal landlords in China in opposition to the bourgeoisie. The most widespread, common, and hated exploiter in the village is the kulak-usurer, the agent of finance capital in the cities.[1] The agrarian revolution is therefore just as much anti-feudal as it is anti-bourgeois in character. In China, there will be practically no such stage as the first stage of our October Revolution in which the kulak marched with the middle and poor peasant, frequently at their head, against the landlord. The agrarian revolution in China signifies from the outset, as it will signify subsequently, an uprising not only against the few genuine feudal landlords and the bureaucracy, but also against the kulaks and usurers. If in our country the poor peasant committees appeared on the scene only during the second stage of the October Revolution, in the middle of 1918, in China, on the contrary, they will, in one form or another, appear on the scene as soon as the agrarian movement revives. The drive on the rich peasant will be the first and not the second step of the Chinese October. . . .

Those objective socio-historical causes which predetermined the 'October' outcome of the Russian revolution rise before us in China in a still more accentuated form. The bourgeois and proletarian poles of the Chinese nation stand opposed to each other even more irreconcilably, if this is at all possible, than they did in Russia, since, on the one hand, the Chinese bourgeoisie is directly bound up with foreign imperialism and the latter's military machine, and since, on the other hand, the Chinese proletariat has from the very beginning established a close bond with the Comintern and the Soviet Union. Numerically the Chinese peasantry constitutes an even more overwhelming mass than the Russian peasantry. But being crushed in the vice of world contradictions, upon the solution of which in one way or another its fate depends, the Chinese peasantry is even less capable of playing a *leading* role than the Russian. . . .

These fundamental and, at the same time, incontrovertible social and political prerequisites of the third Chinese revolution demonstrate not only that the formula of the democratic dictatorship has *hopelessly outlived its usefulness*, but also that the third Chinese revolution, despite the great backwardness of China, or more correctly, because of this great backwardness as compared with Russia, will not have a 'democratic' period, not even such a six-month period as the October Revolution had (November 1917 to July 1918); but it will be compelled from the very outset to

[1] Trotsky's reasoning here shows his complete ignorance of the realities of Chinese society, where the bourgeoisie was rather an emanation of the class of landed proprietors than the reverse, and where the usurer, whether or not he was a 'kulak', was generally linked to the countryside, even though he did not always reside there continually, and in any case was not the agent of 'finance capital'.

effect the most decisive shake-up and abolition of bourgeois property in city and village. . . .

The younger the proletariat, the fresher and more direct its 'blood-ties' with the peasantry, the greater the proportion of the peasantry to the population as a whole, the greater becomes the importance of the struggle against any form of 'two-class' political alchemy. In the West the idea of a workers' and peasants' party is simply ridiculous. In the East it is fatal. . . . The workers' and peasants' party can only serve as a base, a screen, and a springboard for the bourgeoisie. . . .

The peasantry, by virtue of its entire history and the conditions of its existence, is the least international of all classes. What are commonly called national traits have their chief source precisely in the peasantry. From among the peasantry, it is only the semi-proletarian masses of the peasant poor who can be guided along the road of internationalism, and only the proletariat can guide them. . . .

One conclusion, at any rate, is indisputable. The experience of the 'peasant' parties of Bulgaria, Poland, Rumania, and Yugoslavia (i.e. of all the backward countries); the old experience of our social revolutionists, and the fresh experience (the blood is still warm) of the Kuomintang; the episodic experiments in advanced capitalist countries – particularly the LaFollete-Pepper experiment in the United States – have all shown beyond question that in the epoch of capitalist decline there is even less reason than in the epoch of rising capitalism to look for *independent*, revolutionary, anti-bourgeois peasant parties.

The city cannot be equated to the village, the village cannot be equated to the city in the historical conditions of the present epoch. The city inevitably *leads the village*, the village inevitably *follows the city*. The only question is *which* of the urban classes will lead the village.[1]

In the revolutions of the East the peasantry will still play a decisive role, but once again, this role will be neither leading nor independent. The poor peasants of Hupeh, Kwangtung, or Bengal can play a role not only on a national but on an international scale, but only if they support the workers of Shanghai, Canton, Hankow, and Calcutta. This is the only way out for the revolutionary peasant on an *international* road. It is hopeless to attempt to forge a direct link between the peasant of Hupeh and the peasant of Galicia or Dobrudja, the Egyptian fellah and the American farmer.

3. Decisions and Directives of the Communist International Regarding the Chinese Revolution, 1928–31

In these extracts one can see how, throughout the decisive period when

[1] Lenin, *Polnoye Sobraniye Sochinenii*, vol. 40, p. 5.

Mao Tse-tung's tactics of a communist revolution carried out by means of a revolutionary war in the countryside were taking shape, the Comintern ceaselessly complained of the unorthodox character of these developments.[1]

A Extract from the Resolution of the Tenth Plenum of the Executive Committee of the Communist International, February 1928

. . . In leading spontaneous demonstrations by peasant partisans in the different provinces, the Party must bear in mind that these demonstrations can become a starting point for a victorious national uprising only on condition that they are linked with the new upsurge of the tide of revolution in the proletarian centres. Here too, the Party must see its main task as the organization of general and coordinated demonstrations in the country and in the *towns, in a number of* neighbouring provinces, and of other uprisings on a *wide* scale. In this connexion it is essential to combat any trend towards scattered and unconnected partisan struggles, which are doomed to defeat (a danger which existed in Hunan, Hupei and elsewhere).

B Extract from a letter from the Executive Committee of the Communist International to the Central Committee of the Chinese Communist Party, February 1929

. . . In all mass actions, in strikes, peasant demonstrations and anti-imperialist mass movements, communists should participate most energetically in fulfilling the strategic aim of developing the revolutionary initiative of the working class, mobilizing the masses of millions of urban and rural workers around the working class, and thus ensuring the leadership (hegemony) of the proletariat in the liberation movement. In this connexion the Chinese comrades should pay particular attention to the thorough preparation, serious organization and implementation in a given revolutionary situation of methods of proletarian revolutionary struggle such as a general revolutionary strike and a general rail strike, bearing in mind that this form of struggle, which mobilizes all revolutionary elements in the country around the proletariat, can and must play a major role in the Chinese revolution. . . .

C Extract from a letter from the Executive Committee of the Communist International to the Central Committee of the Chinese Communist Party, December 1929

. . . The national crisis and the revolutionary upsurge have their own particular Chinese characteristics. . . . One distinctive characteristic of the national crisis and the revolutionary upsurge in

[1] SOURCE: *Strategiya i Taktika Kominterna v Natsional'no-Kolonial'noy Revolyutsii, na primere Kitaya* (Moscow, 1934), pp. 209–310 *passim.*

China is the peasant war. The counter-revolution of the bourgeoisie and land-owners has not succeeded in suppressing the peasant revolutionary movement once and for all. Uprisings by the Muslims, the 'Red Spears', etc., which are under reactionary leadership but are objectively revolutionary because of their mass nature; in particular the general growth of the mass agrarian movement in most of the Chinese provinces; the remaining areas of Soviet power, which have in recent times been expanding and growing stronger; and the increasing partisan war in the south – these are all in the process of becoming one of the courses along which the mighty upsurge of the all-Chinese revolution will continue to develop. But the truest and most substantial indication of the swelling upsurge is the animation of the workers' movement, which has emerged from its depressed state following the heavy defeats of 1927. The proletariat's economic struggle through strike action is developing. It is showing a tendency to develop towards political battles and street demonstrations. These processes within the workers' movement have already resulted in strengthening the Communist Party. . . .

D Extracts from the Resolution of the Executive Committee of the Communist International on the Chinese Question, June 1930

. . . It is necessary in analysing the present stage of the struggle to start with the fact that as yet there is still not an objective revolutionary situation covering the whole of China. The waves of the workers' movement and the peasants' movement have not yet merged into one. Their total effect is as yet insufficient to ensure the necessary amount of pressure upon imperialism and the Kuomintang régime. The peasant revolutionary struggle is at present developing successfully only in part of the southern provinces. Divisions and internecine strife within the ruling clique of the dominant classes have not yet resulted in weakening them altogether and bringing about their political collapse. But events are moving in such a way that the revolutionary situation will shortly encompass, if not the whole of Chinese territory, then at least the territory of a number of key provinces. The acceleration of this process largely depends on the Communist Party employing correct tactics, primarily on its finding a correct solution for the problems of consolidating its leadership and the further development of the Soviet movement. . . .

. . . The Soviet movement sets the Party a task of the highest importance, namely that of organizing and putting in order the activities of a central Soviet Government. Concerning a workers' and peasants' Soviet Government in China, the Party must base itself on the premise that such a government could acquire the necessary strength and significance provided that a real Red Army, completely subordinate to the leadership of the Communist Party and capable of supporting the government, were established in the best-endowed region. It is thus essential to concentrate on forming and strengthening a Red Army so as to be able in the future, subject to the military and political situation, to be in a position to take over one or several of the industrial and administrative centres. . . .

. . . The Party's work in the Soviet regions must be coordinated with its activities throughout Chinese territory. The Party's fundamental task while the revolutionary upsurge is developing *is to ensure that the hegemony of the proletariat is solid and is exercised consistently*. . . .

The task of accomplishing the hegemony of the proletariat involves the Party in a struggle to extend the development of the strike movement, to organize and lead the economic battles of the Chinese proletariat. In combining economic and political struggle, the Party must make every effort to develop political strikes, moving towards the organization of a general political strike in all industrial centres or in a number of them. . . .

The revolutionary-democratic dictatorship of the proletariat and peasantry in China will be substantially different from the democratic dictatorship envisaged by the Bolsheviks in the revolution of 1905. In the first instance, this difference is connected with the Chinese revolution's international setting, with the existence of the U.S.S.R. . . . On the other hand, the situation taking shape in China permits one to expect that communists will constitute a majority in the government. Thanks to this, the proletariat will succeed in achieving not only ideological but state hegemony over the peasantry. . . .

E Extract from a letter from the Executive Committee of the Communist International on the Statement by Li Li-san, October 1930

. . . Comrade Li Li-san completely fails to understand that we do not yet possess a genuine workers' and peasants' Red Army with working-class commanders and a strong Party backbone. The Red Army's successes are enormous, its growth and its heroic deeds command the admiration of the entire international proletariat. But this same Red Army is still weak and inadequately organized, and is not sufficiently in the hands of the Chinese Communist Party. The social composition of the Red Army is far from satisfactory. Ex-soldiers from militarist armies predominate in a number of armies. Kulaks have infiltrated the Red Army. The Red Army must be transformed into a workers' and peasants' army with proletarian leadership. . . .

F Extracts from the Resolution of the Presidium of the Executive Committee of the Communist International on the Tasks of the Chinese Communist Party, 26 August 1931

. . . The hegemony of the proletariat and the victorious development of the revolution can be guaranteed only on condition that the Chinese Communist Party becomes a proletarian party not only in its political line but in its composition and the role played by the workers in all of its leading organs. To recruit into the Party fearlessly, systematically, and as a matter of top priority, the best elements among the workers must become the major political mission of all Party cells and committees. The Chinese Communist Party must infiltrate its local organizations into large and major enterprises. Party organizations must be re-established and strengthened in all large centres in the country. The Party is duty bound to re-establish contact at the earliest possible moment with groups of Party members in enterprises, who have continued, sometimes for years, waging the struggle without leadership and without contact with Party organizations. The Party's Central Committee must elevate in every possible way the role of the factory cells in Party affairs at large. . . . The best Party officials must be attached to the factory cells, and their work must be made a model for all Party organizations. . . .

The agrarian revolution is showing its anti-imperialist nature more clearly every day. . . . The main bulk of the peasantry is rising up under the leadership of the proletariat to join the struggle against imperialism and to eliminate the political and economic positions of imperialism in China, and is learning from its own experience in the struggle that the victory of the agrarian revolution is impossible unless the country is liberated from imperialism.

The proletariat's leadership in the revolutionary movement is being reinforced. The party of the proletariat – the Chinese Communist Party – is the ruling party of Soviets, the organizer and commander of the workers' and peasants' Red Army, and sole leader of the workers and peasants. The hegemony of the proletariat is being consolidated in the rudiments of state power and constitutes an incipient and transitional stage on the way to the dictatorship of the proletariat.

At the same time, the struggle to create and confirm the preconditions for China's transition to the socialist path of development calls for all-round expansion of the territorial basis of the Soviets and the Red Army, their victory over the armed forces of counter-revolution and the establishment of Soviet power over all territory of crucial importance in China.

Only Soviet revolution can bring about the unification of China as a state. The union of the workers' and peasants' movements, the overthrow of counter-revolutionary power and the establishment of Soviet power in the large proletarian centres will draw into the revolution vast new strata of workers and peasants, and will make the hegemony of the proletariat many times stronger (radically improving the Communist Party's social composition, directly involving the masses of the proletariat in the construction of Soviets, creating numerous leading proletarian cadres for the Soviets and the Red Army, and centralizing the movement) and will thus give the central Soviet government a power and significance that genuinely extend over the whole of China to the whole nation. . . .

SECTION VIII: REVOLUTION IN ASIA IN THE PERIOD OF THE POPULAR FRONT AND THE SECOND WORLD WAR

1. Extract from the Resolutions of the Seventh Congress of the International

When the Seventh Congress met in 1935, the Nazis had taken power in Germany, thanks in part to the sectarian tactics of the International in the years after 1928, which made social democracy the chief enemy. It was decided to abandon the tactics of 'class against class', and to return to the united front. The following passages show the application of this line to the non-European countries.[1]

In the face of the towering menace of fascism to the working class and all the gains it has made, to all toilers and their elementary rights, to the peace and liberty of the peoples, the Seventh Congress of the Communist International declares that *at the present historic stage it is the main and immediate task of the international labour movement to establish the united fighting front of the working class*. . . .

In *the colonial and semi-colonial countries*, the most important task facing the communists consists in working to create an *anti-imperialist people's front*. For this purpose it is necessary to draw the widest masses into the national liberation movement against growing imperialist exploitation, against cruel enslavement, for the driving out of the imperialists, for the independence of the country; to take an active part in the mass anti-imperialist movements headed by the national reformists and strive to bring about joint action with the national-revolutionary and national-reformist organizations on the basis of a definite anti-imperialist platform.

In China, it is indispensable to coordinate the extension of the Soviet movement and the reinforcement of the fighting strength of the Red Army with the development of the people's anti-imperialist movement in the whole country. This movement must be carried out under the slogan of the national-revolutionary struggle of the armed people against the imperialist enslavers, above all against Japanese imperialism and its Chinese lackeys. The Soviets must become the unifying centre of the whole Chinese people in its struggle for liberation.

In the interests of its own struggle for liberation, the proletariat of the imperialist countries must give all possible support to the liberation struggle of the colonial and semi-colonial peoples against the imperialist invaders.

[1] SOURCE: *Rezolyutsii VII Vsemirnogo Kongressa Kommunisticheskogo Internatsionala* (Moscow, Partizdat, 1935), pp. 14, 25–6.

2. *Maurice Thorez on Colonial Problems, 1937–9*

The two following texts illustrate the application of the line recommended by the Seventh Congress of the International to colonial problems and particularly to the Algerian problem. Text VIII 2 A is taken from the report of Maurice Thorez to the Ninth Congress of the French Communist Party, 25 December 1937; Text VIII 2 B is taken from a speech he made in Algiers, 11 February 1939.[1]

A The French Communist Party and Algeria

... Another very important problem of our policy is the attitude of the Popular Front towards the legitimate demands of the colonial peoples. Satisfaction must be given to the colonial peoples, first of all in the very interest of the unfortunate populations of North Africa, Syria, Lebanon, and Indochina. It must be done in the interest of the Popular Front which must merit the hopes, well cooled off today, that the natives of the colonies had laid in it.

It must be given in the interest of France, in order not to give to fascism any longer the demagogic arguments by which it tries to stir up certain strata of the native populations against our country.

For the workers: raise their miserable salaries, ensure the complete application of social laws; for the fellaheen, for the unhappy peasants, grant immediate aid in food, tools, seeds; then in Algeria redistribute the land, give back to the natives the good lands from which they have been expropriated and driven away; then, give water to everyone, to the settlers, to the French, to the natives; consider special measures to help the craftsmen, so numerous in the large cities of North Africa, in Fez as in Tunis, as in Algiers.

We must eliminate the native code, allow the accession of natives to public offices. As the first step towards the right of voting and of being elected for all the natives, the Blum-Viollette bill must be speedily adopted. In Lebanon and in Syria, France cannot go on favouring the activities of the fascists, agents of Mussolini, enemy of the France of the Popular Front, who enforce a reign of terror over a people who want to live in friendship with France.

The fundamental demand of our Communist Party concerning the colonial peoples remains self-determination, *the right to independence.* Recalling a formula of Lenin, we have already told our Tunisian comrades, who approved of our attitude, that *the right to divorce* did not mean *the obligation to divorce.* If the decisive question of the moment is the victorious struggle against fascism, the interest of the colonial peoples lies *in their union* with the French people, and not in an attitude which could favour the undertakings of fascism and, for example, place Algeria, Tunisia and Morocco under the

[1] SOURCE: Maurice Thorez, *Oeuvres* (Paris, Éditions sociales, 1954), Livre troisième, tome XIV, pp. 280–81 and tome XVI, pp. 174–86 *passim.*

yoke of Mussolini or Hitler, or make Indochina a base of operations for militaristic Japan.

B For the Front of all the French

One can sometimes trip up this Popular Front, strike it blows, but it lives and it will triumph. Moreover, it will triumph while expanding. . . .

We have said and we repeat:

Unite all men who want to live free, without distinction of race or religion, all the French of France and all the French of Algeria. When I say French of Algeria, I mean all of you here present, you French by birth, naturalized French, Israelites, and you Arab and Berber Muslims too, all the sons, if not by blood, at least by heart, of the great French revolution which made no distinction between races and religions, when it affirmed that the French Republic was 'one and indivisible'.

. . . Then our contradictors chime in: You are speaking to uneducated beings, to ignorant men who despise you at the bottom. Give them a few liberties and they will keep at it until they have thrown you French into the sea.

I shall repeat in this connexion what we have had the opportunity to state already. Yes, we want a free union between the peoples of France and Algeria. Free union means, to be sure, the right of divorce but not the obligation to divorce. I even add that, in the historical conditions of the moment this right is accompanied by the duty of uniting even more closely with French democracy. . . . But doesn't the same hold true here in Algeria? Where now in your country is the chosen race, the one which could lay claim to an exclusive domination, the one which could say: this land has been the land of my ancestors alone and it must be mine? *There is the Algerian nation which is taking form historically and whose evolution can be facilitated, aided by the efforts of the French Republic.* Would one not find here among you, perhaps, the descendants of those ancient Numidian tribes already civilized to the point of having made their lands the granary of ancient Rome: the descendants of these Berbers who gave to the Catholic Church Saint Augustine, bishop of Hippo, at the same time as the schismatic Donatius; the descendants of those Carthaginians, of those Romans, of all those who, during several centuries, contributed to the blooming of a civilization still attested to today by so many vestiges such as these ruins of Tebessa and Madaure which we visited a few days ago. Here today are the sons of the Arabs who came behind the banner of the prophet, the sons also of the Turks converted to Islam who came after them as new conquerors, of the Jews settled in large numbers on this soil for centuries. All these have mixed together in your land of Algeria, and have been joined by Greeks, Maltese, Spanish, Italians and French, and what French! The French of all our provinces, but in particular the French of the French territories of Corsica and Savoy, those of the French territory of Alsace who came in 1871 in order not to be Prussians.

There is an Algerian nation which is taking form, it too, in the blending of twenty races. . . .

Let us go ahead, calm, serene. Our cause, the cause of Liberty, the cause of Peace and of France will triumph through unity. Long live unity!

3. *Mao Tse-tung: 'On New Democracy'*

Extracts from the book, published early in 1940 under the above title, in which Mao Tse-tung developed at some length his ideas regarding collaboration between the communists and the bourgeoisie during the democratic stage of the revolution. In this text we have employed the system used in *The Political Thought of Mao Tse-tung*, consisting in italicizing all the passages which were eliminated or extensively revised by Mao in preparing the current edition of his selected works. Some details regarding the most important variants are given in the notes. It will be seen that in the original version Mao spoke not of the 'four-class bloc' which had been Stalin's formula a decade and a half earlier, but of a 'three-class bloc'. This detail in itself is not of tremendous importance, since the reality covered by the expression is the same – Mao simply lumps together peasantry and urban petty bourgeoisie under the common term of petty bourgeoisie. It is significant, however, as a reflection of Mao's general tendency, in this book addressed to a wide audience, to de-emphasize themes such as agrarian revolution which might have disturbed some of his non-communist readers. More important in this respect is the fact that he includes among the classes which should participate in the united front not the 'national bourgeoisie', as in the current version, but simply the bourgeoisie. In other words, he includes the big bourgeoisie as well, and even the 'comprador' bourgeoisie, provided it is 'patriotic'. It is also interesting to note a sentence (which has naturally disappeared from the current edition) regarding the possible hegemony of the bourgeoisie in the revolution, and in general a less rigid position than in texts such as *The Chinese Revolution and the Chinese Communist Party* written almost simultaneously, but addressed primarily to Party members. (See *The Political Thought of Mao Tse-tung*, Texts III K and IV H, pp. 229–34 and 262–4.)[1]

The historical characteristic of the Chinese revolution lies in its division into the two stages, democracy and socialism, the first being no longer democracy in general, but democracy of the Chinese type, a new and special type, namely, New Democracy. . . .

. . . This characteristic did not emerge immediately after the

[1] SOURCE: *Chieh-fang*, nos. 98–9, 20 February 1940. The variants are given on the basis of a comparison of this text with that in the current Chinese edition of Mao's works. We have taken as a basis for our translation that in the *Selected Works of Mao Tse-tung* (Peking, Foreign Languages Press, 1965), vol. II, pp. 342–77 *passim*, which is on the whole extremely accurate except where the Chinese text itself has been rewritten by Mao.

Opium War, but took shape later, after the first imperialist world war and the October Revolution in Russia. . . .

Before these events, the Chinese bourgeois-democratic revolution came within the old category of the bourgeois-democratic world revolution, of which it was a part.

Since these events, the Chinese bourgeois-democratic revolution has changed, it has come within the new category of bourgeois-democratic revolutions and, as far as the alignment of revolutionary forces is concerned, forms part of the proletarian-socialist world revolution. . . .

In an era in which the world capitalist front has collapsed in one corner of the globe (a corner which occupies one-sixth of the world's surface), and has fully revealed its decadence everywhere else, in an era in which the remaining capitalist portions cannot survive without relying more than ever on the colonies and semi-colonies, in an era in which a socialist state has been established and has proclaimed its readiness to fight in support of the liberation movement of all colonies and semi-colonies . . . in such an era, a revolution in any colony or semi-colony that is directed against imperialism, i.e., against the international bourgeoisie and international capitalism, no longer comes within the old category of the bourgeois-democratic world revolution, but within the new category. It is no longer part of the old bourgeois and capitalist world revolution, but is part of the new world revolution, the proletarian-socialist world revolution. . . .

Although during its first stage or first step, such a revolution in a colonial and semi-colonial country is still fundamentally bourgeois-democratic in its social character, and although its objective demand is still fundamentally to clear the path for the development of capitalism, it is no longer a revolution of the old type, led *entirely* by the bourgeoisie, with the aim of establishing a capitalist society and a state under bourgeois dictatorship. It is rather a revolution of the new type, led by the proletariat *or with the participation of the proletariat* in the leadership, and having as its aim, in the first stage, the establishment of a new-democratic society and a state under the joint dictatorship of all the revolutionary classes. . . .[1]

Such a revolution attacks imperialism at its very roots, and is therefore not acceptable to imperialism, which on the contrary opposes it. But it is acceptable to socialism, and is supported by the land of socialism and by the socialist international proletariat.

Therefore, such a revolution cannot but become part of the proletarian-socialist world revolution.

The correct thesis that 'the Chinese revolution is part of the world revolution' was put forward as early as 1926–7 during the period of China's Great Revolution. . . .

[1] Here Mao Tse-tung added in 1951: 'Thus this revolution actually serves the purpose of clearing a still wider path for the development of socialism.'

The Chinese communists put forward this correct thesis on the basis of Stalin's theory.

. . . Stalin has again and again expounded the theory that revolutions in the colonies and semi-colonies have broken away from the old category and become part of the proletarian-socialist revolution. The clearest and most precise explanation is given in an article published on 30 June 1925, . . . which contains the following passage:

> . . . The war, on the one hand, and the October Revolution in Russia, on the other, transformed the national question from a part of the bourgeois-democratic revolution into a part of the proletarian-socialist revolution. As far back as October 1916, in his article 'The discussion on Self-Determination Summed Up', Lenin said that the main point of the national question, the right to self-determination, had ceased to be a part of the general democratic movement, that it had already become a component part of the general proletarian, socialist revolution. . . .[1]

From this it can be seen that there are two kinds of revolution. The first belongs to the bourgeois or capitalist category. The era of this kind of world revolution is long past; it came to an end in 1914, when the first imperialist world war broke out, and more particularly in 1917 when the Russian October Revolution took place. The second kind, namely the proletarian-socialist world revolution, thereupon began. This type of revolution has the proletariat of the capitalist countries as its main force, and the oppressed peoples of the colonies and semi-colonies as its allies. No matter what classes, parties or individuals in an oppressed nation join the revolution, and no matter whether they are conscious of this point or understand it subjectively, so long as they oppose imperialism, their revolution becomes part of the proletarian-socialist world revolution and they become its allies.

Today, the Chinese revolution has taken on still greater significance. . . . The Chinese revolution is a great part of the world revolution. . . .

Because the Chinese bourgeoisie[2] is the bourgeoisie of a colonial and semi-colonial country, and because it is oppressed by imperialism, it retains at certain periods and to a certain degree – even in the era of imperialism – a revolutionary spirit which leads it to fight against foreign imperialism and the domestic governments of bureaucrats and warlords (instances of opposition to the latter can be found in the period of the Revolution of 1911 and the Northern Expedition, *that is to say at periods when the bourgeoisie did not itself exercise power*). It can unite with the proletariat and the petty

[1] Stalin, 'The National Question Once Again', *Works* (Moscow, Foreign Languages Publishing House, 1954), vol. VII, pp. 225–7. See also Texts IV 7 and VI 14 B on pp. 185–6 and 227 above.

[2] Here, and generally throughout this text, Mao replaced 'bourgeoisie' by 'national bourgeoisie' in 1951.

bourgeoisie against such enemies as it is ready to oppose. In this respect, the Chinese bourgeoisie differs from the bourgeoisie of the old Russian empire. Since the old Russian empire was itself already a military-feudal imperialism which carried on aggression against other countries, the Russian bourgeoisie was entirely lacking in revolutionary quality. There, the task of the proletariat was to oppose the bourgeoisie, not to unite with it. Because China is a colonial and semi-colonial country which is a victim of aggression, the Chinese bourgeoisie has a revolutionary quality at certain periods and to a certain degree. Here, the task of the proletariat is not to neglect this revolutionary quality of the bourgeoisie; on the contrary, it is possible to establish with it a united front against imperialism and the bureaucrat and warlord governments.

At the same time, precisely because the Chinese bourgeoisie is the bourgeoisie of a colonial and semi-colonial country, it is extremely flabby economically and politically, and it also has another quality, namely a proneness to compromise with the enemies of the revolution. . . . When the European and American countries were still in their revolutionary era, the bourgeoisie of those countries, and especially of France, was comparatively thorough in carrying out the revolution. In China, the bourgeoisie does not possess even this degree of thoroughness. . . .

In China, the situation is extremely clear. Whoever can lead the people in overthrowing imperialism and the feudal forces will be able to win the people's confidence, for the mortal enemies of the people are imperialism and the feudal forces, especially imperialism. Today, whoever can lead the people in driving out Japanese imperialism and introducing democratic government will be the saviour of the people. *If the Chinese bourgeoisie can fulfil this responsibility, no one will be able to refuse his admiration; but if it cannot do so*, this responsibility will inevitably fall on the shoulders of the proletariat. . . .[1]

. . . The multifarious types of state system in the world, classified according to their *social character*,[2] can be reduced to three basic kinds: (1) republics under bourgeois dictatorship; (2) republics under the dictatorship of the proletariat; and (3) republics under the joint dictatorship of several revolutionary classes.

The first kind comprises the old democratic states. Today, after the outbreak of the second imperialist war, there is already not the slightest trace of democracy in *any*[3] of the capitalist countries; they

[1] In the current edition this sentence has been replaced by the flat statement that the bourgeoisie cannot lead this struggle and the proletariat must therefore do so.

[2] In the current edition 'social character' was replaced by 'class character of their political power'.

[3] In the current edition, this sentence is formulated in slightly less sweeping terms; only a part of the capitalist states are accused of being bloody dictator-

have *all* been transformed, or are about to be transformed, into bloody military dictatorships of the bourgeoisie. . . .

Apart from the Soviet Union, the second kind is ripening in all capitalist countries, and in the future it will be the dominant form throughout the world for a certain period.

The third kind is the transitional form of state in the revolutionary colonies and semi-colonies.[1] To be sure, the various colonies and semi-colonies will necessarily have certain different characteristics, but these are only minor differences within the general framework of uniformity. So long as they are revolutionary colonial and semi-colonial countries,[1] their state and governmental structure will of necessity be basically the same, i.e., a new-democratic state under the joint dictatorship of several anti-imperialist classes. In China today, this new-democratic state takes the form of the anti-Japanese united front. . . .

What if it is said that, owing to certain specific conditions (the victory of the bourgeoisie over Greek aggression and the extreme feebleness of the proletariat), a tiny Turkey ruled by a bourgeois dictatorship of a Kemalist type did still emerge after the first imperialist war and the October Revolution? Well, after the Second World War and the completion of socialist construction in the Soviet Union, there can certainly not be another Turkey, still less a Turkey with a population of 450 million. . . . After the defeat of the Great Chinese Revolution[2] in 1927, did not bourgeois elements in China loudly clamour for something called Kemalism? But where is China's Kemal? . . . Besides, even the so-called Kemalist Turkey finally had to throw herself into the arms of Anglo-French imperialism, becoming more and more a semi-colony and a part of the reactionary imperialist world. In the international situation of the 1940s and 1950s, the heroes and brave fellows (*ying-hsiung hao-han*), whoever they may be, in the colonies and semi-colonies must either line up on the imperialist front and become part of the forces of world counter-revolution, or line up on the anti-imperialist front and become part of the forces of world revolution. They must do one or the other, for there is no third way. . . .

. . . The present situation is perfectly clear. If there is no policy of uniting with Russia, if we do not unite with the land of socialism, there will inevitably be a policy of uniting with imperialism, we will inevitably unite with imperialism. Is it not evident that this is

ships. For further details regarding Mao's view of the capitalist states at this time, see *The Political Thought of Mao Tse-tung*, Text IX E, pp. 394–400.

[1] Here Mao now speaks of 'revolution *in* the colonies' rather than 'revolutionary colonies'.

[2] In the current version the 'Great Chinese Revolution' has become the 'First Great Revolution', to distinguish it from the 'second revolution' of 1927 to 1937, and the 'third revolution' of 1945 to 1949.

exactly what happened after 1927? *During the first two years of the anti-Japanese resistance, because the imperialist great war had not yet broken out, one could still utilize the contradictions between Japan and different countries such as England and the United States. After the outbreak of the imperialist great war, these contradictions, although they have not entirely disappeared, have greatly diminished. If we were to make improper use of them, then England and the United States could demand that China participate in their struggle against the Soviet Union. If China then complied with their demand, she would immediately place herself on the side of the reactionary front of imperialism, thus putting an end to all national independence.*[1] Once the conflict between the socialist Soviet Union and *imperialist England and America*[2] grows sharper, China will have to take her stand on one side or the other. This is an inevitable trend. Is it not possible to avoid leaning to either side? No, that is an illusion. The entire globe will be swept into one or the other of these two fronts, and henceforth 'neutrality' will be merely a deceptive term. Especially is this true of China, which is fighting an imperialist power that has penetrated deep into her territory; her final victory is inconceivable without aid from the Soviet Union. . . .

A cultural revolution is the ideological reflection of the political and economic revolution, and is in their service. In China there is a united front in the cultural as in the political revolution.

The history of the united front in the cultural revolution during the last twenty years can be divided into four periods. . . .

The first period extended from the 'May 4th' Movement of 1919 to the founding of the Chinese Communist Party in 1921. The 'May 4th' Movement was its chief landmark.

The 'May 4th' Movement was an anti-imperialist as well as an anti-feudal movement. . . . The 'May 4th' Movement came into being at the call of the world revolution of that time, at the call of the Russian Revolution and of Lenin. The 'May 4th' Movement was a part of the world proletarian revolution of that time. Although at the time of the 'May 4th' Movement the Chinese Communist Party had not yet come into existence, there were already large numbers of intellectuals who approved of the Russian revolution and had the rudiments of communist ideology. In the beginning, the 'May 4th' Movement was a revolutionary movement of the united front of three sections of people – communist intellectuals, revolutionary petty-bourgeois intellectuals, and bourgeois intellectuals (the last forming the right wing of the movement). Its weak point was that it was confined to the intellectuals, and the workers and peasants did not participate in it. But as soon as it developed

[1] This whole passage has been eliminated from the current edition.

[2] In the current edition 'imperialist England and America' has been replaced by 'the imperialist powers', thus masking the fact that in 1940 Mao regarded Chamberlain as worse than Hitler. See the text cited in note 3, p. 254 above.

into the 'June 3rd' Movement,[1] not only the intellectuals but the mass of the proletariat, the petty bourgeoisie and the bourgeoisie joined in, and it became a nation-wide revolutionary movement. The cultural revolution of the 'May 4th' Movement was a movement of thoroughgoing opposition to feudal culture; there had never been such a great and thoroughgoing cultural revolution since the dawn of Chinese history. . . .

In the second period, whose landmarks were the founding of the Chinese Communist Party, the 'May 30th' Movement,[2] and the Northern Expedition, the united front of the three classes formed at the time of the 'May 4th' Movement was continued and expanded.[3] This united front also took form politically, this being the first instance of Kuomintang-Communist cooperation. . . .

The third period was the new revolutionary period of 1927–36. As a result of the changes which had taken place within the revolutionary camp at the end of the previous period, involving the going over of the Chinese bourgeoisie[4] to the counter-revolutionary camp of the imperialist and feudal forces, only *two* of the *three* classes[5] originally composing the revolutionary camp remained. There remained the proletariat and the petty bourgeoisie (*including the peasantry, the revolutionary intellectuals, and other sections of the petty bourgeoisie*). Thus the Chinese revolution inevitably entered a new period, in which it was led by the Chinese Communist Party alone. . . .

The fourth period is that of the present anti-Japanese war. Pursuing its zigzag course, the Chinese revolution has again arrived at a united front of *three* classes. But this time the scope is much broader. Among the upper classes, it includes *all the rulers*; among the middle classes, it includes the petty bourgeoisie *in its totality*;[6] among the lower classes, it includes the totality of the proletarians. All classes and strata of the country have become allies, and are resolutely resisting Japanese imperialism. . . .

. . . If we consider Chinese history as a whole, the progress achieved in the twenty years since the 'May 4th' Movement not only surpasses that of the preceding eighty years, it truly surpasses that

[1] Beginning on 3 June 1919, the merchants and workers in a number of cities came out on strike in support of the 'May 4th' student movement.

[2] The protest movement against the mistreatment of Chinese by the foreign powers which began in Shanghai on 30 May 1925.

[3] Here Mao has added a reference to participation by the peasantry.

[4] In the current text Mao speaks of the 'big bourgeoisie . . ., with the national bourgeoisie trailing after it'.

[5] Here, and throughout the rest of this extract, Mao distinguishes only three classes instead of four, the peasantry being included among the petty bourgeoisie. In the current version he refers to the four-class bloc, the peasants being counted separately.

[6] In the current version, Mao here includes the national bourgeoisie among the middle classes.

of several millennia. Can we not visualize what further progress China will make in another twenty years? The unbridled violence of all the forces of darkness, whether domestic or foreign, has brought disaster to our nation; but this very violence indicates that while the forces of darkness still have some strength left, they are already in their death throes, and that the popular masses are gradually approaching victory. This is true in the Far East, and it is also true in the world as a whole. . . .

SECTION IX: FROM THE SEVENTH CONGRESS OF THE CHINESE COMMUNIST PARTY TO THE DEATH OF STALIN

1. Liu Shao-ch'i on the Sinification of Marxism by Mao Tse-tung

Extracts from Liu Shao-ch'i's report to the Seventh Congress of the Chinese Communist Party, in May 1945, published under the title 'On the Party'. The affirmation, in the programme adopted by this Congress, that 'Mao Tse-tung's Thought' constitutes the sole correct and orthodox theory which must guide all the work of the Party, constituted a decisive stage in the development of the Mao cult.[1]

The General Programme of the Party Constitution stipulates that the Thought of Mao Tse-tung shall guide all the work of our Party. The Constitution itself provides that it is the duty of every Party member to endeavour to understand the fundamentals of Marxism-Leninism and the Thought of Mao Tse-tung. This is a most important historical characteristic of our amendment of the Constitution at this time. I believe that this Congress and the entire Party will heartily support this stipulation.

For over a century, the Chinese nation and people, which have known profound misfortunes, have accumulated immeasurably rich experience in the course of their bloody struggles for their own emancipation. Their practical struggles and the experience thus gained inevitably culminated in the creation of great theories of their own, thus showing that the Chinese nation is not only a nation capable of fighting, but also a nation which has a modern scientific revolutionary theory. . . .

. . . This theory has led our Party and our people to very great victories, and it will continue to lead our Party and our people to ultimate and complete victory and liberation. This is the greatest achievement and glory of our Party and of our people in their long struggles, and it will bring blessings to our nation for generations and generations. This theory is none other than the Thought of Mao Tse-tung – Comrade Mao Tse-tung's theory and policy regarding Chinese history, Chinese society, and the Chinese revolution.

The Thought of Mao Tse-tung is the thought that unites Marxist-Leninist theory with the practice of the Chinese revolution. It is Chinese communism, it is Chinese Marxism.

[1] SOURCE: Liu Shao-ch'i, *Kuan-yü hsiu-kai tang-chang ti pao-kao* (Wuhu, Hsinhua Shutien, n.d. (1945?)), pp. 16–19. Our translation is adapted, with numerous corrections, from the considerably edulcorated version given in Liu Shao-ch'i, *On the Party* (Peking, Foreign Languages Press, 1950).

The Thought of Mao Tse-tung is a further development of Marxism in the national-democratic revolution in the colonial, semi-colonial and semi-feudal countries of the present epoch. It is an admirable model of the nationalization of Marxism (*Ma-k'o-szu-chu-i ti min-tsu-hua*). . . . It is Chinese, and at the same time it is thoroughly Marxist. . . .

The Thought of Mao Tse-tung . . . is our Party's only correct guiding theory and its only correct general line.

The birth, development, and maturity of the Thought of Mao Tse-tung has a long history of twenty-four years. It has been repeatedly tested in the course of numerous bitter struggles of millions upon millions of people, and has been proved to be objective truth, the only correct theory and policy to save China. Numerous historical events in the past have shown that whenever the revolution was under the leadership of Mao Tse-tung and his Thought, it succeeded and developed, and whenever it departed from that leadership it met with failure or decline. The combination of Marxist theory with the practice of the proletarian revolution in the epoch of imperialism, and the practice of the Russian revolution, gave rise to Russian Bolshevism – Leninism-Stalinism, which not only guided the Russian people to win their complete emancipation, but also guided and is still guiding the peoples all over the world to achieve emancipation. What Comrade Mao Tse-tung has done as a disciple of Marx, Engels, Lenin and Stalin is precisely to unite Marxist theory with the practice of the Chinese revolution, thus giving rise to Chinese communism – the Thought of Mao Tse-tung. And Mao Tse-tung's Thought, too, has guided and is guiding the Chinese people to achieve complete emancipation; it will, moreover, make great and useful contributions to the cause of the emancipation of the peoples of all countries, and of the peoples of the East in particular.

The Thought of Mao Tse-tung, from his world view to his style of work, is Sinified Marxism (*Chung-kuo-hua ti Ma-k'o-szu-chu-i*) in the process of development and perfection. . . . These theories and policies are thoroughly Marxist, and at the same time thoroughly Chinese. They are the highest expression of the wisdom of the Chinese nation, and its highest theoretical achievement.

Because of various conditions, such as the very great peculiarities in China's social and historical development and her backwardness in science, etc., it is a unique and difficult task to carry out the systematic Sinification of Marxism, to transform Marxism from its European form to a Chinese form – in other words, to use the Marxist standpoint and method to solve the various problems of the contemporary Chinese revolution. Many of the problems encountered in the process have never been raised or solved by the world's Marxists, for here in China the masses are composed principally of peasants and not of workers, and the fight is directed against foreign imperialist oppression and against the medieval remnants, and not against domestic capital. This can never be accomplished, as some people seem to think, by simply reading Marxist works over and over, reciting them by heart, and quoting from them. It requires the combination of a high level of scientific spirit and a high level of revolutionary spirit. . . . It is none other than our Comrade Mao Tse-tung who has so remarkably and successfully carried out the unique and difficult task of the Sinification of Marxism. This constitutes one of the greatest achievements in the history of the world Marxist movement. It is an unprecedented development of Marxism, the best of all truths, in a nation of 450 millions. This is something for which we should be particularly grateful. Our Comrade Mao Tse-tung is not only the greatest revolutionary and statesman in all of Chinese history; he is also the greatest theoretician and scientist in all of Chinese history. Not only did he dare to lead the entire Party and the entire Chinese people in combats that shook the world; his theoretical culture and his courage in theoretical work were also of the highest. In the theoretical field, he was boldly creative, discarding certain specific Marxist principles and conclusions that were obsolete and ill-adapted to concrete conditions in China, and replacing them with new principles and conclusions adapted to China's new historical conditions. Thus he was able to carry out successfully the difficult and gigantic task of the Sinification of Marxism. . . .

2. *Zhukov: 'The Aggravation of the Crisis of the Colonial System'*

Extracts from an article published under this title by one of the principal Soviet specialists in the political problems of the non-European countries. This text, which appeared in the organ of the Central Committee of the Soviet Communist Party, illustrates the Zhdanovite position hostile to all collaboration with bourgeois nationalism which prevailed in 1947.[1]

The struggle of the peoples of the colonial and dependent countries for their liberation, and against imperialism, has a long history. It is well-known that over the decades the peoples of the colonial countries have on several occasions raised the banner of revolt against the foreign imperialists. But now the nature of the struggle has changed. The upsurge of the national-liberation movement in the colonial and dependent countries since the Second World War has been distinguished by the fact that bourgeois or even semi-feudal elements have been predominant in the movement's leadership. Thus in Turkey the national-liberation struggle was led by the Kemalites, in Egypt by the Wafd party, in India by the Gandhists and in China by the Kuomintang. . . .

Earlier, it was the bourgeoisie and in certain cases dubious

[1] SOURCE: *Bol'shevik*, 15 December 1947.

feudal-clerical prophets who led the national-liberation movement, but now, as a result of the Second World War and the strengthening of the positions of socialism and democracy throughout the world, the powerful force of the anti-imperialist struggle in the colonies and semi-colonies is the working class.

In China, Korea, India and many other countries of the East, communist parties are now the recognized leaders of millions of workers, and fight consistently for their country's national independence and sovereignty. This is how the nature of the national-liberation movement in the colonies and semi-colonies has changed.

Economic transformations in these countries are the most important factor in the change that has come over the general political situation in the colonial and dependent countries.

The imperialists are consciously holding back the development of productive forces in the colonies, hindering the development of competing branches of industry, primarily of industry that makes the means of production, and preventing the introduction of progressive reforms capable of raising the general economic and cultural level of the dependent countries. But as it squeezes raw materials and foodstuffs out of the colonies, imperialism is naturally not opposed to the export of capital into the colonies, or to industry based on local raw materials being developed there, which also enables them to exploit widely the cheap, and in some countries practically free, labour of the 'native' workers. . . .

It is a well-known fact that the Second World War precipitated to a considerable extent the industrial development of a number of colonial countries, of India above all. . . . All of this was bound to have an effect upon the numbers and political activity of the working class of India. . . .

The logic of the class struggle leads to the big national bourgeoisie seeing the workers as a greater enemy than domination by foreign imperialists that limits its scope for profiteering. If for this reason alone, the big national bourgeoisie is willing to strike a bargain with the imperialists to the detriment of the nation's interests. . . .

Thus, in the colonies, it is not only the feudal upper crust but also the bourgeoisie closely bound up with it which, because of its class nature, is incapable of applying itself consistently and utterly to the struggle to rescue the country from the clutches of political and economic backwardness that stems from imperialist enslavement. Spontaneous revolutionary demonstrations by the peasantry frighten the big national bourgeoisie – both comprador and industrial – no less than demonstrations by the proletariat. . . .

Because of the general process of the development of industry in the colonies and semi-colonies and the attendant sharp aggravation of class contradictions, the big national bourgeoisie is getting further and further away from the mass liberation movement, and more and more frequently has recourse to outright betrayal of national interests. . . .

The emergence of the working class as the vanguard force of the national-liberation movement in the colonies and semi-colonies . . . has inevitably led to the elevation of the role of communist parties in the colonies and semi-colonies. In many Eastern countries communist parties have become the guiding spirit and organizer of a bloc of national democratic forces fighting against imperialism for their country's independence, a bloc which unites not only the proletariat and peasantry but the remaining strata of the workers and, in many countries, also a section of the bourgeoisie, chiefly the petty and middle bourgeoisie.

The glorious battle-hardened Chinese Communist Party, with upwards of two million members, is the supreme leader and organizer of the broad masses of the Chinese people, who, under its direction, are striving for the triumph of democratic principles to eliminate China's centuries of backwardness, to free her from the bonds of feudalism that fetter her national development, and to free her from thraldom to imperialism. . . .

A popular, anti-imperialist front has been formed in a number of colonial and dependent countries, representing a coalition of parties whose platform is the liberation struggle with the Communist Party taking the leading part (Indonesia, Vietnam). . . .

Comrade Zhdanov noted in his report that Indonesia and Vietnam adhere to the anti-imperialist camp. In other words, they are a serious factor in shaking the positions of imperialism in the colonies, and a centre of attraction for many millions of colonial slaves who no longer wish to tolerate oppression.

3. *The Struggle of Peoples for Independence within the Framework of the French Union*

Excerpts from the report of the Central Committee of the French Communist Party for the Eleventh National Congress in June 1947. This report retraces the history of the attitude of the French Communist Party in colonial matters since the end of the Second World War; our excerpts have been drawn from the passage dealing with the period from November 1946 to April 1947.[1]

. . . Throughout the world the old colonial system is condemned. The government of the Netherlands has been forced to recognize the Indonesian republic whose peoples it has dominated for centuries.

The British government is forced to announce officially that it will leave India before June 1948. At the time when de Gaulle was president of the government, France, because it did not respect

[1] SOURCE: *Du congrès de Paris au congrès de Strasbourg*. Deux années d'activité pour la renaissance économique et politique de la République française, s.l.n.d., pp. 41–3.

promises made, had to leave Syria and Lebanon, whence England helped to chase it.

These lessons of history must be taken into account. It is in the interest of France to treat with the peoples who claim their elementary democratic freedoms.

Any complications in our relations with the peoples of the French Union can only benefit the foreign imperialists who are always looking for new outlets.

For the Communist Party the presence of France, freely accepted by free peoples within the framework of the French Union written into the constitution, must not be questioned.

The socialist leaders have abandoned the position of the working class in letting the war continue against Vietnam, which is fighting for its independence within the framework of the French Union – a position of the working class which is in conformity with the defence of France's interests and the maintenance of her presence in the Far East.

Indeed, only the communists have refused to be a party to such a policy, and by abstaining at the time of the vote of confidence in the government and the vote of military credits to carry on the war against Vietnam, the Communist Party has strengthened the sympathy it enjoys from all republicans, from all men animated by a progressive spirit.

The repercussion of this honest attitude has had and will not fail to have in the entire world, a happy influence on all the peoples who love liberty and more particularly on the colonial peoples.

However, taking into account the general situation of the country at the present time, of the will of the reaction to do everything to exclude the communists from the government, and of the situation of France on the international level, especially as concerns the meeting of the 'Big Four' in Moscow, the communist ministers could not break government solidarity.

In agreement on all the other points of government policy, it was not possible to abandon the points of agreement for a single point of disagreement which moreover would have changed nothing as regards the substance of the problem of Vietnam – quite the contrary.

After Vietnam, the incidents in Madagascar, the sending of troops and the state of siege in the great island seem to indicate that there, too, the intention is to move towards a policy of force which can only be contrary to French interests.

In carrying out this criminal policy, it is not the maintenance of what some call the 'French Colonial Empire' that one will obtain but the successive loss of countries which their peoples wish to see living freely within the French Union.

The Communist Party has done and will do in the future everything in its power in order that the relations of the overseas populations with the French Republic may be in conformity with the constitution of the Republic and the humane traditions of our country. . . .

4. *Zhukov: 'Questions of the National and Colonial Struggle after the Second World War'*

Extracts from an article of 1949, published under the above title, illustrating the persistence of the sectarian attitude which still saw in Nehru the 'lackey of the Americans'.[1]

The armed struggle of the peoples of several colonial and dependent countries for their national independence and state autonomy is evidence not only of the growing scope of the national-liberation struggle but also of its qualitative improvement. The armed struggle to create independent republics in Indonesia and Indo-china, the armed struggle in Malaya and Burma, the peasant uprisings in India and, lastly, the victorious liberation war waged by the Chinese people, are clear evidence that since the Second World War the national-liberation movement has entered a new, higher stage of development.

The leading role of the working class and its vanguard, the communist parties, is of decisive significance in the national-liberation movement of major colonial countries. We can now state with complete accuracy that in the majority of the colonial countries, and primarily in those countries where the struggle against imperialism has become fiercest, working-class hegemony in the colonial revolution is recognized and the Communist parties lead the national-liberation movement either unaided or through the broader mass organizations.

Clearly, one cannot speak of the development of the national struggle in the colonies and semi-colonies, of the nature, direction and tendencies of that struggle, outside the context of the general international situation. It is not difficult to see that the upsurge of the national-liberation movement and its successes since the Second World War have entirely resulted from the world-wide balance of class forces changing in favour of democracy and socialism and against imperialism, and from the increase in the might of the U.S.S.R. This is borne out by the entire train of post-war historical development. . . .

The scope and success of the popular movements in Asia are seriously disturbing the imperialist camp. They are particularly unpleasant for the Americans, who are seeking world domination, since they expose the adventurism of their plans and stratagems. . . . The monopolists of the U.S.A. consider the colonial possessions of any imperialist power as potentially their own and, using various levers to exert political, economic and military pressure upon the

[1] SOURCE: *Voprosy Ekonomiki*, no. 9, 1949, pp. 54–61.

so-called Marshall-aid countries (Britain, France, Holland, Belgium), they overcome their competitors' resistance and force them, in the majority of colonies, to pursue a policy consistent with the interests of American monopoly capital. . . .

This policy is dictated primarily by the strategic interests of the aggressive Anglo-American imperialist bloc. It is designed to use the human and material resources of the colonies and semi-colonies principally to obtain cheaply or for nothing a labour force, cannon-fodder and military resources in order to prepare a new world war. . . .

The imperialists are increasingly relying not only on feudal-land-owning elements but on the big national bourgeoisie of the colonies and semi-colonies. . . .

Bourgeois nationalism in the colonies and semi-colonies is called upon to keep the popular masses under the ideological and political leadership of the big bourgeoisie which, in most of the colonial countries, has already deserted to the imperialist camp. . . .

This is why ruthless exposure of reactionary bourgeois-nationalist ideology in its various forms – be it Kemalism or Gandhism, Zionism or Pan-Arabism – hastens the process of the national and social emancipation of the peoples of the colonial and dependent countries, and frustrates the provocative machinations of the imperialists and their agents. . . .

Just as right-wing socialists in the developed capitalist countries, who betray the working class, try to spread the putrid idea of the possibility of some 'third', middle road between communism and capitalism, whilst in actual fact they actively serve the forces of imperialist reaction which is plotting war against the U.S.S.R. and the countries of people's democracy, so national-reformists in the colonial and semi-colonial countries falsely assert their desire 'to remain outside' of the struggle between the two camps and their 'neutrality' in respect of what they call the 'ideological conflict' between the U.S.S.R. and the U.S.A., whereas in reality they make common cause with the reactionary bourgeoisie, slander the U.S.S.R. and actively assist the imperialists. . . .

In most of the major colonies the alliance between the Anglo-American colonizers and the national bourgeoisie and its national-reformist followers enables the imperialists to exploit bourgeois-democratic, reformist illusions more widely so as to deceive the masses, and to exchange overt, crude forms and methods of colonial domination for more refined and insidious ones. . . .

India is a particularly convincing example in this connexion. The Indian bourgeoisie now rivals the most reactionary forces in stifling the mass popular movement, in terrorizing progressive elements in the working-class and peasant movement. The metamorphosis undergone by Nehru clearly demonstrates this: Nehru, who has changed from being a leftist congressman who denigrated imperialism, has become a cunning slave serving two masters – Britain and the U.S.A. – the ally of Indian princes and landowners, the bloody destroyer of India's progressive forces. But such is the logic of the class struggle: there can be no 'half-way house' between imperialism and democracy. . . .

In the struggle for people's democracy in the colonies and semicolonies it is not only the workers, peasants, urban petty bourgeoisie and intelligentsia who are joining forces, but even a section of the middle bourgeoisie that is interested in freeing itself from ruinous foreign competition and imperialist domination. Thus, the struggle for people's democracy can unite under the leadership of the working class the great majority of the people. This means that the popular-democratic revolution can easily become a form of national-liberation struggle, of colonial revolution. . . .

. . . In the course of its development, the popular-democratic revolution in the colonies must pass through a number of successive stages and the time taken in these countries to pass to the stage of solving socialist problems and building a socialist economy may prove longer than in other countries of people's democracy which have not been colonies. . . .

The general laws of social development are identical for Eastern and Western countries alike. One can speak only of differences in the pace or in the particular forms of this development. In this sense, people's democracy in the East does not differ in its basic outlines from people's democracy in the West. . . .

The whole course of the national-colonial struggle, and the immense victories won by the democratic forces in East Asia, startlingly confirm the truth of Lenin's and Stalin's teaching on the national-colonial question and demonstrate the triumph of the all-conquering ideas of Marx, Engels, Lenin and Stalin.

5. Astafiev: 'From a Semi-Colony to a People's Democracy'

Extracts from an article published in 1949 by a staff member of the Academy of Sciences, which gives the Soviet viewpoint on the Chinese revolution at the moment when Mao had just won victory.[1]

The great October Socialist Revolution and the Soviet Union – the workers' and peasants' State which it created – has had an enormous and decisive influence on the development of the national-liberation movement in China and throughout the whole world.

The October Revolution broke the imperialist chain which completely encircled China; it inspired the Chinese toilers for the struggle against imperialism and assured them not only of all-round moral support and assistance from the U.S.S.R. but also

[1] SOURCE: *Krizis Kolonial'noy Sistemy.* Natsional'no-osvoboditel'naya Voyna Narodov Vostochnoy Azii (Moskva, Izdatel'stvo Akademiy Nauk S.S.S.R., 1949), pp. 32, 56–7, 82–6.

that the enormous revolutionary experience of the Russian proletariat and its party would be handed on to them. Comrade Stalin has on numerous occasions pointed to all of these circumstances as one of the basic factors which facilitated the development of the revolution in China.[1]

In an article devoted to the twenty-eighth anniversary of the Chinese Communist Party, Mao Tse-tung writes that it is thanks only to the October Revolution that 'the Chinese discovered the universal truth of Marxism-Leninism. . . .

'Before the October Revolution, not only Lenin and Stalin but Marx and Engels were unknown to the Chinese. The salvoes of the October Revolution brought us Marxism-Leninism. The October Revolution helped progressive people throughout the world and in China to adopt the proletarian outlook on the world as a means of determining a country's destiny and re-examining their own problems. Their conclusion was to embark on the path taken by the Russians'. . . .[2]

It is not surprising that the heroic liberation struggle of the Chinese people arouses admiration, sympathy and moral support from all democratic progressive elements throughout the world, and this also is a mark of the link between the Chinese national-liberation movement and the general struggle of the world camp of democracy. . . .

In the words of Mao Tse-tung, 'The Chinese Communist Party is a party built on the example of the All-Union Communist Party (Bolshevik).'[3] It has made wide use of the accumulated revolutionary experience of the Russian Bolsheviks, and is guided in its activities by the strategy and tactics of revolutionary struggle elaborated by the great leaders of the world proletariat – Lenin and Stalin. From the first, its policy has been based on Lenin's teaching concerning imperialism and the characteristics of the revolution in colonial and dependent countries.

The works of Comrade Stalin, and in particular his works on the Chinese question, have been of enormous significance for the Party in its formulating a correct Marxist-Leninist policy. Basing himself in these works on a profound theoretical analysis of the situation in China, Comrade Stalin defined the characteristics of the Chinese revolution, brilliantly predicted its course and indicated the conditions in which it could succeed. . . .

By its successes in the struggle against internal reaction and imperialism, its achievements in the sphere of democratic transformations and economic and cultural construction, the national-liberation movement of the Chinese people exercises an enormous

[1] Stalin, *Sochineniya*, vol. VIII, p. 366; vol. IX, p. 221.

[2] Mao Tse-tung, 'On the People's Democratic Dictatorship', *Selected Works*, vol. IV (Peking, Foreign Languages Press, 1962), p. 413.

[3] *For a lasting peace, for a people's democracy*, 1 November 1948.

revolutionary influence on all the oppressed peoples of South-East Asia. It inspires them for the decisive struggle against imperialism to win freedom, independence and democratic rights.

The peoples of Indochina, Burma and Malaya and even of countries distant from China like the Philippines, Indonesia and India see in the successes of the Chinese people a clear example demonstrating the fact that the forces of imperialism and internal reaction can be crushed, given the close-knit union of the popular masses and a firm resolve to fight to the very end. At the same time, a semi-colonial country which has creatively applied the teachings of Lenin and Stalin on strategy and tactics in the national-colonial revolution and also Comrade Stalin's guidance on the problems of the Chinese revolution, and has made use of the enormous experience of the All-Union Communist Party (Bolshevik) and, basing itself on all of this, has achieved its present successes, is itself a vast treasury of revolutionary experience; this in turn helps all the oppressed peoples of the East to choose the right course in their struggle against imperialism, to avoid numerous errors and to attain their goal with fewer losses and in a shorter space of time.

The experience of the national-liberation movement in China shows the oppressed peoples of the East, and in particular the peoples of South-East Asia, that . . . in present circumstances, the national bourgeoisie is already incapable of playing the part of a major participant in the national-liberation movement, even less that of its leader. . . .

Taking China as an example, one sees particularly clearly the close bond that exists between American imperialism and internal reaction in any country which is an obedient instrument of that imperialism. . . .

And, what is particularly important, the oppressed peoples see from the example of China that American imperialism, indeed the entire imperialist camp, is not invincible, and that even economically underdeveloped peoples can defeat imperialism, if they are united in solidarity and if they fight, relying on the support of the whole democratic camp. . . .

6. *Liu Shao-ch'i on the 'Chinese Way'*

Extracts from Liu Shao-ch'i's opening speech at the meeting of the World Federation of Trade Unions which took place in Peking in November 1949. In this address, he declared most emphatically that the Chinese way was applicable throughout Asia.[1]

Comrades! In the vast territories of Asia and Australasia live over one half of the total world population. In these territories are rich resources, hard-working peoples as well as the most ancient cultures. The people of Asia and Australasia could have built up their

[1] SOURCE: *Hsin-hua yüeh-pao*, vol. I, no. 2, pp. 440–41.

happy and beautiful life and culture according to their own will, but for the unfortunate fact that many of their countries were, for centuries, invaded by imperialism which forced upon them a colonial and semi-colonial system. The imperialists have unrestrictedly exploited the fruits of the labour of the colonial and semi-colonial peoples and ruthlessly repressed their opposition and resistance. It is owing to this fact alone that the peoples, particularly the working class, in these areas have been thrown into the abyss of endless starvation, death and darkness. Nourished by the rich spoils of colonies and semi-colonies in the East as well as other parts of the world, the imperialists became strong enough to oppress the working people of their own countries, throwing them also into unemployment, starvation and an oppressed position. The colonies and semi-colonies are the rear bases of world imperialism, on which it relies for its existence. The so-called 'civilization' of imperialism is built upon its criminal rule over the colonies and semi-colonies. The building of the happiness of the minority on the misery of more than a thousand million people in the colonies and semi-colonies, and in their own countries, is the essence of the so-called 'civilization' of the imperialists. It is therefore necessary for the colonial and semi-colonial people and the working people in the imperialist countries to unite together to fight against their common enemy – imperialism. The mainstay of such a unity should, first and foremost, be the unity of the working class of these countries. This is the only way leading to the liberation of the colonial and semi-colonial countries as well as to the emancipation of the working people in the various imperialist countries.

The brutal oppression and exploitation of the colonies and semi-colonies of Asia and Australasia by the imperialists had, since the very early days, evoked ceaseless opposition and resistance from the colonial and semi-colonial peoples, which has become more intense and better organized with each passing day. Since the founding of the world's first socialist state after the victory of the October Socialist Revolution in the U.S.S.R., the movement of the colonial and semi-colonial peoples against imperialism and for national independence has entered an entirely new stage and acquired a world-wide magnitude and significance. After the victory of the Second World War, owing to the defeat of three imperialist states, Germany, Japan and Italy, and the weakening of two others, Britain and France, the national-liberation movement of the colonies and semi-colonies has been developing more rapidly in scope and strength. As a result of this development, China has been able to achieve a great victory in the unprecedentedly large-scale people's war of liberation against imperialism and its running dogs, the Kuomintang reactionaries, and to liberate one quarter of the world's population. The war of national liberation in Vietnam has liberated 90 per cent of her territory; the war of national liberation in Burma and Indonesia is now developing; the partisan warfare against imperialism and its running dogs in Malaya and the Philippines has been carried on persistently over a long period; and armed struggles for emancipation have also taken place in India. . . .

The armed struggles of the colonies and semi-colonies to resist imperialist attacks and to win national independence are a mighty force in strengthening and defending world peace, just as the victory of the Chinese people's war of liberation has greatly strengthened the forces of world peace and democracy. . . . I think that our Trade Union Conference of Asian and Australasian countries should support the wars of national liberation of these countries in resisting the attack of the imperialists and their running dogs. It is only after the victory of the war of national liberation and the driving out of the imperialists from the oppressed countries in Asia and Australasia that it will be possible to solve in a radical manner such problems as the liberation of the working class, the raising of the workers' living standard, the improvement of working conditions, and the guaranteeing of trade union rights in these countries. . . . To fight for national independence and people's democracy, therefore, is the supreme task of the working class in the colonial and semi-colonial countries.

The way taken by the Chinese people in defeating imperialism and its lackeys and in founding the People's Republic of China is the way that should be taken by the peoples of many colonial and semi-colonial countries in their fight for national independence and people's democracy. This way, which led the Chinese people to victory, is summarized in the following formula:

1. The working class must unite with all other classes, political parties and groups, organizations and individuals, who are willing to oppose the oppression of imperialism and its running dogs, form a broad nation-wide united front and wage a resolute fight against imperialism and its running dogs.

2. This nation-wide united front must be led by and built round the working class which opposes imperialism most resolutely, most courageously and most unselfishly, and its Party, the Communist Party, with the latter as its centre. It must not be led by the wavering and compromising national bourgeoisie or petty bourgeoisie and their parties.

3. In order to enable the working class and its Party, the Communist Party, to become the centre for uniting all the forces throughout the country against imperialism, and to lead competently the national united front to victory, it is necessary to build up through long struggles a Communist Party, which is armed with the theory of Marxism-Leninism, understands strategy and tactics, practises self-criticism and strict discipline and is closely linked with the masses.

4. It is necessary to set up wherever and whenever possible a national liberation army which is led by the Communist Party and is powerful and skilful in fighting the enemies, as well as the bases on which it relies for its activities, and to coordinate the mass struggles in the enemy-controlled areas with the armed struggles. Armed struggle is the main form of struggle for national liberation in many colonies and semi-colonies.

This is the basic way followed and practised in China by the Chinese people in winning their victory. This way is the way of Mao Tse-tung. It may also be the basic way by which the peoples of other colonial and semi-colonial countries where similar conditions prevail achieve emancipation. The situation is very clear.

The imperialists in the colonies and semi-colonies are bandits armed to the teeth. They still have strong forces to dominate the people in all the areas which are under their rule. We must absolutely not underestimate these forces. In these areas, it is impossible for the revolutionary working class and oppressed people to overthrow the oppression of imperialism and its running dogs and establish a people's democratic state by taking any other easier way than that specified above. If anyone attempted to do so, it would be a mistake. At the same time we must realize that the imperialists are isolated, especially among the peoples of the colonies and semi-colonies. And except for their running dogs there are innumerable people opposing them – not only the workers and peasants, but also the petty bourgeoisie, the broad intelligentsia and the national bourgeoisie of the colonies and semi-colonies. Although the proletariat is the class most resolutely opposing imperialism, generally speaking, it constitutes only a minority of the population in the colonies and semi-colonies. Because of these obvious reasons, the working class of the colonies and semi-colonies, if it wants to defeat still powerful imperialism, must unite, and is fully capable of uniting, all the classes, political parties, organizations and individuals who are willing to oppose imperialism and its running dogs in order to form a broad nation-wide united front. Only thus will it be possible to attain victory; otherwise it will be impossible to do so. In this connexion, the first thing for the working class to do is to unite with the peasantry and establish a strong alliance between workers and peasants.

Generally speaking, although the national bourgeoisie in the colonies and semi-colonies is opposed to imperialism at a certain period and to a certain extent, and can be an ally of the working class in the anti-imperialist struggles, its members are weak; they have many connexions with the imperialists; they fear the real revolutionary movement of the masses of people; they are of a vacillating and compromising nature which they themselves cannot overcome. Therefore they cannot play the leading role nor serve as a centre in uniting the whole nation and forming a mighty national united front. Should they lead the movement, they will inevitably compromise half-way at the critical moment in the course of the movement, and lead it on to the road of defeat and suffering. There are many such instances in history which need not be enumerated here. With regard to the petty bourgeoisie, although they are a class resolutely opposed to imperialism, they also cannot be the leading class in the serious revolutionary struggles on account of their many weaknesses. Hence in order to win victory in the present historical stage, the stage of imperialist rule, the national liberation movements of the colonies and semi-colonies can be led only by the proletariat and its Party, the Communist Party.

7. *The Nature and Attributes of People's Democracy in the Countries of the East*

Extracts from an authoritative statement declaring that the Chinese way was *not* applicable throughout Asia.[1]

A Conference on the nature and attributes of the system of people's democracy in the countries of the East was held from 12–23 November 1951 in the Oriental Institute of the U.S.S.R. Academy of Sciences. . . .

The Conference opened with a report by E. M. Zhukov, Corresponding Member of the U.S.S.R. Academy of Sciences, on 'The Attributes of People's Democracy in the East'.

The speaker noted that the road to socialism via people's democracy had proved equally applicable both for economically developed countries and for backward colonial and dependent countries.

The four states of people's democracy established by the peoples of the East – the Chinese People's Republic, the Mongolian People's Republic, the Korean Democratic People's Republic and the Democratic Republic of Vietnam – could be regarded as a single group of Eastern popular-democratic countries, regardless of the diverse conditions in which their individual popular-democratic régimes had originated and developed and of the great difference in their respective economic and cultural levels.

The main distinction between the Eastern and the European countries of people's democracy lay in the fact that in China, Mongolia, Korea and Vietnam, people's democracy at the present stage was resolving the national-liberation and anti-feudal problems of bourgeois-democratic revolution; it was not faced with the immediate prospect of constructing socialism and, consequently, did not function as a proletarian dictatorship.

[1] SOURCE: *Izvestiya Akademii Nauk S.S.S.R., Seriya Istorii i Filosofii*, vol. IX, no. 1, January–February 1952, pp. 80–81.

The main cause of this situation was the recent colonial yoke, which had retarded the economic development of these Eastern countries and prevented the eradication of most barbarous vestiges of the Middle Ages that were particularly intolerable for the peasantry, which constituted the vast majority of Asia's population. . . .

In speaking of the Eastern countries of people's democracy as a unit, the speaker said that the enormous differences between one Eastern popular-democratic country and another should not be forgotten. . . .

The speaker went on to describe the existing states of people's democracy – the Mongolian People's Republic, the Korean Democratic People's Republic, the Democratic Republic of Vietnam and the Chinese People's Republic, emphasizing the need to take account of the peculiarities of each country and to avoid a stereotyped approach to the subject.

The speaker devoted particular attention to the situation in the Chinese People's Republic, notably to the successes achieved in creating a united popular-democratic front, to agrarian reform and the Communist Party's agrarian policy.

The experience of the Chinese revolution is of enormous significance. Traces of its fruitful influence can easily be found in the documents of the Indian Communist Party and the Labour Party of Vietnam. But, recalling the first tactical principle of Leninism, namely that it is imperative to take into account the national distinctions and peculiarities of each different country, it would be dangerous to consider the Chinese revolution as a sort of 'stereotype' for popular-democratic revolutions in other Asian countries.

In particular, it is difficult to imagine that other Eastern countries pursuing the path of people's democracy would necessarily be able to count on acquiring one of the Chinese revolution's most important advantages – a revolutionary army like the one in China.

All of this, of course, in no way means that there will not be thousands of problems in solving which the progressive people of India, Indonesia, or any other Eastern country, will need to take into consideration the specific experience of the Chinese revolution or of the October Revolution in Russia. . . .

8. The New Aspect of the War of National Liberation in the East

Extracts from a small book published in China in December 1950, and reprinted in a revised edition in January 1952, strongly emphasizing the key role of China in the revolution in the East, and the universal validity of the Chinese example.[1]

[1] SOURCE: Meng Hsien-chang, *Tung-fang min-tsu chieh-fang chan-cheng ti hsin hsing-shih* (2nd edn., Shanghai, Commercial Press, January 1952), pp. 1–23, 49–50 *passim*.

A The October Revolution constituted the starting-point for the liberation of the nations of the East

... The great October Socialist Revolution roused the revolutionary energies of the downtrodden masses of the colonial countries; it established a link between their struggle for liberty and national independence and the revolutionary struggles of the working people of all the countries of the world, and hence, it opened the path of liberation to them. As a result, all the movements of national liberation in the East sprang into action. However, their strength was still limited; as Lenin said, 'The fate of the colonies is now being decided, in fact, by the European war.' But later on, 'the movements of national liberation in the East became an integral part of the world proletarian socialist revolution, they have become the allies of the world proletarian socialist revolution' (Mao Tse-tung).[1]

Consequently, 'it (the October Revolution) threw a bridge between the socialist West and the enslaved East. From the western proletariat, through the Russian revolution, to the downtrodden peoples of the East, a . . . revolutionary front against world imperialism has been created.'[2]

B The historical development of the wars of national liberation in the East since the Second World War

During the Second World War, the different English, American, French, Dutch, etc., imperialisms, having suffered from the oppression of the Japanese bandits, retreated in confusion from all the dependent Eastern countries, and then all the oppressed peoples of the East took up arms in order to decide their own destiny. In Indochina, Indonesia, Burma, the Philippines, etc., the communists, the social democrats, the workers, the peasants, and even the national bourgeoisie and a part of the great land-owners, all took part in the creation of clandestine anti-Japanese organizations to wage guerrilla warfare against the Japanese army. After the defeat of Japanese imperialism these clandestine organizations became the mainstay of the various movements of national liberation. The Republic of Indonesia, proclaimed in August 1945, as well as the Democratic Republic of Vietnam, were both formed with the armies of anti-Japanese volunteers as their principal force. . . .

The movements of national liberation in the East after the war can be divided into three periods. The first extends from August 1945 to the end of 1946. During this period the two republics of

[1] See above, Text VIII 3, pp. 252–3.

[2] Stalin, 'The October Revolution and the National Question', *Sochineniya*, vol. IV, p. 166.

Indonesia and Vietnam were set up. The labour movements of India and Burma were at the peak of their prestige. But Dutch and French imperialism crushed the two republics by military force. The second period extends from the beginning of 1947 until March 1948. A policy of leniency on the part of imperialism took form, the big national bourgeoisie of the colonies conspired to bring about an agreement with the imperialists and began to crush the worker and peasant movement. The two dominions of India and Pakistan were born; Burma and the Philippines became 'independent', and the Federation of Malaya was established. . . . In India the Nehru government passed a labour law and suppressed the labour movement. . . . The third period is that which extends from March 1948, when, in particular, the war of liberation of the Chinese people passed from the defensive to the offensive and won one great victory after another, up until the present time. The blows of the people have doubled in strength, while the various imperialisms, headed by American imperialism, even though they make use of the most reactionary and retrograde elements and set up puppet régimes such as that of Chiang Kai-chek in China, Bao Dai in Vietnam, and Syngman Rhee in Korea, cannot prevent the collapse of their position. . . . Since the Chinese and Korean people's armies have inflicted repeated bloody whippings on the invading armies of American imperialism and its satellites, and since the paper tiger of American imperialism has been torn to shreds, the struggle for national liberation in the East has made even greater strides forward, and capitalist imperialism, which has dominated the peoples of the East for four or five centuries, is rapidly heading towards its grave.

C The enormous influence of the victory of the Chinese revolution on the East

The people's democratic revolution in China has already obtained a great victory, a victory of world-wide historical significance. In the future, the victory of the Chinese revolution will influence not only the destiny of all the nationalities making up the Chinese people, but also the world as a whole, and more particularly the historical destiny of the people of all the other Eastern nations. Lenin has already said, 'In the last analysis, the outcome of the struggle will be decided by the fact that Russia, India, China, etc., make up the great majority of the population.'[1] Now, China alone already has a population of 475 millions, which represents roughly one fifth of the population of 2,250 millions of the entire earth and two fifths of the population of Asia, which numbers 1,200 millions. Moreover, from a geographical viewpoint, China lies precisely in the middle, and a great number of Asiatic countries share

[1] See Text V 4, p. 199 above.

common borders with her. From the historical point of view, all these countries have had, in the past, prolonged relations with China. From the cultural viewpoint, the literature and social customs of all these countries are also similar to those of China. What is more, the Chinese abroad make up everywhere a high percentage of the population. . . .

Secondly, the great victory of the Chinese revolution struck new and powerful blows at the whole world-wide system of imperialism. This is the most important defeat that the world-wide system of imperialism as a whole has suffered since the victory of the great October Socialist Revolution in U.S.S.R. and the defeat of Hitler's fascist alliance. . . . As a result, the imperialist camp has been further weakened, the general crisis of capitalism has been further accentuated, and the ineluctable day which will see the end of bourgeois domination, announced by the whole history of the social development of humanity, has been brought even closer. Thus the final victory of the working people and of communism in the entire world will come more quickly. As a result of the Chinese victory, all the Eastern peoples have been greatly encouraged, their confidence in the final victory has been further strengthened, and the war of liberation is unfurling even more rapidly.

The latest and also the most important influence is that of the synthesis worked out by Mao Tse-tung between Marxist-Leninist theory and the experience of the Chinese revolution, that of the new democracy which he was the first to promote. This new democracy is adapted for the use of all the backward, feudal, colonial, semi-feudal and semi-colonial countries, and has been uniformly accepted by all the Eastern peoples. As regards more especially revolutionary strategy, during the period when the Japanese bandits invaded China, the Chinese Communist Party . . . set up a united anti-Japanese national front with the Kuomintang. During that period, the communist parties of all the Eastern countries also set up anti-Japanese national fronts comprising the national bourgeoisie and the great land-owners of their own countries. After the surrender of Japan, the Chiang Kai-chek régime in China, representing the big bourgeoisie and the great land-owners, betrayed the revolution and surrendered to American imperialism. Then the Chinese Communist Party put forward the slogans of national independence and people's democracy in order to unite the workers, the peasants, the petty bourgeoisie and the national bourgeoisie in pursuing the overthrow of the reactionary Kuomintang régime, which represented imperialism, feudalism and bureaucratic capitalism. In the same way, the communist parties of all the countries of the Far East, due to the fact that the big bourgeoisie and the great land-owners had betrayed the revolution, also put forward the national-democratic front and the people's democratic dictatorship. At the time of the meeting in Peking of the conference of trade union representatives of Asia and Australasia, Vice-Chairman Liu Shao-ch'i, analysing the conditions of the revolutionary victory of people's liberation in China, said, 'The path . . . of the Chinese people is that which should be followed by the peoples of many colonial and semi-colonial countries in their struggle for national independence and people's democracy.'

The Indian delegate Shelwaukar said, 'In our struggle for liberation in India, we do not need your aid; we shall simply study your experience, and the Thought of Mao Tse-tung, and then we shall be able to obtain arms from Nehru's army.' The delegate from Ceylon, Wickremasinghe, said, 'The present of China is the future of Ceylon'.

Thus the great victory of the Chinese revolution has exerted a decisive influence on the national-liberation struggles of all the countries of the Far East.

D The common peculiarities of the wars of national liberation in the East

From the point of view of social and economic background, all the Eastern countries are roughly similar, and, moreover, all these countries have accepted the precious experience of the war of liberation waged by the Chinese people under the direction of the Chinese Communist Party. Consequently, all these countries show certain common peculiarities as regards their wars of liberation.

1. *The application of new democracy.* In the period since the First World War and the October Revolution, when the rotten character of capitalism and the glaring superiority of socialism are appearing more clearly every day, new democracy is a transitory stage through which all the backward countries must pass to reach socialism. . . . In the region of Telangana of the state of Hyderabad, there were already in the spring of 1950 2,500 liberated villages, with an area which had reached 130,000 square *li*, and a population of 5 millions. In this liberated region, under the leadership of armed guerrilla detachments of 30,000 men, the agrarian reform has long since been carried out, and the people's own political power has been established. In the long-standing bases in Burma, the agrarian reform has been carried out, and the great capitalist enterprises monopolized by England have moreover been confiscated. In the liberated areas of the Philippines, the agrarian reform has also been carried out successfully. . . . In Indonesia, the agrarian reform has also been carried out successfully in the liberated areas, and the great industrial enterprises have been nationalized, taking the oil wells and rubber plantations away from private property and restoring them to the hands of the people. . . .

2. *Leadership by a Communist Party armed with Marxism-Leninism.* In

the epoch of imperialism, the bourgeoisie of all the colonial countries is weak and inclined to compromise, and cannot assume the difficult task of opposing imperialism. As for the peasantry, it is dispersed and backward and full of conservatism. Consequently, in all the countries, the task of opposing imperialism and feudalism falls on the shoulders of the proletariat and especially on the vanguard of the working class, endowed with an iron discipline and filled with the spirit of struggle, the Communist Party. . . . In Vietnam, although it is the Viet Minh which leads the revolution, within the Viet Minh effective leadership belongs to the Communist Party of Vietnam, founded in 1930. . . . Under the direction of President Ho Chi Minh and of Secretary General Truong Chinh, and by uniting Marxism-Leninism and the Thought of Mao Tse-tung with the experience of the Vietnamese revolution, they are presently developing the struggle against French and American imperialism. . . .

3. *The formation of a national-democratic united front.* The experience of the Chinese people's victorious war of national liberation clearly shows: The working class must unite the totality of the parties and groups which are disposed to fight against imperialism and its running dogs in order to organize a broad united front on a nation-wide scale; it is only in this way that it can defeat imperialism. In order to unite the progressive forces, to win over the intermediate forces and to isolate the reactionary forces, all the countries have created broad national-democratic united fronts of which the Communist Party constitutes the central core. . . .

4. *The armed people opposes the armed counter-revolution.* This means that the principal form of the revolutionary struggle of the Eastern peoples is armed struggle. Under conditions in which the enemy is strong and we are weak, one first of all develops guerrilla warfare in the villages, one transforms the countryside into solid base areas, one makes the guerrilla detachments the core of all revolutionary struggles, one musters his forces and extends his territory, and little by little, in the course of a protracted war, one obtains the final revolutionary victory. . . . The experience of the Chinese revolution has amply demonstrated this: without establishing a strong revolutionary armed force, it is absolutely impossible to strike effective blows at the armed counter-revolutionary forces of the alliance of imperialism with the reactionary forces of different countries, in order to reach the objective of national independence and people's democracy. Outside the Japanese Communist Party . . . and the Siamese people which are not as yet very strong, all the Eastern peoples have powerful and courageous armed forces which are carrying on a heroic struggle against imperialism, feudalism and the *comprador* bourgeoisie. And the present glorious and brilliant successes of Korea in its resistance to American imperialism are an even more exemplary case.

5. *The creation of an anti-imperialist front with the broad popular masses of the imperialist countries.* The liberation of the proletariat within the imperialist countries is inseparable from the victory of the liberation movement in the colonies. . . . Under the direction of the English Communist Party, the working people of England give proof of an internationalist spirit; ceaselessly they unmask the conspiracies of English imperialism, support the people of Malaya and demand that an end be put to 'the savage war of aggression against the people of Malaya who are fighting for their democratic rights and their democratic liberties'.

On 25 January 1950, the French people organized a 'national day to secure peace in Vietnam'; their call for an immediate stopping of the dirty war waged in Vietnam, put forth during a great meeting, received the support of the broad French popular masses. . . .

After American imperialism launched its invasion in Korea, more than 10,000 persons took part in a public demonstration of opposition in New York, and the signatures for peace rapidly passed from the previous 400,000 to 2 millions. . . .

All these cases mentioned above are glorious examples of the union of peace-loving people on the international level. Fraternal and sincere unity between the working people of the West and the revolutionary people of the colonies and dependent countries is being established, and this unity of the countless popular masses is a rock which will crush imperialism.

6. *The contradictions of imperialism and its unity.* Although most of the colonies in the East belong to the English, French, Dutch, etc., imperialists, they have already become satellites of American imperialism. That is why the military aid of American imperialism, as well as its economic aid and projects for development of backward regions in accordance with Point 4, has already made its influence felt everywhere, usurping the place of English, French and Dutch colonialists. As a result, there effectively exist some contradictions between American imperialism and the other imperialisms. . . .

Even though there are some contradictions between the different imperialisms, resulting from the fact that they do not agree on the division of the spoils, they are in complete agreement on the subject of the suppression of the revolutionary movement in the colonies. . . . American imperialism has already become the most savage enemy of the national-liberation movement in the East.

E The Eastern peoples in heroic struggle. . . .

(omitted)

F The glorious future of national liberation in the East

'A new era is already open in all of Asia and great transformations are presently going on in this vast region which comprises more than half of the population of the world. The meaning of this transformation and its irreversible character lies in the fact that it has been accomplished by a profound revolutionary movement of the people of Asia.' These are the words of the war-monger Acheson, Secretary of State of the United States. Certainly these words can be explained by the desire to rid American imperialism of its hideous aspect and to give it a false air of pity, in order to further its dishonest machinations against the peoples of the East. He none the less recognizes that the headlong torrent of the furious tide unleashed by the national-liberation movement in the East is quite capable of engulfing American imperialism. . . . This in no way implies that the nations of the Far East can be excessively optimistic, thereby paralysing themselves; they must, on the contrary, increase their preparations, redouble their vigilance, and get ready to brave rather difficult battles, before one can force imperialism and its running dogs into their coffins. . . . But from the viewpoint of the laws of the historical development of society, socialism is like the sun rising at dawn, while capitalist imperialism is already like the sun setting behind the mountains in the West; it is about to breathe its last. Today, when the relation between the force of the camp of democracy and peace, and that of the camp of aggression on the world level is rapidly changing, all the Eastern peoples, in the near future, will certainly be able, in the wake of the new China, to reap the great and glorious victory of national liberation and people's democracy.

SECTION X: FROM STALIN'S DEATH TO THE GREAT LEAP FORWARD

1. Extracts from the Debates of the Twentieth Congress of the Communist Party of the Soviet Union

The Twentieth Congress of the Soviet Communist Party, which met in February 1956, undertook to find a way out of the political impasse in which the Soviet Union had been trapped as a result of the rigid and dogmatic character of the ideology of the Stalinist period, especially as regarded relations with the newly-independent countries of the non-European world. The extracts from the debates which we give here, as well as the authoritative commentaries which follow (Texts X 2 and X 3) show the desire of the Soviet leaders to recognize the real situation in these countries, where the bourgeoisie finds itself in power, and by so doing to open the way to relations with them.[1]

KHRUSHCHEV: . . . The new period that Lenin predicted in world history when peoples of the East take an active part in settling the destinies of the whole world and become a new, powerful factor in international relations, has arrived. Unlike the situation in the pre-war period, the great majority of the countries of Asia now take their place on the world stage as sovereign states or states tenaciously defending their right to an independent foreign policy. International relations have gone beyond the stage of relations between states populated principally by peoples of the white races, and are beginning to assume the character of genuinely universal relations.

That the peoples of the former colonies and semi-colonies win political freedom is the first and essential precondition of their complete independence, that is to say their achievement of economic independence. The countries of Asia which have gained freedom are working to create an industry of their own, to train their own technical personnel, to raise the living standard of their people, and to re-establish and develop their own centuries-old national culture. . . .

In order to create an independent national economy and to raise the living standard of their peoples, these countries, though not part of the world socialist system, can benefit by its achievements. They now have no need to go begging to their former oppressors for modern equipment. They can obtain such equipment in the socialist countries without any obligation of a political or military character. . . .

Naturally, so-called [American] 'aid' to the underdeveloped

[1] SOURCE: *Dvadtsatiy S'yezd Kommunisticheskoy Partii Sovetskogo Soyuza* (Moscow, 1956), pp. 25–40, 73–82 *passim*, 503.

countries is made available on specific political conditions: the integration of these countries into aggressive military blocs, the signing of joint military pacts, and support for American foreign policy which aims at world domination or, as the Americans themselves call it, 'world leadership'. . . .

With the fundamental changes that have taken place on the world scene, new prospects have also opened up for countries and nations to make the transition to socialism.

On the eve of the Great October Socialist Revolution, V. I. Lenin could write: 'All nations will come to socialism. This is inevitable, but they will not all come in the same manner: each will put the stamp of its own individual character on some form of democracy, some variety of proletarian dictatorship, some tempo of socialist transformation of the various aspects of social life. There is nothing more wretched from the point of view of theory or more ridiculous in practice than "in the name of historical materialism" depicting that future as uniformly grey in colour: the result of a Suzdal daubing, nothing more.'[1]

Historical experience has fully borne out Lenin's brilliant proposition. Today, besides the Soviet form of reorganizing society on socialist principles there is the form of the people's democracy.

In Poland, Bulgaria, Czechoslovakia, and the other European countries of people's democracy this form has thrived. . . .

The Chinese People's Republic, whose economy before the victory of the revolution was extremely backward, semi-feudal and semi-colonial in character, brings to socialist construction much that is original. Having gained the levers of power, the popular-democratic state, in the process of developing the socialist revolution, pursues a policy of peacefully transforming private industry and trade and gradually integrating them into the socialist economy. . . .

In the Federative People's Republic of Yugoslavia, where power belongs to the workers and society is based on public ownership of the means of production, specific original forms of management of the economy and organization of state administration are being established in the process of socialist construction.

It is very probable that forms of transition to socialism will become more and more varied. And it is not necessarily true that pursuit of these forms involves civil war in all cases. . . .

Leninism teaches us that the ruling classes do not give up power of their own free will. But whether the struggle is more severe or less severe, whether violence is employed or not in making the transition to socialism, depends not so much on the proletariat as on the degree of resistance offered by the exploiters and on the employment of violence by the class of exploiters itself.

In this respect the question arises whether it is also possible to

[1] *Sochineniya*, 4th edn., vol. XXIII, p. 58.

make use of the parliamentary path for the transition to socialism. This path was ruled out for the Russian Bolsheviks, who were the first to make the transition to socialism. Lenin showed us another path, that of establishing a republic of Soviets, which was the only correct path in the historical circumstances of the time, and we followed that path and won a historical victory of universal significance.

But since that time radical changes have taken place in the historical situation which allow us to approach this question in a new way. The forces of socialism and democracy have increased immeasurably throughout the whole world, whilst capitalism has become considerably weaker. . . .

In these conditions, the working class, uniting around itself the toiling peasantry, the intellectuals and all patriotic forces, and giving a decisive rebuff to opportunist elements incapable of renouncing the policy of accommodation with the capitalists and landlords, is capable of inflicting a defeat on the reactionary, anti-popular forces and winning a sound majority in Parliament and transforming that organ of the bourgeois democrats into an instrument of the true popular will. . . .

The achievement of a sound parliamentary majority relying on the mass revolutionary movement of the proletariat and workers would create for the working class of a number of capitalist and ex-colonial countries conditions guaranteeing radical social transformations. . . .

The absolute and crucial requirement for all forms of transition to socialism is the political leadership of the working class headed by its vanguard. Without this the transition to socialism is impossible.

It must be very strongly emphasized that if better conditions for the victory of socialism have been created in other countries, it is because socialism has triumphed in the Soviet Union and is triumphing in the countries of people's democracy. . . .

KUUSINEN: . . . It is necessary to note the important political significance of the fact that Comrades N. S. Khrushchev and N. A. Bulganin, in the speeches they made in India, justly recognized the outstanding role played by Mahatma Gandhi in the history of the Indian people. In so doing, Comrades N. S. Khrushchev and N. A. Bulganin in effect took the initiative of correcting the sectarian errors which in previous years had found expression in certain statements made by Soviet orientalists and in the publications of the Communist International. Basing themselves exclusively on criticism of Gandhi's philosophical views which, as is known, are far removed from the concepts of Marxism-Leninism, certain of our journalists at that time had taken so one-sided a view that they completely denied Gandhi any positive role in history.

I wish to add to this that our historians and propagandists have reason to study critically and revise certain other publications of ours too, the celebrated theses of the Sixth Comintern Congress on the colonial question, for example.[1] I am thinking specifically of the definition and evaluation made in these theses of the role of the national bourgeoisie in colonial and semi-colonial countries. Even at the time when the said theses on the colonial question were drafted, this evaluation was already somewhat tainted with sectarianism. In the changed conditions of the present day, now that the authority of the Soviet Union has greatly increased, such an evaluation in no way corresponds to reality. . . .

2. *The Twentieth Congress of the Communist Party of the Soviet Union and Problems Concerning the Study of the Contemporary East*

Extracts from an editorial of the scholarly journal of Soviet orientalists criticizing their previous work in this domain.[2]

. . . The state of ideological work was subjected to thorough criticism at the Twentieth Congress. . . .

Fully-deserved criticism was levelled at the Institute of Oriental Studies of the U.S.S.R. Academy of Sciences. In his address at the Twentieth Congress A. I. Mikoyan said with complete justification, 'The entire East may have awakened during our time but this Institute is still asleep to this day. Has the time not come for it to match up to present-day requirements?'

Oriental studies have been greatly harmed by a failure to understand the nature and depth of the contradictions existing between the forces of imperialism and internal reaction, on the one hand, and those of national progress in the non-socialist Eastern countries, on the other. Our orientalist economists have studied mainly the activity of foreign capital in the economy of the Eastern countries. However, internal processes have not been analysed sufficiently carefully, and no adequate assessment has been made of the objective tendency towards independent capitalist development which has undermined the dominant position of imperialism. . . .

In the circumstances arising since the Second World War out of the radically changed balance of forces at the international level, the dominant position occupied by foreign capital in the economies of certain Eastern countries no longer means that imperialism necessarily dominates the political life of those countries. For example, countries such as Indonesia or Saudi Arabia, which are not yet free from economic interference by imperialism, are now pursuing a sovereign policy. . . .

[1] See Text VII 1 C, pp. 237–9 above.

[2] SOURCE: *Sovetskoye Vostokovedeniye*, no. 1, 1956, pp. 6–9.

. . . Facts show that as national capitalist enterprise expands in the Eastern countries, so the contradictions marking off the local bourgeoisie from foreign finance capital and the feudal land-owner grow sharper. Failure to understand the objective logic of these economic contradictions has been one of the main reasons why certain orientalists have not succeeded in their attempts to expound the essential nature of many major political processes.

As O. V. Kuusinen stated in his speech at the Twentieth Congress, certain statements made in the past by Soviet orientalists contained sectarian errors in that they described and assessed incorrectly the role of the national bourgeoisie in the Eastern countries.

It is a well-known tenet of Marxism-Leninism that during the phase of the general crisis of capitalism it is possible for the proletariat of colonial and dependent countries where capitalism is comparatively developed to assume hegemony over the national-liberation and anti-feudal revolution. This tenet is brilliantly confirmed by the great victory of the Chinese people and the peoples of the other popular-democratic Eastern countries.

However, from this indisputably correct premise it has been wrongly concluded that proletarian leadership alone can ensure victory in the struggle for national independence. For this reason, when India, Burma, Indonesia, Egypt and certain other Eastern countries where hegemony of the proletariat, the vanguard of the patriotic forces, was not yet possible, won their sovereignty under the leadership of the national bourgeoisie, many orientalists were unable to appreciate sufficiently objectively the great significance of this event in the history of the East. Worse still, certain writings labelled this way of winning sovereignty the 'final accommodation with the big bourgeoisie and imperialism'.

Obviously there is a difference in principle, especially as far as the ultimate aims of the liberation movement are concerned, between gaining independence under the leadership of the proletariat, which alone fights consistently to the very end for national and social liberation, and gaining sovereignty under the leadership of the national bourgeoisie. However, this is no justification for adopting a negative attitude towards numerous important processes which have taken place and are now taking place in the countries of the East.

Inability to understand the nature of the objective contradictions existing between the national bourgeoisie and imperialism has led to its political stance sometimes being defined as nothing but fear of the class struggle of the masses. In this way the dialectical concept of the ambivalent nature of the national bourgeoisie has given way to a one-sided view of the national bourgeoisie as imperialism's faithful ally against its own country's working masses. From this standpoint, the political activity of the national bourgeoisie could be portrayed only as a series of capitulations, betrayals and demagogic manoeuvres. And this, in fact, is how the political line of the Indian bourgeoisie and the National Congress led by M. K. Gandhi was portrayed for several years. . . .

Underestimation of the contradictions existing between the national bourgeoisie and imperialism has led to outright denial of the incontestable fact that at certain stages of the anti-imperialist struggle the interests of this bourgeoisie largely coincided with those of the majority of the people. For this reason the patriotic demands contained in the programme put forward by the bourgeois leaders during their negotiations with the colonizers objectively reflected the interests of the people, who had risen up for the liberation struggle. In making concessions, the colonizers were giving way in actual fact to the pressure of the popular masses, not to the diplomacy of the bourgeois leaders. . . .

Sectarian errors also manifested themselves occasionally in a failure to notice the diversity of forms of national-liberation struggle in the countries of the East and, particularly, the possibility of winning independence, in certain historical circumstances, by peaceful means.

No heed was taken of the individual peculiarities of certain Eastern countries nor of the decisive change that had taken place both internationally and within the Eastern countries themselves in the balance between the forces of reaction and the forces of progress. Facts show that the increased authority of the Soviet Union, the considerably increased strength of the whole socialist camp, especially since the formation of the Chinese People's Republic, the defeat of the imperialist armies in Korea and Vietnam, the powerful development of solidarity movements between the workers in the metropolitan countries and the peoples of the colonies and, lastly, the general upsurge of the national-liberation struggle in the East, where the decisive role belongs to the working class and peasantry, are forcing the colonizers to yield in certain cases without starting large-scale colonial wars. . . .

3. Zhukov: 'The Collapse of the Colonial System of Imperialism'

Extracts from an article published under the same title. Mr Zhukov continues, as he had done in 1947 and 1949 (Texts IX 2 and IX 4), to predict the collapse of the colonial system. At the same time, he adapts himself to the line of the Twentieth Congress as regards the tactics which will best contribute to hastening the process.[1]

The great October Socialist Revolution initiated the crisis of the colonial system and seriously shook and weakened imperialism's grip on the colonies and semi-colonies. But it is only comparatively recently – in the years immediately following the end of the Second

[1] SOURCE: *Partiinaya Zhizn'*, no. 16, August 1956, pp. 41–8.

World War, when, as a result of the defeat of fascism, a number of imperialism's colonies and semi-colonies had attained political independence and embarked upon the path of autonomous development (Vietnam, Indonesia, Syria, Lebanon and others) – that the collapse of the colonial system began. This progressive historical process greatly broadened its scope with the victory of the Chinese revolution in 1949 and the establishment of the sovereign Republic of India in 1950. . . .

The collapse of the colonial system is a complex and intricate process. Liberation from colonial oppression occurs in varying ways in different countries. In certain cases, peoples achieve full independence, that is to say political and economic independence, all at once and aim at carrying out not only democratic but also socialist transformations. In these cases the new sovereign states are organized as people's democracies, and the working class enjoys undisputed leadership in the class alliance of the democratic forces of the people. This was the end achieved by the victory of the national-liberation struggle in China where the mighty Chinese People's Republic was formed, in Vietnam where the Democratic Republic of Vietnam is flourishing, and in Korea where the Korean People's Democratic Republic successfully fought a terrible battle for its existence. . . .

Everywhere the active role played in the anti-imperialist movement by the working class and its militant vanguard – the communist parties – is on the increase and it is naturally to be expected that in the future the working class will everywhere win leadership of this struggle. But it is a long and complicated process.

The workers are not the only force waging the struggle for national liberation against imperialism. In the colonial and dependent countries peasants, artisans, tradesmen, industrialists, the intelligentsia, including students, minor functionaries and army officers take an active part in this struggle.

Sometimes even certain feudal elements (khans and princes) mingle in the general current of the national-liberation movement in the colonies and semi-colonies, if only for a certain length of time. This happens particularly when the imperialists are plotting a colonial war with the aim of completely enslaving one people or another or when they confiscate lands belonging to particular tribes or nationalities which preserve pre-capitalist relations. . . .

The most numerous section of the population of the colonies and semi-colonies is the peasantry. As the largest stratum of people, it is subjected to the worst exploitation, primarily by feudal elements, and epidemics. The peasantry in the colonies and semi-colonies is an enormous revolutionary force. However, the peasants' struggle against local and foreign oppressors is, as a rule, of the traditional type. The peasantry practically never enters the political scene with a political programme of its own. The reason for this is that, although the peasantry constitutes the vast majority of the population, it is too dispersed and internally divided, and does not represent a single tight-knit mass.

It is largely for this reason that, in those countries of Asia and Africa where the working class has not yet attained the status of recognized leader of the national-liberation struggle, the movement is most often headed by representatives of the national bourgeoisie. And this is not accidental. The national bourgeoisie is an organized force which possesses the best-trained cadres in the greatest numbers and puts forward a political programme of its own. It therefore aspires to the leadership of the anti-imperialist struggle of the whole nation.

At the present time in many former colonies and dependent countries which have gained political independence, the leadership belongs to the national bourgeoisie and its parties. This is the situation in India, in Egypt, in Indonesia and in many other countries which have recently embarked on the path of independent national development. . . .

Political independence is not complete independence. It should not, however, be forgotten that the political independence of recent colonies and semi-colonies is of special significance in the present international situation. If the capitalist system still ruled undivided, as was the case until 1917, then no political independence won by any colony would be secure. It would inevitably be but conditional and formal. But since the victory of the great October Socialist Revolution and particularly in the present state of development and consolidation of the states of the socialist system, the nature of political independence won by the peoples in the struggle with imperialism has changed substantially. The new sovereign states do not remain isolated in opposing the powerful capitalist world which gave birth to the colonial system. The liberated colonies and semi-colonies can rely on the support of the socialist states, which, by the very fact of their existence, lighten the struggle against colonialism. . . .

The construction of state industrial enterprises according to a precise plan (India, Egypt) is a fact of extreme importance, characteristic of the aspiration of young sovereign states to attain economic independence. Obviously, the policy of industrializing a country – and industrialization is the only sound guarantee of economic independence – is not pursued in the same manner in socialist countries (China) as in non-socialist countries (India). In India, state-capitalist enterprises are established. The state sector of the Indian economy is not socialist in character. Nevertheless, the development of state industry in India, and also in other countries that have recently won their independence, is of extremely positive significance. . . .

The imperialists plan to exploit the fact that in many countries the national bourgeoisie enjoys hegemony in the anti-imperialist front. However, the supposition that the national bourgeoisie would never fail, whatever the circumstances, to seek accommodation with the imperialists has proved untrue.

In these conditions the problem of establishing correct relationships within the united anti-imperialist front, and in particular the problem of the attitude of the working class and its party towards the national bourgeoisie, assumes great importance. It must be noted that the outstanding successes of the national-liberation struggle in Asia and Africa owe much to the correct tactics of the revolutionary organizations, and particularly to their having overcome the dangerous sectarian errors of the past. . . .

V. I. Lenin harshly condemned the adoption of a high-handed, doctrinaire attitude towards any of the masses' revolutionary activities which bear the stamp of any sort of prejudice, backwardness or lack of political awareness:

> The more backward a country is, the stronger in it are small-scale agricultural production, patriarchalism and ignorance, which inevitably cause the deepest of petty-bourgeois prejudices, viz., the prejudices of national egoism and national narrowness, to become particularly strong and tenacious.[1]

Were revolutionary organizations to ignore this fact, it would inevitably lead to sectarianism, isolation from the masses, and ultimately to the slackening of the struggle against colonialism.

In his speech to the Twentieth Congress of the C.P.S.U., Comrade Kuusinen remarked on the mistakes made in the past concerning Gandhi, that important national leader of India. Gandhi opposed British rule in India and was a great organizer of the national struggle against British imperialism and was therefore exceptionally popular among the broadest strata of the Indian people. Many of those who today lead the Indian State consider themselves pupils of Gandhi.

Naturally, concentration on criticizing the reactionary aspects of Gandhi's philosophy and ignoring the positive role which he played as one of the leaders of the national anti-imperialist movement in India were manifestations of sectarianism. The attacks made on Gandhi, particularly in the Soviet press, in actual fact played into the hands of the imperialists, who were extremely anxious to hinder mutual understanding between the peoples of India and the U.S.S.R. and to provoke mutual distrust and a feeling of alienation between them.

It should be admitted that similar sectarian errors were perpetrated in certain Soviet publications also in respect of other bourgeois leaders of national movements, for example in the case of Kemal, the leader of the Turkish national-liberation movement.

[1] See Text III 3, p. 155 above.

In their anxiety to delay the collapse of the colonial system, the imperialists constantly pass themselves off as the 'friends' of the peoples of Asia and Africa, posing as champions of 'nationalism', which they set up in opposition to 'communism'. Where does the truth of the matter lie? Obviously nationalism and communism are two distinct ideologies. Bourgeois nationalism is profoundly alien to the working class. But it should not be forgotten that the national bourgeoisie plays an active part in the struggle against imperialism. Its ideology is bourgeois nationalism. The national bourgeoisie cannot have a communist, proletarian ideology. But to the extent that the national bourgeoisie shows itself to be an active participant (sometimes even the leader) of the anti-imperialist struggle of the whole nation, its nationalist ideology may not be an insuperable obstacle barring the working masses from cooperation and alliance with it against imperialism. In this case nationalism is opposed to imperialism, which tries to enslave nations and is the worst enemy of free national development. . . .

The nineteenth century was marked by the dominance of the industrial countries of Europe and the U.S.A., which developed largely at the expense of the peoples of the colonial and dependent countries. There would seem to be every reason for the twentieth century's becoming the century of the rise of the countries of Asia and Africa, the gradual elimination of their economic backwardness, their liberation from alien domination, their industrialization and the flowering of their national culture. In all this, the key to genuine independence is industrialization. . . .

The imperialists fear the industrial development of the ex-colonies and semi-colonies like the plague, for this is the way towards eliminating their backwardness, that is to say the means of abolishing actual inequality and thus of finally assuring the national independence of these countries. . . .

4. The Aim of Revolution is to Set Free the Productive Forces of Society

Extracts from a summary of Mao's speech of 25 January 1956 to the Supreme State Conference presenting his twelve-year programme for agricultural development. This text shows the relative moderation and emphasis on technical factors which characterized Mao's position at that time. It also reveals the tremendous stress he placed on agriculture as the key to China's future. We have appended to Mao's remarks the last three of the forty points of the programme, which likewise illustrate the importance he attached to the countryside.[1]

Chairman Mao said that the country was at that moment caught up in the high tide of the great socialist revolution. The founding

[1] SOURCE: *Jen-min jih-pao*, 26 January 1956.

of the Chinese People's Republic symbolized the transition of the Chinese revolution from the stage of bourgeois-democratic revolution to that of socialist revolution. In other words, it had marked the beginning of the period of transition from capitalism to socialism. The work of the first three of the past six years had been concentrated mainly on restoring the national economy and carrying out various social reforms – first and foremost land reform – left incomplete in the first stage of the revolution. Since last summer socialist transformation, that is, socialist revolution, had developed on a vast scale with far-reaching results. This socialist revolution, he said, could be completed in the main and on a national scale in about three more years.

The object of socialist revolution, said Chairman Mao, was to set free the productive forces of society. It was quite certain that the change-over from individual to socialist, collective ownership in agriculture and handicrafts, and from capitalist to socialist ownership in private industry and commerce would lead to an ever greater release of productive forces; this laid the social basis for an enormous expansion of industrial and agricultural output.

Our method of carrying out the socialist revolution, continued Chairman Mao, was a peaceful one. In the past many people, both inside and outside the Communist Party, doubted if that was possible. But since the great high tide of the cooperative movement in the countryside last summer, and the high tide of socialist transformation in the towns and cities in the past few months, their doubts had been largely resolved. Conditions in China were such that it was not only possible, by using peaceful methods, i.e. methods of persuasion and education, to turn individual into socialist, collective ownership, but also to change capitalist into socialist ownership. The speed of socialist transformation in the past few months had been far more rapid than we had expected. There were people who had worried that it would not be easy to get through the 'difficult pass' to socialism. It now looked, said Chairman Mao, as if this pass would not be so difficult to get through after all.

Chairman Mao said that a fundamental change had taken place in the political situation in China. Up to last summer there had been many difficulties in agriculture, but things were quite different now. Many things that had seemed impracticable were now quite feasible. It was possible to fulfil ahead of time or to overfulfil the country's First Five-Year Plan. The task of this National Programme for Agricultural Development for 1956 to 1967 was to outline the prospects for agricultural production and rural work and set a clear-cut goal before China's peasants and all who work in agriculture, on the basis of this high tide in socialist transformation and socialist construction. A spurt must also be made in other kinds of work besides agriculture, in order to keep in step with the new situation arising from this high tide of socialist revolution.

In conclusion, Chairman Mao said that the people of our country must have a far-reaching, comprehensive plan of work in accordance with which they could strive to wipe out China's economic, scientific and cultural backwardness within a few decades and rapidly get abreast of the most advanced nations in the world. To achieve this great goal, the decisive factor was to have cadres, to have an adequate number of excellent scientists and technicians. At the same time they had to go on strengthening and extending the people's democratic united front, by uniting all forces that could be united. The Chinese people would ally themselves with the people of all the countries of the world to fight for the preservation of world peace. . . .

(38). Young people in the countryside should be given every encouragement to show zeal in their work, and in studying to acquire culture, as well as scientific knowledge and skill. The young people in the countryside should become the activists and the shock force in productive, scientific and cultural work in the countryside.

(39). Starting from 1956, in the next five to seven years steps should be taken in the light of local conditions to wipe out unemployment in the cities and provide work for all urban unemployed. The unemployed can find work not only in the cities but also on the outskirts of towns and cities, in the countryside proper, in areas where land reclamation is going on or in mountainous regions, in agriculture, forestry, live-stock breeding, subsidiary occupations, fishing, or in the fields of science, culture, education and health in the rural areas.

(40). Workers in the cities and peasants in the cooperatives must give each other mutual support. The workers must turn out more and better industrial goods to satisfy the peasants' needs, and the peasants must grow more and better grain and industrial raw materials to satisfy the needs of industry and the town-dwellers. Besides this, workers in the cities and peasants in the cooperatives should arrange get-togethers, visit one another, and write to each other. They should keep in constant touch, give each other encouragement and exchange experience so as to promote the development of industry and agriculture and help consolidate the alliance between the workers and the peasantry led by the working class.

5. *Mao Tse-tung on Learning from the Soviet Union*

Extracts from Mao Tse-tung's opening address to the Eighth Congress of the Chinese Communist Party on 15 September 1956, illustrating the manner in which he formulated the compromise line prevailing at that time, particularly in the field of international relations.[1]

The task of this Congress is to sum up the experience gained since the Seventh Congress, to unite the whole Party and to unite with all those forces at home and abroad that can be united with to build a great, socialist China. (*Applause.*)

In the eleven years since the Seventh Congress we have, in this great country with its vast territory, huge population and complex conditions, completed the bourgeois-democratic revolution and we have also gained a decisive victory in the socialist revolution. It has been proved in practice in these two revolutions that the line followed by the Central Committee of the Party from the Seventh Congress up to the present time is correct and that our Party is a great Marxist-Leninist party which has attained political maturity. (*Applause.*) Our Party is now more united, more consolidated than at any time in the past. (*Applause.*) It has become the core uniting the people throughout the country for socialist construction. (*Applause.*) We have achieved great success in every field of work. We have done our work correctly, but we have also made some mistakes. At this Congress we must sum up the main experience in our work, including both successes and mistakes, so that we can popularize our successful experience and draw lessons from our mistakes.

So far as internal conditions are concerned, our victories are due to the fact that we have relied on the worker-peasant alliance led by the working class and that we have extensively united all the forces that can be united. Great and heavy tasks lie ahead of us in carrying on the great work of construction. Although there are over 10 million members in our Party, they still constitute a very small minority of the country's population. In the various organs of state and in public affairs a lot of work has to be done by non-Party people. It is impossible to get the work well done unless we are good at relying on the masses and cooperating with non-Party people. . . .

Internationally, our victories are due to the support of the camp of peace, democracy and socialism headed by the Soviet Union (*applause*) and the profound sympathy of peace-loving people throughout the world. (*Applause.*) At present, developments in the international situation have become even more favourable to the work of construction in our country. We and all the socialist countries want peace; the peoples of all the countries of the world want peace. The only ones who crave for war and do not want peace are certain monopoly-capitalist circles in a handful of imperialist countries which look to aggression for their profits. As a

[1] SOURCE: Mao Tse-tung, *Chung-kuo Kung-ch'an-t'ang ti-pa-tz'u ch'üan-kuo tai-piao ta-hui k'ai-mo-tz'u*, Peking, Jen-min ch'u-pan-she, 1956, 8 p.

result of the unceasing efforts of the peace-loving countries and peoples, there has been a trend towards relaxation of tension in the international situation. (*Applause.*) To achieve a lasting peace in the world, we must further develop our friendship and cooperation with the fraternal countries in the camp of socialism (*applause*) and strengthen our solidarity with all peace-loving countries. (*Applause.*) We must endeavour to establish normal diplomatic relations on the basis of mutual respect for territorial integrity and sovereignty, and equality and mutual benefit, with all countries willing to live together with us in peace. We must give active support to the national independence and liberation movement in countries in Asia, Africa and Latin America as well as to the peace movement and righteous struggles in all countries throughout the world. (*Applause.*) We firmly support the entirely lawful action of the Government of Egypt in taking back the Suez Canal Company, and resolutely oppose any attempt to encroach on the sovereignty of Egypt and start armed intervention against that country. (*Applause.*) We must completely frustrate the schemes of imperialism to create tension and prepare for war. (*Prolonged applause.*)

The victories of the revolution and construction in our country are victories of Marxism-Leninism. Close integration of Marxist-Leninist theory with the practice of the Chinese revolution is the ideological principle consistently followed by our Party. For many years, especially since the campaign in 1942 to rectify the style of work in the Party, we have done much to strengthen Marxist-Leninist education within the Party. Compared with the time before this campaign, our Party has raised its level of Marxist-Leninist theory by another step. But we still have serious shortcomings. Among many of our comrades there are still standpoints and styles of work which are contrary to Marxism-Leninism, namely, subjectivism in their way of thinking, bureaucracy in their way of work, and sectarianism in organizational questions. Such standpoints and such styles of work alienate us from the masses, cut us off from reality and harm unity both within and without the Party. They obstruct the advance of our cause and the progress of our comrades. Such serious shortcomings in our ranks must be vigorously corrected by strengthening ideological education in the Party. (*Applause.*)

After the October Revolution, Lenin put forward the task of study, and again study, before the Communist Party of the Soviet Union. Our Soviet comrades and the Soviet people have acted according to this behest of Lenin. The time has not been long, but their achievements have been most glorious. (*Prolonged applause.*) At its twentieth Congress held not long ago, the Communist Party of the Soviet Union formulated many correct policies and criticized shortcomings which were found in the Party. It can be confidently asserted that very great developments will follow on this in its work. (*Prolonged applause.*)

The tasks confronting us today are in general similar to those confronting the Soviet Union in the early period following its foundation. In transforming China from a backward, agricultural country into an advanced, industrialized one, we are confronted with many strenuous tasks and our experience is far from being adequate. So we must be good at studying. We must be good at learning from our forerunner, the Soviet Union, (*applause*) from the People's Democracies, (*applause*) from the fraternal parties in other parts of the world (*applause*) as well as from the peoples the world over. (*Applause.*) We must never adopt a conceited attitude of great-nation chauvinism and become arrogant and complacent because of the victory of the revolution and some successes in the construction of the country. Every nation, big or small, has its own strong and weak points. Even if we had achieved extremely great successes, there is no reason whatsoever to feel conceited and complacent. Humility helps one to make progress whereas conceit makes one lag behind. This is a truth we must always bear in mind. (*Applause.*)

Comrades, you and I all believe that the strength of the liberated Chinese people is inexhaustible. Besides, we have the assistance of our great ally the Soviet Union and the other fraternal countries (*applause*) and we have also the support of all the fraternal parties (*applause*) and all sympathizers throughout the world. (*Applause.*) We have no feeling of standing isolated. Thus we shall assuredly be able to build our country step by step into a great socialist industrialized state. (*Applause.*) Our Congress will give a great impetus to the cause of construction in our country. (*Applause.*)

We have among us today delegates from the Communist Parties, Workers' Parties, Parties of Labour and People's Revolutionary Parties of more than fifty countries. (*Prolonged applause.*) They are all Marxist-Leninists and share a common language with us. (*Applause.*) Inspired by the spirit of noble friendship, they have undertaken long journeys to come to our country to take part in this Congress of our Party. This is a great encouragement and support to us. (*Applause.*) We extend our warm welcome to them. (*A long standing ovation*). . . .

6. Chou En-lai on the Nationalist Path

Extracts from Chou En-lai's report of 5 March 1957 to the Chinese People's Political Consultative Conference, on the journey he had just made to a number of countries in Europe and Asia.[1]

When Western colonialism penetrated . . . into the East, this vast

[1] SOURCE: *Hsin-hua pan-yüeh-k'an* no. 7, 1957, p. 7.

[Asiatic] continent, which in former times illuminated the ancient world with its wisdom, was plunged into suffering and disaster.... Our nations were humiliated and our people reduced to slavery. The independent development of our political life, of our economy, and of our culture was arrested and trampled upon, and the links between us, which date back for several millennia, were artificially broken. This common experience of suffering aroused in our peoples feelings of mutual sympathy. And these sentiments of sympathy have been further deepened by the struggles which we have carried on against a common enemy.

Following the Second World War, our long and arduous anti-colonialist struggles were at length victorious. The colonial system began to crack under the repeated onslaughts of these struggles. In Asia and Africa, one country after another, which had been reduced to the status of a colony, regained its independence. . . .

The paths which we Asian and African countries have followed in winning our independence are, of course, not . . . the same. It is under the leadership of the communists that the peoples of China, Mongolia, the People's Democratic Republic of Korea and the Democratic Republic of Vietnam won their independence. Now they are advancing on the socialist path. It is under the leadership of the nationalists that many other Asian and African countries embarked on the path of independence and development. We do not wish to hide the fact that our respective social and political systems are not at all the same, and that we are not of the same opinion on many questions. But such divergences do not prevent us from establishing friendly cooperation with one another. All the Asian and African peoples who have achieved independence wish to consolidate this independence, to defend world peace, and to promote friendly collaboration among themselves. In this respect, our aspirations are identical.

We must . . . struggle unremittingly to defend the sovereignty and independence of our countries. Moreover, our independence is still imperfect, since we have not yet freed ourselves from the economic and cultural backwardness which is the heritage of imperialism. Consequently, we are all resolved to develop our native lands and reach the level of modern states, for it is only in this way that we can really consolidate our independence. . . .

7. Liu Shao-ch'i on the Acceleration of the Revolution

Extracts from Liu Shao-ch'i's speech of 5 May 1958, at the Second Session of the Eighth Congress of the Chinese Communist Party, in which he proclaimed the policy of the 'Great Leap Forward' and the 'permanent revolution'.[1]

. . . Throughout the country, the broad masses are full of confidence

[1] SOURCE: *Jen-min jih-pao*, 27 May 1958.

in the leap forward in production; they are determined further to speed up socialist construction. They are eager to remove the obstacles placed in their way by technical and cultural backwardness. In view of the fact that basically the victory of the socialist revolution has already been achieved on the economic, political and ideological fronts, the Central Committee of the Party and Comrade Mao Tse-tung consider that the time is ripe to set new revolutionary tasks for the whole Party and the whole people, that now is the time to call for a technical revolution and, along with it, a cultural revolution.

Marx, Engels and Lenin often pointed out that the fighting slogan of the working class should be 'permanent revolution'. In putting forward new revolutionary tasks in good time, so that there is no half-way halt in the revolutionary struggle of the popular masses, the revolutionary fervour of the popular masses will not cool with interruptions in the revolution, and Party and state functionaries will not rest content with the success won and grow arrogant or apathetic, the Central Committee of the Communist Party and Comrade Mao Tse-tung have long guided the Chinese revolution by this Marxist-Leninist theory of permanent revolution. Already on the eve of the victory of the democratic revolution, the Central Committee of the Party, in a resolution adopted in March 1949 . . . clearly put forward the task of 'transforming the new-democratic state into a socialist state'. After the founding of the People's Republic of China and immediately following the completion of land reform, the Central Committee, in December 1951, pointed out the road to collective farming through the mutual-aid and cooperative movement, and in 1953 carried out extensive propaganda among the people for the socialist transformation of agriculture, handicrafts and private industry and commerce. After the socialist revolution in the ownership of the means of production had basically achieved victory, the Central Committee launched the socialist revolution on the ideological and political fronts. All this has enabled the revolution to advance at the opportune moment from one stage to another, scoring one victory after another. . . .

. . . Some say that speeding up construction makes people feel 'too tense', and so it's better to slow down the tempo. But are things not going to get tense if the speed of construction is slowed down? Surely one should be able to see that a frightfully tense situation would exist precisely if more than six hundred million people had to live in poverty and cultural backwardness for a prolonged period, had to exert their utmost efforts just to eke out a bare living, and were unable to resist natural calamities effectively, unable to put a quick stop to possible foreign aggression, if they found themselves in a passive situation in which they were utterly unable to master their own fate. It was to get rid of such a situation that hundreds of millions of people summoned up their energies to throw themselves, full of confidence, into the heat of work and struggle. This is simply common revolutionary practice to which we should give our heartiest approval. This kind of 'tension' is nothing at all to be afraid of. . . .

8. The People's Communes and the Transition to Communism

Extracts from the 'Resolution on Some Questions Concerning the People's Communes' adopted by the Sixth Plenum of the Central Committee of the Chinese Communist Party on 10 December 1958. This text illustrates the blend of utopian aspirations and prudence in ideological claims which followed the boundless enthusiasm of the summer of 1958.[1]

In 1958 a new social organization appeared, fresh as the morning sun, above the broad horizon of East Asia. This was the large-scale people's commune in the rural areas of our country which combines industry, agriculture, trade, education and military affairs and in which government administration and commune management are integrated. Since their first appearance the people's communes with their immense vitality have attracted widespread attention.

The movement to set up people's communes has grown very rapidly. Within a few months starting in the summer of 1958, all of the more than 740,000 agricultural producers' cooperatives in the country, in response to the enthusiastic demand of the mass of peasants, reorganized themselves into over 26,000 people's communes. Over 120 million households, or more than 99 per cent of all China's peasant households of various nationalities, have joined the people's communes. This shows that the emergence of the people's communes is not fortuitous; it is the outcome of the economic and political development of our country, the outcome of the socialist rectification campaign conducted by the Party, of the Party's general line for socialist construction and the great leap forward of socialist construction in 1958.

Although the rural people's communes were established only a short while ago, the mass of the peasants are already conscious of the obvious benefits they have brought them. Labour power and the means of production can, on a larger scale than before, be managed and deployed in a unified way to ensure that they are used still more rationally and effectively, and consequently the development of production will be further facilitated. Under the unified leadership of the commune, industry, agriculture (including farming, forestry, animal husbandry, side-occupations and fisheries), trade, education and military affairs have been closely coordinated and developed rapidly. In particular, thousands and

[1] SOURCE: *Jen-min jih-pao*, 19 December 1958.

tens of thousands of small factories have mushroomed in the rural areas. To meet the pressing demands of the masses, the communes have set up large numbers of community dining-rooms, nurseries, kindergartens, 'homes of respect for the aged' and other institutions for collective welfare, which have, in particular, completely emancipated women from thousands of years of kitchen drudgery and brought broad smiles to their faces. As the result of the bumper crops many communes have instituted a system of distribution that combines the wage system with the free supply system; the mass of peasants, both men and women, have begun to receive their wages and those families which in the past constantly worried about their daily meals and about their firewood, rice, oil, salt, soya sauce, vinegar and vegetables are now able to 'eat without paying'. In other words they have the most important and most reliable kind of social insurance. For the peasants, all this is epoch-making news. The living standards of the peasants have been improved and they know from practical experience and the prospects of the development of the communes that they will live much better in the future.

The development of the system of rural people's communes has an even more profound and far-reaching significance. It has shown the people of our country the way to the gradual industrialization of the rural areas, the way to the gradual transition from collective ownership to ownership by the whole people in agriculture, the way to the gradual transition from the socialist principle of 'to each according to his work' to the communist principle of 'to each according to his needs', the way gradually to lessen and finally to eliminate the differences between town and country, between worker and peasant and between mental and manual labour, and the way gradually to lessen and finally to eliminate the internal function of the state. . . .

People's communes have now become the general rule in all rural areas inhabited by our people of various nationalities (except in Tibet and in certain other areas). Some experiments have also begun in the cities. In the future urban people's communes, in a form suited to the specific features of cities, will also become instruments for the transformation of old cities and the construction of new socialist cities; they will become the unified organizers of production, exchange and distribution and of the livelihood and well-being of the people; they will become social organizations which combine industry, agriculture, trade, education and military affairs, organizations in which government administration and commune management are integrated. There are, however, certain differences between the city and the countryside.

Firstly, city conditions are more complex than those in the countryside.

Secondly, socialist ownership by the whole people is already the main form of ownership in the cities, and the factories, public institutions and schools, under the leadership of the working class, have already become highly organized in accordance with socialist principles (with the exception of some of the family members of the workers and staffs). Therefore, the switch-over of cities to people's communes inevitably involves some requirements different from those in the rural areas.

Thirdly, bourgeois ideology is still fairly prevalent among many of the capitalists and intellectuals in the cities; they still have misgivings about the establishment of communes – so we should wait a bit for them.

Consequently, we should continue to make experiments and generally should not be in a hurry to set up people's communes on a large scale in the cities. Particularly in the big cities, this work should be postponed except for the necessary preparatory measures. People's communes should be established on a large scale in the cities only after rich experience has been gained and when the sceptics and doubters have been convinced. . . .

The people's commune is the basic unit of the socialist social structure of our country, combining industry, agriculture, trade, education and military affairs; at the same time it is the basic organization of the socialist state power. Marxist-Leninist theory and the initial experience of the people's communes in our country enable us to foresee now that the people's communes will quicken the tempo of our socialist construction and constitute the best form for realizing, in our country, the following two transitions.

Firstly, the transition from collective ownership to ownership by the whole people in the countryside; and,

Secondly, the transition from socialist to communist society. It can also be foreseen that in the future communist society, the people's commune will remain the basic unit of our social structure.

From now on, the task confronting the people of our country is: through such a form of social organization as the people's commune, and based on the general line for socialist construction laid down by the Party, to develop the social productive forces at high speed, to advance the industrialization of the country, the industrialization of the communes, and the mechanization and electrification of agriculture; and to effect the gradual transition from socialist collective ownership to socialist ownership by the whole people, thus fully realizing ownership by the whole people in the socialist economy of our country and gradually building our country into a great socialist land with a highly developed modern industry, agriculture, science and culture. During this process, the elements of communism are bound to increase gradually and these will lay the foundation of material and spiritual conditions for the transition from socialism to communism. . . .

On the question of transition from socialism to communism, we must not mark time at the socialist stage, nor should we drop into the Utopian dream of skipping the socialist stage and jumping over to the communist stage. We are advocates of the Marxist-Leninist theory of permanent revolution; we hold that no 'Great Wall' exists or can be allowed to exist between the democratic revolution and the socialist revolution and between socialism and communism. We are at the same time advocates of the Marxist-Leninist theory of the development of revolution by stages; we hold that different stages of development reflect qualitative changes and that these stages, different in quality, should not be confused. The Political Bureau of the Central Committee has pointed out clearly in its August Resolution on the Establishment of People's Communes in the Rural Areas: in the case of the people's communes,

> the transition from collective ownership to ownership by the whole people is a process, the completion of which may take less time – three or four years – in some places, and longer – five or six years or even more – elsewhere. Even with the completion of this transition, people's communes, like state-owned industry, are still socialist in character, i.e. the principle of 'from each according to his ability and to each according to his work' prevails. Some years after that the social product will become very abundant; the communist consciousness and morality of the entire people will be elevated to a much higher degree; universal education will be achieved and the level raised; the differences between worker and peasant, between town and country, between mental and manual labour – the legacies of the old society that have inevitably been carried over into the socialist period – and the remnants of unequal bourgeois rights which are the reflection of these differences will gradually vanish; and the function of the state will be limited to protecting the country from external aggression; and it will play no role internally. At that time Chinese society will enter the era of communism in which the principle of 'from each according to his ability and to each according to his needs' will be practised.

In order to clear up misconceptions about the people's communes and ensure the healthy development of the people's commune movement, extensive and repeated publicity and education based on this Marxist-Leninist point of view must be carried out seriously throughout the Party and among all the people of China. . . .

In running a people's commune well the fundamental question is to strengthen the leading role of the Party. It is only by strengthening the Party's leading role that the principle of 'politics in command' can be realized, that socialist and communist ideological education among the cadres and commune members and the struggle against all kinds of erroneous tendencies can be conducted in a thoroughgoing way and that the Party's line and policy can be implemented correctly. There are some people who think that with the emergence of the commune the Party can be dispensed with, and that they can practise what they call 'merging the Party and the commune in one'. This kind of thinking is wrong. . . .

In all its work, the Party should hold fast to the principle of combining revolutionary zeal with a scientific spirit. The great leap forward in 1958 has won an unprecedented victory for socialist construction in our country. Now even our enemies find it impossible to deny the significance of this victory. But we must never overlook our small weak points because of big achievements. On the contrary, the bigger the achievement the more we need to remind our cadres to keep cool-headed and not be carried away by the flood of news of victory and become unable or even unwilling to see the weak points in their work. One tendency which deserves our attention in the present work of socialist construction is exaggeration. This is incompatible with the practical working style of our Party, and is harmful to the development of our socialist construction.

9. Extracts from the Debates of the Twenty-First Congress of the Communist Party of the Soviet Union

The Twenty-First Congress, which met in January 1959, adopted a less clearly defined position than the Twentieth Congress, emphasizing the precarious nature of the national front and the inevitability of class conflicts. But the more moderate line adopted at the Twentieth Congress was by no means abandoned, as the praise of the Indian government suffices to show.[1]

KHRUSHCHEV: The whole of progressive mankind can be satisfied with the way events have developed in the countries of the Near and Middle East. We welcome the national-liberation movement of the Arab peoples and other peoples of Asia and Africa who have rid themselves of colonial oppression. . . .

When the peoples fight for their national independence, against the colonizers, all patriotic forces combine in a united national front.

Such was the situation, for example, in the period when the Egyptian people and other Arab peoples were struggling to free themselves from oppression by the imperialist colonizers. . . .

After the expulsion of the colonizers, when problems involving the whole nation have largely been solved, the peoples seek an answer to the social problems that life poses. This means firstly the agrarian-peasant question and the struggle of labour against capital. In the ranks of the national-liberation movement social processes begin to occur which inevitably give rise to differing opinions

[1] SOURCE: *Vneocherednoy XXI S"yezd Kommunisticheskoy Partii Sovetskogo Soyuza.* Stenograficheskiy Otchet (Moscow, 1959), vol. 1, pp. 78–80, 397–8, 158.

as to the path of future development to be taken by the State in question.

Our country, like the other socialist countries, has supported and will continue to support the national-liberation movement. The Soviet Union has not interfered and does not intend to interfere in the internal affairs of other countries, but we cannot keep to ourselves our attitude to the fact that a campaign is being waged against the progressive forces in certain countries under the false slogans of anti-communism. In so far as statements have recently been made in the United Arab Republic against the ideas of communism, and accusations have been made against communists, I, as a communist, consider it necessary for me to state at our Communist Party's Congress that it is incorrect to accuse communists of assisting in weakening or disuniting the national effort in the struggle against imperialism. On the contrary, there is no one more staunch or more dedicated to the cause of the struggle against the colonizers than communists. . . .

The questions of the development of society should be considered more profoundly. Objective laws of social development exist. They state that within a nation there exist classes with disparate interests. After the elimination of imperialist oppression from the colonial countries, the workers want to secure a shorter working day and higher wages; the peasants want more land and the chance to enjoy the fruits of their labours, and both of them want political rights. But the capitalists want higher profits and the landlords want to keep the land which they hold. The progressive forces strive for the development of the country along the path of social progress, try to reinforce its national independence, and protect it from the intrigues of the imperialists. Internal reactionary forces, frequently incited from outside by the imperialists, wage a struggle against this.

These processes taking place in countries which have freed themselves from imperialist oppression occur not through the will or at the wish of this or that party but because of the existence of classes and their different interests. We, as communists, and all progressive people, naturally sympathize with those who fight for social justice. We do not hide the fact that we and certain leaders of the United Arab Republic hold different views in the sphere of ideology. But in matters concerning the struggle against imperialism, on the question of strengthening the political and economic independence of countries which have liberated themselves from colonialism, in the struggle against the danger of war, our positions and those of the same leaders coincide. Differences in ideological views must not hinder the development of friendly relations between our countries and our joint struggle against imperialism. . . .

MUKHITDINOV: Anti-imperialist revolutions have given many peoples national independence, which is their greatest victory, and an historic one. But for the solution of economic, political and social problems, national independence alone is not enough, even though it is the principal condition of independent development.

The aspiration of the countries of the East to wipe out their backwardness now shows itself in the policy of nationalizing industry and introducing agrarian reforms, which are of extremely great significance, encouraging the state sector, and in attempting to make use of planning principles in the economy. But, in a number of countries, reaction, fearing for its privileges, is sabotaging these measures and does not even draw the line at concluding direct alliances and doing deals with the imperialists.

The peoples of the East oppose the imperialist front with their own front. The Bandung Conference was an important stage on this path, for it demonstrated the great solidarity of the countries of Asia and Africa in the struggle against imperialism. The strength of the ideas of Bandung, which were confirmed anew at the Cairo and Tashkent Conferences, lies in the fact that they express the spirit and the vital needs of the contemporary period. The desire of the Arabs, Africans and other peoples of the East for unity is historically justified and legitimate, and the Soviet people fully shares this just desire of theirs. But as they say in the East, the kind of unity which corresponds with the interests of the peoples is the kind which allows an even wider extension of the struggle to eradicate all the vestiges of colonial dependence. Anti-imperialist content – this is its main criterion. Unity can be fruitful if it is created on a voluntary basis, takes into account the historical, economic and social peculiarities of each people, and is based on equality and respect for independence and sovereignty.

For the countries which have freed themselves from colonial oppression the all-round expansion of democracy and the union of all strata of the populace are of exceptionally great importance. In this respect India's development is interesting. Undoubtedly India still has much to do in order to eliminate the consequences of colonialism once and for all and ensure social and economic progress. But there is also no doubt that, as a result of the far-sighted policy of the outstanding statesman of the East, Prime Minister Jawaharlal Nehru, and of his government, and also the activity of all her progressive forces, India has achieved in a short historical period notable successes in industrial development, in agriculture, the economy as a whole and in securing national unity and increasing the country's international prestige. . . .

KUUSINEN: The international significance of the Seven-Year Plan is not only that it contributes to world peace. The implementation of the plan will indisputably make a serious *contribution to the struggle of the colonial and underdeveloped peoples for liberty, economic, social and cultural progress*. . . .

SECTION XI: THE MOSCOW CONFERENCE OF 1960 AND ITS SEQUELS

1. Documents regarding the November 1960 Moscow Conference

It was at the Moscow Conference that the first great debate took place among the Soviet and Chinese communists and the partisans of the various intermediate positions. At the time, however, very little filtered through to the outside world, and even now the documentation on the Conference is far from complete. Nevertheless, the French, Italian, and Indian parties have published the speeches of their representatives, and other parties, including the Chinese, have published summaries of the debates. The first text in this series of extracts, taken from the Statement published at the time, illustrates the compromises which were reached on two important points: the problem of national independence within the communist bloc, and the originality of each country (especially the non-European countries) on the cultural level. The texts which follow give some idea of the way in which these compromises were reached. Text XI 1 B is extracted from Thorez's first speech, and Text XI 1 D is taken from the written declaration which he made in the name of the French delegation later in the Conference. In the interval, the Secretary General of the Communist Party of India also spoke on these themes (Text XI 1 C).[1]

A Extracts from the Statement of the Communist and Workers' Parties

One of the greatest achievements of the world socialist system is the practical confirmation of the Marxist-Leninist thesis that national antagonisms diminish with the decline of class antagonisms. In contrast to the laws of the capitalist system, which is characterized by antagonistic contradictions between classes, nations and states leading to armed conflicts, there are no objective causes in the nature of the socialist system for contradictions and conflicts between the peoples and states belonging to it. Its development leads to greater unity among the states and nations and to the consolidation of all the forms of cooperation between them. . . .

[1] SOURCE: Text XI 1 A: *World Marxist Review*, December 1960.

Text XI 1 B: *Problèmes du Mouvement Communiste International* (Paris, édité par le Comité Central du Parti communiste français, January 1963), pp. 34–5.

Text XI 1 C: *The India-China Border Dispute and the Communist Party of India.* Resolutions, Statements and Speeches, 1959–63 (New Delhi, Communist Party Publication, 1963), pp. 32–7, 43–4.

Text XI 1 D: *Problèmes du Mouvement Communiste International*, pp. 42–3.

Fraternal friendship and mutual assistance of peoples, born of the socialist system, have superseded the political isolation and national egoism typical of capitalism. . . .

The Declaration of 1957 points out quite correctly that undue emphasis on the role of national peculiarities and departure from the universal truth of Marxism-Leninism regarding the socialist revolution and socialist construction prejudice the common cause of socialism. The Declaration also states quite correctly that Marxism-Leninism demands creative application of the general principles of socialist revolution and socialist construction depending on the specific historical conditions in the country concerned, and does not permit of a mechanical copying of the policies and tactics of the communist parties of other countries. Disregard of national peculiarities may lead to the party of the proletariat being isolated from reality, from the masses, and may injure the socialist cause.

Manifestations of nationalism and national narrow-mindedness do not disappear automatically with the establishment of the socialist system. If fraternal relations and friendship between the socialist countries are to be strengthened, it is necessary that the communist and workers' parties pursue a Marxist-Leninist internationalist policy, that all working people be educated in a spirit of internationalism and patriotism, and that a resolute struggle be waged to eliminate the survivals of bourgeois nationalism and chauvinism. . . .

National-liberation revolutions have triumphed in vast areas of the world. About forty new sovereign states have arisen in Asia and Africa in the fifteen post-war years. The victory of the Cuban revolution has powerfully stimulated the struggle of the Latin-American peoples for complete national independence. A new historical period has set in in the life of mankind: the peoples of Asia, Africa and Latin America that have won their freedom have begun to take an active part in world politics.

The complete collapse of colonialism is imminent. The breakdown of the system of colonial slavery under the impact of the national-liberation movement is a development ranking second in historic importance only to the formation of the world socialist system.

The Great October Socialist Revolution aroused the East and drew the colonial peoples into the common current of the world-wide revolutionary movement. This development was greatly facilitated by the Soviet Union's victory in the Second World War, the establishment of people's democracy in a number of European and Asian countries, the triumph of the socialist revolution in China, and the formation of the world socialist system. The forces of world socialism contributed decisively to the struggle of the colonial and dependent peoples for liberation from imperialist oppression. The socialist system has become a reliable shield for the independent national development of the peoples who have won freedom. The national-liberation movement receives powerful support from the international working-class movement.

. . . Communists have always recognized the progressive, revolutionary significance of national-liberation wars; they are the most active champions of national independence. The existence of the world socialist system and the weakening of the positions of imperialism have provided the oppressed peoples with new opportunities of winning independence.

The peoples of the colonial countries win their independence both through armed struggle and by non-military methods, depending on the specific conditions in the country concerned. They secure durable victory through a powerful national-liberation movement. The colonial powers never bestow freedom on the colonial peoples and never leave of their own free will the countries they are exploiting. . . .

The alliance of the working class and the peasantry is the most important force in winning and defending national independence, accomplishing far-reaching democratic transformations and ensuring social progress. This alliance forms the basis of a broad national front. The extent to which the national bourgeoisie participates in the liberation struggle also depends to no small degree upon its strength and stability. . . .

In present conditions, the national bourgeoisie of the colonial and dependent countries unconnected with imperialist circles, is objectively interested in the accomplishment of the principal tasks of anti-imperialist, anti-feudal revolution, and therefore can participate in the revolutionary struggle against imperialism and feudalism. In that sense it is progressive. But it is unstable; though progressive, it is inclined to compromise with imperialism and feudalism. . . .

After winning political independence the peoples seek solutions to the social problems raised by life and to the problems of reinforcing national independence. Different classes and parties offer different solutions. Which course of development to choose is the internal affair of the peoples themselves. As social contradictions grow, the national bourgeoisie inclines more and more to compromising with domestic reaction and imperialism. The people, however, begin to see that the best way to abolish age-long backwardness and improve their living standard is that of non-capitalist development. . . .

In the present situation, favourable domestic and international conditions arise in many countries for the establishment of an independent national democracy, that is, a state which consistently upholds its political and economic independence, fights against imperialism and its military blocs, against military bases on its territory; a state which fights against the new forms of colonialism and the penetration of imperialist capital; a state which rejects dictatorial and despotic methods of government; a state in which the people are ensured broad democratic rights and freedoms (freedom of speech, press, assembly, demonstrations, establishment of political parties and social organizations), the opportunity to work for the enactment of an agrarian reform and other domestic and social changes, and for participation in shaping government policy. The formation and consolidation of national democracies enables the countries concerned to make rapid social progress and play an active part in the people's struggle for peace, against the aggressive policies of the imperialist camp, for the complete abolition of colonial oppression.

The class-conscious workers of the colonial powers, who realized that 'no nation can be free if it oppresses other nations', fought consistently for the self-determination of the nations oppressed by the imperialists. Now that these nations are taking the path of national independence, it is the internationalist duty of the workers and all democratic forces in the industrially developed capitalist countries to assist them vigorously in their struggle against the imperialists. It is their duty to assist them in their struggle for national independence and its consolidation, and in effectively solving the problems of their economic and cultural rebirth. In so doing, the workers defend the interests of the people of their own countries. . . .

B Maurice Thorez on 'Chinifying' Marxism

. . . The Declaration of 1957 reminds us that 'Marxism-Leninism demands that the general principles of the revolution and of socialist construction be applied with due account of the concrete historical conditions of each country. . . . Lenin insisted many times on the necessity of correctly *applying* the fundamental principles of communism in accordance with the specific traits of each nation, of each national state.' This thesis, which is profoundly correct, has nothing to do with the curious theories defended by our Chinese comrades about the 'Chinification' of Marxism-Leninism, or even, if one sticks to their own translation into French, about the 'adaptation' of Marxism-Leninism to China. What would remain of the universal principles of Marxism-Leninism after its 'Chinification' by some, its 'Frenchification' by others, or its 'Russification' – to employ the terms used by the social democrats in criticizing Lenin?

Each communist party contributes, in the conditions of its country, to the enrichment of our theory and not to its 'adaptation', that is to say, finally, to its impoverishment, to its narrow limitation to the framework of a specific country. . . .

C Extracts from the Speech of Ajoy Ghosh, Secretary General of the Communist Party of India

We fail to understand why there should be any divergence on the issue of war and peace and on peaceful coexistence. . . .

By fighting for disarmament and by resolutely upholding the cause of peace, the socialist countries, with the U.S.S.R. at their head, are continuously isolating the imperialists and winning the moral leadership of the people of the world. . . .

The forces of world socialism have not merely played the decisive role in frustrating the drive of imperialists towards war – they have also enormously helped the struggle of the colonial and dependent peoples for national liberation. Of great importance in this connexion, as the Draft Declaration points out, was the People's Democratic Revolution of China which helped to change the correlation of forces on world scale and had powerful impact on the peoples of the countries of Asia, Africa and Latin America.

This great role of China in accelerating the process of disintegration of the world colonial system and in giving a powerful impetus to the national liberation movement is universally acknowledged. On a world plane, the Soviet Union has been delivering blow after blow against imperialism, whose worldwide collapse is unthinkable without the gigantic role of the C.P.S.U. and the Soviet Union. It baffles and pains us when it is suggested that the Soviet Union has been half-hearted in its support to the freedom struggle of the colonial peoples and that it embellishes and appeases imperialism. It is a totally baseless allegation.

The peoples of Asia and Africa, both those who have won political independence and are striving to defend and strengthen it and those who are still struggling to be free have always found in the Soviet Union an unfailing friend and a reliable ally. The entire record of the Soviet Union proves this conclusively. Hence the deep love entertained by the oppressed peoples for the Soviet Union.

Comrades, the victories of the national liberation movement in recent years have been phenomenal in scope and significance. Hundreds of millions of people who, the arrogant imperialists thought, were destined to remain for ever hewers of wood and drawers of water, have awakened to a new life. . . .

In many of these countries, imperialists still retain very strong positions. But it is equally true that many of these countries, even though capitalist régimes prevail there, have already ceased to be under imperialist control. They oppose colonialism, they stand for peace, they are striving for economic independence. One of the most important of these countries is the Republic of India – a country of 400 million people, which together with the People's

Republic of China was the author of the historic Panch Sheel.[1]

We, Indian communists, have never entertained illusions about the Indian national bourgeoisie. The National Congress, the ruling party in India, looks upon our party as its chief enemy. The leaders of the ruling party, including Nehru, never miss an opportunity to malign and attack our party. Radical agrarian reforms are an urgent necessity for the rebuilding of our economy. Our Party is fighting determinedly against feudal and semi-feudal survivals and for genuine agrarian reforms. . . .

While waging a determined struggle against its anti-people and anti-democratic policies, we nevertheless realize that the Indian government, led by Nehru, constitutes a very significant force for world peace, despite its vacillations. We are also conscious of the big influence that India exerts over many countries of Asia and Africa. That is why we strive our utmost to strengthen the independent and peace-loving policy of the Indian government. We support every single move of the Indian government that strengthens peace and weakens imperialism while at the same time, criticizing its vacillations. We constantly press for closer cooperation between India and the countries of the socialist world.

In the struggle to uphold peace and isolate the instigators of a new world war, the newly-independent countries of Asia and Africa can play a great role. The Soviet Union and other countries of the socialist world have been fully conscious of this fact. The significance of the emergence of the peace zone which includes these countries was emphasized in the Moscow Declaration of 1957. Here I would like to mention the disinterested aid given by the socialist countries and, above all, by the U.S.S.R. to India and the other newly-independent countries. This aid has immensely helped India to build basic industries like the Bhilai steel plant. We attach great importance to such economic aid from socialist countries. It helps the development of the economy of the countries of Asia and Africa and enables them to resist imperialist pressure as well as overcome economic dependence on imperialism. It has thus a profoundly anti imperialist content.

We have already said that China, together with India, put forward the historic Panch Sheel. The Bandung Conference was such a resounding success primarily because the two great countries of Asia acted unitedly there. We must also mention the fact that for no country in the world has there been in India such warm sentiments of friendship as for the People's Republic of China. We have always held and still hold the Communist Party of China and its leaders in great respect for their titanic achievements, for their contributions in the sphere of theory and practice, which have

[1] The five principles of peaceful coexistence formulated for the first time in the Sino-Indian Treaty of April 1954.

meant so much to the people of the whole world, especially the peoples of Asia and Africa, for the valuable advice and assistance they have given to our party on many occasions.

It is all the more painful for us therefore to point out to the Chinese comrades that some of the positions taken by them today are not in conformity with what they themselves preached and practised in the past. . . .

Imperialists are striving to disrupt the peace zone. The socialist states must do everything in their power to prevent this.

In our opinion, in recent periods, the Communist Party of China has underestimated the importance of this task, and in relation to India, they have not acted in a way so as to strengthen the peace zone. . . .

It has been argued by the Chinese comrades that in accordance with the tactics of unity and struggle in relation to the national bourgeoisie, they waged the necessary struggle when the Indian government acted wrongly against China. The argument, in this context, is not convincing. Evidently the main forces in the struggle against the bourgeois rulers of India are the mass of Indian people. It follows, therefore that China's tactics – including the way in which the struggle is waged even against the Nehru government and the method and manner of waging it – had to be such as helps to isolate the bourgeois rulers and not help them to rally the masses. It had to be tactics that help the Indian democratic movement. This, we regret to say, was not kept in mind.

D Maurice Thorez on the Susceptibility of Liberated Peoples

. . . Rightly, the draft statement stresses that 'the conscious workers of the mother countries have persistently fought for the self-determination of the nations enslaved by imperialism, understanding that *a people which oppresses others cannot be free*. Now that these peoples are embarking on the path of national independence, the international duty of the workers and of all the democratic forces of the advanced capitalist countries is to grant them a maximum aid in their struggle against the imperialists, to impart to them, on a basis of completely free consent, their experience and their knowledge in order that they may successfully resolve the problems raised by economic and cultural rebirth. By acting in this way, they defend the interests of the popular masses of their countries.' We believe that this important idea must not be called into question.

To be sure, we understand that the exactions of imperialism have left a deep wound in the heart of the peoples yesterday oppressed, and that their sensitivity about these questions is particularly sharp. We, who have struggled since the foundation of our Party and in the light of the October Revolution against the crimes of colonialism and for the independence of the enslaved peoples, share without reserve the hatred of these peoples for imperialism, its methods and its men.

However, if one called into question the idea of the statement regarding the practical support afforded the former colonial peoples by the democratic elements of the imperialist countries, this would seem to us false in principle and in contradiction with practice.

This thesis is false in principle because it lumps together the imperialists and the elements which, under the direction of the working class, struggle against imperialism in the mother countries. This thesis leads to the negation of this great fact that the proletariat of the mother countries is the ally of the colonial peoples struggling for independence; its final result is therefore to weaken this struggle itself.

Experience invalidates this thesis as well. This is shown by the example of Guinea, a country completely liberated from the oppression of French imperialism and which has adopted in general a democratic orientation. Answering the appeal of the Guinean government, a rather large number of progressive communist French technicians are working with profit for the Guinean people. It is the French reactionary government which is disturbed by this situation and which takes sanctions against these men. This attitude of the reaction of the mother country is enough to show where the interest of the liberated peoples lies. Their interest is to use the progressive technicians of the formerly dominant countries. . . .

2. *The Dangers of Nationalism within the Communist Bloc*

Extracts from the new programme of the Communist Party of the Soviet Union, as it was submitted to the Twenty-Second Congress of the Party in October 1961.[1]

. . . The experience of the world socialist system has confirmed the need for the *closest unity* of countries that have broken away from capitalism, for their united effort in the building of socialism and communism. The line of socialist construction in isolation, detached from the world community of socialist countries, is theoretically untenable because it conflicts with the objective laws governing the development of socialist society. It is harmful economically because it causes waste of social labour, retards the growth rate of production and makes the country dependent on the capitalist world. It is reactionary and dangerous politically because it does not unite but divides the peoples in face of the united front of imperialist forces, nourishes bourgeois-nationalist

[1] SOURCE: *Programma Kommunisticheskoy Partii Sovetskogo Soyuza* (Proyekt) (Moscow, Gospolitizdat, 1961), pp. 21–2, 24.

tendencies and may ultimately lead to the loss of the socialist gains. . . .

. . . The experience of the Soviet Union and the People's Democracies has confirmed the accuracy of Lenin's thesis that the class struggle does not disappear in the period of the building of socialism. The general trend of class struggle within the socialist countries when socialist construction is going forward successfully leads to consolidation of the position of the socialist forces and weakens the resistance of the remnants of the hostile classes. But this development does not follow a straight line. Changes in the domestic or external situation may cause the class struggle to intensify at certain junctures. This calls for constant vigilance in order to frustrate in good time the designs of hostile forces within and without, who persist in their attempts to undermine people's power and sow strife in the fraternal community of socialist countries.

Nationalism is the chief political and ideological weapon used by international reaction and the remnants of the domestic reactionary forces against the unity of the socialist countries. Nationalist sentiments and national narrow-mindedness do not disappear automatically with the establishment of the socialist system. National prejudice and survivals of former national strife are the province in which resistance to social progress must be protracted and stubborn, bitter and insidious. . . .

3. The Duty of the Western Proletariat towards the Non-European Peoples

Extracts from the Chinese editorial of 4 March 1963, entitled 'Once More on the Differences between Comrade Togliatti and ourselves'.[1]

. . . Without support from the revolutionary struggles of the oppressed nations and peoples of Asia, Africa and Latin America, it will be impossible for the proletariat and the people in capitalist Europe and America to rid themselves of the calamities of capitalist oppression and of the menace of war arising from imperialism. Therefore, the proletarian parties of the metropolitan imperialist countries are duty bound to heed the voice of the revolutionary people in these regions, study their experience, respect their revolutionary feelings and act in concert with their revolutionary struggles. They have no right whatsoever to flaunt their seniority and primogeniture before these people, to put on lordly airs, to carp and cavil like Comrade Thorez of France, who so arrogantly and disdainfully speaks of them as being 'young and inexperienced'.[2] Much less have they the right to take a social-

[1] SOURCE: *Hung-ch'i*, no. 3–4, 1963, pp. 19, 27.

[2] Report of Maurice Thorez to the Central Committee of the French Communist Party, 15 December 1960. *Problèmes du Mouvement Communiste International*, p. 53.

chauvinist attitude, slandering, cursing, intimidating and obstructing the revolutionary struggles of the people of these regions. . . .

Since the imperialists and reactionaries incessantly foment wars in various regions of the world to serve their own political ends, it is impossible for anybody to prevent the oppressed people and nations from waging wars of resistance against oppression.

Certain self-styled 'Marxist-Leninists' may not regard the wars cited above as wars at all. They acknowledge only wars which take place in 'highly developed civilized regions'. Actually, such a viewpoint is nothing new.

Lenin long ago criticized the absurd view that 'wars outside Europe are not wars'. Lenin said sarcastically in a speech in 1917 that there were '. . . wars which we, Europeans, do not consider to be wars, because too often they resemble not wars, but the most brutal slaughter, extermination of unarmed peoples'.[1]

People exactly like those Lenin criticized really do exist today. They think that all is quiet in the world so long as there is no war in their own locality or neighbourhood. They do not consider it worth their while to bother whether the imperialists and their running dogs are ravaging and slaughtering people in other localities, or engaging in military intervention and armed conflicts or provoking wars there. They only worry lest the 'sparks' of resistance by the oppressed nations and people in these places might lead to disaster and disturb their own tranquillity. They see no need whatsoever to examine how wars in these places originate, what social classes are waging these wars, and what the nature of these wars is. They simply condemn these wars in an indiscriminating and arbitrary fashion. Can this viewpoint be regarded as Leninist? . . .

4. *The Indian Communist Party and Nehru's Socialism*

Extracts from a Chinese editorial of 9 March 1963, entitled 'A Mirror for Revisionists', attacking the President of the Indian Communist Party, S. M. Dange, in the dual context of the struggle against 'modern revisionism' and of the Sino-Soviet conflict.[2]

. . . Dange and company are assisting the Nehru government to hoodwink the people with its sham 'socialism'. They laud Nehru as 'the symbol of national unity' and say, 'When you have such a person at the head of the nation, and we [Dange and company] adopt a correct attitude inside the common front, the front grows into a leading force for future development. What future development? The realization of socialism!'

The Moscow statement clearly states that communists should

[1] See Lenin, 'War and Revolution', *Polnoye Sobraniye Sochinenii,* vol. XXXII, p. 80.

[2] SOURCE: *Jen-min jih-pao,* 9 March 1963.

expose the fraudulent use by bourgeois politicians of socialist slogans. But Dange and company have done nothing to expose Nehru's socialism; on the contrary, they have tried to persuade the Indian communists and the Indian people that Nehru is really pursuing a policy of socialism and should be given unconditional support. They have publicly asked the Congress Party to cooperate with the Indian Communist Party in order to build socialism in India under the leadership of the Nehru government. We would like to ask: If the Dange clique believe that Nehru and his Congress Party can be depended upon to realize socialism, is not the Communist Party controlled by Dange and company superfluous? . . .

5. *We Do Not Want to Follow the Chinese Way*

Extracts from the article entitled 'Neither Revisionism nor Dogmatism is our Guide', by which Mr Dange replied to the Chinese attacks contained in the preceding text.[1]

It is well known that all world parties in their Party Constitutions abide by Marxism-Leninism. But the Chinese Party found it necessary to add something else to it, basing themselves on their own experience and the needs of their revolution.

In the Constitution of their Party adopted at the Seventh National Party Congress in June 1945, Article 2, under the head 'Duties of a Party Member', lays down the following:

(*a*) to endeavour to raise the level of his consciousness and to understand the fundamentals of Marxism-Leninism and the Thought of Mao Tse-tung.[2]

It may be pointed out that the 'Thought' is with a capital T and hence is something very concrete.

So the Chinese Party has, in addition to the fundamentals of Marxism-Leninism, also the 'Thought' of a great national leader of theirs, Comrade Mao Tse-tung. What other parties enjoy such good fortune! We certainly are nowhere within the neighbourhood of such a personality or its cult and 'Thought'. . . .

. . . Why should we be asked to follow Chinese lessons of 'thirty years before', which have no validity for us? And if we do not do so, why, please, why interfere in our work and force on us the 'Thought of Mao Tse-tung' to the exclusion of our own, which, however poor it may be, is our own understanding of our situation and Marxism-Leninism?

[1] SOURCE: *The Great Debate. Selected Writings on Problems of Marxism-Leninism Today* (New Delhi, People's Publishing House, 1963), pp. 358–9.

[2] Liu Shao-ch'i, *On the Party* (Peking, Foreign Languages Press, 1950), p. 163. Mr Dange cites another English edition, of which the pagination is slightly different. In any case, the ironic reference in the next sentence to the capital T in 'Thought' applies only to the translations, since there are no capitals in Chinese.

SECTION XII: THE SINO-SOVIET RUPTURE

1. Apologists of Neo-Colonialism

In the middle of 1963, the Soviet and Chinese positions were defined in the letter of the Central Committee of the Chinese Communist Party dated 14 June, and in the open letter of 14 July addressed by the Central Committee of the Communist Party of the Soviet Union to party organizations and to all communists in the Soviet Union. These statements, while they were very important at the time, have lost a good deal of their interest as a result of the subsequent publication of even more explicit and categorical declarations; we have therefore omitted them here. The Chinese position on all aspects of the controversy was systematically set forth in the nine successive 'replies' to the Soviet open letter of 14 July 1963. The following extracts are taken from the fourth reply, which appeared under the title given above. The authors of this text (to which Mao Tse-tung himself certainly gave close attention, if he did not actually write passages here and there) manifest both their ideological radicalism, and their almost visceral feeling of solidarity with the peoples of the non-European countries.[1]

... The storm of the peoples' revolution in Asia, Africa and Latin America requires every political force in the contemporary world to take a stand. This mighty revolutionary storm makes the imperialists and colonialists tremble and the revolutionary people of the world rejoice. The imperialists and colonialists say: 'An awful mess!' The revolutionary people say: 'Very good indeed!' The imperialists and colonialists say: 'It is rebellion, which is forbidden.' The revolutionary people of the whole world say: 'It is revolution, which is the people's right and an inexorable current of history.'

An important line of demarcation between the Marxist-Leninists and the modern revisionists is the attitude taken towards this issue, the sharpest of contemporary world politics. The Marxist-Leninists firmly side with the oppressed nations and actively support the national-liberation movement. The modern revisionists in fact side with the imperialists and colonialists and repudiate and oppose the national-liberation movement in every possible way.

In their words, the leaders of the C.P.S.U. do not dare as yet to discard completely the slogans of support for the national-liberation movement, and at times, for the sake of their own interests, they even take certain measures which create the appearance of

[1] SOURCE: *Hung-ch'i*, no. 20, 22 October 1963, pp. 1–15 *passim*.

support. But if we probe to the essence and consider their views and policies as a whole over a number of years, we see clearly that their attitude towards the liberation struggles of the oppressed nations of Asia, Africa and Latin America is a passive or scornful or negative one, and that they serve as apologists for neo-colonialism. . . .

Abolition of the Task of Combating Imperialism and Colonialism

. . . The leaders of the C.P.S.U. have . . . created the 'theory' that the national-liberation movement has entered upon a 'new stage' having economic tasks as its core. Their argument is that, whereas 'formerly, the struggle was carried on mainly in the political sphere', today the economic question has become the 'central task' and 'the basic link in the further development of the revolution'.

The national-liberation movement has indeed entered a new stage. But this is by no means the kind of 'new stage' described by the leadership of the C.P.S.U. In this new stage, the level of awareness of the Asian, African and Latin American peoples has risen higher than ever and the revolutionary movement is surging forward with unprecedented intensity. They urgently demand the thorough elimination of the forces of imperialism and its running dogs in their own countries and strive for complete political and economic independence. The primary and most urgent task facing these countries is still the further development of the struggle against imperialism, old and new colonialism, and their running dogs. This struggle is still being waged fiercely in the political, economic, military, cultural, ideological and other spheres. And the struggles in all these spheres still find their most concentrated expression in political struggle, which often unavoidably develops into armed struggle when the imperialists resort to direct or indirect armed suppression. . . .

. . . This theory of a 'new stage' advocated by the leaders of the C.P.S.U. is clearly intended to whitewash the aggression against and plunder of Asia, Africa and Latin America by neo-colonialism, as represented by the United States, to cover up the sharp contradiction between imperialism and the oppressed nations and to paralyse the revolutionary struggle of the people of these continents. . . .

Prescriptions for Abolishing the Revolution of the Oppressed Nations

In line with their erroneous 'theories' the leaders of the C.P.S.U. have sedulously worked out a number of nostrums for all the ills of the oppressed nations. Let us examine them.

The first prescription is labelled peaceful coexistence and peaceful competition. . . .

. . . The leaders of the C.P.S.U. hold that the victories of the national-liberation revolution are not due primarily to the revolutionary struggles of the popular masses of each country and that the popular masses cannot emancipate themselves, but must wait for the natural collapse of imperialism through peaceful coexistence and peaceful competition. In fact, this is equivalent to telling the oppressed nations to put up with imperialist plunder and enslavement for ever, and not to rise up in resistance and revolution.

The second prescription is labelled aid to backward countries. . . .

. . . The leaders of the C.P.S.U. openly propose cooperation with U.S. imperialism in 'giving aid to the backward countries'. Khrushchev said in a speech in the United States in September 1959:

> Your and our economic successes will be hailed by the whole world, which expects our two great powers to help the peoples who are centuries behind in their economic development to get on their feet more quickly.

Look! the principal bastion of modern colonialism can after all help the oppressed nations 'to get on their feet more quickly'! Moreover, the leaders of the C.P.S.U. are not only willing but even proud to be associated with the neo-colonialists. This is indeed startling.

The third prescription is labelled disarmament.

Khrushchev has said:

> . . . Disarmament would create the necessary conditions for a tremendous increase in the scale of assistance to the newly established national states. If a mere 8–10 per cent of the 120,000 million dollars spent for military purposes throughout the world were turned to the purpose, it would be possible to end hunger, disease and illiteracy in the distressed areas of the globe within twenty years. . . .

Khrushchev here sounds just like a priest delivering a sermon. Downtrodden people of the world, you are blessed! If only you are patient, if only you wait until the imperialists lay down their arms, freedom will descend upon you. Wait until the imperialists show mercy, and the poverty-stricken areas of the world will become an earthly paradise flowing with milk and honey! . . .

This is not just the fostering of illusions, it is opium for putting the people to sleep. . . .

Opposition to Wars of National Liberation

If the leaders of the C.P.S.U. have been thus trying by every means to make the people of Asia, Africa and Latin America abandon their revolutionary struggle it is because although they talk about supporting the movement and wars of national liberation, in reality they tremble with fear before the revolutionary storm.

The leaders of the C.P.S.U. have the famous 'theory' that 'even a tiny spark can cause a world war', and that a world war must necessarily be a thermonuclear war, which means the annihilation of mankind. Therefore, Khrushchev roars that ' "local wars" in our time are very dangerous', and that 'we will work hard . . . to put out the sparks that may set off the flames of war'. Here Khrushchev makes no distinction between just and unjust wars and betrays the communist stand of supporting just wars. . . .

To curry favour with the French imperialists, the leaders of the C.P.S.U. did not dare to recognize the Provisional Government of the Republic of Algeria for a long time; not until the victory of the Algerian people's war of resistance against French aggression was a foregone conclusion and France was compelled to agree to Algerian independence did they hurriedly recognize the Republic of Algeria. This clownish attitude caused the socialist countries to lose face. . . .

The Areas in which Contemporary World Contradictions are Concentrated

. . . The open letter of the Central Committee of the C.P.S.U. accuses the Chinese Communist Party of putting forward a 'new theory'. It says:

. . . according to this theory the main contradiction of our times is, after all, not the contradiction between socialism and imperialism, but that between the national-liberation movement and imperialism. The decisive force in the struggle against imperialism, the Chinese comrades hold, is not the world socialist system, not the struggle of the international working class, but again the national-liberation movement. . . .

Our view is crystal clear.

In our letter of 14 June we discussed the revolutionary situation in Asia, Africa and Latin America and the significance and role of the national-liberation movement. This is what we said:

1. The various types of contradictions in the contemporary world are concentrated in the vast areas of Asia, Africa and Latin America; these are the most vulnerable areas under imperialist rule and the storm centres of the world revolution which is dealing direct blows at imperialism at the present time.

2. The national-democratic revolutionary movement in these areas and the international socialist revolutionary movement are the two great historical currents of our time.

3. The national-democratic revolution in these areas is an important component of the contemporary proletarian world revolution.

4. The anti-imperialist revolutionary struggles of the people in Asia, Africa and Latin America are pounding and undermining seriously the foundations of the rule of imperialism and colonialism, old and new, and are now a mighty force in defence of world peace.

5. In a sense, therefore, the whole cause of the international proletarian revolution hinges in the last analysis on the outcome of the revolutionary struggles of the people of these areas, who constitute the overwhelming majority of the world's population.

6. Therefore, the anti-imperialist revolutionary struggle of the people in Asia, Africa and Latin America is definitely not merely a matter of regional significance but is one of overall importance for the whole cause of proletarian world revolution.

These are all Marxist-Leninist theses. They are all conclusions drawn by scientific analysis from the realities of our time.

No one can deny that an extremely favourable revolutionary situation now exists in Asia, Africa and Latin America. Today the national-liberation revolutions in Asia, Africa and Latin America are the most important forces dealing imperialism direct blows. The contradictions of the world are concentrated in Asia, Africa and Latin America.

The centre of world contradictions, of world political struggles, is not fixed and immutable but shifts with changes in the international struggles and the revolutionary situation. We believe that, with the development of the contradiction and struggle between the proletariat and the bourgeoisie in Western Europe and North America, the momentous day of battle will arrive in these homes of capitalism and heart-lands of imperialism. When that day comes, Western Europe and North America will undoubtedly become the centre of world political struggles, of world contradictions. . . .

An Example of Social-Chauvinism

According to the principle of proletarian internationalism the proletariat and the communists of the oppressor nations must actively support both the right of the oppressed nations to national independence and their struggles for liberation. Only with the support of the oppressed nations will the proletariat of the oppressor nations have a better chance of victory in its revolution. . . .

However, some self-styled Marxist-Leninists have abandoned Marxism-Leninism on this very question of fundamental principle. The leaders of the French Communist Party are typical in this respect. . . .

For the past ten years and more, the leaders of the French Communist Party have followed the colonial policy of the French imperialists and served as an appendage of French monopoly capital. In 1946, when the French monopoly capitalist rulers played a neo-colonialist trick by proposing to form a French Union, they followed suit and proclaimed that 'we have always envisaged the French Union as a free union of free peoples' and that 'the French Union will permit the regulation, on a new basis, of the relations between the people of France and the overseas peoples formerly dependent on France'.[1] In 1958, when the French Union collapsed and the French government proposed the establishment of

[1] See R. Barbé's articles in *Cahiers du Communisme*, no. 10, 1946, pp. 971–9, and no. 5, 1947, pp. 399–403.

a 'French Community' to preserve its colonial system, the leaders of the C.P.F. again followed suit and proclaimed 'we believe that the creation of a genuine community will be a positive event'. . . .

On the question of Algeria, the national-chauvinist stand of the leaders of the C.P.F. is all the more evident. They have recently tried to justify themselves by asserting that they had long 'recognized the legitimate demand of the people of Algeria for freedom'. But what are the facts?

For a long time the leaders of the C.P.F. absolutely refused to recognize Algeria's right to national independence; they followed the French monopoly capitalists, crying that 'Algeria is an inalienable part of France',[1] and that France 'should be a great African power, now and in the future'. Thorez and others were primarily concerned about the fact that Algeria could provide France with 'a million head of sheep' and large quantities of wheat yearly to solve her problem of 'the shortage of meat' and 'make up our deficit in grain'.[2]

Just see! What feverish national-chauvinism on the part of the leaders of the C.P.F.! Do they show an iota of proletarian internationalism? Is there anything of the proletarian revolutionary in them? By taking this national-chauvinistic stand they have betrayed the fundamental interests of the international proletariat, the fundamental interests of the French proletariat and the true interests of the French nation.

Against the 'Theory of Racism' and the 'Theory of the Yellow Peril'

Having used up all their magic weapons for opposing the national-liberation movement, the leaders of the C.P.S.U. are now reduced to seeking help from racism, the most reactionary of all imperialist theories. They describe the correct stand of the C.P.C. in resolutely supporting the national-liberation movement as 'creating racial and geographical barriers', 'replacing the class approach with the racial approach', and 'playing upon the nationalist and even racist prejudices of the Asian and African peoples'. . . .

In the last analysis, the national question in the contemporary world is one of class struggle and anti-imperialist struggle. Today the workers, peasants, revolutionary intellectuals, anti-imperialist and patriotic bourgeois elements and other patriotic and anti-imperialist enlightened people of all races – white, black, yellow or brown – have formed a broad united front against the imperialists, headed by the United States, and their running dogs. . . .

When they peddle the 'theory of racism', describing the national-liberation movement in Asia, Africa and Latin America as one of

[1] See the bill signed by Thorez, Billoux and Marcel Paul in the *Journal Officiel* of 26 September 1946.

[2] Maurice Thorez, report to the Tenth Congress of the French Communist Party, June 1945, *Oeuvres* (Paris, Éditions sociales, 1963), Part V, vol. 21, p. 68.

the coloured against the white race, the leaders of the C.P.S.U. are clearly aiming at inciting racist hatred among the white people in Europe and North America, at diverting the people of the world from the struggle against imperialism. . . .

Anyone with a little knowledge of modern world history knows that the 'theory of the Yellow Peril' about which the C.P.S.U. leadership has been making such a noise is a legacy of the German Emperor William II. Half a century ago, William II stated, 'I am a believer in the Yellow Peril. . . '.

When William II spread this 'theory of the Yellow Peril' the European bourgeoisie was extremely rotten and reactionary, and democratic revolutions were sweeping through China, Turkey and Persia and affecting India, around the time of the 1905 Russian revolution. That was the period, too, when Lenin made his famous remark about 'backward Europe and advanced Asia'. . . .

Fifty years have gone by; imperialism in Western Europe and North America has become still more rotten and reactionary, and its days are numbered. Meanwhile, the revolutionary storm raging over Asia, Africa and Latin America has grown many times stronger than in Lenin's time. It is hardly credible that today there are still people who wish to step into the shoes of William II. This is indeed a mockery of history. . . .

2. *The Indian Viewpoint on the Relative Importance of Revolution in Asia and in Europe*

Extracts from the resolution adopted in October 1963 by the National Council of the Communist Party of India regarding the ideological controversy within the world communist movement.[1]

. . . The main content of our epoch is that it is an epoch of transition from capitalism to socialism. The most distinctive feature is that the world socialist system is becoming the decisive factor in the development of human society.

The C.P.C. leadership discounts, if not virtually ignores, these two highly important aspects of the present epoch. . . .

The National Council of the C.P.I. notes that the C.P.C. leadership has radically revised the collective, Marxist-Leninist standpoint about the main contradiction in modern society. According to the C.P.C. leaders, the principal contradiction is not between capitalism and socialism but between imperialism and national liberation. This departure on the question of main contradiction leads to another erroneous conclusion. The Chinese leaders contend that the focal points of the contradiction in the world are concentrated in the vast areas of Asia, Africa and Latin

[1] SOURCE: *Resolutions of the National Council of the Communist Party of India*, New Delhi, 14–19 October 1963 (New Delhi, Communist Party Publication, 1963), pp. 18–21.

America, where the national liberation struggles are being conducted. The Chinese leaders have gone to the length of saying that the whole cause of the international proletarian revolution hinges on the outcome of the revolutionary struggles in these areas. All this is a complete misinterpretation of the contradictions in the modern world and is contrary to the propositions of the Moscow Declaration and the Moscow Statement.

Even before the world socialist system came into existence, the contradiction between capitalism and socialism was regarded by Marxist-Leninists as the main contradiction. With the emergence of the world socialist system and the tremendous manner in which it is influencing the world developments, as well as the advance of the international working class movement, this contradiction has immensely sharpened. It is astonishing that the C.P.C. leadership should have abandoned the correct Marxist-Leninist understanding now of all times.

The National Council of the C.P.I. fully acknowledges the great revolutionary role of the national liberation movements in Asia, Africa and Latin America and the shattering blows they are delivering to imperialism. There must be no underestimation of this great revolutionary force. But with all these, the decisive role in the development of human society and the world revolutionary process is not played by the national liberation struggles but by the international working class and its chief creation – the world socialist system. It is not difficult to see that the national liberations by themselves do not end the socio-economic basis of imperialism – state-monopoly capital – in the imperialist countries. This is a task for the revolutionary working class of these countries to accomplish. Further, it is the international working class movement and the socialist camp which ensure the success of national liberation.

The Chinese view of the focal points of contradictions is again wrong and contrary to Marxism-Leninism. The National Council is of the opinion that the focal points are precisely those where the main contradictions of our epoch are being resolved – that is, the contradictions between capitalism and socialism. These are being resolved, first and foremost where the most organized and powerful forces of socialism stand face to face with the forces of imperialism. This means that the contradictions between the world socialist system and the world capitalist system are focal points, if one would prefer this description. The line of the C.P.C. seeks to replace the social class standpoint by a geopolitical approach. The National Council naturally rejects this view of the Chinese leaders.

The National Council notes the new proposition of the so-called 'intermediate zone' which the Chinese leaders have advanced. At the very outset, the Council considers it necessary to point out that such a concept does not find even a mention in the Moscow Declaration and the Moscow Statement.

The Chinese leaders put the U.S.A. in one bracket and all the other imperialist powers, advanced capitalist countries and the newly liberated nations in another bracket to describe them as constituting the so-called 'intermediate zone'. This is a perverse and politically misleading picture of the present-day world. No one will deny the inter-imperialist contradictions between the U.S.A. and other imperialist powers, nor the U.S. designs of world domination. But it is highly misleading to present the other imperialist powers as if they are mere objects of such designs of the U.S. imperialists.

. . . The Chinese concept of 'intermediate zone' is liable to lead to an under-estimation of dangers posed by the imperialist blocs and to the blunting of vigilance against them. This thesis of the C.P.C. underplays the neo-colonialism of Britain, France, West Germany, Japan and so on. It underplays the grave threat arising from the revenge-seeking West German imperialism to which the Moscow Statement draws particular attention. The National Council cannot accept this wholly wrong and harmful thesis of 'intermediate zone'.

In this connexion, the National Council cannot but point out that, while inventing an unrealistic and harmful thesis about the so-called 'intermediate zone', the Chinese leaders and the 14 June Letter do not say a word about the vast peace zone, comprised of the socialist countries and the non-aligned, newly liberated nations pursuing the broad policy of anti-imperialism and anti-colonialism in the world arena. Their contributions are highly appraised by the Moscow Declaration and the Moscow Statement but the C.P.C. leaders seem to have written them off.

3. *The Struggle of the Communist Party of the Soviet Union for the Unity of the International Communist Movement*

Extracts from Suslov's report to the Plenum of the Central Committee of the Communist Party of the Soviet Union, on 14 February 1964, published in April of the same year under the above title. This report was the starting-point for the ideological offensive against the Chinese communists which was launched in the spring of 1964 in the Soviet press.[1]

. . . The radical changes that took place in the world after the Second World War are linked chiefly with the rise and development of a world system of socialism. The countries of the socialist commonwealth are the main bulwark of all the revolutionary forces of modern times, a reliable champion of the cause of world peace. The struggle between world socialism and world imperialism is the principal content of our epoch, the pivot of the class struggle on a world scale.

[1] SOURCE: *O bor'be za splochennost' mezhdunarodnogo kommunisticheskogo dvizheniya. Doklad na plenume Ts.KKPSS, 14 fevralya 1964 goda.* Politizdat. 1964.

There was a time when the Chinese leaders subscribed to this major proposition of Marxism-Leninism. Lately, however, the C.P.C. leadership have been setting up the national-liberation movement against the socialist system and the working-class movement in the capitalist countries, proclaiming it as the main force in the struggle against imperialism and undermining the unity of the revolutionary forces of modern times. . . .

An editorial article carried by *Jen-min jih-pao* and *Hung-ch'i* on 22 October 1963, states: 'The national-liberation revolutions in Asia, Africa and Latin America are the most important forces dealing imperialism direct blows.'[1]

This clearly revises the Marxist teaching on the historical role of the working class and belittles the working-class movement in the developed capitalist countries. As regards the world socialist system, the Chinese theoreticians apportion to it only the role of a 'strongpoint' for supporting and developing the revolution of the oppressed nations and peoples of the whole world. . . .

This interpretation of the role and significance of the world socialist system does not conform with the actual balance of forces in the world and directly contradicts the conclusions drawn by the fraternal parties in their Statement of 1960.

The idea that modern world development is based on the contradiction between socialism and capitalism belongs to V. I. Lenin. He said: '. . . the relations between peoples and the entire world system of states are determined by the struggle of a small group of imperialist nations against the Soviet movement and the Soviet states headed by Soviet Russia. If we lose sight of that we shall be unable correctly to formulate a single national or colonial question, even if it concerned the most remote corner of the world. Only by proceeding from this standpoint can the communist parties correctly formulate and resolve political problems both in the civilized and in the backward countries.'[2]

This was said during the early years of Soviet power. In our day, when instead of only one socialist state there is a mighty socialist camp, its influence on 'the relations between peoples', on 'the entire world system of states' and, in the final analysis, on the world revolutionary process, has grown tremendously.

Attaching the utmost significance to the national-liberation movement, Marxist-Leninists at the same time hold that the main content, the main trend and the main features of the historical development of human society in the modern epoch are determined by the world socialist system, by the forces struggling against imperialism, for the socialist reorganization of society. The most organized class forces, primarily the bulk of the working class, the most advanced class of modern society which, as our teachers –

[1] See Text XII 1 above, p. 321.
[2] *Sochineniya*, vol. XXXI, p. 216 (note by Suslov).

Marx, Engels and Lenin – pointed out, is the grave-digger of capitalism, are concentrated at this very bridge-head.

The prime role of the world revolutionary process is played by the socialist countries. . . .

What is the attitude of the C.P.C. leadership towards Lenin's conclusion that socialist countries influence the development of the world revolution mainly by their economic achievements? Do the C.P.C. leaders stand for peaceful economic competition?

The C.P.C. leadership, misrepresenting the issue, tries to argue that economic competition means that 'the oppressed peoples and nations have no need at all to fight and to rise in revolt . . .', and that 'they have merely to wait quietly until the Soviet Union outstrips the most developed capitalist country in level of production and standard of living. . . '.

It would never occur to a Marxist-Leninist, however, to affirm that peaceful economic competition 'can take the place of the struggle of the peoples of different countries for their emancipation', or that the achievements of socialism in economic competition will lead to the 'automatic' collapse of capitalism and release the peoples from the necessity of waging class and national-liberation struggles. . . . The fact is that Marxist-Leninists see the revolutionizing effect of the victories of socialism in economic competition precisely in the fact that these victories stimulate the class struggle of the working people and make them conscious fighters for socialism. Not only does peaceful economic competition not doom the people to waiting passively, but it arouses their revolutionary activity.

Questions of War, Peace and Revolution

Facts show that time and again the C.P.R. government has come forward in the world arena as a force opposing the peaceful foreign policy of the socialist countries and disorganizing the common anti-war front. It has happened time and again that when the world has been faced with an acute situation in which unity of action among the socialist countries and all peace-loving forces was particularly imperative, the Chinese leaders have become active. But against whom? Against the Soviet Union and other socialist countries seeking a relaxation of tension. Moreover, it has been noted that Peking has been unable to conceal its irritation and annoyance every time the situation has been restored to normal and a military conflict avoided. This was the case, for example, during the Caribbean crisis. . . .

It is a fact that when the Caribbean crisis was at its height the C.P.R. government extended the armed conflict on the Sino-Indian frontier. . . .

While allowing relations with India, which as everyone knows is not a member of military blocs, to deteriorate sharply, the

Chinese leadership at the same time actually entered into league with Pakistan, a member of S.E.A.T.O. and C.E.N.T.O., which are threatening the peace and security of the Asian peoples. It is a fact that having discarded their 'revolutionary phrase - mongering' the Chinese leaders have in reality adopted a line that is hard to reconcile with the principled position of the countries of the socialist commonwealth with regard to imperialist blocs. . . .

The essence of the C.P.C. leadership's present concepts of the problem of revolution consists in the rejection of the Leninist teaching of the socialist revolution as being the result of a mass struggle by the people, in relying solely on armed uprisings everywhere and in all cases without taking any account of the mood of the masses, their preparedness for revolution, without taking into account the internal and external situation. . . . Has this kind of action anything in common with Marxism-Leninism and is this not the popularization of long-since rejected Blanquist and Trotskyite ideas? . . .

The C.P.C. Leaders' Policy of Isolating the National-Liberation Movement from the International Working Class

. . . It is particularly typical of the Chinese leaders that they completely ignore the immense variety of conditions prevailing in the countries of Asia, Africa and Latin America. . . .

Marxist-Leninists consider that the main tasks of the former colonies where the political rule of the imperialists is done with – and these countries constitute a majority – are to strengthen the independence achieved, uproot colonial practices in their economy and develop it at a fast rate, achieve economic independence, and follow the road of social and economic progress. Among the primary general national problems are the expulsion of foreign monopolies, the implementation of agrarian reforms in the interests of the peasants, the promotion of a national industry, above all by setting up a state sector, and the democratization of social and political life. In a number of countries, conditions are already being created, as these tasks are fulfilled, for development along non-capitalist lines, for taking the socialist road. . . .

Marxist-Leninists have always supported armed risings against the colonialists and tyrannical régimes, and have supported the liberation wars of oppressed peoples. But they have always opposed standardized tactics based on the dogmatic use of one given form of struggle, irrespective of the actual conditions. Such tactics are particularly harmful now that in most of the Asian, African and Latin American countries national governments have come to power that are pursuing an anti-imperialist policy. In these circumstances, to advance the slogan of armed struggle as a universal method means causing double harm, disorienting the forces of national liberation and distracting them from the struggle against imperialism.

After all, it is absurd to say that the working people of Algeria, Ghana, Mali and certain other countries are faced with the task of starting an armed revolt. Such an idea amounts to an appeal to back the reactionaries, who are intent on overthrowing the governments of those countries. And what else but harm can one expect from an attempt to put this idea into effect in such countries as, for example, Indonesia or Ceylon? . . .

In the question of the prospects of the historical development of the liberated countries the Chinese leaders oppose such cardinal principles of the communist movement as Lenin's thesis on the possibility of a non-capitalist way of development for the liberated countries.

Speaking at the Moscow bilateral meeting in July 1963, Teng Hsiao-p'ing, Secretary-General of the Central Committee of the Chinese Communist Party, said outright that the thesis of the non-capitalist path was 'meaningless talk', although every communist knows that this thesis was put forward by V. I. Lenin and has been borne out by the experience of a number of peoples that in the past were colonial.

The idea of the non-capitalist path is gaining ground among the peoples of Asia, Africa and Latin America, and for the peoples of a number of countries it has become a call for practical action. This is a tremendous achievement for socialism! Capitalism has discredited itself in the eyes of the peoples, and the appeal of socialist ideas in the newly-free countries is so strong that the advanced forces and national leaders of many countries advocate taking the socialist path and are taking practical steps in this direction, counting with good reason on support from the socialist countries and the Marxist-Leninist parties. . . .

But the C.P.C. leaders do not confine themselves to slander. In the steps they take officially and in various world democratic organizations, they concentrate not on furthering the unity of the anti-imperialist forces but on the struggle against the U.S.S.R. and other socialist countries. That was how Chinese delegates behaved, in particular, at the Afro-Asian Solidarity Conference in Moshi.

At the Conference, Liu Ning-i, head of the Chinese delegation, said in an interview with our delegates: 'East European countries should not interfere in Asian and African affairs. . . . We regret the fact that you came here at all. Who wants you here? It is an insult to the solidarity movement of the Afro-Asian countries. . . . You may do as you will, but we will be against you.' The Chinese delegates at that Conference suggested to Asian and African delegates that since Russians, Czechs and Poles are whites, 'they cannot be trusted', that they would 'always come to terms with the American whites', and that the peoples of Asia and Africa had special interests of their own and must form their own separate associations.

Lately, the Chinese leaders have virtually begun to form separate (trade union, journalistic, writers', student, sports, etc.) organizations, which they plan to set up against the World Federation of Trade Unions and other international associations.

In the light of the practical activities of the Chinese leaders in recent years, the true political meaning of their slogan – 'The East wind is beginning to prevail over the West wind' – has become particularly clear. It will be recalled that at the meeting of 1960 this slogan was sharply criticized as a nationalist slogan substituting a geographic, even racial, approach for the class approach. It is clearly an attempt to minimize the role of the world socialist system, the working class and the peoples of Western Europe and America.

. . . The Chinese leaders are counting on being able to set the peoples of the former colonies and semi-colonies against the socialist countries and the working people of the developed capitalist countries, and on representing themselves as the sole defenders of the interests of these peoples. For, if we are to expose the secret design behind the Chinese slogan and reveal the far-reaching aim of the C.P.C. leaders, it is as follows: China, according to them, is the largest country of the East, it embodies the interests of the East, and it is here that the 'winds of history' spring up that are to 'prevail over' the winds 'from the West'.

In other words, this slogan is nothing but the ideological and political expression of the Chinese leadership's aspirations for hegemony. . . .

4. Extracts from Kuusinen's Speech at the February 1964 Plenum of the Central Committee of the Communist Party of the Soviet Union

This text was published in *Pravda* in May 1964, after the death of Otto Kuusinen, who had been one of Stalin's oldest comrades and had been responsible for many theoretical texts both before and after Stalin's disappearance. This text merits particular attention both because of the personality of the author, and because of the extreme position adopted, which casts doubt not only on the specificity of the revolution in the East, but on certain fundamental postulates of Leninism.[1]

Comrades, seeing that the erroneous, anti-Marxist position adopted by the Chinese leadership has already been extensively covered in Comrade M. A. Suslov's report, may I be permitted to deal with one question only, namely the nature of the dictatorship that now exists in China?

Nobody, of course, is in any doubt that there is a dictatorship in China. But what sort of dictatorship is it?

[1] SOURCE: *Pravda*, 19 May 1964.

It is essential to have a precise understanding on this point for reasons both of theoretical principle and of practice. For the question of the dictatorship of the proletariat is one of the fundamental questions of Marxism-Leninism. It serves as a gauge of a communist party's attitude towards the various classes of society. . . .

The Chinese leaders themselves give a deliberately confused definition of the dictatorship that they have established. In the period immediately following the victory of the revolution they defined their state system as 'a democratic dictatorship of the people'. The term 'the people' was understood to mean the working class, the peasantry, the petty bourgeoisie and the national bourgeoisie.

According to the explanation of Mao Tse-tung, China's state system was a dictatorship of *an alliance of all these classes*. Mao Tse-tung repeatedly stressed during those years that there was a difference of principle between this Chinese 'dictatorship of the people' and the dictatorship of the proletariat as always understood by Marxists.

He need hardly have bothered to say this! Even an inexpert eye could see that his theoretical hypothesis had nothing in common with Marxism-Leninism. In Marxist theory there never has been, nor is there now, any such concept as 'the dictatorship of the people'. This expression has an odour strongly reminiscent of petty bourgeois revolutionary phraseology. It smacks particularly of the kind of language favoured by the *Narodnaya Volya* and Socialist Revolutionaries of old Russia.

Had the Chinese leaders wanted to define in Leninist terms the class nature of their state system during the period immediately following the victory of the revolution, they could have spoken, for example, of a revolutionary-democratic dictatorship of the working class and peasantry developing, under the leadership of the working class, into a dictatorship of the proletariat. Such a form of dictatorship would have left them sufficient scope in actual practice for attracting representatives of the loyal strata of the national bourgeoisie to play a part in this or that organ of power. But for some reason (we shall see why later), Mao Tse-tung found it necessary to hail China's national bourgeoisie as a class that bears the functions of dictatorship. This, then, is the crux of the matter!

Somewhat later, however, the Peking leaders were obliged to consider improving upon their definition of the dictatorship in China, which was a patent revision of Marxism. 'Our state,' said Mao Tse-tung this time, 'is a democratic dictatorship of the people, led by the working class and founded on an alliance of the workers and peasants.'

This already sounded better. There was now a reference to the leading function of the working class. But the comments which followed again spoiled the whole tune: '*Who exercises dictatorship?*' asked Mao Tse-tung. And he replied, 'The working class, of course, and the people that it leads, all people having civil rights, united by the working class, and primarily the peasants, exercise dictatorship over the reactionary classes. . . .'[1]

One wonders – surely the national bourgeoisie in China possesses civil rights? Yes, of course it does; at least this is true for the vast majority. It therefore follows from Mao Tse-tung's statement that the vast majority of the Chinese national bourgeoisie exercises dictatorship in the country together with the workers and the peasants. Thus Mao Tse-tung's new, amended formula retains his former little opportunist idea. And the meaning of this idea is that after winning power the working classes cannot exercise dictatorship alone but must share it with the national bourgeoisie.

One might ask why the Chinese leaders, these ultra-revolutionaries, show such great concern for the rights of the bourgeoisie. Who can know for sure? But it is very probable that they are counting on this making it easier for them to flirt with the bourgeois nationalists in other countries, and particularly the bourgeois of Chinese nationality in various parts of Asia and Africa. March with us – the Peking leaders seem to be saying to these elements – and we shall make it our business to give you an honourable place in the system of dictatorship which we have invented.

The decisive question, however, in evaluating China's state system is the role assigned there to the working class. We have seen that on paper the Chinese leaders have now recognized not only the proletariat's participation but its leadership in the Chinese 'dictatorship of the people', although they have done so in a most general and abstract form. But what is the situation in reality?

It must be noted that, in the system of state power, the Chinese working class does not in reality occupy the place assigned to it by Marxism-Leninism. And furthermore, the policy of the Chinese leaders towards the urban proletariat bears the stamp of distrust and alienation. It is difficult to rid oneself of the impression that the leaders of the Chinese Communist Party somehow fear an increase in the influence of the working class. This has been fully apparent primarily in its attitude towards the Chinese trade unions. Attempts of the trade unions to attract attention to the legitimate demands of the workers, to the need for some improve-

[1] All of these quotations are from Mao's essay 'On People's Democratic Dictatorship', published in July 1949, which is likewise the source of the ideas which Kuusinen describes earlier as having been put forward 'immediately following the victory of the revolution'. It is not apparent why he thus broke up a single text and described part of it as an 'amended formula' invented by Mao 'somewhat later'. Perhaps he had read the essay only in bits and pieces quoted by other writers, and did not know they came from the same source.

ment in their financial situation, have been resolutely cut short by the leaders of the C.P.C. This perfectly normal trade union activity has been branded as a manifestation of the dangerous 'deviations' of 'economism' and 'syndicalism'.

Instead of the working masses being trained in class consciousness and to understand their lofty historical mission as the builders and leading force of the new society, the workers in China are being asked simply for blind submission. It is impressed upon them that they should content themselves with the dumb role of 'little cogs'. The Chinese leaders see their chief support and all of their political hopes in the peasantry and not in the working class.

This wrong, in fact negligent, approach of the C.P.C. leadership to the development of the workers' movement in their country is not something new. In its time it provoked justified criticism by the Communist International. I am far from thinking that all the decisions of the Comintern, including those on the Chinese question, have always been faultless. But on this important question of principle the Comintern was a hundred per cent correct.

Exaggeration of the role of the peasantry in the socialist revolution and simultaneous underestimation of the role and possibilities of the working class which, from the point of view of Marxism, is the only class in society that is revolutionary through and through – are typical of this system of petty-bourgeois views which is being intensely disseminated in China. Even during the period prior to the accession to power, the leaders of the Communist Party of China did not pay due attention to the proletarian stratum within the party's ranks, and did little work among the urban proletariat. And later the Chinese leaders complained that, for example, in such an important working-class centre as Shanghai the Kuomintang was more influential than the Communist Party, and blamed the workers for this.

The extent to which the Chinese leaders prefer the revolutionary potential of the peasantry can also be judged from the testimony of such a passionate propagandist of the Chinese régime as the American journalist Anna Louise Strong. In her book she says, for instance, that Liu Shao-ch'i, in conversation with her, praised to the skies the revolutionary strength of the 'peasant lads', who were superior to any proletarian revolutionary. According to Liu Shao-ch'i, 'Marx never knew men like these. . . . They are even more disciplined and dedicated than the industrial proletariat.'

Of course, the Chinese peasantry embarked with great ardour on the revolutionary struggle to throw off the feudal yoke and to achieve national liberation. But what Marxist-Leninist would on these grounds set the peasantry in opposition to the working class, belittle the revolutionary potential of the proletariat and, moreover, 'correct' Marx on the subject?

However, in order not to display openly their break with

Marxist theory, the Chinese leaders prattle about the participation and the leadership of the proletariat in the Chinese dictatorship. But in precisely what form this role of the proletariat is expressed in Chinese conditions – this they are unable to explain. On the contrary, the facts show that the Chinese working class is now in a disenfranchised, not to say disastrous, state. But in stating this fact, I do not doubt for one moment that the glorious Chinese working class will, in the future course of the revolution, fight successfully for its vital rights, for the leading role which the laws of history have cast for it.

In order to get out of the difficult situation in which they have placed themselves as a result of their crude distortions of Lenin's teaching on the dictatorship of the proletariat, the Chinese leaders and propagandists are resorting to the following most naïve explanation: since we have a Communist Party, and since, in the final analysis, it is the party that settles all of the country's important affairs, then, by the same token, both the leadership and the dictatorship of the working class are being implemented. Mao Tse-tung wrote that the 'democratic dictatorship of the people' established in China 'is led by the working class *through the Communist party*'. And Liu Shao-ch'i, in his report to the Eighth Congress of the C.P.C., stressed that with the formation of the Chinese People's Republic 'the Chinese Communist Party has become a ruling political party, and the democratic dictatorship of the people has become in reality one of the forms of the *dictatorship of the proletariat*'.[1] The leadership and dictatorship of the proletariat have here been actually equated with the leadership of the Communist Party. Is this correct?

No, it is not correct. The Chinese leaders completely forget great Lenin's teaching to the effect that by no means every party that calls itself communist is really the vanguard and recognized leader of the working class. According to Lenin's teaching, it can be a genuine vanguard of the working class only if it pursues a correct policy consonant with the interests of the proletariat, and if it is closely linked with the proletariat, shares the proletariat's life, trusts it and enjoys its absolute trust. These stipulations made by Lenin apply not only to the communist parties of the old capitalist countries but to those of colonial and semi-colonial countries where a working class exists. Lenin included China among such countries.

Do those at the top of the Chinese Party heed Lenin's stipulations here? No, they do not. As I have already said, the Chinese leaders do not trust the working class, disregard its interests and ask of it only uncomplaining obedience. Not without reason has the Central Committee of the C.P.C. recently been thrusting upon

[1] For this passage in Liu's report see *Eighth National Congress of The Communist Party of China* (Peking, Foreign Languages Press, 1956), vol. I, p. 19.

the workers' collectives and trade unions certain slogans typical of militarized organizations such as: 'Politics is the commanding force', 'The Secretary of the Party Committee is the production commander', etc. The All-China Conference on Industrial Questions, held in Peking early in 1964, called on all workers 'to learn from the People's Liberation Army'. Thus the line that the leaders of the C.P.C. are pursuing towards the working class is not to persuade the workers but barefacedly to demand obedience and military discipline. What chance is there here for the proletariat to fulfil its leading role?

On the most important international questions, too, Peking's policy is incorrect, non-Marxist, and is not the policy of proletarian internationalism. Does a policy that is rife with great-power aspirations, that substitutes chauvinism for proletarian internationalism and puts the policy of undermining and splitting the unity of the socialist countries and the world communist movement before that of strengthening that unity – does such a policy conform with the interests of the Chinese proletariat? The leaders of a party which pursues such a nationalistic policy simply cannot be deemed to be expressing the will of the working class.

For this reason the Chinese C.P. cannot be considered the genuine vanguard of the working class, capable of really fulfilling the proletariat's leading role.

In actual fact there is at present no dictatorship of the people in China, no dictatorship of the proletariat, and the proletariat has no leading role and the party no vanguard role. The pseudo-Marxist terminology used by the Chinese leaders is all mere camouflage to hide the real nature of the dictatorship that exists there. This is dictatorship by the leaders or, more precisely, *personal dictatorship*.

The Party leaders have in fact shaken off all control by the Party. It is many years now since the C.P.C. last held congresses and the party's representative organs are to an increasing extent playing a merely decorative role. The Chinese leaders have also consigned to oblivion the decision of the Communist International which back in 1926 required the C.P.C. to 'steadfastly pursue *collective leadership* within the party, from the C.C. down to the factory and street cells'.

It is significant too that in attacking our party's programme the C.P.C. leaders turn with particular fury upon the provisions which envisage the utmost development of intra-party and Soviet democracy and the increasing participation of the workers in the management of the state. In China, democracy is either not mentioned at all or formal lip-service is paid to it. And this is not surprising! Socialist democracy is a flower that will not grow in the shadow of the personality cult. . . .

SECTION XIII: RECENT TENDENCIES

1. On Khrushchev's Phoney Communism and its Historical Lessons for the World

Extracts from the Ninth Chinese reply to the Soviet letter of 14 July 1963, dated 13 July 1964. (See above the introductory paragraph to Text XII 1.) This article is remarkable not only for the violence with which it denounces the betrayal of the Soviet 'new class', but above all for the affirmation that it will require two or three centuries, even in China, in order to transform human nature in the direction required for a communist society. In a sense, this text may be regarded as the starting-point for the current 'Great Proletarian Cultural Revolution'.[1]

. . . Going forward to communism means moving towards the abolition of all classes and class differences. A communist society which preserves any classes at all, let alone exploiting classes, is inconceivable. Yet Khrushchev is fostering a new bourgeoisie, restoring and extending the system of exploitation and accelerating class polarization in the Soviet Union. A privileged bourgeois stratum opposed to the Soviet people now occupies the ruling position in the party and government and in the economic, cultural and other departments. Can one find an iota of communism in all this? . . .

Going forward to communism means moving towards enhancing the communist consciousness of the popular masses. A communist society with bourgeois ideas running rampant is inconceivable. Yet Khrushchev is zealously reviving bourgeois ideology in the Soviet Union and serving as a missionary for decadent American culture. By propagating material incentives, he is turning all human relations into money relations and encouraging individualism and selfishness. Because of him, manual labour is again considered sordid and love of pleasure at the expense of other people's labour is again considered honourable. Certainly, the social ethics and customs promoted by Khrushchev are far removed from communism, as far as far can be. . . .

Khrushchev's 'communism' is in essence a variant of bourgeois socialism. He does not regard communism as completely abolishing classes and class differences but describes it as 'a bowl accessible to all and brimming with the products of physical and mental labour'. He does not regard the struggle of the working class for communism as a struggle for the thorough emancipation of all

[1] SOURCE: *Hung-ch'i*, no. 13, 1964, pp. 23–32. With a few minor changes, we have taken over the translation published in *Peking Review*, no. 29, 17 July 1964, pp. 21–6.

mankind as well as itself but describes it as a struggle for 'a good dish of goulash'. There is not an iota of scientific communism in his heart, but only the image of a society of bourgeois philistines. . . .

There is nothing new about such 'communism'. It is simply another name for capitalism. . . .

It is thus easily understandable why Khrushchev's 'communism' is appreciated by imperialism and monopoly capital. The U.S. Secretary of State, Dean Rusk, has said:

> . . . to the extent that goulash and the second pair of trousers and questions of that sort become more important in the Soviet Union, I think to that extent a moderating influence has come into the present scene.

We would advise the imperialist lords not to be happy too soon. Notwithstanding all the services of the revisionist Khrushchev clique, nothing can save imperialism from its doom. The revisionist ruling clique suffer from the same kind of disease as the imperialist ruling clique; they are extremely antagonistic to the masses of the people who comprise over ninety per cent of the world's population, and therefore they, too, are weak and powerless and are paper tigers. Like the clay Buddha that tried to wade across the river, the revisionist Khrushchev clique cannot even save themselves, so how can they endow imperialism with long life? . . .

Is our society today thoroughly clean? No, it is not. Classes and class struggles still remain, the activities of the overthrown reactionary classes plotting a comeback still continue, and we still have speculative activities by old and new bourgeois elements and desperate forays by embezzlers, grafters and degenerates. There are also cases of degeneration in a few primary organizations; what is more, these degenerates do their utmost to find protectors and agents in the higher leading bodies. We should not in the least slacken our vigilance against such phenomena but must keep fully alert. . . .

How can the restoration of capitalism be prevented? On this question Comrade Mao Tse-tung has formulated a set of theories and policies, after summing up the practical experience of the dictatorship of the proletariat in China and studying the positive and negative experience of other countries, mainly of the Soviet Union, in accordance with the basic principles of Marxism-Leninism, and has thus enriched and developed the Marxist-Leninist theory of the dictatorship of the proletariat.

The main contents of the theories and policies advanced by Comrade Mao Tse-tung in this connexion are as follows:

First, it is necessary to apply the Marxist-Leninist law of the unity of opposites to the study of socialist society. The law of contradiction in all things, i.e., the law of the unity of opposites, is the fundamental law of materialist dialectics. It operates everywhere, whether in the natural world, in human society, or in human thought. The opposites in a contradiction both unite and struggle with each other, and it is this that forces things to move and change. Socialist society is no exception. . . .

Second, socialist society covers a very long historical period. Classes and class struggle continue to exist in this society, and the struggle still goes on between the socialist road and the capitalist road. The socialist revolution on the economic front (in the ownership of the means of production) is insufficient by itself and cannot be consolidated. There must also be a thorough socialist revolution on the political and ideological fronts. Here a very long period of time is needed to decide 'who will win' in the struggle between socialism and capitalism. Several decades won't do it; success requires anywhere from one to several centuries. On the question of duration, it is better to prepare for a longer rather than a shorter period of time. On the question of effort, it is better to regard the task as difficult rather than easy. . . . During the historical period of socialism it is necessary to maintain the dictatorship of the proletariat and carry the socialist revolution through to the end if the restoration of capitalism is to be prevented, socialist construction carried forward and the conditions created for the transition to communism.

Third, the dictatorship of the proletariat is led by the working class, with the worker-peasant alliance as its basis. This means the exercise of dictatorship by the working class and by the people under its leadership over the reactionary classes and individuals and those elements who oppose socialist transformation and socialist construction. Within the ranks of the people democratic centralism is practised. Ours is the broadest democracy beyond the bounds of possibility for any bourgeois state.

Fourth, in both socialist revolution and socialist construction it is necessary to adhere to the mass line, boldly to arouse the masses and to unfold mass movements on a large scale. . . .

Fifth, whether in socialist revolution or in socialist construction, it is necessary to solve the question of whom to rely on, whom to win over and whom to oppose. The proletariat and its vanguard must make a class analysis of socialist society, rely on the truly dependable forces that firmly take the socialist road, win over all allies that can be won over, and unite with the masses of the people, who constitute more than ninety-five per cent of the population, in a common struggle against the enemies of socialism. . . .

In the light of the historical lessons of the dictatorship of the proletariat Comrade Mao Tse-tung has stated:

Class struggle, the struggle for production and scientific experiment are the three great revolutionary movements for building a mighty socialist country. These movements are a sure guarantee that communists will be free from bureaucracy and immune against revisionism and dogmatism, and will forever remain invincible. They are a reliable guarantee that the proletariat will be able to unite with the broad working masses and realize a democratic dictatorship. If, in the absence of these movements, the landlords, rich peasants, counter-revolutionaries, bad elements and ogres of all kinds were allowed to crawl out, while our cadres were to shut their eyes to all this and in many cases fail even to differentiate between the enemy and ourselves but were to collaborate with the enemy and become corrupted, divided and demoralized, if our cadres were thus dragged into the enemy camp or the enemy were able to sneak into our ranks, and if many of our workers, peasants, and intellectuals were left defenceless against both the soft and the hard tactics of the enemy, then it would not take long, perhaps only several years or a decade, or several decades at most, before a counter-revolutionary restoration on a national scale inevitably occurred, the Marxist-Leninist party would undoubtedly become a revisionist party or a fascist party, and the whole of China would change its colour.[1]

Comrade Mao Tse-tung has pointed out that, in order to guarantee that our party and country do not change their colour, we must not only have a correct line and correct policies but must train and bring up millions of successors who will carry on the cause of proletarian revolution.

In the final analysis, the question of training successors for the revolutionary cause of the proletariat is one of whether or not there will be people who can carry on the Marxist-Leninist revolutionary cause started by the older generation of proletarian revolutionaries, whether or not the leadership of our party and state will remain in the hands of proletarian revolutionaries, whether or not our descendants will continue to march along the correct road laid down by Marxism-Leninism, or, in other words, whether or not we can successfully prevent the emergence of Khrushchevite revisionism in China. In short, it is an extremely important question, a matter of life and death for our Party and our country. It is a question of fundamental importance to the proletarian revolutionary cause for a hundred, a thousand, nay ten thousand years. Basing themselves on the changes in the Soviet Union, the imperialist prophets are pinning their hopes of 'peaceful evolution' on the third or fourth generation of the Chinese Party. We must

[1] A footnote to the editorial attributes this quotation to Mao's 'Note on the Seven Well-Written Documents of Chekiang Province Regarding Participation by Cadres in Productive Labour', dated 9 May 1963. An editorial in no. 10, 1967, of *Hung-ch'i* attributes a portion of this quotation to a Draft Decision of the Central Committee of the Chinese Communist Party on Rural Work elaborated under Mao's direction in May 1963, and cites an additional sentence. The full text of this decision, commonly known as the 'Early ten points', is to be found in R. Baum and F. C. Teiwes, *Ssu-ch'ing. The Socialist Education Movement of 1962–66* (University of California, Center for Chinese Studies, 1968), pp. 58–71.

shatter these imperialist prophecies. From our highest organizations down to the grass-roots, we must everywhere give constant attention to the training and upbringing of successors to the revolutionary cause.

2. *On the Necessity for a Realistic Analysis of the Revolution in the Developing Countries*

The following document represents the conclusion of the debates which took place in the spring of 1964 at the Institute of International Relations (Moscow). Five years ago, the positions expressed in the course of these discussions appeared to reflect the thinking of a few isolated theoreticians. The evolution which has taken place in the last five years has shown that regarding the evaluation of the national liberation movements, and of various socialist doctrines, the debates of 1964 marked the starting-point for the subsequent ideological developments in the U.S.S.R.[1]

Numerous interesting and often new questions were raised during the discussion and even more new approaches to 'old' problems were found. Moreover the most important thing is that the problems discussed here are of quite recent origin and as yet lack definition. It is considerably more complicated to answer these questions and evaluate them scientifically than to analyse phenomena and events established over a great number of years. . . .

National-liberation revolutions in the great majority of countries have not yet developed into socialist revolutions, and most of them are at the national-democratic stage. This stage is bourgeois-democratic in its socio-economic content. But in the scope of their tasks national-democratic revolutions exceed the limits of classical bourgeois-democratic revolution. In contemporary conditions they differ from both in their tasks and in their motive forces. The fundamental task of bourgeois-democratic revolution in the independent countries has been to overthrow absolutism. But it is not only bourgeois-democratic problems that are resolved in the course of the development of national-liberation revolutions. Their aim is to overthrow domination by imperialism, to win national independence, to resolve the agrarian problem in a revolutionary manner, to break the colonial economic structure and attain economic independence, and to democratize the whole of socio-political life. The revolution is thus national and democratic in character. Its class content is far from exhausted when it has met the demands of the bourgeoisie. It goes beyond this. And even when the bourgeoisie comes to power, it is unable to keep the revolution within capitalist bounds. Having entered the move-

[1] SOURCE: *Mirovaya Ekonomika i Mezhdunarodniye Otnosheniya*, no. 6, 1964, pp. 77–82 (summing up by V. Tyagunenko).

ment, the popular masses do not stop until the anti-imperialist, anti-feudal, democratic revolution is carried through to its conclusion. But the accomplishment of these tasks is inevitably directed against capitalism. At the same time the national-liberation movement does not yet set up for itself as its prime task the socialist reconstruction of society.

It must not be imagined that the development of these revolutions must of necessity follow a steady course, without ups and downs. To present the situation this way is to pass off the desirable for the actual.

In certain speeches the idea cropped up that in the main the tasks of the bourgeois-democratic revolutions have been resolved, and that these countries were now faced with socialist revolutions. One can hardly agree with such a view.

Such an approach could lead us to look too far ahead, a danger which often lies in wait for us when we study present-day national-liberation revolutions.

Quite recently, some four or five years ago, the view was current in our literature that in the majority of former colonies and semi-colonies it was the national bourgeoisie who had installed itself in power. No distinction was made as to which strata of the bourgeoisie it was who were in power. The expression 'the national bourgeoisie' covered representatives of the middle and even the big industrial bourgeoisie, who share power with land-owners and feudal elements, and the petty and middle commercial bourgeoisie and even the petty-bourgeois intelligentsia. From this it was concluded that in the countries where there were representatives of the bourgeoisie the prerequisites existed for the accelerated development of capitalism and that further revolutionary development was possible only if the working class took over leadership of the movement. Where there was no hegemony of the working class, it was essential to struggle to achieve it; and where, in the author's opinion, it did exist, socialist revolution could be accomplished at any moment.

In extending these deductions to all the former colonies and semi-colonies, their authors were in fact denying the real possibility of intermediate stages of development in the national-democratic revolution, rejecting the possibility of the revolution deepening under the leadership of non-proletarian strata – revolutionary democrats, progressive intelligentsia, etc. . . . However, life has toppled these theories.

The idea of the possibility of a non-capitalist stage of development in national-democratic revolutions and of the creation of a state of national democracy as a political form of non-capitalist development which was put forward at the Conference of Representatives of Communist and Workers' Parties in 1960 was an important contribution to the theory of the development of the national-liberation revolution. Events since 1960 have fully confirmed these views. . . .

One of the main characteristics of the present period is the fact that the extraordinary increase in political activity by the peoples is giving rise to an enormous variety of forms in the democratic progressive movement. The existence of a powerful socialist system and a strong international communist and working-class movement is creating the conditions for the transition from one social organization to another, not directly, but through a series of intermediate stages. It is no accident, therefore, that in the course of the development of national-democratic revolutions various forms of development for liberated countries have come into being.

This does not mean, of course, that the direct transition to socialism is impossible. In countries where a revolutionary situation exists or is rapidly being created, the working class is naturally called upon to exploit it and to take power into its own hands. But revolutionary development equally cannot come to a stop in countries where, at present, conditions do not exist for a socialist revolution. The coexistence of two world systems and the all-round influence of world socialism on the nature and prospects of the liberated countries are creating new possibilities for a gradual development of revolution, stage by stage, the possibility of non-capitalist development towards socialism.

In the liberated countries there is a complicated interplay of diverse situations and events. The social situation has not become stabilized and the balance of class forces is changing rapidly. To locate and select among these complex processes those which foster the movement of these countries along the non-capitalist path of development or their transition on to that path, to discover and analyse the forces which oppose this movement, is one of our most important tasks. It is a very serious and complex task. It is complex primarily because the development is taking place at great speed and its manifestations are very diverse and transitory – hence there is a great danger of taking a superficial view, of confusing the reality of these processes with external, superficial appearances.

A second danger, no less great, which flows from the first, consists in overestimating one set of factors and underestimating another . . . , underestimating the influence of the progressive forces inside these countries.

This underestimation manifests itself in the fact that we frequently fail to notice measures or events that are objectively progressive in the young states or we judge them to be reactionary simply because their authors are representatives of non-proletarian strata. Frequently we fail to see in good time the evolution in the views and actions of particular leaders of the national-liberation movement; we fail to see the changes in them and their leftward changes of direction.

A third danger threatens from another quarter, and certain comrades here have pointed it out. It consists in the fact that in all these countries, to a varying degree, a rapid development of private capitalism is taking place. Its strength must not be underestimated, for it is encouraged, and frequently openly imposed, by imperialism and its agents. Small-scale production has been and remains the economic basis of the newly independent countries. In some countries it is already commercialized, and in others it is only becoming so. Private ownership interests have begun to grow rapidly in many countries, whilst in others they are being artificially cultivated. In certain circumstances, if the development of capitalist relations is not checked, if this force is not controlled in time, it may reproduce capitalism on a large scale, and may engulf entire countries, even continents.

It seems to me, however, that it would hardly be expedient to put a total ban on the development of private capital, even in countries which have already moved further than others along the path of social progress. The public sector is not yet able to guarantee a country the necessary goods. So great is these countries' backwardness that it is necessary to use all available resources, under state control, of course, for economic development. Total prohibition of private capital might also do political damage. The revolution is at a democratic stage. This would be a sectarian policy, which might result in the defeat of the progressive forces and ultimately in the victory of imperialism. A great part of our discussion was devoted to analysing the socialist doctrines now current in the ex-colonies and semi-colonies. It was correctly emphasized that this was only a first attempt at rationalizing the ideological shifts now taking place in the minds of those who are fighting in the national-liberation movement, in their actual recognition of the greatness of Marxism-Leninism and the bankruptcy of bourgeois ideology.

The multiplicity and the rapid spread of socialist doctrines in recent years reflect the new stage reached by national-liberation revolutions and the contradictory situation which has arisen since the ex-colonies achieved independent statehood.

In the period of the struggle for political independence, the leaders of the national bourgeoisie put forward nationalist slogans which were at the time a sign of the unity of all patriotic forces and the goal for which they were struggling. However, after the elimination of the colonial régimes, the ideology of nationalism, which is essentially bourgeois, ceased to satisfy the needs of the masses. The aspiration of the workers for the further development of the revolution found expression in the advancement of new slogans, now painted in socialist colours. What these doctrines have in common is that they contain a mixture of the ideology of nationalism and non-proletarian theories of socialism, in varying proportions.

A large place in the conglomeration of socialist doctrines now in circulation is occupied by different variants of 'democratic socialism', which the local bourgeoisie is trying to adapt to the conditions of the newly-independent countries. . . . However, among socialist doctrines there are some that spring from the sincere desire of their authors to bring about radical changes in the existing socio-economic structure in the interests of the broad popular masses. The ideologues and purveyors of these doctrines are generally representatives of the peasantry, the urban petty bourgeoisie, the progressive intelligentsia and patriotic army circles.

Expressing the inherent aspiration of the majority of the population of the newly-independent countries – the peasantry – for social justice, material welfare, public forms of production and distribution, the socialist doctrines disseminated by progressive representatives of the middle strata are the ideological expression of the transitional nature of the existing socio-economic structure in these countries. In a number of cases these doctrines signify simply a determination to make the transition to socialism and not at all a recognition of new economic methods as socialist. But even when democratic transformations are declared to be socialist, the socialist doctrines reflect the transitional nature of socio-economic relations. . . .

But at present . . . when the national-democratic revolution is growing more and more profound, socialist doctrines in a number of countries are being relieved of the weight of petty-bourgeois prejudices. This unburdening is particularly actively encouraged by revolutionary practice, which, as the experience of development in the U.A.R., Burma, Algeria and Mali and certain other countries shows, precedes ideological doctrines. Not infrequently socio-economic transformations in these countries are more profound and radical than the theories which 'explain' them. This habit of theory lagging behind revolutionary practice, when theory can hardly manage to 'realign itself' and define the current situation that has been reached, when it in fact follows at the heels of the movement, is inevitable when the revolutionary struggle is led, not by representatives of the proletariat equipped with Marxist-Leninist theory, but by revolutionary democrats, whose ideology is usually eclectic. The most consistent leaders of the revolutionary-democratic movement strive not to lose touch with the revolutionary struggle of the masses, give support in one form or another to the creative initiatives of the workers, and learn from the experience of the masses in revolutionary struggle, assimilating their advanced ideology. . . .

The development of national-democratic revolutions into socialist revolutions is accompanied by the transfer of power into the hands of the most revolutionary forces of the working class and peasantry or representatives of the intelligentsia who express the interests of these classes. In order to become the movement's leader, it is necessary to organize it and create a united front of all revolutionary forces. But it is impossible to create a united front without lengthy, daily, painstaking work by the progressive forces. A sound and effective united front cannot be created merely through agreements made at the top. It must be supported by concerted action, that is to say it must be forged through mass action from below, following joint action by various class and social groups.

A united national-democratic front is created when there is a certain conjuncture of social forces. The force which becomes its leader is, of course, the one which at the given moment wields the greatest authority and influence among the broad masses. A united democratic front may be created also when hegemony does not belong to the working class. But a united democratic front cannot be created by the bourgeoisie. In present conditions unity can and must be achieved not around the bourgeoisie but with its participation.

3. *The Role of the Army in the Revolution*

Extract from a recent Soviet article on the role of classes and class struggle in the developing countries. The interest of this article lies in the fact that, even as they reaffirm the basic role of the proletariat and of its vanguard, the Communist Party, in the revolution in the developing countries, the authors have endeavoured to consider above all the reality of the social relations in these countries and the role of the political forces which actually intervene, namely of the army.[1]

The army is not a class. But it should not be thought that, since the army consists of representatives of specific classes, each man serving in it necessarily expresses the interests of the class to which he belongs. Similarly, it would be incorrect to say that the army in the developing countries automatically and entirely expresses the interests of the class that is in power. We said earlier that during the stage of the transition from colonial domination to independence, political power can become divorced from its class basis and, for a certain time, exist without directly expressing the interests of a particular class. The army in these countries represents an *incomparably more independent* force than in the advanced capitalist

[1] SOURCE: G. Mirskiy, T. Pokataieva, 'Klassy i klassovaya bor'ba v razvivayushchikhsya stranakh.' Second part of article in *Mirovaya Ekonomika i Mezhdunarodniye Otnosheniya*, no. 3, 1966, pp. 64–8.

countries. It is not simply the aggregate of a certain number of men of peasant or petty-bourgeois origin: on military service these men all acquire a new quality and merge into a new organism.

The post-war history of the countries of Asia, Africa and Latin America has not yet known a case in which even remotely serious political changes have been brought about against the will of the army, provided that it was acting unanimously. Nor has there been a case in which any other forces have removed military authorities from power – again provided that those authorities enjoyed the complete support of the army (in the Sudan in 1964 the military dictatorship was overthrown, but this was made possible only because a considerable portion of the middle and junior officers sided with the revolutionary movement). On the other hand, there have been numerous cases in which an army has imposed its will on a country which had no wish at all for military rule. Of course, the army does objectively express class interests, but these are, firstly, not necessarily the interests of a single class and, secondly, incorporated in them are the interests of the army itself as a sort of corporation or particular institution within the state.

Among the causes which have contributed to thrust the army into the forefront of political life in the developing countries we would note the following: the army is, in fact, the *only all-national institution* in a society in which the nation in the true sense of the term is passing through the formative stage and common national links are still weak (the rise of nationalism is explained in large measure by the need to develop these links). Ties of family, kinship, tribe and region still determine people's attitudes more than any feeling of belonging to a single national entity. From time immemorial people have seen the state as an organ of administrative coercion rather than a facet of national sovereignty. People have become accustomed to thinking in terms of kin, the tribe, the village, the caste, and the religious sect. The army has been an organism in which all strata of the populace, people from various regions and members of tribal and social groups, have been mingled. The army has given people a national consciousness and has been a symbol of the nation's unity, the bringer of the idea of sovereignty, and this has set it apart as a special institution within the state and has given it unique advantages. Moreover, it has been the *most modern institution in society*. Even in a backward country the army has inevitably been obliged to conform, at least to some extent, to generally-accepted modern standards and to keep itself informed about the state of military science and technology. The administration, the educational system, culture and science and, ultimately, social life – all of this could remain at a most primitive, medieval level, and yet the state could continue to exist, especially if isolated from the world outside. In all these spheres of social life it has not been essential to be the equal of other states. But for the army this has been indispensable. . . .

No one could be more sharply aware of the state's backwardness than an officer, who, in the course of his military training, has become acquainted not only with the state of affairs in the armies of other, more developed, states, but also with the state of their economies, and also their scientific and cultural achievements, as these things are inextricably bound up with each other. And to discover the causes of backwardness in a country that is under foreign control is not a very difficult matter.

The army – a modern organism that frequently contrasts with the other institutions in a backward society – moves officers who are constantly aware of this contrast to think of the need to overcome backwardness on a state-wide scale, of putting an end to domination by the colonizers and their associates, the local privileged upper-crust. In a backward society the army becomes a factor for national consolidation. Conscious of its unique situation in the state, the army begins to cultivate its role as the 'vanguard and bearer of a historical mission'. It is only one step from this to its taking upon itself the functions of *supreme arbiter*, the only 'supra-class' force, symbolizing the nation as a whole, in the stage following the achievement of independence.

But it is here that differentiation begins to take place. The senior officers, as a rule, are rooted in the 'establishment' and are concerned for its preservation, not to mention the fact that in most cases they have received their military education in the academies of the metropolitan countries, are imbued with conservative views, and are inclined to be pro-Western in orientation. The fact that their generals have originally come from the lower and middle strata is not important, as they have had time to abandon their earlier contacts long ago and to attach themselves to the privileged upper-crust of society. Conversely, the young officers hold more radical views and show dissatisfaction with stagnant, stereotyped systems and are favourably inclined towards changes. It is easy for them to establish contact with the progressive intelligentsia, with anti-imperialist and nationalistically-inclined petty-bourgeois and peasant strata.

At all events, the army carries out a *coup* wherever and whenever there are considerable social forces which are interested in making changes, but the *coup* may be staged either to the benefit of these forces, as was the case in Egypt, and in Iraq (1958), and Burma, or, on the other hand, to prevent them from growing stronger (the Sudan, 1958). The army always acts under the slogan of defending the nation's interests as a whole, and sometimes this is actually true.

Thus, in Egypt in 1952 a group of officers proved themselves representative of the will of the entire Egyptian nation, and took upon themselves the mission of ridding the country of imperialist domination and of the despotism of the land-owners and the court in circumstances in which no other force was able to do so.

In the armies of Asia and Africa, the officers, as a rule, come from the families of reasonably comfortable peasants, low-grade officials, the intelligentsia. . . . Nasser is the son of a country postman, and Ne Win the son of a small-town civil servant. According to available statistics, ninety per cent of the officers in the Syrian army come from humble backgrounds. It is not surprising that it was officers who pushed the Baa'thists in the direction of radical social transformations. . . .

All of this, however, does not mean that those who think that the army everywhere in the African and Asian countries is a democratic and revolutionary force are right. Of the fifty-one countries in Asia and Africa, it is only in a few that the army has played a revolutionary-democratic role (Egypt, Burma, Algeria, Yemen, Syria and Iraq), and in Iraq this role was very short-lived. In a very much larger number of African and Asian countries (not to mention Latin America), the army is fulfilling the function of protector of conservative, sometimes even pro-imperialist, reactionary régimes. In itself, the fact of a military *coup d'état* is no criterion of the army's revolutionary or reactionary nature. The complexity of the conditions in which the young states are becoming established renders useless any rigid blueprints and over-categorical formulae. For instance, many Iraqi officers who in July 1958 stormed the royal palace took part a few years later in a cruel, destructive war against the Kurds or in repressive measures against their former communist allies. *Nationalism is a two-edged weapon*; it has its anti-imperialist side but is also capable of being turned against the democratic forces, the clearest example of this being the present events in Indonesia.

However, it is just in this way that nationalism manifests itself in the behaviour of all middle, intermediary, petty-bourgeois strata, which, depending on circumstances, may become the foundation of revolutionary-democratic movements or the mainstay of reactionary, chauvinistic forces. This same social instability is characteristic also of the political representative of these forces – the intelligentsia. And the officers are the military intelligentsia. As a rule, this intelligentsia expresses the interests of the middle social reaches, and has the weaknesses and instability characteristic of that milieu.

4. The Basic Stages in the Development of Humanity are Everywhere the Same

Extracts from the concluding remarks of Nikiforov, one of the sceptics regarding the use of the concept of the Asiatic mode of production, at the conference on this subject held in Moscow in May 1965.[1]

I repeat: a serious scientific discussion must not be reduced to a mere quarrel about words. If it is held that a class society in which there are slaves and private property in land, and in which the oppressed are for the most part members of the commune exploited by means of state taxation – if it be held that such a society should be called the Asiatic system – then I am an 'Asiatic'. . . . But it is not merely a matter of words; we are debating questions of substance. When it is said that there is no such thing as an Asiatic system, this means that there is not and there could not arise an antagonistic society without a class of private owners of the means of production; that there could not arise a state in a society where classes had not arisen – in any case so far we are not aware of any facts regarding such a development.

The only concrete example of an 'Asiatic' society in the course of our discussions was put forward by I. L. Andreev, speaking about Mali. By 'Asiatic system' he understands the transitional period between the primitive communal system and class society. I have already said in my report that one cannot deny either the existence of such a period or the particular role played in this period by the state power, but there are no grounds for regarding this period as a particular socio-economic formation.

There is no particular form of exploitation peculiar to the transitional period from classless society to class society, and belonging to it alone, which could be distinguished from the domination of the individual by violence (which is typical of the slave-holding formation), from exploitation on the basis of a monopoly in the ownership of land (which is typical of the feudal formation), from wage labour (which is the dominant form of exploitation under capitalism). In early class society these forms develop more or less in parallel.

Which of them is the leading form? Usually it is possible to determine this only later, at a higher level of development. It is clear that during the early stages of world history there is not the accumulation of immense capital in the hands of a few individuals; in other words, the conditions for the transition to capitalism do not exist. There is not the accumulation in the hands of a few

[1] SOURCE: V. N. Nikiforov, 'Zakliuchitel'noe Slovo po Doklady', in *Obshchee i Osobennoe v Istoricheskom Razvitii Stran Vostoka* (Moscow, Izdatel 'stvo 'Nauka', 1966), pp. 236–7, 243.

individuals of great landed possessions – such being the indispensable pre-condition of feudalism. During the period of the disintegration of the primitive communal system, there is usually much free land, and land does not have great value, unlike the situation which obtains under feudalism in which land constitutes the principal form of wealth. It is the methods of direct violence, of the seizure and enslavement of individuals, which are in the foreground and by means of which certain individuals can force others to work for them, and to hand over to them the fruits of their labour. Economic dependence and economic forms of exploitation also exist, but they are in the background.

Thus it is the slave-holding tendency which predominates. It is difficult and often impossible to determine which of the three tendencies predominates under the conditions of early class society, in view of the fact that they are as yet only feebly expressed, and are still in an embryonic state.

Moreover, the simultaneous development of different class tendencies is obviously characteristic, not only for the period of the emergence of the first antagonistic class formation, but also for any antagonistic formation at the stage of its emergence. I will remind you only of the genesis of capitalist relations in Russia: as a result of the disintegration of feudal relations there developed the progressive capitalist régime, which was the leading form in these circumstances, but at the same time there was a parallel development of feudal exploitation itself which took the form of serfdom – of semi-slave and fully slave relations. Is not the process noted by L. B. Alaev in the development of the Indian community analogous to this? Is it not the same thing – the rebirth of slave forms on the eve of transition to a new formation – which we encounter in the West Indies and in other countries in the epoch of primitive accumulation? Is it not this same tendency in Russia which confused G. V. Plekhanov, who declared, as is well known, that Russian serfdom corresponded to the Asiatic mode of production, and which also confused the Soviet author G. M. Dubrovskii, who, in 1929, made of serfdom a particular formation which was supposed to be distinct from feudalism? . . .

Our discussions have shown that in the historical development of the countries of the East, as compared to the development of the Western European countries, there exist essential peculiarities. In the history of the East in the pre-capitalist period, state centralization and despotic power played a very great role. The development of commercial and monetary relations in antiquity did not lead in the East to such a high level of classical slave-holding, nor to such a highly developed communal-slave-holding democracy, as we find in certain Mediterranean cities. These are peculiarities common to all the civilizations of the ancient East, despite the tremendous differences among them. One can also say that such are the peculiarities of the development of the Western European countries as compared to the East.

Nevertheless, in my opinion these peculiarities do not justify us in speaking of an Asian socio-economic formation, nor in saying that from the most ancient times the countries of Asia have known only the feudal system. On the contrary, the further we go in our research the more we perceive the common character of the basic stages through which humanity has passed in the course of world history.

5. *The Asiatic Mode of Production is not Peculiar to Asia*

Extracts from an article published in 1966 by one of the protagonists of the Asiatic mode of production, in which he attempts to evade the embarrassing problem of Marx's condescending attitude towards the backward and unprogressive character of non-European civilizations by denying that there is any definite link between the concept of the Asiatic mode and the history and society of a particular geographical area.[1]

In Marxist historiography, both in the Soviet Union and in foreign countries, the discussion of the question began with the study of the theoretical heritage of K. Marx regarding the problem of the Asiatic mode of production. And this is natural. Various viewpoints regarding the content of the concept 'Asiatic mode of production' in the works of Marx have already been expressed. A particular, independent, and universal mode of production – a transitional stage from primitive society to class society, an early class society marked by specific types of exploitation different from those of the slave-holding formation – such is the first viewpoint, which is shared by the great majority of the participants in the discussions which have taken place during the last few years in the Institute of Philosophy, the Institute of History and the Institute of the Peoples of Asia. In general, we are agreed that K. Marx in the course of his investigations was led to consider the problem of the establishment of a society, and of an early class system, distinct from the slave-holding system. But it appears to us that it is impossible to go beyond this statement. The attempts to construct a particular mode of production from the 'secondary indices' sketched out by K. Marx (the community, state property in the land, irrigation, despotism, and so on) contradict Marx's own teaching about types of relations of production. Research oriented in this direction also runs the risk of leading science on to the path of dogmatism. It creates an insoluble 'enigmatic situation' and strengthens belief in the localized character of the concept of the Asiatic mode of production.

[1] SOURCE: Iu. M. Garushiants, 'Ob Aziatskom Sposobe Proizvodstva' *Voprosy Istorii* no. 2, 1966, pp. 97–8.

The second point of view (which, incidentally, was first set forth by Soviet historians as early as the beginning of the 1930s) treats the Asiatic mode of production as the primitive communal system. The origin of this viewpoint can be understood if we remind ourselves of the considerations which led K. Marx to introduce the notion of an 'Asiatic formation' in his teaching regarding the stages in the development of society. However, this viewpoint does not enable us to find an answer to the questions raised by the new materials which have been accumulated by historical science.

The third interpretation of the Asiatic mode of production, which makes of it a geographical concept, a localized concept, appears to us altogether feeble. This viewpoint can be demonstrated only by doing absolute violence to the corresponding texts [of Marx]. Moreover, the partisans of such an interpretation have never presented a well-developed argument in favour of their position based on the creative research of K. Marx. In particular they base their views on the fact that they do not find the Asiatic mode of production in European history, thus confounding the principle of universality with universal geographic extension. As N. B. Ter-Akopian has quite justifiably objected, 'If you take your stand on such a viewpoint, even the capitalist mode of production cannot be considered universal. The universality of any given mode of production consists above all in the necessity of this stage for the development of human society. In some places society enters on this stage in its fully developed form, in other places they will pass through it in a weakened form. The peoples who have entered later into history will sometimes leap completely over one or another stage.'

The partisans of the 'geographic' interpretation of Marx's category also commit a grave methodological error when they wish to construct a particular mode of production from the traits of the 'Asiatic formation' sketched out by Marx, or even from a single one of these traits. Ia. A. Lentsman in particular proceeds in this way. He regards the Asiatic mode of production as a localized phenomenon, if only because he does not find in Mycenaean Greece either the property of the sovereign in the land or a strong imperial power (despotism). Let us note that in this case the partisans of the continental conception of the problem derive their arguments in large part from authors whose interpretation of K. Marx is on the whole correct, but who absolutize all his statements, seeking to discern in the community, in despotism, and so on, an independent formation, without recognizing at the same time the hypothetical character of Marx's theories on this subject.

Finally, we must consider as an obvious misunderstanding the viewpoint which makes the Asiatic mode of production the Asiatic variant of slave-holding society and of feudalism. We are profoundly convinced that such an interpretation results from mixing up two different problems, which K. Marx solved on the basis of materials from the socio-economic history of the Asiatic countries: the question of early class society, and the problem of the survival of modes of production deformed by colonialism. The partisans of this viewpoint derive their arguments from Marx's statements about the specific paths of the development of Eastern society; this has nothing to do with the way in which K. Marx understood the Asiatic mode of production.

6. The International Significance of Mao Tse-tung's Theory of People's War

In this passage from his article of September 1965, entitled 'Long Live the Victory of the People's War', Lin Piao sets forth his global revolutionary strategy for the encirclement of the 'cities' of the world by the 'rural areas'.[1]

The Chinese revolution is a continuation of the Great October Revolution. The road of the October Revolution is the common road for all people's revolutions. The Chinese revolution and the October Revolution have in common the following basic characteristics: (1) Both were led by the working class with a Marxist-Leninist Party as its nucleus. (2) Both were based on the worker-peasant alliance. (3) In both cases state power was seized through violent revolution and the dictatorship of the proletariat was established. (4) In both cases the socialist system was built after victory in the revolution. (5) Both were component parts of the proletarian world revolution.

Naturally, the Chinese revolution had its own peculiar characteristics. The October Revolution took place in imperialist Russia, but the Chinese revolution broke out in a semi-colonial and semi-feudal country. The former was a proletarian socialist revolution, while the latter developed into a socialist revolution after the complete victory of the new-democratic revolution. The October Revolution began with armed uprisings in the cities and then spread to the countryside, while the Chinese revolution won nation-wide victory through the encirclement of the cities from the rural areas and the final capture of the cities. . . .

Comrade Mao Tse-tung's theory of people's war has been proved by the long practice of the Chinese revolution to be in accord with the objective laws of such wars and to be invincible. It has not only been valid for China, it is a great contribution to the revolutionary struggles of the oppressed nations and peoples throughout the world. . . .

In the last analysis, whether one dares to wage a tit-for-tat struggle against armed aggression and suppression by the imperialists and their lackeys, whether one dares to fight a people's

[1] SOURCE: *Hung-ch'i*, no. 10, 1965, pp. 17–20.

war against them, is tantamount to whether one dares to embark on revolution. This is the most effective touchstone for distinguishing genuine from fake revolutionaries and Marxist-Leninists.

In view of the fact that some people were afflicted with the fear of the imperialists and reactionaries, Comrade Mao Tse-tung put forward his famous thesis that 'the imperialists and all reactionaries are paper tigers. . . .'

The imperialists are extremely afraid of Comrade Mao Tse-tung's thesis that 'imperialism and all reactionaries are paper tigers', and the revisionists are extremely hostile to it. They all oppose and attack this thesis and the philistines follow suit by ridiculing it. But all this cannot in the least diminish its importance. The light of truth cannot be dimmed by anybody. . . .

It must be emphasized that Comrade Mao Tse-tung's theory of the establishment of rural revolutionary base areas and the encirclement of the cities from the countryside is of outstanding and universal practical significance for the present revolutionary struggles of the oppressed nations and peoples in Asia, Africa, and Latin America against imperialism and its running dogs.

Many countries and peoples in Asia, Africa and Latin America are now being subjected to aggression and enslavement on a serious scale by the imperialists headed by the United States and their running dogs. The basic political and economic conditions in many of these countries have many similarities to those that prevailed in old China. As in China, the peasant question is extremely important in these regions. The peasants constitute the main force of the national-democratic revolution against the imperialists and their running dogs. In committing aggression against these countries, the imperialists usually begin by seizing the big cities and the main lines of communication, but they are unable to bring the vast countryside completely under their control. The countryside, and the countryside alone, can provide the broad areas in which the revolutionaries can manoeuvre freely. The countryside, and the countryside alone, can provide the revolutionary basis from which the revolutionaries can go forward to final victory. Precisely for this reason, Comrade Mao Tse-tung's theory of establishing revolutionary base areas in the rural districts and encircling the cities from the countryside is attracting more and more attention among the people in these regions.

Taking the entire globe, if North America and Western Europe can be called 'the cities of the world', then Asia, Africa and Latin America constitute 'the rural areas of the world'. Since the Second World War, the proletarian revolutionary movement has for various reasons been temporarily held back in the North American and West European capitalist countries, while the people's revolutionary movement in Asia, Africa, and Latin America has been growing vigorously. In a sense, the contemporary world revolution also presents a picture of the encirclement of cities by the rural areas. In the final analysis, the whole cause of world revolution hinges on the revolutionary struggles of the Asian, African and Latin American peoples who make up the overwhelming majority of the world's population. The socialist countries should regard it as their internationalist duty to support the people's revolutionary struggles in Asia, Africa and Latin America. . . .

7. *Extracts from the Decision of the Central Committee of the Chinese Communist Party concerning the Great Proletarian Cultural Revolution (adopted on 8 August 1966)*

This decision, adopted ten days before the first official appearance of the 'Red Guards', lays down the basic guidelines for the 'cultural revolution', as regards both content and methods of organization.[1]

1. A New Stage in the Socialist Revolution

The great proletarian cultural revolution now unfolding is a great revolution that touches people to their very souls and constitutes a new stage in the development of the socialist revolution in our country, a deeper and more extensive stage.

At the Tenth Plenum of the Eighth Central Committee of the Party, Comrade Mao Tse-tung said: To overthrow a political power, it is always necessary, first of all, to create public opinion, to do work in the ideological sphere. This is true for the revolutionary class as well as for the counter-revolutionary class. This thesis of Comrade Mao Tse-tung's has been proved entirely correct in practice.

Although the bourgeoisie has already been overthrown, it is still trying to use the old ideas, culture, customs and habits of the exploiting classes to corrupt the masses, capture their minds and endeavour to stage a come-back. The proletariat must do just the opposite: it must meet head-on every challenge of the bourgeoisie in the ideological field and use the proletariat's own new ideas, culture, customs and habits to change the mental outlook of the whole of society. At present, our objective is to struggle against and crush those persons in authority who are taking the capitalist road, to criticize and repudiate the reactionary bourgeois academic 'authorities' and the ideology of the bourgeoisie and all other exploiting classes and to transform education, literature and art and all other parts of the superstructure that do not correspond to the socialist economic base, so as to facilitate the consolidation and development of the socialist system.

2. The Main Current and the Zigzags

The masses of the workers, peasants, soldiers, revolutionary intellectuals and revolutionary cadres form the main force in this

[1] SOURCE: *Hung-ch'i*, no. 10, 1966, pp. 1–7.

great cultural revolution. Large numbers of revolutionary young people, previously unknown, have become courageous and daring pathbreakers, they are energetic and intelligent. Through the media of big-character posters and great debates, they argue things out, expose and criticize thoroughly, and launch resolute attacks on the open and hidden representatives of the bourgeoisie. In such a great revolutionary movement, it is hardly avoidable that they should show shortcomings of one kind or another, but their main revolutionary orientation has been correct from beginning to end. This is the main current in the great proletarian cultural revolution. It is the main direction along which the great proletarian cultural revolution continues to advance.

Since the cultural revolution is a revolution, it inevitably meets with resistance. This resistance comes chiefly from those in authority who have wormed their way into the party and are taking the capitalist road. It also comes from the force of the habits of the old society. At present, this resistance is still fairly strong and stubborn. However, the great proletarian cultural revolution is after all the trend of the times, which cannot be held back. There is abundant evidence that such resistance will crumble fast once the masses become fully aroused.

Because the resistance is fairly strong, there may be reversals and even repeated reversals in this struggle. There is no harm in this. It tempers the proletariat and other toiling masses, and especially the younger generation, teaches them lessons and gives them experience, and makes them understand that the revolutionary road is a zigzag one, and not plain sailing.

3. Put Daring Above Everything Else and Boldly Arouse the Masses

The fate of this great cultural revolution will be determined by whether or not the party leadership dares boldly to arouse the masses. . . .

What the Central Committee of the Party demands of the party committees at all levels is that they give firm and correct leadership, put daring above everything else, boldly arouse the masses, change the state of weakness and incompetence where it exists, encourage those comrades who have made mistakes but are willing to correct them to cast off their [mental] burdens and join in the struggle, and dismiss from their leading posts all those in authority who are taking the capitalist road and so make possible the recapture of the leadership for the proletarian revolutionaries. . . .

9. Cultural Revolutionary Groups, Committees and Congresses[1]

Many new things have begun to emerge in the great proletarian

[1] Parts 4 to 8 are omitted

cultural revolution. The cultural revolutionary groups, committees and other organizational forms created by the masses in many schools and units are a new phenomenon of great historic importance.

These cultural revolutionary groups, committees and congresses are excellent new forms of organization whereby under the leadership of the Communist Party the masses are educating themselves. They are an excellent bridge to keep our party in close contact with the masses. They are organs of power of the proletarian cultural revolution.

The struggle of the proletariat against the old ideas, culture, customs and habits handed down by all the exploiting classes for thousands of years past will necessarily take a very, very long time. Therefore, the cultural revolutionary groups, committees and congresses should not be temporary organizations but permanent standing mass organizations. They are suitable not only for schools and administrative organs, but generally also for factories, mines, other enterprises, urban districts and villages.

It is necessary to institute a system of general elections, like that of the Paris Commune, for electing members to the cultural revolutionary groups and committees and delegates to the cultural revolutionary congresses. The lists of candidates should be put forward by the revolutionary masses after full consideration, and the elections should be held after the masses have discussed the lists over and over again.

The masses are entitled at any time to criticize members of the cultural revolutionary groups and committees and delegates elected to the cultural revolutionary congresses. If these members or delegates prove incompetent, they can be replaced through election or recalled by the masses after discussion. . . .

8. *On Bourgeois Authority and Proletarian Authority*

This text is composed of extracts from two editorials entitled respectively 'On the Proletarian Revolutionaries' Struggle to Seize Power' and 'On Revolutionary Discipline and Revolutionary Authority of the Proletariat'. They spell out most explicitly the conceptions which have prevailed in China since the beginning of the cultural revolution, according to which authority is vested in the loyal followers of Chairman Mao's correct line and not in the existing Party organs.[1]

Proletarian revolutionaries are uniting to seize power from the handful of persons within the Party who are in authority and taking the capitalist road. This is the strategic task for the new stage of the great proletarian cultural revolution. It is the decisive battle between the proletariat and the broad masses of labouring

[1] SOURCE: *Hung-ch'i*, No. 3, 1967, pp. 13–21.

people on the one hand and the bourgeoisie and its agents in the Party on the other. . . .

Chairman Mao has pointed out: 'Make trouble, fail, make trouble again, fail again, and so on till their doom; that is the logic of the imperialists and all reactionaries the world over in dealing with the people's cause, and they will never go against this logic.' This is also true of the handful of persons within the Party who are in authority and taking the capitalist road. We must 'cast away illusions, prepare for struggle' in accordance with Chairman Mao's teaching. . . .

The current seizure of power from the handful of persons within the Party who are in authority and taking the capitalist road is not effected by dismissal and reorganization from above, but from below by the mass movement called for and supported by Chairman Mao himself. Only in this way can the leading organs of our Party and state, enterprises and undertakings, cultural bodies and schools be regenerated and the old bourgeois practices be thoroughly eradicated. . . .

A number of units, where a handful of persons within the Party who are in authority and taking the capitalist road have entrenched themselves over a long period, have become rotten. There these persons have been exercising not proletarian dictatorship, but bourgeois dictatorship. The Marxist principle of smashing the old state machine must be put into practice in the struggle for the seizure of power in these units.

In summing up the experience of the Paris Commune, Marx pointed out that the proletariat must not take over the existing bourgeois state machine but must thoroughly smash it. Practice in the international communist movement has proved this to be a great truth. Since a number of units, in which a handful of persons within the Party who are in authority and taking the capitalist road have entrenched themselves, have been turned into organs for bourgeois dictatorship, naturally we cannot take them over ready-made, resort to reformism, combine two into one and effect peaceful transition. We must smash them thoroughly.

The great mass movement to seize power from the handful of persons within the Party who are in authority and taking the capitalist road has begun to create and will moreover continue to create new organizational forms for the state organs of the proletarian dictatorship. Here, we must respect the initiative of the masses and boldly adopt the new forms, full of vitality, that emerge in the mass movement to replace the old practices of the exploiting classes and in fact to replace all old practices that do not correspond to the socialist economic base. It is absolutely impermissible merely to take over power while letting things remain the same and operating according to the old rules. . . .

To arouse from below the masses in their hundreds of millions, to seize power from the handful of persons within the Party who are in authority and taking the capitalist road, to smash the old practices and create new forms, opens up a new era in the international history of the world proletarian revolution and in the international history of the dictatorship of the proletariat. It will greatly enrich and develop the experience of the Paris Commune, greatly enrich and develop the experience of the Soviets, and greatly enrich and develop Marxism-Leninism.

The struggle by the proletarian revolutionaries to seize power from the handful of persons within the Party who are in authority and taking the capitalist road is being carried out under the conditions of the dictatorship of the proletariat. In the course of the seizure of power, the dictatorship of the proletariat must be strengthened. This is an indispensable condition for the establishment of the new proletarian revolutionary order. . . .

In his celebrated article 'On the People's Democratic Dictatorship', Chairman Mao points out that in dealing with the reactionaries, we must 'enforce dictatorship . . . suppress them, allow them only to behave themselves and not to be unruly in word or deed. If they speak or act in an unruly way, they will be promptly stopped and punished. . . .'

All revolutionary comrades must firmly bear in mind these teachings of Chairman Mao. In dealing with the reactionaries we will not give them even limited democracy, not to speak of extensive democracy, not one iota. Towards them, only dictatorship should be carried out!

A group of ghosts and monsters have now come out to set up counter-revolutionary organizations and carry out counter-revolutionary activities. These counter-revolutionary organizations must be resolutely eliminated. Counter-revolutionaries must be dealt with in accordance with the law without hesitation.

Chairman Mao has called on the People's Liberation Army actively to support and assist the genuine proletarian revolutionaries and resolutely to oppose the Rightists. The great People's Liberation Army created by Chairman Mao himself has warmly responded to his call. The People's Liberation Army is making new, great contributions to the cause of socialism in the great proletarian cultural revolution. This is the glorious task of the People's Liberation Army. . . .

Comrade Mao Tse-tung, the greatest Marxist-Leninist in the present era, discovered the law of class struggle in socialist society. It is he who personally initiated and is leading the great proletarian cultural revolution and the struggle of the proletarian revolutionaries to form a great alliance and unite the broad masses of people to seize power from the handful of persons within the Party who are in authority and are taking the capitalist road. . . .

The handful of persons within the Party who are in authority and are taking the capitalist road are the most dangerous and the main enemy. An important weapon of these reactionary elements for preserving their reactionary rule is illegally to use the name of the Party and turn Party discipline into bourgeois discipline to repress the masses and oppose revolution. This counter-revolutionary discipline must be thoroughly smashed.

All revolutionary cadres must step forth, stand with the revolutionary masses and carry out resolute struggle against the handful of persons within the Party who are in authority and are taking the capitalist road, and pay no attention to their 'discipline'. They are no longer revolutionary superiors, on the contrary they are counter-revolutionary revisionists. During war, when a commander turns traitor and surrenders to the enemy, a revolutionary fighter absolutely cannot obey his commands but on the contrary should turn his gun on him. True during war, this should also be so in political struggle.

The proletarian revolutionary fighters must smash counter-revolutionary discipline and, at the same time, consciously observe proletarian revolutionary discipline. . . .

Basing himself on the principles of Leninism, Chairman Mao has always stressed revolutionary discipline. He has pointed out many times that petty-bourgeois ultra-democracy and unrestrained liberalism which undermines discipline must be firmly opposed. . . .

There is no authority which is above class. We must thoroughly overthrow bourgeois authority and firmly establish proletarian authority. By no means do we oppose all authority. . . .

Engels pointed out in *On Authority* that combined action means organization and that it is impossible to have organization without authority. Engels thoroughly criticized the anti-authoritarians. He wrote:

> Have these gentlemen ever seen a revolution? A revolution is certainly the most authoritarian thing there is; it is the act whereby one part of the population imposes its will upon the other part by means of rifles, bayonets and cannon – authoritarian means, if such there be at all; and if the victorious party does not want to have fought in vain, it must maintain this rule by means of the terror which its arms inspire in the reactionaries. Would the Paris Commune have lasted a single day if it had not made use of this authority of the armed people against the bourgeois? Should we not, on the contrary, reproach it for not having used it freely enough? . . .

Without authority there can be no organized revolutionary action, let alone victory in the revolution. This was true in the years of revolutionary war and is equally true today when, under the conditions of the dictatorship of the proletariat, the proletarian revolutionaries are waging the struggle to seize power from the handful of persons in the Party who are in authority and are taking the capitalist road.

Marxism-Leninism, Mao Tse-tung's thought, is the highest authority of the proletariat. The proletarian revolutionary line that Chairman Mao represents is the highest authority in the great proletarian cultural revolution. All provisional organs of power that carry out this correct line in directing the struggle to seize power should naturally have authority and certainly do have it. Proletarian revolutionaries should take it as their obligation to assume such authority. This is the authority of the proletariat. . . .

We must bear in mind the lesson that the Paris Commune made insufficient use of its authority. The provisional organs of power and their responsible members who carry out Chairman Mao's revolutionary line in directing the struggle to seize power must display the courage and resourcefulness of proletarian revolutionaries, make full use of the revolutionary authority of the proletariat, guide the broad masses, and victoriously accomplish the historic task of the struggle to seize power.

9. *Revolutionary Committees are Fine*

These extracts from a joint *People's Daily-Red Flag-People's Liberation Army Daily* editorial of the same title spell out very clearly the combination of mass participation and military control which is an essential feature of the 'dictatorship of the proletariat' as practised in China today.[1]

A year ago, when the new-born revolutionary committees had just appeared on the eastern horizon, our revered and beloved leader Chairman Mao, with his great proletarian revolutionary genius, pointed out with foresight:

> In those places or units where power must be seized, it is necessary to carry out the policy of the revolutionary 'three-in-one' combination in establishing a provisional organ of power which is revolutionary and representative and enjoys proletarian authority. This organ of power should preferably be called the Revolutionary Committee.

Our great leader Chairman Mao again recently pointed out:

> The basic experience of revolutionary committees is this – they are three-fold: they have representatives of revolutionary cadres, representatives of the armed forces and representatives of the revolutionary masses. This forms a revolutionary 'three-in-one' combination. The revolutionary committee should exercise unified leadership, do away with redundant or overlapping administrative structures, have 'better troops and simpler administration' and organize a revolutionized leading group which is linked with the masses.

Chairman Mao's brilliant directive sums up the experience of revolutionary committees at all levels and gives the basic orientation for building revolutionary committees. . . .

This 'three-in-one' organ of power enables our proletarian

[1] SOURCE: *Jen-min jih-pao*, 30 March 1968

political power to strike deep roots among the masses. Chairman Mao points out: 'The most fundamental principle in the reform of state organs is that they must keep in contact with the masses.' The representatives of the revolutionary masses, particularly the representatives of the toiling masses – the workers and peasants – who have appeared in great numbers in the course of the great proletarian cultural revolution are revolutionary fighters with practical experience. Representing the interests of the broad revolutionary masses, they participate in the leading groups at various levels. This provides the revolutionary committees at these levels with a vast mass foundation. Direct participation by the revolutionary masses in the running of the country and the enforcement of revolutionary supervision from below over the organs of political power at various levels play a very important role in ensuring that our leading groups at all levels always adhere to the mass line, maintain the closest relations with the masses, represent their interests at all times and serve the people heart and soul.

This 'three-in-one' organ of power strengthens the dictatorship of the proletariat. 'If the army and the people are united as one, who in the world can match them?' The great Chinese People's Liberation Army is the main pillar of the dictatorship of the proletariat and a Great Wall of steel defending the socialist motherland. The revolutionary 'three-in-one' combination carries our army-civilian unity to a completely new stage. . . . As a result of the direct participation of P.L.A. representatives in the work of the provisional organs of power at all levels, our dictatorship of the proletariat is better able to withstand storm and stress, better able to smash the plots of all enemies, domestic or foreign, and play a more powerful role in the cause of socialist revolution and socialist construction.

Revolutionary leading cadres are the backbone of the 'three-in-one' organs of power. They have rich experience in class struggle and are a valuable asset to the Party and people. By going through the severe test of the great proletarian cultural revolution and receiving education and help from the broad masses, they were touched to the soul and remoulded their world outlook further. The combination of the revolutionary leading cadres and representatives of the P.L.A. and of the revolutionary masses in the revolutionary committees makes them better able to carry out Chairman Mao's proletarian revolutionary line, grasp and implement the Party's policies, and correctly organize and lead the masses forward. At the same time, veteran cadres and young new cadres work together in the revolutionary committees, learn from each other and help each other so that, as Chairman Mao teaches, *the veterans are not divorced from the masses and the young people are tempered.* Organizationally, this guarantees the work of training successors to the proletarian revolutionary cause. . . .

10. Absorb Fresh Blood From the Proletariat – An Important Question in Party Consolidation

These extracts from a *Red Flag* editorial published in October 1968 illustrate graphically the basic dilemma of the cultural revolution: How to make use of the political skills of the former Party cadres without allowing them to subvert the revolution by following their own revisionist bent.[1]

Chairman Mao has solved the problem of continuing the revolution under the dictatorship of the proletariat. He points out that the struggle between the two classes and the two roads continues for a long time under the dictatorship of the proletariat, that the main danger of capitalist restoration comes from the handful of Party capitalist roaders who reflect the interests of the bourgeoisie, and that it is essential to enforce all-round dictatorship of the proletariat not only in the political field but also in the ideological and cultural fields. Starting from firm faith in the overwhelming majority of the people and, first of all, the overwhelming majority of the workers, peasants and soldiers, Chairman Mao personally initiated and is leading the first great proletarian cultural revolution. He lets Communists, together with the broad revolutionary masses, 'face the world and brave the storm' in the great tempest of the turbulent and extremely complicated revolutionary mass movement, expose the capitalist roaders, expose the counter-revolutionaries, criticize and repudiate revisionism and bourgeois ideas, take a correct attitude towards the masses and, in different forms of struggle, learn to distinguish and handle correctly the contradictions between ourselves and the enemy and the contradictions among the people under the conditions of the dictatorship of the proletariat. This has greatly raised the communist consciousness of the broad masses of Communist Party members, clearly indicated the direction for continuing the revolution under the dictatorship of the proletariat, swept away the bureaucratic airs corrupting the revolutionary will, and brought about closer ties between the Party and the working masses. As a result, the Left – i.e. the genuine proletarian revolutionaries – has been discovered and tempered, the wavering middle-of-the-roaders educated, and the Rightists, that is, the bourgeois reactionaries serving imperialism and the Kuomintang, isolated and exposed. Only by implementing this proletarian revolutionary line of Chairman Mao's and carrying out a Party rectification movement of a mass character, not a movement behind closed doors, can it be guaranteed that the leadership of the Party organizations at all levels is truly in the hands of those Communist Party members who are loyal to Chairman Mao, to Mao Tse-tung's thought and

[1] SOURCE: *Hung-ch'i*, No. 4, 1968, pp. 5–12.

to Chairman Mao's proletarian revolutionary line; only in this way can the Party always maintain its character as the vanguard of the proletariat, lead the broad masses forward and fulfil the glorious historical task set by the dictatorship of the proletariat, the task of completely eliminating the bourgeoisie (the last exploiting class in the history of mankind), eliminating class differences and realizing communism.

A question that demands attention in the present work of Party rectification is the question of absorbing fresh blood from the proletariat.

Talking about Party consolidation, Chairman Mao has said:

> A human being has arteries and veins through which the heart makes the blood circulate, and he breathes with his lungs, exhaling carbon dioxide and inhaling fresh oxygen, that is, getting rid of the stale and taking in the fresh. A proletarian party must also get rid of the stale and take in the fresh, for only thus can it be full of vitality. Without eliminating waste matter and absorbing fresh blood the Party has no vigour.

This vivid analogy by Chairman Mao embodies profound dialectics. Chairman Mao teaches us to look at the proletarian revolutionary Party as an organization developing through the process of metabolism of the revolution, and not as a static and immutable organization.

'Eliminating waste matter' means resolutely expelling from the Party the proven renegades, enemy agents, all counter-revolutionaries, obdurate capitalist roaders, class-alien elements and degenerate elements. As for apathetic persons whose revolutionary will has declined, they should be advised to leave the Party.

'Absorbing fresh blood' consists of two inter-related tasks: taking into the Party a number of outstanding rebels, first of all advanced elements from among the industrial workers, and selecting outstanding Communist Party members for leading posts in the Party organizations at all levels.

Tempered in the great proletarian cultural revolution, a number of rebel fighters with proletarian consciousness have emerged from among the broad revolutionary masses, first of all among the labouring masses, the workers, peasants and soldiers. They have these characteristics: a high level of consciousness in the struggle between two lines, a keen sense of class struggle, boldness in stepping to the forefront of the struggle in defence of Chairman Mao's revolutionary line and, especially, firmness in opposing revisionism. These are very valuable revolutionary qualities. They also have shortcomings, but these can be overcome through education. . . .

During the period of socialist revolution, attention must be paid to Party building among the workers and to developing revolutionary vigour. This has been Chairman Mao's consistent thinking. . . . In June 1950, in his report 'Fight for a Fundamental Turn for the Better in the Financial and Economic Situation in China' made at the Third Plenary Session of the Seventh Central Committee of the Party, Chairman Mao . . . pointed out clearly, 'attention must be paid to drawing politically-conscious workers into the Party systematically, expanding the percentage of workers in the Party organization.' In July 1957, in the article 'The Situation in the Summer of 1957', Chairman Mao again pointed out: 'A Communist must be full of vigour, he must have a strong revolutionary will, he must defy all difficulties and overcome them with an unyielding will, he must get rid of individualism, departmental egoism, absolute equalitarianism and liberalism, otherwise he is not a Communist in the real sense.' In 1967, at the time when decisive victory has been won in the great cultural revolution, Chairman Mao again pointed out: 'The Party organization should be composed of the advanced elements of the proletariat; it should be a vigorous vanguard organization capable of leading the proletariat and the revolutionary masses in the fight against the class enemy.'

In order to do a good job in admitting new Party members in accordance with Chairman Mao's revolutionary line, it is . . . necessary to have a new leading body which is a revolutionary three-in-one combination and resolutely carries out Chairman Mao's proletarian revolutionary line. Those comrades who are good at creatively studying and applying Mao Tse-tung's thought, truly devote themselves to proletarian revolution and are really full of vigour, should be selected for leading posts in the Party organizations, and a unified leadership should be formed gradually.

Oppose the restoration of the old. It is impossible to do a good job in admitting new Party members in any place where the leading body is composed entirely of former personnel, has not drawn fresh blood from the proletariat, has no revolutionary three-in-one combination. Such leading bodies cannot maintain close ties with the revolutionary masses. It is, therefore, very possible that they would admit into the Party some 'middle-of-the-roaders' or 'good old chaps'. It is even possible that they would let some bad elements, whose words do not tally with their deeds, and opportunists sneak into the Party while excluding comrades who dare to make frontal attacks on the class enemies and persevere in principled struggle. . . .

In some places there is conservatism in regard to the activists applying for Party membership. There are cases where good comrades who are all right as regards class origin and ideology have been kept out of the Party for five or six years, although they have applied many times. Such things should be corrected.

Blind faith in elections is also a form of conservative thinking. Chairman Mao pointed out recently:

Who is it that gives us our power? It is the working class, the poor and lower-middle peasants, the labouring masses comprising over 90 per cent of the population. We represent the proletariat and the popular masses and have overthrown the enemies of the people, and therefore the people support us. Direct reliance on the broad revolutionary popular masses is a basic principle of the Communist Party.

This most important instruction of Chairman Mao's penetratingly points out the mass basis of the mighty power of the dictatorship of the proletariat, criticizes and repudiates the formalism of having blind faith in elections, and gives the basic orientation for building the Party and revolutionary committees.

The revolutionary committee is the most representative revolutionary organ of power of the dictatorship of the proletariat since the liberation. But it originates not from elections, but from direct reliance upon action by the broad revolutionary masses. The revolutionary committees of the twenty-nine provinces, municipalities and autonomous regions under the leadership of the proletarian headquarters headed by Chairman Mao and with Vice-Chairman Lin Piao as its deputy leader have about 4,000 members; about half are representatives of the revolutionary masses, and the overwhelming majority are representatives of the revolutionary workers, peasants and soldiers. These 4,000 or so comrades were tested and tempered in the revolutionary storms and were selected as a result of repeated arguments, deliberations, consultations and examinations. The cadres are discussed and examined by the revolutionary masses and approved of by the leadership, and besides there are always partial replacements or adjustments. When a revolutionary committee is set up, the number of people attending the mass celebration rally ranges from over a hundred thousand to hundreds of thousands. Everyone knows about it and is overjoyed. Has any Party committee or government council or People's Congress in any part of the country in the past ever had such a vast mass character? Has any one of them gained the understanding of and received supervision by the broad revolutionary masses to such a vast extent? What decides the nature of a leading organ is the line it carries out and the class interests it reflects, not the form it takes. Democracy has class character. The revolutionary organ of power – including among its workers revolutionary cadres, old and new, from various fields – which is created in the revolutionary movement by following a thoroughgoing mass line, conforms better to proletarian democracy and democratic centralism, and reflects more profoundly the interests of the proletariat and the working people than those organs of power produced in the past only by means of elections. This experience should also be drawn upon in regard to Party life. . . .

CHRONOLOGY

1818	5 May: Birth of Karl Marx
1820	28 November: Birth of F. Engels
1839–42	Opium War waged by England against China
1848	February: The *Communist Manifesto* is published in London
1851–64	Taiping Rebellion
1857–9	Nationalist movements in India
1864	September: The World Labour Congress, meeting in London, founds the First International
1867	Publication of the first volume of *Capital*
1870	22 April: Birth of Lenin
1871	18 March–28 May: The Paris Commune
1883	14 March: Death of Karl Marx
1885	Foundation of the Indian National Congress
1889	July: The Second International is founded at a congress in Paris
1891	Second congress of the Second International in Brussels
1893	Third congress of the Second International in Zurich
1894	Sun Yat-sen founds the Revive China Society (Hsing Chung Hui)
1895	5 August: Death of Engels
1896	Fourth congress of the Second International in London
1898	13–15 March: First congress of the Russian Social Democratic Workers' Party in Minsk
1899–1900	In China the Boxer Rebellion is repressed by the great powers
1900	Fifth congress of the Second International in Paris
1902	Lenin writes *What is To Be Done?*
1903	17 July: Second congress of the Russian Social Democratic Workers' Party in Brussels and later in London
	10 August: Appearance of the 'Bolshevik' and 'Menshevik' tendencies
1904	Sixth congress of the Second International in Amsterdam
1904–5	Russo-Japanese War
1905–7	Revolution in Russia. The government makes concessions to the liberals which are finally withdrawn in June 1907, with the dissolution of the Second Duma elected six months earlier
1905–11	Constitutional revolution in Iran
1905	Foundation of the United League (T'ung Meng Hui) by Sun Yat-sen
1907	Seventh congress of the Second International in Stuttgart
1908	Revolution of the 'Young Turks'
	General strike of the workers in Bombay

1908 Foundation in Indonesia of the Budi Utomo (Noble Effort), a nationalist organization of revolutionary tendencies

1910 Eighth congress of the Second International in Copenhagen

1911 October: Beginning of the Republican revolution in China

1912 15–17 January: Sixth congress of the Russian Social Democratic Workers' Party in Prague. The party takes the name of Russian Social Democratic Workers' Party (Bolsheviks)

September: Foundation of the Kuomintang by Sun Yat-sen
Foundation of the Sarekat Islam (Islamic Union) in Indonesia

1914 28 July: Germany declares war on Russia

31 July: Jaurès is assassinated

3 August: The German Social Democrat deputies vote the war credits

26 August: In France Jules Guesde becomes Minister

November: In Russia the Central Committee of the Russian Social Democratic Workers' Party (Bolsheviks) publishes a manifesto against the imperialist war

December: In Germany the revolutionaries regroup themselves around Karl Liebknecht and Rosa Luxemburg

1915 5–8 September: International socialist conference in Zimmerwald

1916 April: International socialist conference in Kienthal

July: Lenin finishes writing *Imperialism: the Highest Stage of Capitalism*

Rebellion in Ireland

1917 27 February (8 March[1]): Revolution breaks out in Russia. Fall of Tzarism, appearance of Soviets of workers', peasants' and soldiers' deputies

25 October (7 November): Bolshevik revolution in Russia

2 (15) December: Russo-German armistice. Beginnings of the peace negotiations of Brest-Litovsk; the treaty is finally signed on 3 March 1918

1918 January: strikes in Germany and Austria/Hungary

9 November: Proclamation of the republic in Germany

1919 27 March: First congress of the Third International (Comintern) in Moscow

January–May: Massacre of the communists in Berlin

4 May: Beginning of the 'May 4th Movement' in China

May: Liquidation of the Bavarian Soviet Republic

August: Liquidation of the Hungarian Soviet Republic

1920 April: In Turkey Kemal Atatürk is elected President of the Grand National Assembly

[1] From the outbreak of the February revolution until February 1918 we give two dates for events taking place in Russia, the first being that of the Julian calendar, which was used in Russia, and the second being that of the Gregorian calendar. In February 1918 the Soviet government adopted the Gregorian calendar.

1920 21 July–6 August: Second Congress of the Comintern in Petrograd

August: The Red Army, led by Tukhachevskii, attacks Warsaw. The Poles counter-attack

1–5 September: First Congress of the Peoples of the East in Baku

1921 February: Soviet–Iranian treaty

16 March: Soviet–British commercial treaty

18 March: Soviet–Polish peace treaty

March: Soviet–Turkish treaty

22 June–12 July: Third Comintern Congress

July: First Congress of the Chinese Communist Party in Shanghai

November: Soviet–Afghan treaty

1922 January: First Congress of the Toilers of the Far East in Moscow and Petrograd

3 April: Stalin becomes Secretary General of the Soviet Communist Party

August: At a plenum of the Chinese Communist Party Maring pushes through the policy of individual membership in the Kuomintang

4 November–5 December: Fourth Congress of the Comintern

26–30 December: The Tenth All-Russian Congress of Soviets votes a resolution in favour of creating a Union of Soviet Socialist Republics, and as a result the U.S.S.R. is formally established

1923 September: Failure of the insurrection in Bulgaria
Failure of an attempt at revolution in Germany

October: Arrival of Borodin in Canton as counsellor to Sun Yat-sen

November: Failure of Hitler's *putsch* in Munich

1924 21 January: Death of Lenin

January: In Canton the First Congress of the Kuomintang officially adopts the policy whereby communists will join the party 'as individuals'

17 June–8 July: Fifth Comintern Congress

December: Stalin announces the policy of 'socialism in one country'

1925 15 March: Foundation of the Sun Yat-sen University in Moscow

Rif War against French domination in Morocco

1926 March: First incident between Chiang Kai-shek and the communists

1927 April: Chiang Kai-shek massacres the workers in Shanghai

September–December: In China, failure of the 'Autumn Harvest Uprising' in Hunan. Mao Tse-tung takes refuge with the remnants of his troops on the Chingkangshan and establishes a revolutionary base there.

1927 December: The 'Canton Commune', established on orders from Stalin, is crushed in blood

1928 July–September: The Sixth Congress of the Comintern and the Sixth Congress of the Chinese Communist Party are held concurrently in Moscow

1931 18 September: Japanese aggression against Mukden

1933 30 January: Hitler takes power in Germany

1934 October: In Spain: 'Commune' in Asturia
In China: beginning of the Long March

1935 25 July–20 August: Seventh Comintern Congress

October: End of the Long March

1936 February: Victory of the Popular Front in the Spanish elections

June: Victory of the Popular Front in the French elections

July: Civil war breaks out in Spain

August: First Moscow trial (Zinoviev, Kamenev, etc). The trials continue until the end of 1938

1937 July: Beginning of the second Japanese war of aggression against China. Establishment of cooperation between the Kuomintang and the Chinese Communist Party to fight Japan

1939 February: End of the Spanish Civil War

23 August: Nazi–Soviet pact

1 September: Beginning of the Second World War

1941 15 April: Soviet–Japanese neutrality pact

22 June: Hitler attacks the Soviet Union

14 August: Signature of the Atlantic Charter

11 December: The United States enters the war

1942 February: Beginning of the rectification campaign in the Chinese Communist Party

1943 2 February: Soviet victory at Stalingrad

10 June: Dissolution of the Comintern

28 November–3 December: Roosevelt, Churchill and Stalin confer in Teheran

4 December: Tito forms a government in Yugoslavia

1944 6 June: Allied landing in Normandy

1945 4–11 February: Yalta conference

8 May: Germany surrenders

14 August: Treaty of alliance between the U.S.S.R. and Nationalist China

2 September: Japan surrenders

1946 Beginning of Zhdanovism in the U.S.S.R.

September: Outbreak of civil war in Greece

December: War begins in Indo-China

1947 March: Rebellion in Madagascar

5 June: Beginning of the Marshall Plan

1947	5 October: Establishment of the Cominform
	December: Full-scale civil war begins in China
1948	June: Emergency declared in Malaya
	September: Madiun affair in Indonesia
1949	31 January: Peking is occupied by the People's Liberation Army
	1 October: Proclamation of the Chinese People's Republic
	November: Chiang Kai-shek moves the seat of the Nationalist government to Taiwan
1950	14 February: Sino-Soviet treaty
	June: Outbreak of the Korean War
1951	November: Riots in Morocco
1952	February: Strikes and riots in Tunisia
	5–12 October: Nineteenth Congress of the Communist Party of the Soviet Union
1953	6 March: Death of Stalin
	June: Strikes and riots in East Germany
	August: The Armistice is concluded in Korea
	September: Khrushchev becomes First Secretary of the Communist Party of the Soviet Union
1954	February–March: Battle of Dien Bien Phu
	April: Sino-Indian treaty embodying the 'five principles' of peaceful co-existence (*Panch Sheel*)
	26 April: International conference on Korea in Berlin
	8 May–21 July: International conference on Indo-China in Geneva
	1 November: Beginning of the Algerian revolution
1955	April: Bandung conference
1956	14–25 February: Twentieth Congress of the Communist Party of the Soviet Union
	June: Strikes in Poland
	October: Uprising in Hungary and intervention of the Soviet Army to support the Kadar government
	October: Egypt nationalizes the Suez Canal Anglo-Franco-Israeli expedition into Egypt
1957	27 February: Mao Tse-tung gives a talk 'On the correct handling of contradictions among the people'
	November: At the first meeting of the communist parties in Moscow, Mao Tse-tung proclaims that 'The East wind prevails over the West wind'
1958	May: At the Second Session of the Eighth Congress of the Chinese Communist Party Liu Shao-ch'i proclaims the 'Great Leap Forward' and the theory of the 'permanent revolution'
	July: Political crisis in Syria and the Lebanon followed by Western intervention
	August: The Chinese People's Republic begins shelling the offshore islands
	December: Khrushchev makes fun of the Chinese communes in a conversation with Humphrey

1959 January: Fidel Castro takes power in Cuba

27 January–5 February: 21st Congress of the Communist Party of the Soviet Union

1960 April: The Chinese publish a new attack on revisionism under the title 'Long Live Leninism'. Withdrawal of Soviet technicians from China

November: Cuba is proclaimed a 'socialist republic'

10 November–1 December: Second conference of the eighty-one communist and workers' parties in Moscow

1961 17–31 March: 22nd Congress of the Communist Party of the Soviet Union

1962 October: Sino-Indian border clash

1963 14 June: Letter from the Chinese Communist Party to the Communist Party of the Soviet Union, referred to as 'letter in 25 points'

14 July: 'Open letter' of the Central Committee of the Communist Party of the Soviet Union in reply to the Chinese letter of 14 June

25 July: Nuclear test ban treaty initialled in Moscow

6 September: Publication of the first of the nine Chinese replies to the Soviet letter of 14 July

22 November: Assassination of President Kennedy

December: Chou En-lai embarks on a voyage throughout Africa

1964 1 February: In China, beginning of the campaign to 'learn from the People's Liberation Army'

14 February: In a report to the plenum of the Central Committee of the Communist Party of the Soviet Union, Suslov denounces the nationalist deviations of the Chinese

May: The General Political Department of the People's Liberation Army publishes the first edition of *Quotations from Chairman Mao.*

14 July: Publication of the ninth and last Chinese reply to the Soviet letter of 14 July 1963 containing Mao's warning against the danger that China might 'change colour' if the class struggle is not carried on without ceasing, and if successors to the revolutionary cause are not properly trained

21 August: Death of Togliatti in Yalta

14 October: Fall of Khrushchev

1965 February: Beginning of the American bombing of North Vietnam

March: The majority of the communist parties having refused to associate themselves with an open condemnation of the Chinese, a 'consultative' meeting is held in Moscow

19th June: Fall of Ben Bella

26 June: The second Afro-Asian conference is postponed

August–September: Indo-Pakistani war

16 September: Chinese ultimatum to India

30 September: *Coup* and counter-*coup* in Indonesia

1965 November: In China, beginning of the attacks on Wu Han which constitute the prologue to the cultural revolution

1966 2 January: Fidel Castro denounces the economic pressures exercised by China on his country

3–15 January: 'Tri-Continental' conference in Havana

4–9 January: At the Tashkent conference Kosygin endeavours to mediate between India and Pakistan

29 March–8 April: 23rd Congress of the Communist Party of the Soviet Union, to which the Chinese Communist Party had refused to send representatives

April–May: New attacks against 'bourgeois' tendencies in China

1 June: Appearance of the term Great Proletarian Cultural Revolution

8 August: The Eleventh Plenum of the Central Committee of the Chinese Communist Party adopts the '16 point decision' on the cultural revolution

18 August: A million people participate in a meeting in Tien An Men Square in Peking where for the first time Mao Tse-tung meets the Red Guards. (Similar meetings continue until November)

August–September: The Red Guards beat up party secretaries in Peking and elsewhere

12 December: A plenum of the Central Committee of the Communist Party of the Soviet Union adopts a 'resolution on the international policy of the U.S.S.R. and the struggle of the Communist Party of the Soviet Union for the cohesion of the communist movement', which condemns 'the anti-Soviet power politics of Mao Tse-tung and his group'

1967 January: In China the 'January revolution' marks the beginning of a new phase of the cultural revolution in the course of which the 'Triple Union' (new activists, People's Liberation Army and cadres faithful to Mao) endeavour to seize power from the hands of the party and state authorities, headed by Liu Shao-ch'i, who are 'taking the capitalist road'

26–30 January: The Red Guards lay siege to the Soviet Embassy in Peking

April: Beginning of criticism of Liu Shao-ch'i in the officia press, under the thin disguise of 'China's Khrushchev'

August: The British Legation in Peking is burned in retaliation for the action of the police in Hong Kong

1968 15 August: Mao Tse-tung issues a directive proclaiming that the working class must take the lead in everything

September: The Chinese press hails the establishment of Revolutionary Committees in all provinces of China except Taiwan. (The last two, set up on 5 September, were those in Tibet and Sinkiang)

October: The 12th plenum of the Eighth Central Committee of the Chinese Communist Party denounces Liu Shao-ch'i by name as a 'renegade, traitor and scab', and

1968 adopts a draft Party Constitution for submission to the Ninth Party Congress

1969 March: Following the Sino-Soviet border clash Evtushenko publishes a poem on the yellow peril

April: The Ninth Congress of the Chinese Communist Party hears a political report by Vice-Chairman Lin Piao and finally adopts, with minor changes, the new Party Constitution

BIBLIOGRAPHY

This does not pretend to be an exhaustive bibliography. It is rather a brief bibliographic essay designed to guide the reader who wishes to make a more thorough study of certain aspects of the problems discussed in this book. Given this limited aim, we refrain from including a systematic list of the primary sources on the basis of which we have selected and translated the materials which appear in our anthology. Information on this subject can be found in the notes to each of the extracts.

1. *Marx, Lenin and the Evolution of Marxism down to the present day*

Let us begin at the beginning, that is to say with Marx. The edition of the works of Marx and Engels published in the course of the past few years in German in East Berlin, and in Russian in Moscow, is marred by unfortunate omissions, but it is the only virtually complete edition which exists. (The publication of the *Marx-Engels Gesamtausgabe* or 'M.E.G.A.', generally considered to be an almost perfect critical edition, was never carried to completion.) Those who do not read German can find in Maximilien Rubel's *Bibliographie des oeuvres de Karl Marx avec en appendice un répertoire des oeuvres de Friedrich Engels* (Paris, Rivière, 1956), a list of all the available translations. The supplement to this bibliography published in 1960 contains, apart from a certain number of other titles and editions, indications regarding those of Marx's political writings which have been omitted from the early volumes of the recent Soviet edition because they were too hostile to Russia.

Among the studies of Marx's thought the most complete and well documented are those of George Lichtheim, *Marxism. An Historical and Critical Study* (2nd edn, London, Routledge & Kegan Paul, 1964), and of Jean-Yves Calvez, *La Pensée de Karl Marx* (Paris, Les Editions du Seuil, 1956). These two works are complementary, the first having been written by a non-Christian humanist, and the second by a Catholic theologian. Also useful are the books of Alfred Meyer, *Marxism: The Unity of Theory and Practice* (Cambridge, Mass., Harvard University Press, 1954), and Henri Lefebvre, *Pour connâitre la pensée de Karl Marx* (Paris, Bordas, 1947).

If we turn to writings on Lenin, the authors of the last two books on Marx mentioned above have each written a book on Lenin as well. That of Alfred Meyer, *Leninism* (Cambridge, Mass., Harvard University Press, 1957), is in our opinion more adequate than that of Henri Lefebvre, *La Pensée de Lénine* (Paris, Bordas, 1957), because Lefebvre endeavours, in conformity with his own personal interests, to make of Lenin a philosopher – something which in our opinion he definitely was not. As for Lenin's work, there still does not exist a satisfactory edition of the Russian text; the fifth, which we have used as the basis for our anthology because it is relatively accessible, must be completed by reference to the third edition and to the *Leninskii Sbornik* (*Leniniana*). The *Collected Works* published in Moscow beginning in 1960 by the Foreign Languages Publishing House are translated from the fourth Russian edition published in Stalin's time, and now completely discredited even in the Soviet Union. They are, however, useful in the absence of any more complete English edition.

Two particularly valuable anthologies are available dealing specifically with the writings of Marx and Engels in the domain covered by this volume. These are *Marx on China 1853–1860: Articles from the New York Daily Tribune*, edited by Dona Torr (London, Lawrence & Wishart, 1951), and K. Marx and F. Engels, *On Colonialism* (Moscow, Foreign Languages Publishing House, n.d.). On the Asiatic mode of production the best known work is, of course, that of Karl A. Wittfogel, *Oriental Despotism* (New Haven, Conn., Yale University Press, 1957). One can read with profit the important critical introduction of P. Vidal-Nacquet to the French edition of Wittfogel's book, *Le despotisme oriental* (Paris, Les Editions de Minuit, 1964). A recent article of G. Sofri, 'Sul modo di produzione asiatico', *Critica storica*, nn. 5–6, pp. 704–810, contributes to the discussion not only a thorough analysis of the controversies to which this concept has given rise over the years, but also a very useful bibliography.

As for 'Leninism' as it is professed today in the Soviet Union, two contrasting interpretations can be found, on the one hand in the official textbook *Fundamentals of Marxism-Leninism* (Moscow, Foreign Languages Publishing House, 1961), and on the other hand, in the study of Gustav Wetter, *Dialectical Materialism* (revised edn, London, Routledge & Kegan Paul, 1958). The latter is extremely learned and rigorous, but of a narrowly philosophical character. Herbert Marcuse's work *Soviet Marxism: a Critical Analysis* (London, Routledge & Kegan Paul, 1958), is a brilliant and original analysis of the Soviet version of Marxism as an ideology fulfilling certain functions in Russian society.

Among the works that deal with the history and doctrine of communism from Marx to the present day, it is not always easy to distinguish between those which are primarily of ideological interest, and those which are above all historical, since in this domain facts and ideas are closely intermingled. The overall study which places the greatest emphasis on the theoretical aspect is perhaps that of R. N. Carew Hunt, *The Theory and Practice of*

Communism (5th revised edn, Harmondsworth , Penguin Books, 1963).

If we turn now to the aspect of Marxist thought dealt with in this volume, the most useful overall study is undoubtedly that of Demetrio Boersner, *The Bolsheviks and the National and Colonial Question* (Paris, Minard, 1957). Despite its title, this volume gives considerable space to Marx and Engels, and to the history of Marxist thinking about the problems of the non-European world prior to 1917. It is marred by some gaps (Boersner seems to be ignorant of certain basic texts of Marx regarding the role of the Orient in the strategy of the world revolution, such as 'Revolution in China and in Europe') and some errors (he talks about the 'Shanghai Commune' instead of the 'Canton Commune'). Nevertheless, this volume is required reading for everyone interested in the subject.

Adam Ulam's book *The Unfinished Revolution. An Essay on the Sources of Influence of Marxism and Communism* (New York, Random House, 1960), is a controversial but very interesting attempt to present Marxism as the ideology corresponding to the 'anarchist' phase in societies undergoing the process of industrialization, when the population rebels against the disaggregation of traditional life brought about by economic change.

2. *History of the Internationals*

On the Second International and the colonial question one can consult a special issue of the journal *Le Mouvement social*, n. 45, October–December 1963, and also the work of Georges Haupt, *La IIe Internationale socialiste 1889–1914* (Paris, Mouton, 1965), which contains an annotated bibliography of the sources.

Regarding the Third International, Enrica Collotti Pischel and Chiara Robertazzi have compiled an immense bibliography, *L'Internationale Communiste et les Problèmes Coloniaux* (Paris, Mouton, 1968), which includes annotations regarding the content of each of the 3,691 items listed. On the International in general, there does not exist as yet a complete history dealing with the whole period of its existence superior to that of Franz Borkenau written in 1939 and recently re-published as a paperback, *World Communism. A History of the Communist International* (Ann Arbor, University of Michigan Press, 1962), despite the highly partisan character of this work and the gaps in its documentation. One can, however, find the equivalent of a history in the three volumes of documents collected and annotated by Jane Degras, *The Communist International 1919–1943, Documents* (London, Royal Institute of International Affairs 1956–65.)

On the history of the Communist International and of the

communist movement from 1917 to recent times, a convenient synthesis is that of H. Seton-Watson, *The Pattern of Communist Revolution. An Historical Analysis* (2nd edn, London, Methuen, 1960). Seton-Watson's book, while not startlingly original, is useful because of its completeness and its solidly documented character.

3. History of the Soviet Union

On the Russian revolution and the beginnings of the Soviet régime, the best starting point is E. H. Carr's monumental *History of Soviet Russia* of which seven volumes have hitherto been published covering the period from 1917–26: *The Bolshevik Revolution, 1917–1923*, in three volumes (London, Macmillan, 1950–53); *The Interregnum 1923–1924* (London, Macmillan, 1954); *Socialism in One Country 1924–1926*, in three volumes, of which the third is divided into two parts (London, Macmillan, 1958–64). The scope of this work is, incidentally, wider than the history of the U.S.S.R. as such, since it deals at considerable length with the communist movement in a dozen countries.

Two histories of the Soviet Communist Party deserve mention: that of Leonard Schapiro, *The Communist Party of the Soviet Union* (London, Eyre & Spottiswoode, 1960), and that of Rudolf Schlesinger, *Il Partito Comunista nell'U.R.S.S.* (Milan, Feltrinelli, 1962). The Soviet historians have so far produced only a single textbook, *History of the Communist Party of the Soviet Union* (Moscow, Foreign Languages Publishing House, 1960), which reinstates only a small proportion of the verities hidden in Stalin's day, and that only very timidly. The Stalinist 'truth' is to be found in the famous *History of the Communist Party of the Soviet Union (Bolsheviks)* (Short Course. Moscow, Foreign Languages Publishing House, various editions.) A useful complement to the history of the Communist Party as an organization is provided by Bertram D. Wolfe's vivid work *Three Who Made a Revolution* (London, Thames & Hudson, 1956).

A useful study of Moscow's strategy both diplomatic and revolutionary in the East down to 1927 is that of X. J. Eudin and R. C. North, *Soviet Russia and the East 1920–1927* (Stanford, Stanford University Press, 1957). On national problems within the U.S.S.R. the historical survey of R. Pipes, *The Formation of the Soviet Union 1917–1923* (Cambridge, Mass., Harvard University Press, 1954), can usefully be consulted. For more detailed analyses of the specific aspects of the national problem in the regions inhabited by Muslim populations, and of the interaction between Islam and revolutionary ideas, see H. Carrère d'Encausse, *Réforme et Révolution chez les musulmans de l'Empire russe, Bukhara 1867–1924* (Paris, Armand Colin, 1966), and also A. Bennigsen and C.

Quelquejay, *Les Mouvements nationaux chez les musulmans de Russie: le Sultangaliévisme au Tatarstan* (Paris, Mouton, 1960).

4. The Chinese Revolution

An extended bibliography of materials on modern China and on the history and ideology of the Chinese Communist Party is to be found in Stuart R. Schram's book *The Political Thought of Mao Tse-tung* (enlarged and revised edn, Harmondsworth, Penguin Books, 1969) pp. 448–56.

On the Sino-Soviet conflict the first solid study was that of Donald Zagoria, *The Sino-Soviet Conflict 1956–1961* (Princeton, Princeton University Press, 1961). Although it is now somewhat out of date, this book still retains a good part of its value. More recent accounts bringing the problem up to date are those of W. E. Griffith, *The Sino-Soviet Rift* (Cambridge, Mass., M.I.T. Press, 1964), and the sequel to this in his article 'Sino-Soviet Relations 1964–65' in *The China Quarterly*, No. 25, 1966, p. 3–143.

INDEX